A GUIDE TO **COBOL** PROGRAMMING

D. D. McCracken and U. Garbassi

    A Guide to COBOL Programming, 2nd Edition

D. D. McCracken
    FORTRAN with Engineering Applications
    A Guide to FORTRAN IV Programming
    A Guide to ALGOL Programming
    A Guide to IBM 1401 Programming
    A Guide to FORTRAN Programming
    Digital Computer Programming

D. D. McCracken and W. S. Dorn

    Numerical Methods and FORTRAN Programming

F. J. Gruenberger and D. D. McCracken

    Introduction to Electronic Computers:
    Problem Solving with the IBM 1620

D. D. McCracken, H. Weiss, and T. H. Lee

    Programming Business Computers

DANIEL D. McCRACKEN
McCRACKEN ASSOCIATES, INC.

UMBERTO GARBASSI
ESSO MATHEMATICS AND SYSTEMS, INC.

a guide to
COBOL
programming

SECOND EDITION

WILEY-INTERSCIENCE, A DIVISION OF
JOHN WILEY & SONS   NEW YORK   LONDON   SYDNEY   TORONTO

Library of Congress Catalogue Card Number: 79-116770

ISBN 0 471 58243 3

Printed in the United States of America

10 9 8 7 6 5 4 3 2 1

We shall not cease from exploration
And the end of all our exploring
Will be to arrive where we started
And know the place for the first time.

PREFACE

This book is written for the person who wants to get a rapid grasp of the application of computers to the problems of business. COBOL is one of the most widely used languages for such work and is an excellent vehicle for the study of computer applications.

All of the essential COBOL matters are explained fully within the framework of realistic applications. The book is therefore considerably more than a simple text on COBOL.

* It presents much background information on the data-processing needs and methods of business in an introductory chapter and in case studies.

* It presents as much background on computer characteristics as is needed to understand COBOL and to use it in practical work with computers.

* There are three extended case studies, which, besides illustrating COBOL methods and showing typical applications of computers in business, describe the way of going about solving a business problem with a computer. The reader thus gets an over-all view of the complete task of going from a problem statement to a running program, including many of the fundamental principles of application system design.

* All case study programs and major illustrative programs have been run on a computer, and the output shown is that actually produced by the machine.

* The important subject of object program efficiency is emphasized throughout the text and in a separate chapter.

* Most chapters contain extensive sets of review questions that allow the reader to test his knowledge of what he has just studied; answers to all questions are given immediately following the questions. The book thus gains many of the advantages of a programmed text. Other exercises at the end of several chapters allow the reader to try his hand at applying COBOL material; answers to about half are given at the end of the book.

* The book is organized so that each reader can easily select the material of value to him. The person who wants only a quick picture of programming in general, having no background in computers, can study Chapters 1 to 4, which include a realistic case study; Chapters 5 to 8 develop the rest of the COBOL material and illustrate a full-scale application; Chapter 9 discusses object program efficiency; the case study in Chapter 10 describes another application area and outlines the complete process of going from a problem statement to a successful long-term operation. The person who already knows programming and is interested only in a quick explanation of COBOL can skip Chapters 1 and 2 and skim the case studies; he will have no difficulty in picking out the half of the text material that relates specifically to COBOL. In general, the sequence of topics has been chosen to facilitate learning, in contrast to the order in which they are usually presented in a reference manual.

* The revisions made in the second edition bring in the experience of heavy use of COBOL in the years since it was introduced.

Emphasis is laid on the options that people really use, and special warnings are given about errors that experience shows are commonly made. Suggestions from many instructors clarify troublesome points and explanations have been added wherever classroom experience has shown it is needed. The changes in COBOL itself are fully reflected in the second edition. Material on disks, in particular, has been added, and there is a discussion of operating systems.

In addition to the obvious usefulness of this book for self-study of COBOL and business-data processing in general, it is hoped that because of the organization, review questions, and exercises it will find application in several types of formal course.

1. It can be used as the text for a course in COBOL programming, preferably with a term problem if a computer is available.

2. It can be used as the text for a three-semester-hour course in business-data pro-

cessing and programming. (Such a course is now recognized as an essential part of the training of any graduate in commerce, accounting, business administration, etc.)

3. Students in industrial courses in COBOL programming will find it useful as an elaboration of the necessarily terse presentation in the reference manuals and as a guide to the ways in which COBOL and computers can be applied to the solution of realistic problems.

It is a pleasure to acknowledge the many and varied contributions of Bill Donally, Dean Earnest, Fred Gruenberger, Jack Jones, Dick McCoy, Stan Naftaly, Steve Wright, and, in the preparation of the second edition, Neil Armann, Bill Bell, Barron Cashdollar, Frank Claffey, and Carol Fernsler.

DANIEL D. McCRACKEN
UMBERTO GARBASSI

Ossining, New York
Tripoli, Libya
January, 1970

ACKNOWLEDGMENT

The presentation of COBOL in this book is based on the COBOL standard developed by the American National Standards Institute (ANSI). In response to their request the following acknowledgment is reproduced in its entirety:

CONTENTS

A GUIDE TO **COBOL** PROGRAMMING

1. ELECTRONIC DATA PROCESSING AND **COBOL**

1.1 Introduction

Electronic computers are widely used in the solution of the problems of science, engineering, and business in applications ranging from a relatively simple inventory-control system for a small wholesaler to the complex calculations of launching a satellite. Their use is based on the ability to operate at great speed, to produce accurate results, to store large quantities of information, and to carry out long and complex sequences of operations without human intervention.

In this book we shall investigate *commercial*, or *business*, data-processing applications. As we shall see, this work is interesting and challenging, even though the calculations are not usually so difficult as those needed in the design of a nuclear reactor or when predicting in a matter of seconds whether a satellite orbit will be satisfactory. Because of the volume of data often involved, commercial data processing presents many challenges in organizing the work so that the needed results can be produced on schedule with a minimum of cost and in guaranteeing that the results will be correct.

Solving a problem with a computer requires a number of steps which may be outlined as follows.

Problem identification and goal definition —feasibility studies. In any computer project it is necessary first to acquire a clear idea of the nature of the company's business. We must then determine several things: why a computer should be used on a particular application (to save time, to save money, to produce more accurate or more complete results, etc.), how this application ties in with other jobs, the origin of the data, how and by whom the results are to be used, and how any exceptional conditions are to be handled. This preliminary analysis, usually called a computer feasibility study, is a sizable undertaking and may lead to many wrong decisions if it is not done properly. In this book we can only suggest some of the considerations that enter into this phase of computer work. The following section outlines the data-processing needs of an illustrative manufacturing company; the case studies in Chapters 4, 7, and 10 point out additional factors.

Systems analysis and system design. There are, as a rule, many ways to approach a particular computer application. Decisions must be made on the timing of data arrival and of computer processing, data formats (arrangements) must be planned to save time and to tie in properly with other applications, provision must be made for recovery from possible machine or operator errors, plans must be laid for getting the whole system started effectively, and various checking techniques must be applied to prove the accuracy of processing—to name only a few of the aspects of this subject. A complete treatment would easily fill a longer book than this one; here we shall try to point out the principles of system design in the case studies.

Computer programming and COBOL. Computers basically execute only very simple instructions, such as "add two numbers," "read a card," or "determine whether two numbers are equal." To do useful work with a computer requires the preparation of a *program* of these instructions; a complete commercial application requires at least hundreds of them and more commonly thousands.

Different types of computers, in general, have different sets of basic instructions, and even when different machines do the same things, such as adding two numbers, they usually have different formats for the coded instructions. This means that a program for one machine will not run on a machine of a different type, which leads to the high cost of preparing completely new programs when a user gets a faster or bigger computer.

COBOL, which stands for COmmon Business Oriented Language, was designed to solve or at least to ease a number of problems in the areas of program writing, computer compatibility, program testing, program modifications, and system documentation. In fact, COBOL simplifies the preparation of a program of thousands of computer instructions by allowing us to write the procedures that the computer is to follow in terms similar to ordinary English, which is then translated, as we shall see at the end of this chapter, into the computer's basic instructions.

Because of the relative simplicity of its English-like sentences, COBOL helps anyone with a reasonably logical mind to write a moderately complex program after a matter of some weeks of training. To accomplish this, however, knowledge of the programming language must be supplemented by some understanding of the computer environment. Consequently, in this book we not only give a complete explanation of most of the features of the COBOL language but also explain as much about the computer as the COBOL programmer needs to know in order to do an effective job.

COBOL also lessens the cost of changing machines because a program written in COBOL can be translated into the instructions of almost any computer after only relatively small changes are made in the COBOL program to reflect the differences between the two computers.

Program checkout and testing. There are so many chances of making mistakes in programming that most programs do not work when first tested. COBOL alleviates this problem because the program is written in English-language form and is therefore somewhat easier to check before trying it on the computer and easier to "debug" during testing. Systematic methods are nevertheless required to detect and locate any errors and to ensure that the program actually does produce correct results. We consider this topic more fully in the case study in Chapter 10.

Production. Finally, after all the preceding steps have been completed successfully, the program can be combined with data for the computer to process. In a typical situation the program is used many times, usually periodically, such as every week or every month. This step may take a few minutes to many hours, depending on the problem, the volume of data, and the speed of the computer.

Good *documentation* of the entire system and its programs is now required to keep the job running smoothly. Again, COBOL simplifies this task, because its English-like instructions are to a certain extent self-documenting—certainly much more so than instructions in machine language.

Finally, it is the destiny of every system to be modified sooner or later. When this occurs, programs written in COBOL can much more easily be understood and changed. This feature is particularly valuable when this task is assigned to a new programmer, that is, one who did not write the original programs.

Several conclusions may be drawn from this discussion. First, the computer does not "solve problems"; it only follows carefully defined computational or logical procedures. Second, a computer does not in any way relieve the user of the responsibility of planning the work carefully; in fact, the computer demands much more careful planning—which is often valuable in itself. The computer is faster and more accurate than a human, but it cannot decide how to proceed, what to do with results, or do many things a human can do, such as detecting an unusual condition for which it had not been "instructed" to test or seeing at a glance that a customer is in a bad mood.

Third, a computer does not in any way reduce the need for a full and detailed understanding of the problem area or of the business procedures in it. Finally, it should be realized that the programming phase—the primary subject of this book—is only one part of the complete process; it may not even take a majority of the time.

This is not meant to minimize the importance of programming nor to suggest that it can be done haphazardly. Programming can be a sizable task and is frequently fascinating in its own right. We simply wish to suggest that programming be viewed in the perspective of the full range of activities.

1.2 The Data-Processing Activities of Business

We are concerned with business data-processing requirements and how they can be filled with computers and COBOL. Let us begin by exploring some of the data-processing activities of a medium-sized manufacturing company.

Figure 1.1 shows in schematic form some of the flow paths of information and materials in a company that manufactures a line of products, some of which are sold from stock and some built specially to the customer's order. This diagram outlines only the major paths, for it omits a variety of other activities, as we shall see later. What are some of the major flows of data through these channels?

First consider what happens when a customer orders a product that the company stocks, ready to ship. The customer's order goes to Sales, which sends notices of it to Accounting, Production Control, and the Stockroom. Accounting uses the information as advance notice for billing and for accounts receivable. Production Control is prepared to update inventory records. The Stockroom makes up the order and sends it to Shipping, accompanied by a packing slip (prepared by Sales), which is sent to the customer. Shipping sends Sales a notification that the order was indeed shipped, noting any shortages, and forwards the same information to Accounting. Sales is then able to update sales

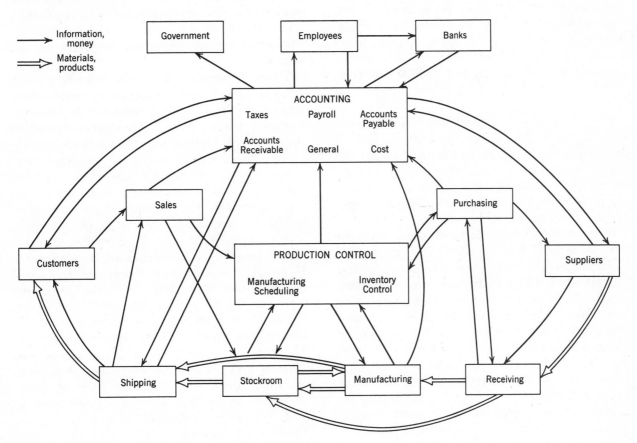

Figure 1.1. Some of the information paths of a manufacturing company.

statistics and to handle the back ordering of any out-of-stock items. Accounting prepares a bill for the customer and the customer returns a check.

The reader may already have thought of several places in which the amount of data transmitted could be reduced, but basically all of the information sent to the various parts of the company really is necessary. In talking about how a computer can be used in such an operation, we are concerned with eliminating as much duplication of data as possible and with cutting down the number of times the same information has to be transmitted. However, there is no major reduction possible in the number of functions of the business that must be undertaken in such a transaction.

Now let us follow the paths of an order for a product that is not stocked but must be manufactured specially to the customer's order, either because the item is sold too infrequently to be worth stocking or because it requires a special design. This time Sales must send data on the customer's order to Production Control, possibly after getting a design from Engineering (not shown). Production Control computes the raw materials to be taken from stock and schedules the manufacturing operations needed to produce the item. Properly timed orders go out to the Stockroom and then to Manufacturing to build the product. When it is completed, it is sent to Shipping, where the chain of action is as before.

This is a highly simplified sequence of operations, of course. We assume, for instance, that all raw materials and subassemblies required for the special order are in stock, that a price can be quoted to the customer by the salesman, and that the price is not so high that special payment provisions are required.

Next let us see what happens when materials must be ordered from suppliers. This process can be initiated either by the requirements of a special product or by a signal from the inventory-control process that some raw materials or finished goods have fallen below their *reorder points*, meaning that more should be ordered. The initiation of the chain of events in buying supplies can thus come either from Sales or the Stockroom; either way, it funnels through the Inventory-Control section of Production Control. Word goes to Purchasing regarding what is needed and when. Purchasing selects a vendor and places the order; at the same time notification is sent to Accounting and Receiving. Accounting makes note of the order in its accounts-payable operation and is also prepared to pay the bill when it arrives. Receiving is forewarned what to expect and when the order is supposed to come; when the materials arrive, Receiving inspects them and sends to Purchasing the supplier's packing slip, the original notice from Purchasing, and the inspection report. The materials go either directly into the Manufacturing shop or to the Stockroom. The supplier submits his bill and Accounting sends a check.

Since there seems to be the temptation sometimes to assume that business thrives on paperwork for its own sake, let us emphasize once again that all of these operations are necessary, although they are not always done in exactly this way. There clearly has to be a careful control of inventory; the penalty for not having control is either the high cost of too much stock or the cost of lost time and lost sales. Purchasing is clearly essential; the choice of vendors and the negotiation of payment terms is a highly specialized function that must be done by experts. Accounting functions are required both by good business practice and by law: bills have to be paid, records of commitments must be maintained, and costs of inventory have to be computed according to methods permitted by government tax regulations.

There are several other major information flow paths here, even in this simplified model of a business. A great deal of data is generated by the manufacturing process. Data on production times and materials must be funneled into Accounting for figuring costs of special orders, for preparing statements of earnings, and for general management control of the shop operations. Labor costs go into these operations, and, of course, labor data is required in considerable volume to compute pay. This naturally is true for all employees, and payroll is usually a major computer application. However, it is of special concern in the actual manufacturing operations, in which frequently there are complex payment formulas based on various kinds of work that each employee may perform and on a variety of incentive payment plans. The computer payroll system accepts inputs from Manufacturing, from the employees themselves, and from various other sources; it prepares checks, statements of earnings, a variety of deduction reports, tax reports, and payments of funds accumulated from deductions.

Banking relations produce considerable data-processing work. Checks issued by the company to employees, suppliers, stockholders, and others must be reconciled with check registers when the checks are returned from the bank. Checks from customers and other miscellaneous sources must be deposited and properly accounted for.

Government regulations require much data processing. The accounting for taxes must be supported by many reports covering income, expenses, inventory valuation, credit losses, and capital gains. Withholding tax and Social Security reports must be prepared for every employee. Dividends to stockholders must be reported.

And this is not all by any means. We have omitted from this discussion, among other things, the information flow paths for branch offices, shipments returned from customers or to suppliers, advertising, market research and forecasting, credit investigation and approval, engineering of special or new products, inspection and quality control, maintenance of plant and equipment, capital expenditures, employee cash-advance and expense accounts, accounting for various employee benefits such as discount sales, complete relations with stockholders and bondholders, and a wide variety of management and government reporting such as budgeting and budget variance, balance sheets, profit-and-loss statements, and auditing.

In recent years there has been a great increase in the demand for reports that fall into a category called management-information services. These reports may include not only management-oriented revisions of those mentioned above, but also special reports on personnel skills, company properties, and even reports on all the reports issued by a company.

In many instances these "selective information" reports are meant to satisfy requests of the type "Give me the names of those employees who are older than 28, earn more than $12,000 per year, and have a Master's degree." We shall see that COBOL is well equipped with logical decision-making features and that it can be employed very effectively in providing this kind of information.

We may close this first look at what business requires of the computer by observing that the manufacturing company discussed here has been chosen as being more or less typical of business data processing, but it is by no means the only kind of organization that uses computers for such purposes. Here is a partial list of other areas in which computers are heavily used: electric utilities, transportation, insurance, retail sales, control of industrial manufacturing processes, banking, government, and education.

In addition to these areas of application of what we have called business data processing, there is a wide range of use in scientific and engineering work. Although it is of great importance, it is not covered in this book, since we are concentrating on business data processing. Furthermore, there are other "user-oriented" programming languages—like FORTRAN and ALGOL—which are better geared to the solution of problems of a mathematical, statistical, and scientific nature.

1.3 Data-Processing Operations

We can begin to get a better insight into what business data processing entails—and how a computer can assist in it—by trying to identify the basic operations. This can be done conveniently by continuing our investigation of the typical business organization in Section 1.2 and by looking in particular at some of the aspects of inventory-control activity.

Collection of data is necessary before it can be processed. In the inventory-control situation this would mean gathering the requests for materials and subassemblies from Manufacturing, the orders from Sales to issue finished goods to Shipping, and acknowledgments from Purchasing that a purchase recommendation has been acted on. In many situations the gathering of data involves the physical movement of paper forms; in some cases it can be set up for transmission electrically. Data collection is not nearly so routine as it might appear. Procedures must be employed to ensure the accuracy of the data as recorded on the paper forms, and pains must be taken to prevent its loss; data must be scheduled to reach the computing center when needed, and any that is unavoidably late must be handled in some acceptable manner.

In most cases the data cannot be "read" by the computer in the form in which it appears in the *source documents* (paper forms). It must first be *recorded* in some *machine-sensible* form. "Machine-sensible" means a form that can be used as input to a computer. Probably the most common method is to punch cards containing the data. Alternatively, data may be recorded directly onto magnetic tape or a strip of paper tape can be punched. Often the source information on cards or paper tape is next transferred onto magnetic tape. In a few instances devices are used to make specially printed source documents directly readable by the computer; these devices are usually called *character readers* and operate either by sensing magnetized particles in the ink or by optical methods. For some applications data is entered directly into the computer from typewriter or other keyboard terminals.

Sometimes the information, now in machine-sensible form, is immediately entered into the computer for processing. In other cases, in which accuracy is a major concern, the input records are *verified* by repeating the operations of preparing the computer input from the source documents but using a special machine that only checks for errors in the input. This, of course, increases the data-preparation costs, but in some applications the detection and correction of errors is so important that the cost is justified.

Just what is done next depends, of course, on the nature of the job and how it has been organized; one possibility is that *calculations* are performed. In the inventory-control example calculation would require the following, among other things. If a shipment has been received from a supplier, the quantity of the shipment must be added to the quantity on hand for that item. If materials have been issued to Manufacturing, the quantity issued must be subtracted from the quantity on hand. If the system keeps track of average usage, a division will be required. In most business data processing the computations are not usually complicated; complexity develops more because of some of the following operations.

Decisions can be made by a computer if the "logic" of the decision can be stated in terms of things a computer can do. For instance, when Manufacturing requests materials from the inventory-control system, the decision whether there is enough on hand to fill the request must be made. It is likewise necessary to determine whether more of an item should be ordered; this, too, can be done by comparing the reorder point (the point at which more should be ordered) with the sum of the quantity on hand and the quantity already on order. Similarly, a computer can determine whether two numbers are equal, which of two names comes earlier in the alphabet, whether a man has worked more than 40 hours in a week, or whether a salary change raises a man's salary more than 50%. By combining simple tests of this sort a computer can make rather complex decisions.

At various stages during the processing data is

validated and *edited*. In the *validation* step source data is checked for validity and accuracy before it is processed. If a part number ought to be completely numeric (contain nothing but digits), it is simple to check that no letters or punctuation symbols appear in the input. The number of hours worked in any one day can be tested for plausibility: there is a clear-cut error if the input shows more than 24 hours and a strong indication of inaccuracy if it shows more than 16. What the computer system does when it detects an error or an unusual condition depends, naturally, on how the system has been designed to operate: the bad data might be rejected and ignored until re-entered in correct form, the data might be accepted and used but a warning notice printed, or any of many other possible actions might be taken.

In the *editing* step data or results are rearranged for printing, with spaces and punctuation inserted and perhaps with leading zeros deleted. For instance, a number that appears within the computer as 00057834 might need to be printed as $578.34; the Social Security number 535221583 might need to be printed as 535-22-1583; the letters JBSMITH might need to be printed as J. B. SMITH. Planning for output editing can be a sizable portion of the work of getting a computer system going.

Data must frequently be *rearranged,* but this has two rather different meanings. In the first it is often necessary to alter the way the data for one item in the system is organized. As an example, an input card may list a man's payroll number first, followed by his name; the printed output might be more readable if his name were printed first. It turns out, perhaps surprisingly, that rearranging data in this sense is a rather large part of electronic data processing.

In the second meaning of rearrangement individual data items are left unchanged, but collections of items called *records* are rearranged. It is often necessary to get a group of transactions into ascending sequence on part number or alphabetically by employee name. The case studies involve this kind of data rearrangement, which is usually called *sorting.*

Data must be *stored* for varying lengths of time. It must be stored at least for the interval of time between reading it from an input device of the computer until it is actually processed; this is one of the functions of the *internal storage* of the computer. In most applications it must also be stored for much longer periods of time; for example, from week to week or from month to month. This is the function of *file storage,* which is most commonly done with decks of punched cards or, in the computer situation, with magnetic tapes or disks.

One of the most important functions in working with a file-storage medium like magnetic tape, in which the records must be inspected in sequence (sequential-file processing), is the process of locating the master-file record that corresponds to a particular transaction-file record. Consider the inventory-control example again. We assume that the transaction records (issue requests, receipt notices, inventory recounts, etc.) have already been sorted into the same ascending sequence on part numbers as the master file. Now we read the first transaction record, but it may not be for the first part number in the master file: there may have been no issues or receipts for that particular part number. We must therefore search through the master-file records until we find the one that does correspond to the first transaction record. When it has been processed, we read the next transaction record, which could be for the same part number as the first, for the next part number in the master file, or for a part number somewhere later in the master file. So we search the master file again until we find correspondence. The basic concept of *sequential-file data processing* is that there can never be a transaction record that requires us to go *backward* in the master file: this is guaranteed by having both files in the same ascending sequence. On the other hand, we shall see that some applications call for the adoption of a different technique called *random processing* of a master file. In this case the file is stored on a *random access* medium, such as a magnetic disk, and records are accessed in a sequential or nonsequential manner, the latter being more important.

The last data-processing operation is that of preparing *reports.* Some reports are what the word implies: stock status, sales statistics, checks outstanding, accounts receivable, or insurance policies that have lapsed. However, we are using the term "report" in a general sense for any results that a data-processing system produces, and thus it includes checks to employees and suppliers, earnings statements to employees, packing slips, bills to customers, back-order notices, or anything else that a computer system might produce. In a sense the production of reports is the goal of all data processing: the system has not served any useful purpose until some person is able to act because of the computer's output. In fulfilling this function, the data-processing system does all of the other things we have listed: the output must be rearranged and edited; new input data must be combined with stored file information; the results of calculations and decisions are eventually presented on some suitable medium, most commonly a printed report.*

In conclusion our task in setting up a data-processing system can be characterized as that of gathering all the information needed for the preparation of reports (including source data and master-file information), organizing it (rearranging and editing), matching new input with file information, performing the necessary calculations and decisions, and doing it all in such a way that as little human and computer effort as possible is used.

1.4 Data Characteristics and Organization

In order to discuss data processing intelligently, we need to know a little more about the data and, in particular, how it is organized. In this context data refers to almost any information that can exist in a computer system: source data, permanent master-file data, or data to be printed. This is slightly different from the common usage of the term, when data refers more to *input* information as distinguished from semipermanent reference (*master-file*) information or output results. Here we use the one term for all kinds and whenever necessary qualify it by saying *source* data, *master-file* data, *sorted* data, *edited* data, etc.

The most elementary unit of data, for our purposes now, is a *character,* which may be a numeric digit, a letter of the alphabet, or any of the special characters that may be allowed on a particular computer, such as a dollar sign, decimal point (period), comma, parentheses, or number sign. It will turn out that we need to regard a *blank* (also called a *space*) as a "character" too: it may seem nonsensical to call "nothing" a "character," but when it comes to storing data or printing reports the computer must have a way of representing the "char-

---

* Although printed reports are by far the most common kind of output, they are being replaced by other media in some applications. Rather than being printed, the output may be presented on a cathode-ray-tube display device for visual inspection, for instance, or transferred directly to microfilm.

acter" that results from reading a blank column on a card or that will result in printing nothing in a given position on a report.*

A *data item*, otherwise called a *field*, is composed of one or more characters. Examples of data items: an account number, an employee's home address, a quantity on hand, the amount of an insurance policy, and a total of all hours worked in a deck of time cards. Data items that contain only the digits 0 through 9 (and perhaps a plus or minus sign) are called NUMERIC†; data items that contain only letters of the alphabet and the space character are called ALPHABETIC; data items that may contain numeric and/or alphabetic characters and/or special characters are called alphanumeric.

We have spoken so far of two characteristics of data items: length and class (NUMERIC, ALPHABETIC, or alphanumeric). In Chapter 5 on the COBOL DATA DIVISION we shall find that several other characteristics must be described for effective computer processing. For now we may note one other feature of data items that we need: each must have a *name* so that we can conveniently refer to the data contained in it without actually knowing *what* data is there at any given moment. Following COBOL terminology, we call the name of a data item a *data name*; "data" is included here to distinguish the name of a data item from a number of other things that can be named in COBOL.

Most students have at least some difficulty in remembering always to make the crucial distinction between a data item and a data name. A *data item* is a piece of actual information that is processed. A *data name* is a symbol by which we refer to a data item. A common analogy is to compare a data name with a house number and a data item with the people who currently live in the house having that number. The distinction is necessary because, still following the analogy, we want to

refer to the people who currently live in the house (the data item) in terms of their address (data name); we will say "move the contents of 123 Main Street to 456 Maple Drive," by which we will mean that *whoever* occupies 123 Main Street *at this moment* should be moved. If we may stretch the comparison one more step, this is necessary because we want to be able to "process" whoever happens to come to town, without knowing who they are. In other words, we want to set up general data-processing procedures that will handle *any* data, within reasonable limits, without knowing at the time we write the procedures what the exact value of the data is.

A *record* is composed of data items. For instance, an inventory-control master-file record would ordinarily contain at least the following data items:

Part number
Quantity on hand
Quantity on order
Quantity reserved for future use on specific projects
Reorder point, below which more should be ordered
Quantity to order when an order is placed
A condensed verbal description

Depending on the nature of the company and the products stocked, such a record might contain many other data items.

An employee master-payroll record would ordinarily contain at least the following data items:

Employee number
Name
Address
Department
Pay rate
Sex
Age
Years with company
Pension-plan contribution
Accumulated pension-plan contributions
Number of dependents
Amount contributed so far this year to Social Security (year-to-date SS)
Year-to-date withholding tax
Amount of union dues
Timeclock location
Location to which check is sent
Year-to-date sick leave
Year-to-date sick pay

---

* The "character" space creates other problems: how do you "write" it when presenting examples in a text? The usual answer is to use some symbol to represent it with the understanding that this other symbol would obviously not be printed. Thus to indicate the number 123 preceded by three spaces we might let "b" stand for "blank" (or space) and write bbb123.

† Words shown in capitals have precise meaning in a COBOL program and are called *reserved words*. In most cases we shall not need the precise definitions until later, but the reader should become accustomed to the fact that these words have special meaning.

1.5 What Is a Program?

There obviously could be many others. A typical master-payroll record might contain in the neighborhood of 500 characters; in some systems the number exceeds a thousand.

Records are also assigned names for the same reasons that data items are.

A *file* consists of records. This is a formally correct definition, but it leaves out a number of points about the way most files are organized and used that are quite important to us. We should first add the qualification that almost any particular file in practice is composed of records *directed toward some one purpose.* They all consist of the information from time cards, they all contain information about insurance policies, or they all contain records from which paychecks will later be printed, and so on.

Second, with almost no exceptions each record in a file contains a *key* or *control field* or *tag* by which it can be identified for processing; for instance, the part number in an inventory-control master record is used to determine whether this is the record corresponding to a given transaction record; the file is normally in sequence on the part numbers of the records.

Third, a file often contains special records at the beginning and the end. For a magnetic tape, for example, the one at the beginning is called the beginning-file label, or header label; it contains identifying information about the file, such as file name, and creation date. The one at the end is called ending-file label, or trailer label.

Finally, many files are assumed to be in ascending or descending sequence on some key in each record. This is not an essential part of the definition of a file, but it is usually crucial to know whether the file is in sequence and on which item or combination of items.

Files are also assigned names and are further distinguished between input and output files.

A file may contain only a few records or it may contain millions; there are realistic examples of both extremes. A typical file size for the case studies that we shall be investigating later would be in the range of thousands to tens of thousands.

Some of the concepts discussed in the preceding paragraphs may not be entirely clear at this point, but most of them will fall easily into place at some later stage. As of now, a conceptual understanding of the terms record, record name, and file and file name will suffice to take us through the first elementary example of a COBOL program.

In many cases our feasibility study of an operation indicates that it can indeed be "computerized," namely, that some or all of its steps, procedures, and requirements can be better satisfied by one or more computer runs. If so, our systems-analysis and system-design work leads to the writing of a computer program, or a suite (otherwise called a series or system) of computer programs. A computer program can be defined as a set of declarative and procedural statements (instructions) organized in a prescribed fashion, which tells the computer, in a very precise form, the steps it must perform to produce a desired output from a given input.

Before writing a program we chart the series of main logical steps that describe the processing in a fashion that clarifies them *to us.* This can best be done with a *block diagram,* also called *flow chart* or *flow diagram.* Let us start with an elementary example.

Suppose we have a file and that for some reason we want to duplicate it; that is, we want to write a program that takes each record from an input file and reproduces it onto an output file, changing neither the record sequence nor any of the data.

We can draw a tentative block diagram that might look like that shown in Figure 1.2.

This logical overview of the processing to be performed would not change, regardless of the programming language we intend to use for writing our program; it merely breaks down the operation into a series of sequential steps. If we now write our program in COBOL, these steps could be represented by the corresponding statements:

```
READ FILE-A.
MOVE RECORD-A TO RECORD-B.
WRITE RECORD-B.
```

We can see already some of the features of a COBOL program. For one thing English words are used to give the desired commands. The meaning of the words used to describe the action to be taken—called *verbs* in COBOL—is usually self-

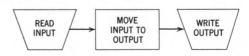

Figure 1.2. Skeleton block diagram of an illustrative file-processing program.

explanatory: READ, MOVE, and WRITE are the same words that we would normally use in the block diagram. FILE-A is the data name that we have chosen for the input file; RECORD-A is the data name that we have chosen for the input record. Why didn't we say READ RECORD-A, since it is actually a record that we want? The answer is that every COBOL verb has syntax rules that specify the types of word that can be used with it. The syntax rule for READ states that the name of an *input file* must follow the verb.

Notice that the syntax rules for WRITE are not the same as for READ. Write requires the name of a *record* to follow and, furthermore, it must be a record of an *output* file. Remember that in COBOL we must READ a file and WRITE a record.

The MOVE verb has a still different set of syntax rules. We not only have to specify *what* is being moved but *where* it is being moved to. From the information presented so far we could deduce part of the syntax rules for the verb MOVE: it must be followed by a data name, and the word TO in the MOVE statement is also necessary, as is the second data name after TO. We can deduce some of the more general COBOL rules: each statement ends with a period and, incidentally, there must be at least one space after the period before we can start another statement.

Let us now digress briefly to give a preliminary over-all view of the structure of a COBOL program. A COBOL program consists of four parts called DIVISIONS: IDENTIFICATION, ENVIRONMENT, DATA, and PROCEDURE. The IDENTIFICATION DIVISION is quite elementary and contains such information as the programmer's name and program identification data. The ENVIRONMENT DIVISION describes the computer on which the program will be compiled and executed, two important concepts that we shall discuss shortly, and ties together the input and output devices of the computer and the data files to be processed. In the DATA DIVISION we describe, among other things, the format and the data layout of the files and assign data names to them. Finally, the PROCEDURE DIVISION contains the instructions that will create a set of desired output data from a given set of input data.

The procedural statements of our example ("READ FILE-A." "MOVE RECORD-A TO RECORD-B." "WRITE RECORD-B.") all belong in the PROCEDURE DIVISION of our program. But the fact that we have decided to call our input file FILE-A, our input record RECORD-A, and our output record RECORD-B would be reflected in the DATA DIVISION. These data names are called *user-defined* or *programmer-supplied* words, and we usually make them up to be as descriptive as possible within a set of rules that is fully stated in Chapter 3. READ, MOVE, and WRITE are instead COBOL *reserved words* that must always be spelled in a fixed and prescribed manner.

Let us now go back to our example. The reader may already have noticed that the three-statement program written above is not a workable one. What happens after the WRITE statement? Nothing, because we did not say what was to be done next. So we must add something. While doing so let us also assume that we no longer like the data names we chose for our files and record—perhaps they were not sufficiently descriptive—and we therefore wish to use some new ones. (We can always change data names in the PROCEDURE DIVISION as long as we change them in the DATA DIVISION as well. The data names in the two divisions must be consistent.)

Now the block diagram and the COBOL statements would be as shown in Figure 1.3, and the program would look like this:

```
READ-ROUTINE.
    READ FILE-IN.
    MOVE RECORD-IN TO RECORD-OUT.
    WRITE RECORD-OUT.
    GO TO READ-ROUTINE.
```

A new COBOL verb has been introduced. Notice that this verb has two words: GO, followed by TO. We could not say GO READ-ROUTINE. After GO TO there must be a *procedure name*; in this case we have decided to use READ-ROUTINE. Procedure names may also be called *paragraph names*, or *paragraph headers*, since they break the COBOL program into separate paragraphs, which can then be referenced individually by certain COBOL verbs, such as GO TO. They are user-

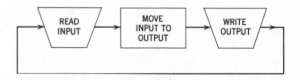

Figure 1.3. The block diagram of Figure 1.2, modified to repeat indefinitely.

defined; we could have selected for our routine a paragraph name like ROUT-45-ONE, in which case we would have said GO TO ROUT-45-ONE.

The next action that will be taken by our program after it executes the statement GO TO READ ROUTINE is READ FILE-IN. The name READ-ROUTINE is just a name, not a command, and it serves merely as an entry point to which the control of the program can be transferred. What we said for data names also applies to paragraph names: they must be formed according to a set of rules that we will find in Chapter 3.

Even with the GO TO statement, our program would still fail to work properly; it would go on forever. What we need is to stop the run when all the records have been duplicated; namely, when the end of the input file has been reached.

In COBOL the test for the "end of file" is made part of the READ statement. Therefore we can rewrite the block diagram as shown in Figure 1.4, and the program could be

```
READ-ROUTINE.
      READ FILE-IN, AT END GO TO END-
      RUN.
      MOVE RECORD-IN TO RECORD-OUT.
      WRITE RECORD-OUT.
      GO TO READ-ROUTINE.
  END-RUN.
      STOP RUN.
```

When the end-of-file condition is reached, and only then, the GO TO END-RUN instruction will be activated, thus causing the STOP RUN statement to be executed. Notice that there is a comma after FILE-IN; this is one of the punctuation marks that can be used in COBOL at the programmer's discretion.

The verb STOP does exactly what it says: it stops the execution of the program. The word RUN, used after STOP, is another COBOL reserved word which indicates that the program has been executed to its completion; the computer is now free to execute another job.

The program as now written seems to be logically sound. There are, however, still a few details left. Before a file can be read it must be *opened,* and at the end it must be *closed.* The COBOL verbs OPEN and CLOSE take care of these steps, as discussed more fully in Chapter 3. The specific actions that the computer will take in executing these commands will vary according to whether the file type is magnetic tape, punched cards, printed output, or disk. (The entries describing the types of file used by a COBOL program are provided in the ENVIRONMENT DIVISION.)

We can now look at the complete block diagram (Figure 1.5) and PROCEDURE DIVISION of our sample program:

```
PROCEDURE DIVISION.
HOUSEKEEPING.
      OPEN INPUT FILE-IN.
      OPEN OUTPUT FILE-OUT.
READ-ROUTINE.
      READ FILE-IN, AT END GO TO END-
      RUN.
      MOVE RECORD-IN TO RECORD-OUT.
      WRITE RECORD-OUT.
      GO TO READ-ROUTINE.
  END-RUN.
      CLOSE FILE-IN.
      CLOSE FILE-OUT.
      STOP RUN.
```

Notice that the syntax rules for OPEN require that this verb be followed by the COBOL reserved words INPUT or OUTPUT—as the case applies—and then by the data names of the files, whereas CLOSE must be followed only by the file names.

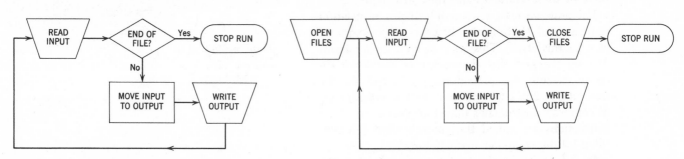

Figure 1.4. The block diagram of Figure 1.3, modified to include a test for the completion of processing.

Figure 1.5. The completed block diagram of an illustrative file-processing program, including opening and closing of files.

Notice also that the title of the division—PRO-CEDURE DIVISION—must appear at the beginning of it.

1.6   How Does COBOL Actually Work?

Once a COBOL program has been duly written on COBOL coding sheets—as we explain in detail in Chapter 3—the PROCEDURE DIVISION, as well as the other three DIVISIONS of the program that we have ignored so far, are transferred onto some medium that a computer can read—generally punched cards.

At this point we may think that the computer could actually be "instructed" by the COBOL program, but that is not quite correct. A computer cannot follow a procedure of this sort just as it stands; there must be an intermediate translation step first. A computer does not "understand" words like READ, MOVE, or WRITE; its vocabulary includes only the *codes* for these actions in which 01 might stand for reading a card or M 207 756, for moving a particular data item.

Furthermore, some of the COBOL verbs cannot be translated into a single computer operation: in many machines, for instance, the instruction "AT END GO TO" would require at least two elementary computer operations. A most important part of the translation from the language of COBOL to the language of the machine is the combination of the actions in the PROCEDURE DIVISION with the data descriptions in the DATA DIVISION. If the two data items in a MOVE are of different lengths, a number of computer operations may be required to add or delete zeros or spaces. Finally, every data item in the computer must have a location in the *storage* of the machine and all operations are actually specified in terms of the contents of storage locations. We shall investigate some of these matters more fully in Chapter 2.

For now we need realize only that a translation is necessary. Fortunately, however, the computer can do this itself. This may seem like a contradiction: we said that the computer could not directly execute the procedure, yet it can do the translation. The explanation is that a *separate* set of computer instructions does the translation; these instructions are called the *compiler* and are supplied by the computer manufacturer.

It cannot be emphasized too strongly that *the compiler is itself a computer program* and a rather sophisticated one at that. The operation is called *compilation* and can be schematically described as shown on Figure 1.6. Notice that one of the two outputs of the compilation is a listing of the program; as we shall see later, this listing contains more than the COBOL cards did. The program, as written in COBOL, is called the *source program*; the set of basic computer instructions produced by the compiler is called the *object program*. It is the object program that is actually executed by the computer to read data, do processing, and produce results. Stated otherwise, *we write a source program; the source program is translated into an object program; the computer executes the object program.* Usually the same computer that translates the program (source computer) will also execute it later, acting as the object computer. (We say usually the same computer because in principle it is possible for one computer to translate programs that will then be run on a different one. In fact, the ENVIRONMENT DIVISION of a COBOL program makes specific allowance for such a possibility.)

The word "COBOL" refers both to the source-programming language and to the compilers that translate programs written in this language into the language of a particular computer.

One of the advantages of COBOL is that the various COBOL compilers accept basically the same source-program language. In some cases

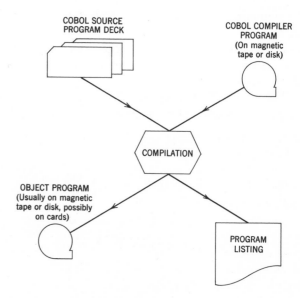

Figure 1.6.   The process of compilation.

there may be features in one compiler that are not found in others, and the characteristics of the object computers may require some changes beyond those always required in the ENVIRONMENT DIVISION. Once these changes are made, however, the same source program can be compiled to run on any machine for which there is a COBOL compiler—which is almost all computers except the smallest.

Thus a computer user is able to change computers with much less cost of reprogramming than if all programs were written in the language of the machine itself. Since different machines are so different in their basic languages, it is generally impossible to change machines without a complete reprogramming job if machine language has been used.

Historically, COBOL grew out of this desire to develop a language that would be *compatible,* that is, acceptable as a source-program language by any computer for which there is a COBOL compiler. This work began in 1959 under the direction of a group of computer experts, many of whom had worked on somewhat similar "English-language" systems, as alluded to in the acknowledgment at the front of the book. The maintenance and orderly development of the language was established as one of the functions of a group called the Conference on Data Systems Languages, which is abbreviated CODASYL.

The first formal report defining COBOL was issued in 1960; that version of COBOL is therefore referred to as COBOL-60. This book reflects subsequent versions—particularly COBOL-61, COBOL-65, and the ANSI (American National Standards Institute) COBOL of 1968—as well as some COBOL extensions recently implemented by a number of computer manufacturers.

A few points should be made in this regard. As in the case of our everyday language, COBOL does not stand still: some words become obsolete, whereas other words are created to express new concepts or to give a name to a new device.

The changes in COBOL in recent years have mainly reflected two facts of life:

As we shall see in Chapters 3 and 5, the original and the present COBOL languages often offer several options for doing the same thing. Too much flexibility tends to create confusion, and therefore many COBOL users have decided to adopt a streamlined set of instructions and strongly urge

their programmers not to use the excluded ones. The adoption of such COBOL *subsets* reduces the amount of training, creates uniform standards for all programs written within the same installation, and reduces the burdens of testing the performance of new compiler versions.

Also, if the compiler for computer A is able to take care of options X and Y, whereas the compiler for computer B is able to translate only option Y, the standards group of an installation that uses both computers would rule option X as illegal and would make option Y compulsory. The reason is obvious: a COBOL program using option Y would work on both computers. On their part the computer manufacturers contributed to this streamlining trend by eliminating from their compilers those options that were not actively used.

On the other hand, there are same factors that contribute to the expansions of COBOL options and reserved words. For instance, the addition of new devices and techniques (disk files and random access) has made it necessary to create new COBOL options to take care of the manipulations that they entail.

In view of the above it is almost impossible—and hardly useful—to cover every minute detail of every possible COBOL option. The purpose of this book is to provide a subset of COBOL options as large as necessary to acquire an understanding of COBOL programs and methods and to write programs that would be accepted by most compilers. The reader who will be using COBOL for actual computer work clearly must have a copy of the manufacturer's reference manual for his compiler.

1.7 Conclusion

It has been our intention in this chapter to give the reader an overview of the data-processing task and the place of COBOL in it. It has *not* been our intention to present any of the material in enough detail to make it completely understandable or usable without further study. This is said in a frank attempt to encourage those who may, at this point, feel some confusion or even discouragement. Not that we *planned* it that way, but it *is* normal.

If the reader has a *general* idea of what has been going on, we would urge him to press on, with the assurance that every attempt has been made to explore fully in succeeding chapters the matters that have been introduced here.

REVIEW QUESTIONS

1. True or false:
   a. COBOL stands for COMPILER ORIENTED BASIC ORGANIZED LISTING.
   b. A COBOL compiler translates a COBOL source program into an object program.
   c. A COBOL compiler must be written in COBOL.
   d. All COBOL compilers are perfectly identical.
   e. A COBOL program consists of four DIVISIONS: IDENTIFICATION, ENVIRONMENT, DATA, and PROCEDURE.
   f. OPEN, CLOSE, READ, and WRITE are examples of COBOL verbs.
   g. If we wished to read every second record of the input file in the sample program in Section 1.5, it would be permissible to write a COBOL instruction like READ EVERY SECOND RECORD OF FILE-IN. (Guess or cheat; at this point you cannot really know.)
   h. A file consists of records, a record consists of data items (otherwise called fields), and a data item consists of characters.

2. Which of the following are generally regarded as advantages of COBOL over machine or assembly language?
   a. COBOL is more machine-independent and therefore allows for easier program conversion from one computer to another.
   b. COBOL offers better documentation.
   c. COBOL is easier to learn.
   d. In performing the same task, an object program generated by a COBOL compiler is much faster than a program written in machine or assembly language.

ANSWERS

1. a. If you have answered "yes" to this question, have another chance at making a correct guess: does COBOL stand for Common Bargain Oriental Language?
   b. True.
   c. False. In fact, it never is.
   d. False! They may vary in number of options and features.
   e. True.
   f. True, and, as such, they are COBOL reserved words and must therefore be spelled and used in a prescribed manner.
   g. False. We can do many things in COBOL, but this would not be a legal COBOL instruction. As we proceed through this book, we shall study the legal COBOL options and the syntax rules that govern them: improvisation in this field is pointless.
   h. True.

2. a, b, and c are regarded as advantages of COBOL, d is not.

2. PUNCHED CARD AND COMPUTER EQUIPMENT

2.1 Punched Card Concepts and Equipment

A COBOL programmer needs a certain amount of knowledge about punched cards because they are commonly used to enter data and programs into the computer and because certain punched-card machines still appear in most data-processing installations. This is true despite the fact that punched-card calculating devices are not classified as computers and COBOL cannot be used as a source programming language for them.

It is not uncommon for a COBOL programmer to "write" his program directly onto cards by using a card punch without ever putting pencil to paper. And even when this is not done the programmer almost always has occasion to punch program corrections and modifications himself.

Accordingly, we begin this survey of computer equipment with a study of how information is represented on cards and what some of the more common punched-card devices are—which may also have a certain historical interest. We then turn to the question of what a computer is composed of and very generally how it works.

A punched card is a piece of light flexible cardboard $7\frac{3}{8}$ wide and $3\frac{1}{4}$ inches high. In what is commonly called the IBM card information is represented with rectangular holes arranged in 80 columns. Sometimes portions of cards less than $7\frac{3}{8}$ inches wide

and having fewer than 80 columns are used, especially in consumer applications in which the customer returns a portion of the bill with his payment. Other configurations, such as the Remington Rand card with its 90 columns and round holes, have been largely supplanted.

The 80 vertical columns are numbered 1 to 80, from left to right. Each column may contain one of the digits 0 to 9, the letters A to Z, or any of the special characters such as dollar or percent sign. There are 12 vertical punching positions in each column, of which those for 0 to 9 are identified by preprinting on the card. Numerical information is recorded by punching a single hole in a given column in the position representing that digit.

Alphabetic information is represented by a combination of two punches, a *numerical* punch and a *zone* punch. Positions 1 to 9 are referred to as the numerical positions. There are three zone punching positions:

12 zone—at the top edge of the card.
11 zone—just below the 12-zone position.
Zero zone—just below the 11-zone position (zero zone and numerical zero are the same position).

The 12- and 11-zone positions are not identified by preprinting on the card because this part of the card is set aside for printing the contents of the columns. Some card punches can print at the top of the card the data punched in each column and a separate machine is available to do essentially the same thing.

The codes (combinations of punches) for the letters of the alphabet are shown in Figure 2.1. To understand the basic idea of this coding* it may be helpful to note that the letters A through I are made up of a 12-zone punch and one of the digits 1 through 9; the letters J through R are made up of an 11-zone punch and one of the digits 1 through 9; the letters S through Z are composed of a zero-zone punch and one of the digits 2 through 9.

The combination of a zero zone and a numerical 1 is used to represent the symbol / (slash). The other special symbols are made up of a 12 zone or an 11 zone alone or the combinations 8-3, 8-4,

---

* Called Hollerith coding after Dr. Herman Hollerith, who invented a similar system for use in the 1890 United States census.

8-5, or 8-6, either alone or with the various zone punches. Thus an ampersand (&) is represented by a 12 zone only; a minus sign (—), by an 11 zone only. The percent sign is represented by the combination of an 8, 4, and zero zone. The combinations used for digits, letters, and some of the most commonly used special characters on the IBM-360 are shown in Figure 2.2; configurations and availability of special characters vary in different equipment, and there are variations even within the equipment of the same manufacturer.

There is no need to memorize these codes because they are automatically punched by the depression of the keys on the card punch and are read automatically by the various machines that accept information from cards. Furthermore, a card punch can be equipped with a printing device that prints at the top of the card the character represented by each column. For cards punched by some other means than a card punch, such as a computer, the characters represented by selected columns can be printed at the top of the card by a machine called an *interpreter*.

Figure 2.3 shows an IBM-29 Card Punch. This device can also be used to reproduce a card, either entirely or partially, a feature that is extremely useful to a COBOL programmer. Also, a double-check, or verification, can be performed on input data: the same card is "punched" again by a different operator on a sister machine, and a special

A	12 and 1	J	11 and 1	S	0 and 2
B	12 and 2	K	11 and 2	T	0 and 3
C	12 and 3	L	11 and 3	U	0 and 4
D	12 and 4	M	11 and 4	V	0 and 5
E	12 and 5	N	11 and 5	W	0 and 6
F	12 and 6	O	11 and 6	X	0 and 7
G	12 and 7	P	11 and 7	Y	0 and 8
H	12 and 8	Q	11 and 8	Z	0 and 9
I	12 and 9	R	11 and 9		

Figure 2.1. Card codes for the letters of the alphabet.

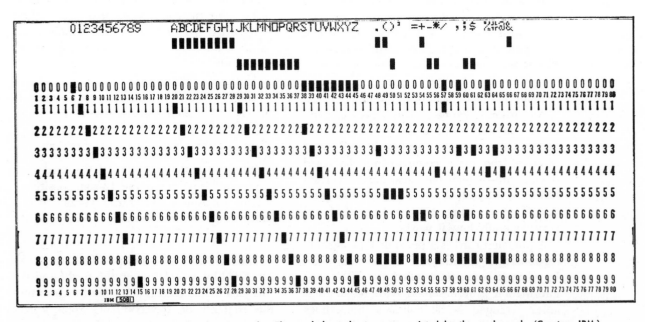

Figure 2.2. A punched card showing the character codes. The symbols at the top were printed by the card punch. (Courtesy IBM.)

Figure 2.3. An IBM Model 29 Card Punch. (Courtesy IBM.)

mark is automatically punched on the margin of the card if the verified columns coincide.

In normal usage columns on a card are grouped into data items, or fields, as discussed in Section 1.4. Data-item assignments, of course, change from one job to the next. The group of columns regarded as one data item in one job might contain parts of several data items in another. There is nothing built into the various card-handling machines that automatically regards any set of columns as being a data item. This assignment must be planned by the user and the various machines instructed accordingly. In COBOL this is one of the functions of the DATA DIVISION.

The handling of data items on a card provides us with an example of a most important concept in data processing: how the equipment handles data depends on how the user *wants* the equipment to handle it. Suppose, for instance, that the four columns 20 to 23 contain punches representing the digits 4397. If we are simply given a card containing these punches, we do not know whether they represent 4397 bolts, $43.97, a $4.397 tax per $100 assessed valuation, or almost anything else. The simple yet fundamental fact is that we have no way of knowing what the digits mean without knowing what they were *intended* to mean. It is the responsibility of the persons planning the data-processing operations—the system analyst or the programmer—to assign the desired meaning to

these columns: to provide punching instructions that will tell the card-punch operators how to punch data in the data item, to set up the card-handling equipment so that the digits in the data item will be handled in the intended way, and to write COBOL DATA DIVISION entries and procedure statements (in our case) so that the desired operations will be properly executed; for example, the operations necessary to process $4397 properly may be considerably different from those required to process $4.397. In our case a suitable DATA DIVISION entry would result in appropriate object-program instructions for either case. Apart from what we say in instructions to computer operators or in the COBOL DATA DIVISION, the data-processing equipment has no way of knowing anything about the difference.

Another good example of this principle is in the variety of meanings attached to an 11 punch in a column. An 11 punch by itself in a column is sometimes used to distinguish the card from other types of card in the same application. In another situation it might cause a printer to print a minus sign or hyphen (-) or it might be used in combination with a numerical punch to represent one of the letters J through R. Again, it might be used in the units position (rightmost column) of a data item with one of the digits 0 to 9 to signal that the entire data item is a credit amount or, mathematically, a negative number. What an 11 punch is taken to mean is entirely up to the person planning the application.

As we have already seen in Chapter 1, one of the most frequent data-processing operations is to sort a set of records into ascending (or descending) sequence on a control key contained in the records. This is most commonly done with magnetic tapes, or disks, at least in the larger computing systems, but it can also be done with a *card sorter*. In data processing based entirely on punched-card methods all sorting is, of course, done with a card sorter, but even in modern computer systems card files are sometimes sorted before entering the data into the computer.

The card sorter, such as the IBM-83 in Figure 2.4, may be seen to have a card hopper and 13 pockets. As the card leaves the hopper, it moves past the *reading station*. This consists of a *brush* that may be set to detect a hole in any one of the 80 columns. When the brush senses a hole in the column, it directs the card to the correspondingly

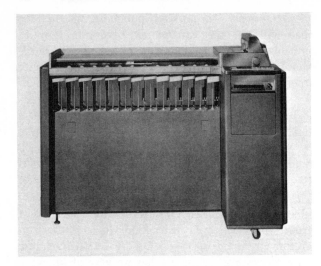

Figure 2.4. An IBM Model 83 Sorter. (Courtesy IBM.)

numbered pocket. If there is no hole in the column, the card is sent to the reject pocket. This sorter can feed cards at a rate of 1000 per minute.

The single brush in a sorter can read only one column at a time. To sort a deck of cards into ascending sequence on a *control key* of several digits requires several passes of the deck through the sorter. The first sort pass is made on the least significant (rightmost) digit of the key, after which the cards are picked up from the pockets in sequence. This puts all the cards with a zero in the least significant digit at the front of the deck, all the ones next, etc. Then the deck is run through the sorter again, this time sorting on the next most significant digit. When the deck has been sorted on all columns of the key, starting from the least significant and ending with the most significant, the deck will be in sequence on the entire key.

The reader should satisfy himself by experimenting with an example that it is necessary to start with the least significant digit, not the most significant, remembering that after each sort pass the entire deck is picked up from the pockets and reassembled; that is, it is not normal procedure to keep the cards from each pocket separate after a sort pass.

Sorting cards on an alphabetic control data item is somewhat more complex and requires either two complete passes on each column or special circuitry in the sorter.

A *collator* can determine whether one deck of cards is properly in sequence. It can *merge* two sequenced decks, which means to combine them into one deck that is also in sequence. It can *match* two decks, which means all cards in one deck with keys that are not the same as those of cards in the other deck are selected out; the matched cards from the two decks may be left separate or combined as desired.

A typical application of a card collator would be as follows. We start with a master file of cards in sequence on part number and a deck of transaction cards, also in sequence on part number. The two decks are placed in the two hoppers of the collator. All transaction cards for which there is no corresponding master are selected into a special pocket; likewise, all masters for which there is no transaction card are selected out. The former is an error, probably indicating a mispunched transaction card; the latter simply means that transactions were not made for every master record. The matched cards are combined so that each matched master is followed by the associated transaction. This example shows that, among other things, a collator could perform the data-processing operation of matching corresponding records in two files, which, as we saw in Section 1.3, is one of the fundamental operations. Data-processing systems based on punched-card equipment make heavy use of the collator for this purpose.

A card *reproducer* is a simple device that can make a copy of a card. Actually, it can do considerably more, such as rearranging the fields during reproduction or *gang punching* (duplicating) the information from one card into several subsequent cards.

A *tabulator* basically performs two functions, although it can do them in a great variety of ways: it *lists* (prints) the information and *summarizes* (totals) data from cards. By the use of a control panel containing wires that direct the machine's operations these basic functions can be varied in many ways. Totals may be broken down by categories, controlled by punching in the cards themselves, page headings and page numbers may be produced, and the handling of card information may be made dependent on codes in the cards.

In a computer data-processing system that uses COBOL a tabulator would probably be needed only for listing cards so that they could be checked.

Punched card *calculators* read card data, compute results, and punch them into cards. These devices, which are not called computers because their instructions are not stored within the machine but instead consist of control panel wiring, can do arithmetic operations, rearrange data, accumulate totals, and make elementary decisions, all at very slow speeds.

2.2   The Parts of a Computer

One of the advantages of COBOL is that the programmer using it does not have to know so much about how the machine operates as he does when programming in the machine's own language. Nevertheless, it is not possible to do a really effective job without learning certain facts about the computer in order to know what can and cannot be done, the reasons for some of the powers and restrictions of the COBOL language, and to avoid doing things in a way that is legal and will produce correct results but is still very wasteful of computer time.

We begin by considering the over-all organization of a computer of the kind that is used with COBOL.* Figure 2.5 shows schematically the major parts of such a machine.

The *input* section handles the entry into the machine of data and the coded instructions that control the machine's actions. This is the phase of the computer's operation that is called *reading*; by

this we mean that information is accepted in some machine-sensible form, such as punched cards, and translated into the form in which it is stored inside the machine, which is usually some type of magnetic storage. The input section also performs a "speed translation," in that things like card readers and tape readers are always at least partly mechanical and therefore much slower than the internal electronic operations.

Punched cards are widely used for the entry of information into a computer. Figure 2.6 shows the IBM 2501 Card Reader. This device can read cards at the rate of 1300 per minute, which is perhaps a little faster than average; a typical rate for punch-card reading might be about 800 cards per minute, which is equivalent to 1100 characters (14 cards) per second.

Punch-card data may be read by the main computer and processed "on-line," either directly or after it has been transferred to magnetic tape or disk; or, if we wish to restrict the use of a large computer to more important processes, cards may be

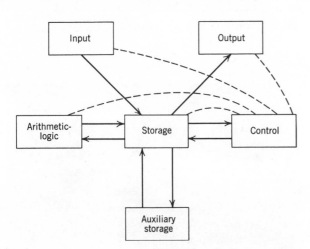

Figure 2.5. The functional parts of a stored program computer.

* We are excluding *analog* computers, which represent information by establishing *analogies* between numbers and voltages or shaft rotations and therefore have limited accuracy and also do not deal with the alphabetic information that is so important in business data processing. We are thus restricting ourselves to *stored program digital* computers; the meanings of these terms will become clear shortly.

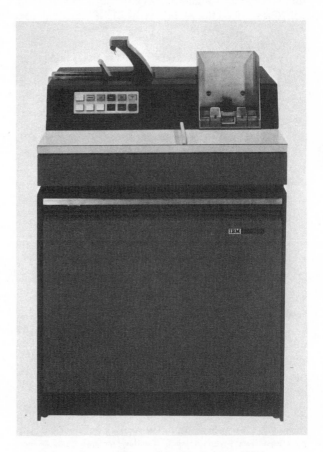

Figure 2.6. The IBM 2501 Card Reader. (Courtesy IBM.)

read "off-line" on a small peripheral computer, which creates a magnetic tape or disk which is then accepted by the larger (and more costly) main computer.

To eliminate the steps of punching the cards and transferring them to tape it is possible to employ a device—called a *data recorder* or *data encoder*— which enables us to write the original input directly onto magnetic tape. Figure 2.7 shows the Mohawk Data Sciences Model 6401 Data-Recorder. Its keyboard is very similar to that of a card punch, but the depression of a key, instead of perforating a card, causes a character to be registered on a magnetic tape. Other data-recorder models have the added capability of transmitting data over telephone lines, thereby making available to a central computer input data from several distant sources.

Another device—generally called an *optical scanner*—permits the bypassing of the card-creation step. This device can transfer to magnetic tape —or directly to the computer core—information that it reads directly in printed form. If this step is based on sensing powdered metallic particles in the ink, it is called Magnetic Ink Character Recognition (MICR). If ordinary ink is used, it is called Op-

tical Character Recognition (OCR). Several companies (Farrington, Control Data, and IBM, among others) have developed OCR devices. Figure 2.8 shows the Control Data Model 915 page reader. MICR is presently employed primarily in banking applications for reading and processing checks. OCR is used in a variety of high-input-volume applications.

Punched paper tape is also used as an input medium. Figure 2.9 shows a section used with the National Cash Register Century Series Computers. Figure 2.10 shows the paper tape reader (left) and the paper tape punch used with the Burroughs B6500 computer. Reading rates vary between 100 and 1000 characters per second; the 350 per second of the Burroughs reader is representative.

Paper tape is used as the *primary* input medium only on some smaller computers, but it is available as an optional method, along with others, for a number of larger machines.

Typewriters, usually an integral part of a computer console, can be used to enter minor amounts of information into the computer at the (relatively) extremely slow rates of human typing. Figure 2.11 shows the operator's console for the Xerox Data Systems Sigma 7.

A typewriter can serve also as an *output* device at a speed of about 15 characters per second. As we shall see, this is a great deal slower than tape writing and line printing; the use of a console type-

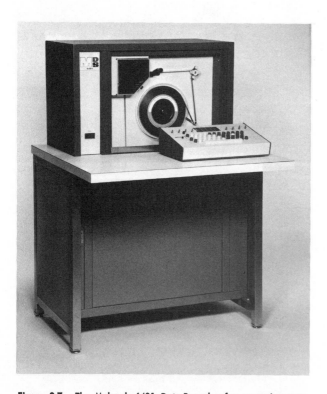

Figure 2.7. The Mohawk 6401 Data-Recorder for preparing magnetic tape from keyboard input. (Courtesy Mohawk Data Sciences Corporation.)

Figure 2.8. The Control Data Corporation Model 915 optical page reader. (Courtesy Control Data Corporation.)

Figure 2.9. A section of paper tape used with National Cash Register Century Series computers. (Courtesy National Cash Register Company.)

Figure 2.10. The paper tape reader *(left)* and paper tape punch used with the Burroughs B6500 computer. (Courtesy Burroughs Corporation.)

writer is therefore limited to messages that are both short and pertinent to the control of the computer operations.

Some sophisticated typewriter models are used as remote *terminals,* in which case they communicate with a computer over telephone lines. In such a system a computer is programmed to service a certain number of remote users and provides them with answers to their individual queries. This environment is known as *time sharing,* since the computer is actually shared by many users, and is found especially in *real-time* applications—another fashionable expression meaning, in general, "fast response" to an inquiry. Statistical and engineering problems are good examples of applications in which a quick turnaround of, let us say, 20 or 30 seconds may prove to be of great value.

Input-output devices related to the processing of

Figure 2.11. Operator's console for the Xerox Data Systems Sigma 7, with paper tape and magnetic tape units visible in background. (Courtesy Xerox Data Systems.)

magnetic tapes and disks are described in Section 2.5, in which we discuss these important media at length.

The *output* section has the obvious function of presenting results within the computer in a readable form, carrying out in reverse the same two translations of medium and speed that the input section does. The most common device for output is a *line printer*, that is, a printer that can print one complete line at a time. The maximum number of characters per line varies with the printer model and is usually 132, 120, or 100. A typical speed for line printing is about 900 lines per minute or, at 132 characters per line, about 2000 characters per second. Figure 2.12 shows the General Electric PRT 201 printer, which prints 1200 lines per minute.

Another output device is the *card-punch*, which

punches out cards from information processed by the computer. A typical speed for this operation is about 350 cards per minute or, at 80 characters per card, about 500 characters per second. Figure 2.13 shows the IBM 2540 Card Read-Punch which accommodates under the same frame a card reader and a card-punch.

Punched paper tape can be produced by some machines at a typical rate of 50 characters per second and then printed with a special typewriter or used directly to operate teletype or other equipment.

In recent years we have witnessed the ascendancy of some interesting nontraditional output media, which aim at replacing printed reports. Although nothing seems to be more readable than a printed page, the producing, handling, and storing of reams and reams of paper create quite a few problems. To

Figure 2.12. The General Electric PRT201 Printer. (Courtesy General Electric Company.)

Figure 2.13. The IBM 2540 Card Read-Punch. (Courtesy IBM.)

computer storage to a microfilm at a speed of the order of 60,000 characters per second. This number of characters is roughly equivalent to five pages of printed output which would normally require about 15 seconds of computer time. A bulky 3000-page report is thus replaced by 3000 microfilm frames, which fit nicely in a pocket-size cartridge. As usual, there is a price to pay: microfilms enable us to save time and space but require the use of special viewers for the perusal of the data. Figure 2.14 shows the DatagraphiX 4440 Micromation Printer.

CRT devices work like TV sets. Selected information is transferred from computer storage to the CRT video and is displayed on it for a number of seconds. This technique is particularly useful in some real-time applications such as inventory control, credit-account management, and airline-ticket reservations. Figure 2.15 shows the RCA Video Data Terminal.

The *storage* section of a computer serves two purposes. It holds the data currently being processed (as distinguished from the data waiting to be read and processed or the data in auxiliary storage that must be brought into internal storage before it can be processed). It also holds the coded instructions that direct the operation of the entire system. These instructions are coded with letters and/or digits so that the instructions can be stored

circumvent them there are at least two techniques that produce nonprinted output: microfilming and CRT (cathode ray tube) displays.

The microfilming process we are referring to transfers information from magnetic tape or from

Figure 2.14. The DatagraphiX 4440 Micromation Printer. (Courtesy Stromberg DatagraphiX, Inc., a General Dynamics subsidiary.)

Figure 2.15. The RCA Video Data Terminal. (Courtesy RCA.)

in precisely the same storage locations that in another problem might hold data.

The main internal storage of a computer, called *core storage* or *memory*, is composed of many thousands of magnetic cores, each of which can be magnetized in one of two "directions": characters can then be represented by combinations of individual cores in a manner that we shall investigate in Sections 2.3 and 5.7.

Computers range in core-storage capacity from a minimum of a few thousand characters to a typical figure of perhaps 60,000 and to a maximum that today may reach several million. Core-storage capacity is usually measured in units of K's. One K used to be equal to 1000, but it is now generally used to mean 2^{10}, or 1024. A 32K computer therefore has a memory of 32,768 characters. One character or, more commonly, one group of 5 to 10 characters can be obtained from core storage and moved to the arithmetic-logical section or to the control section in a representative time of one *microsecond* (millionth of a second).

The *arithmetic-logic* section of a computer does the actual processing of data. It is able to carry out arithmetic operations and can make simple decisions of the type mentioned in Chapter 1, which accounts for the "logic" part of the name. Two data items can be compared for equality or to decide which is larger, among other things. The outcome of such a decision determines which of two groups of instructions will be executed, the groups having been set up in the program to handle the different cases properly. The arithmetic-logic section can shift numbers right or left, or perform something

equivalent, to match up data items of different lengths and decimal-point positions. It can usually perform many operations that have to do with the detailed actions of a particular computing system.

The *control* section has the responsibility of getting instructions from storage in correct sequence, interpreting them, and sending properly timed signals to the rest of the machine, telling it what to do. This function takes up a large part of the electronic equipment of a computer.

Although we are not primarily concerned in this book with the hardware of which computers are constructed, it may be of interest to show (Figure 2.16) a picture of some internal circuitry of which a computer can be made. This view, here magnified approximately 40 times, is of an *integrated circuit* that, in this case, is part of the arithmetic-logic portion of a computer. Within the anticipated useful life of this book, such technology will advance to the point of being able to pack electronic com-

Figure 2.16. An integrated circuit element used in computers, with grains of table salt to show scale. The chip shown here, which is about a tenth of an inch in length, can contain about 5000 transistors. (Courtesy Electronic Arrays, Inc.; McCracken Associates photo.)

ponents somewhat more densely than neurons in the human brain.

Auxiliary storage is used to store data and instructions that take up too much space to be contained in core storage. This topic leads into a number of important concepts and is discussed fully in Section 2.5.

2.3 Representation and Storage of Information

Two things that are quite important for a COBOL programmer to know about computers are how information is stored and how it is represented because these matters are significant in setting up the DATA DIVISION, which in turn greatly influences the speed of the object program. We shall consider the most common representations of numeric and alphabetic characters and some important variations, the grouping of characters into units called words, and the way words are addressed (referred to).

Information is represented in a computer in a form that requires each storage or processing element to be able to take on only two distinct states. For instance, magnetic cores are built into storage systems so that each core is always fully magnetized in one direction or the other; a core is not allowed to operate so that its magnetization is anywhere between these two extremes. Thus each core can be used to represent exactly two symbols.

Since there are 10 digits, 26 letters, and a number of other characters to be processed, a character must be represented within the computer by a combination of individual cores. Four cores, logically associated, would be adequate to represent the digits from 0 to 9 and six cores would be adequate for all of the characters, since there are 64 different combinations of the directions of magnetization of six cores. But for reasons that we shall investigate shortly the prevailing number of cores logically associated for the purpose of representing characters is either seven or nine.

It would be inconvenient to talk for long in terms of "combinations of directions of magnetization of magnetic cores." We therefore look for some simpler way to describe the two directions of magnetization. Actually, any two convenient symbols or terms would do: north and south, or on and off, or yes and no. The conventional way is to call them zero and one, which is simply a convenience of ter-

minology and has nothing to do with the question whether the character represented by a *combination* of individual cores is zero or one or even numeric. A device or condition that has exactly two possible states is described as *binary*. It is then said to represent a *binary digit*, which is commonly abbreviated *bit*. We speak of the method of coding the various characters with six bits as *binary coding* or *binary coded decimal*. Figure 2.17 shows the binary coding of the 48 characters allowed in the IBM 1401 and 1410. Bits 1, 2, 4, and 8 stand for 2^0, 2^1, 2^2, and 2^3, namely, the first four powers of 2. A and B are usually called "zone bits" and their function parallels that of the zone punches in the cards.* The seventh bit, designated "C," is called the *parity bit*. The word parity is used here in the sense of oddness or evenness; a study of Figure 2.17 will show that

Character	Binary Code		Character	Binary Code	
	C	BA 8421		C	BA 8421
0	1	00 1010	O	0	10 0110
1	0	00 0001	P	1	10 0111
2	0	00 0010	Q	1	10 1000
3	1	00 0011	R	0	10 1001
4	0	00 0100	S	1	01 0010
5	1	00 0101	T	0	01 0011
6	1	00 0110	U	1	01 0100
7	0	00 0111	V	0	01 0101
8	0	00 1000	W	0	01 0110
9	1	00 1001	X	1	01 0111
A	0	11 0001	Y	1	01 1000
B	0	11 0010	Z	0	01 1001
C	1	11 0011	&	1	11 0000
D	0	11 0100	.	0	11 1011
E	1	11 0101	¤	1	11 1100
F	1	11 0110	-	0	10 0000
G	0	11 0111	$	1	10 1011
H	0	11 1000	*	0	10 1100
I	1	11 1001	/	1	01 0001
J	1	10 0001	,	1	01 1011
K	1	10 0010	%	0	01 1100
L	0	10 0011	#	0	00 1011
M	1	10 0100	@	1	00 1100
N	0	10 0101	blank	1	00 0000

Figure 2.17. Binary coding of the 48 characters used in the IBM 1401 and 1410 computers. (Courtesy IBM.)

* The core-storage representation of characters may be visualized by employing some analogies. The function of an individual core parallels that of a punching position in a card. The function of a combination of cores parallels that of a column in a card: both represent or "contain" a character. Finally, the address of a character in core storage is defined by a *storage address*, which performs a function analogous to that of a column number.

the representation of a character in this system always has an *odd* number of ones: the parity bit, by being a one or a zero, keeps it odd throughout the scheme. Parity is used to check the accuracy of machine operations at certain crucial points within the machine. The number of ones in each character passing by these points is counted to determine whether it is odd. If it is not, an error is signaled on the console of the computer. Parity checking provides a high degree of assurance that the machine is operating correctly; compensating errors are possible of course, but in practice they are rare.

The seven bits in a character are seen in this case to have designations that are more or less conventional: CBA8421. Sometimes the coding of a character is discussed by listing the designations of the bit positions that are one for that character; thus, instead of saying that the letter P is coded as 1100111, we would write CB421. The difference is one of preference only and has no bearing on what happens inside the machine.

We should note that in a computer that uses the binary-coded decimal system of coding, each digit, letter, or symbol is represented separately: the two-digit number 17 would be stored as the following pattern of bits:

```
C BA 8421    C BA 8421
0 00 0001    0 00 0111
```

In other words, every character is represented by exactly seven bits.

There are several important variations of the seven-bit coding scheme. In one, which is no longer widely applied, the computer is able to represent only the digits from zero to nine, which require only four bits. Letters and other symbols are then coded as two-decimal digits. In the IBM 7070, for instance, the letter P is represented as the two digits 77, A is 61, and Z is 89. This system is called *two-digit alphanumeric coding*.

A coding scheme that is quite fashionable nowadays is the Extended Binary-Coded Decimal Interchange Code (EBCDIC). It is based on nine-bit configuration and is found in such computers as the IBM 360 and the RCA Spectra 70. Each logical group of nine bits—called a *byte*—contains one parity bit; the remaining eight bits may be used to represent one character (letter, special character, or digit) or *two* digits, each represented by four bits. In other words, a byte may be used *whole* or *split*. The latter case, known as *packed decimal* represen-

tation, provides a very efficient use of core storage. All this is very important in COBOL because there is a USAGE clause in the DATA DIVISION that deals specifically with these representations. We shall return to this subject in Section 5.7.

EBCDIC also makes full use of the 16* different combinations (0 through 15) that can be obtained from a set of four bits. (The number 15 is obtained when all four bits are "on," since $2^3 + 2^2 + 2^1 + 2^0 = 15$.) This permits a byte to represent 16×16, or 256, possible characters.

Almost all of the more modern computers permit numeric characters to be coded in what is called *pure binary*, in which an *entire* number is put into binary form rather than coding each digit separately. In this scheme the number 23 would be written 10111; the ones, reading from the left, stand for 16, 4, 2, and 1, which are powers of 2; if the bits of one byte (or any other combination of bits) are not sufficient to accommodate a number, the bits of the logically adjacent byte may be used to represent consecutively higher powers of 2. This system therefore allows large numbers to be represented with fewer bits than any system of coding individual digits and speeds up arithmetical operations considerably. It cannot, however, represent letters or other symbols in any convenient fashion, and conversion between pure binary and binary coded decimal is required whenever numbers are to be presented in a readable form.

Used judiciously, pure binary can save space and time in an object program; used unwisely, it can waste huge amounts of time because of the conversions required. Again the USAGE clause in COBOL is used in connection with this particular representation, a subject to which we shall return in Section 5.7.

Characters within a computer are grouped into units called *words*. In many computers the number of digits or characters in a word is fixed, and we speak of them as *fixed-word-length* computers. The Remington Rand UNIVAC II has 12 alphanumeric characters in a word; the Honeywell 800 has a word of 48 bits that may be used as pure binary, as 11

---

* This number system is therefore called hexadecimal. Notice that a number system takes its name from the number of numbers, including zero, that can be represented with one-symbol expressions: binary from 2, octal from 8, decimal from 10, hence hexadecimal from 16. The hexadecimal set is represented by 16 symbols: 0 through 9, plus A,B,C,D,E, and F for 10, 11, 12, 13, 14, and 15, respectively.

decimal digits and a sign, or as 8 alphanumeric characters; the RCA 3301 has a 10-character word length; the IBM 360 has a word of 4 bytes, a "double-word"* of 8 and a "half-word" of 2.

Other computers are designed so that the number of characters in a word can be any number (in principle) from one up to the number of characters in storage: we speak then of *variable-word-length* or *character-addressable* computers. Naturally some system must be devised to indicate the length of a word for processing. In the IBM 1401 and 1410 each character position has an eighth bit called the *word mark* for this purpose; in the RCA 501 the end of a word is indicated by a special symbol that in most cases takes up a character position; in the IBM 7080 the sign of a NUMERIC data item is used to indicate the end of the particular data item, and alphanumeric data item lengths are controlled by the length of certain devices in the arithmetic-logic section of the machine. The IBM 360 can, optionally, operate in this mode as well.

Variable-word-length machines are in some ways easier to work with because the storage for a data item always constitutes one word no matter how many character positions are required. Since there is little wasted storage space, they are able to get by with a little less storage. Yet nothing is free: since each character must in most cases be obtained from storage separately, instead of getting the entire word at once as fixed-word-length machines do, the variable-word-length machine tends to be slower in operation for the same basic storage speed. Furthermore, variability of data-item lengths creates some problems of its own; a fixed-word-length machine may not be so flexible, but it is perhaps a little more straightforward in its basic operations.

Each word location in a fixed-word-length machine or each character location in a variable-word machine must be identifiable: when we place something in storage, we want to be able to go back to the same place later to retrieve the information. The identification of the "same place" is handled by assigning to each word or character location an *address*, which is simply a number that identifies the location. In the machine's basic language all references to storage are in terms of addresses. If we say, for instance, in COBOL, "MOVE TRANS-

ACTION-QUANTITY TO MASTER-QUANTITY," what the machine actually does is to move† the contents of the *storage location* that has been assigned to TRANSACTION-QUANTITY to the *storage location* that has been assigned to MASTER-QUANTITY. Literally all that appears in the completed object program are the instructions that specify the *addresses* of information and the operation to be performed. The object program simply operates on whatever it finds in the locations, which will be data that has been read by the program or results that it has produced earlier.

This brings us back to what we already saw in Chapter 1, that we must specify all processing in advance. The object program is completely indifferent to the data it receives. It consists of instructions to add the contents of two storage locations named by address only, to read a card into specified locations, to test the contents of two locations for equality, or whatever. It will do whatever it is supposed to do, including, of course, any testing that has been built into the source program, but nothing more. If an incorrect time card says that a man worked 27 hours in one day and the source program does not check the reasonableness of the data, the object program will blindly compute the pay for 27 hours, following whatever rules for overtime it has been given.

What we are driving at, and the reason for including this chapter in the book, is the way in which the characteristics of the machine interact with the needs of the business and with the characteristics of the COBOL language to determine the approach to the task of setting up a data-processing system.

A particularly important characteristic of the machine in this context is that everything must eventually be expressed in the machine's "language" of elementary instructions, a subject first discussed in Chapter 1 and on which we now elaborate.

2.4 Instructions and Programming

A data-processing system, no matter how complex it may be in over-all action, is directed by

---

* It would appear at first sight that double words could be defined best as the elementary components of double-talk, but industry representatives have consistently refused to endorse this definition.

† "Move," incidentally, is a misleading term, since the contents moved from a location are "moved" but not lost. After a MOVE, therefore, the information is available in two places in storage.

individual computer instructions, each of which does only a minute fraction of the complete work.

An instruction may take many different forms, depending on the computer in question. Probably the most common type has just two parts: an *operation code* and an *address part*. The operation code tells the control section *what* to do, and the address part specifies where in storage to find the data item to be operated on. A hypothetical instruction might read 32 1629; the 32 is the operation code, standing for "add," and the 1629 is the address in storage of the number that should be added to whatever is already in an arithmetic register, called the *accumulator*. The instruction 49 2380 might mean to store whatever is in an accumulator in the storage location with the address 2380. The instruction 67 1800 might mean to write on the printer a line consisting of 12 words, the leftmost of which has the address 1800.

A machine having instructions of this sort would be called a *single-address* or *one-address* computer. The Remington Rand UNIVAC II, the Philco 2000 series machines, the Bendix G-20, and the IBM 7080, among many others, were designed according to this scheme. Instructions in the IBM 1401 and 360, on the other hand, may have two addresses, which will specify, for instance, where to find a quantity and also where to store it in a "move" operation. A computer may have three addresses, as have the Honeywell H800, the National Cash Register 304, and the Burroughs 280. An add instruction in one of these machines might specify where to find the two numbers to be added and where to place the result.

In every computer it must be possible, for a number of purposes, to refer to the locations of instructions themselves. We commonly want to return from almost the end of a program to almost its beginning, to repeat some of its routines; this was done in the example in Chapter 1, when we said in the COBOL source program GO TO READ-RTN; in the object program this becomes a *transfer of control* instruction, which specifies the address of the instruction to be executed next, instead of simply executing the succeeding instruction in sequence, as would normally happen. The addresses of instructions are also used in computer decision making. In COBOL, as we shall see, we can write conditional instructions, like IF TOTAL-PRICE IS GREATER THAN 100.00 PERFORM DISCOUNT-CALCULATION. In the object program of a computer with two-address instructions,

for example, this would become two instructions: one to compare the contents of the storage location containing the total price just computed, with a location containing the number 100.00, and a second to transfer control to the discount routine if the total price was greater (and to continue on in sequence if not).

If programming is to be done in the machine's language, or something close to it, it is obviously necessary to know in detail how the machine operates. *Assembly languages* (which are close to machine languages and allow for easier and faster programming than machine language, but still have to be translated by an *assembler*) have already lessened this need for detailed knowledge. A "high-level" programming language like COBOL saves us the time required to learn all of these details and also makes the writing of the source program even faster, but it would be a mistake to assume that we can ignore the machine entirely. As we proceed we shall encounter many examples in which a certain minimum knowledge of the computer is essential. A programmer for a particular computer may want to learn considerably more about his equipment than we are able to sketch here.

2.5   Auxiliary Storage Devices

In commercial data processing there is frequent need for the storage of far more data than can be contained in core storage. Four types of medium are used for this purpose: magnetic drums, data cells, disks, and tapes, the latter two being much more common. Since all of them allow information to be moved from the storage device into core storage and vice versa, they can be viewed as input and output media also. This applies particularly to magnetic tape.

A *magnetic drum* consists of a rotating cylinder, on the surface of which information can be recorded in the form of magnetized areas. A typical capacity is three million characters and a typical reading and writing rate is 300,000 characters per second.

A *data cell* is a drum supplemented by several hundred magnetic strips, each containing some hundreds of thousands of characters. During processing each strip containing the desired information is mechanically picked up, wrapped around the drum, and later released. Capacity is in the order of 400 million characters (2000 strips with 200,000 characters each). Transfer speed is in the range of 55,000 characters per second.

Magnetic disks are shaped like phonograph records and are usually assembled together in groups of six or more on *disk packs*. These devices rotate on disk drives at a speed of the order of 2400 revolutions per minute. Each disk pack is subdivided into *cylinders* and *tracks*. The capacity of a pack varies from 7 million to 70 million characters, depending on the number and size of the disks. Transfer speed is in the order of 200,000 characters per second. Figure 2.18 shows two disk packs used with the National Cash Register Century Series computers.

Each disk surface contains a number of concentric tracks, identifiable by consecutive numbers. The set of all the tracks in a pack having the same number is called a cylinder (cylinder 1 consists of

Figure 2.18. Disk storage units used with the NCR Century Series computers. (Courtesy National Cash Register Company; Black Star photo.)

all tracks number 1, cylinder 2, of all tracks number 2, and so on). The number of tracks on a disk surface—and therefore the number of cylinders in a pack—is in the order of 200 in the common models.

By far the most common auxiliary storage medium is *magnetic tape*, which is also heavily used as the medium for input and output of major quantities of data. The tape systems for different computers may vary in some of their characteristics; since we are concerned with basic ideas rather than with the details of any machine, we present a composite picture of tape features.

Magnetic tape is most often made of a ribbon of plastic, usually ½-inch wide, with a coating of magnetic oxides that can retain data. One reel a little less than a foot in diameter contains a tape typically 2400 feet long. For reading or writing a tape reel is mounted on a device called a *tape unit* or *tape drive*. One reel of tape can hold in the range of 10 to 20 million characters, which can be read at a typical rate of 100,000 per second. Figure 2.19 shows a tape unit for the Honeywell computer equipment.

Information is recorded on a tape with a binary coding system that is the same as or similar to that used in core storage. There are 7-channel tape drives and 9-channel tape drives, which read and write the 7- and 9-bit configurations discussed in Section 2.3.

Characters are written in *blocks*. In a variable-word-length computer a block may contain any number of characters; in a fixed-word-length machine the number of characters must be a multiple of the number of characters in a word; that is; only complete words may be written on the tape. A typical *recording density* is 800 characters to the inch; that is, on one inch of tape, with its seven parallel channels, 800 characters can be written. Thus the information on one 80-column card could be written on about one tenth of an inch of tape at this density; the information in a box of 2000 cards could in principle be written on about 17 feet of tape.

The "in principle" in the last sentence brings up one of the most important aspects of programming for magnetic tapes. We could not in practice write one block of tape containing all of the information on 2000 cards, which would be 160,000 characters, because it is necessary to have all data present in core storage before starting to write the block. Not all computers have core storage for 160,000 char-

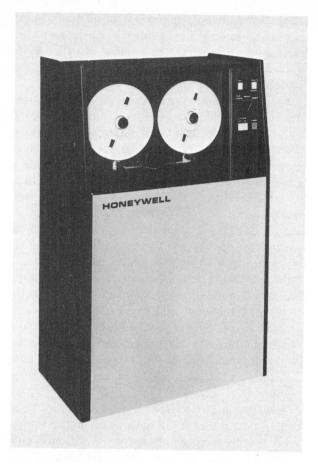

Figure 2.19. A tape drive for Honeywell computer equipment. (Courtesy Honeywell.)

acters, and even in those that have we would seldom wish to use it that way. Similarly, there would usually not be sufficient space to read such a block into storage.

Blocks on magnetic tape must therefore be kept to some reasonable size, depending on the amount of storage available and on the difficulty of handling certain programming matters that we shall investigate later. This brings us to a characteristic of most magnetic tape systems that becomes a major factor in programming: each tape block is separated from the adjacent block by a section of blank tape, typically about ½ or ¾ inch long.

This space, which we shall call the *interblock gap*, effects tape utilization in two important ways. The first factor is that the interblock gap, of course, contains no information; this can result in a tape that contains much less than the maximum amount of information if the blocks are short. Suppose, for instance, that each block of a 2400-foot tape contains 80 characters, that the recording density is 500 per inch, and that the interblock gaps are ½

inch. Then each block of 80 characters requires about ⅔ inch of tape; ⅙ for the data and ½ for the gap. A full reel could therefore hold about 43,000 blocks and 3.5 million characters. This is considerably less than the maximum capacity quoted earlier of 10 to 20 million characters; the reason, of course, is that three quarters of the tape consists of interblock gaps.

The second factor is that the presence of so much blank tape will ordinarily waste computer time in processing the information. The primary purpose of the interblock gaps is to allow the tape units time to get the tape moving at full speed before starting to read or write it. (Tape speed is typically 10 feet a second.) Similarly, when the end of a block is reached in reading or writing, the tape cannot be stopped instantaneously (as would be required in order to stop between character positions), and a little space must be provided for tape movement during the braking of its motion. The time required to get a tape moving at full speed before starting to read or write a block or the time to stop the tape after reaching the end of the block is called the *start/stop time*. If the computer must wait on the tape system during this time, or even part of it, without being able to process any other data, then naturally the entire system is delayed.

Wasted tape space is of some concern in itself: a reel of tape costs about $40 and many installations have hundreds or even thousands of reels. More important, however, is the waste of time of an expensive data-processing system. If the system must wait while tapes are changed or while blank tape is moved, then, in effect, the short blocks cause a waste of time of a system that costs perhaps $200 per hour to operate.

The most common solution to this basic problem is to make the blocks longer by placing several *records* in one *block*. The terminology must be clear: a *block* is a physical group of characters on tape, separated from the preceding and following blocks by interblock gaps, whereas a *record* is a "logical" group of characters giving information about one item in a file. A block is thus a physical tape-recording concept; a record is a logical data-processing concept. In order to make this distinction clear, we sometimes speak of a record as a *problem record* or a *logical record* and of a block as a *physical record*. The number of logical records in one physical record is called *blocking factor*.*

---

* This terminology is unfortunately by no means standard. At least one important computer manufacturer uses the term

As we shall see, the latter is indicated in a COBOL program by a clause in the DATA DIVISION (BLOCK CONTAINS xxxx RECORDS).

A few more matters of tape use and organization will round out what we need to know about the subject.

Both for tape-unit design reasons and for programming considerations it is necessary to be able to detect the beginning and end of usable tape. These points are signaled by some markings, usually small strips of aluminum that are sensed by photoelectric cells and are therefore called *photosensing markers*. (To an operator the one at the beginning of a reel is known as the "reflective spot" or the "load point.")

The basic idea is that when the end-of-reel mark is sensed an indicator within the computer is turned on; suitable instructions can be used to determine the status of this indicator. After every writing operation, therefore, it is necessary in most computers to test the indicator to decide whether the end of the reel has been reached. If it has, there is still space to write another short block called the *trailer block*, or some such name, containing certain information about the tape. In some tape systems it is also necessary at this point to write on the tape a magnetic indication that the end of the tape has been reached; in IBM terminology this is called the *tape mark* and is also used to indicate an end of file when it occurs before the end of the reel. When the tape is read, the tape mark, not the photosensing marker, is used to indicate that the end of the recorded information has been reached; this also is done with suitable instructions.

In COBOL the various steps that must be taken to handle the conditions that develop at the end of a file are triggered by the AT END clause.

The marker at the beginning of a tape is used in *rewinding* a tape, which means to return a tape from the middle or end to its beginning. Most tape systems have two modes of rewinding. One permits further processing of tape, for example, when the purpose of rewinding was simply to position the tape to its beginning or when further processing is to be done. The other, which is called rewinding with *lock* or *interlock*, makes it impossible to do anything further with the tape until an operator takes certain actions at the tape unit. Rewind with lock is ordinarily used when a tape ought to be dismounted to prevent destroying newly recorded

information. In COBOL the two modes are reflected by two distinct options: CLOSE File-Name (which we have already seen in Chapter 1) and CLOSE File-Name WITH LOCK.

The tape reels for most systems contain some sort of file-protection device, typically a removable ring on the back of the reel, which makes it impossible to write on that reel. This is used when working with a master file of information that would be difficult to reconstruct if the file were accidentally destroyed by writing on the tape.

Tape systems are subjected to considerable checking for accuracy. Parity checking is used on every character, and there is ordinarily at least one additional parity bit for each channel in a block.

Magnetic drums, data cells, and disks are usually called *random-access* or *direct-access* devices because, in contrast to tape, information can be obtained from them in a more or less "random" fashion. With tape it is not possible to get from one part of a reel to another without physically "passing" the tape between the two parts; with direct-access devices, on the other hand, the read-write mechanisms can move *directly* from one place to another. As in the case of a magnetic-tape recorder, it is impossible to reach the fourth song or speech without passing through the first three, but it is possible, instead, to position the pickup arm of a phonograph directly on the fourth band of a record. What this means in data processing is that with tape it is necessary to process records in the order in which they appear in the file (sequential-file processing); with direct-access devices records can be processed in any convenient order (random-access-file processing).

Direct-access devices are considerably more expensive for the same amount of storage than magnetic tapes. Yet they are used with increasing frequency because in certain applications they greatly reduce the computer processing time.

One additional topic should be mentioned here, that of *buffering*. Without some form of buffering the entire data-processing system must wait while data is read or written. This represents a considerable waste of time; we would much rather be able to process data while additional data is being read or while previous results are being written. Buffering makes this possible. In a typical situation, once the scheme has started, we are at any given time processing one set of input while the next set is being read and the preceding set of results is being written. This ordinarily requires two input and two output areas in core storage. While

---

"inter-record gap" for what we have just called an inter-block gap.

one of the input areas is being filled, the data previously read into the other is processed. When the first area has been filled and the data in the second has been processed, the functions of the two are reversed: the new data now in the first is processed and the second is filled. A similar scheme is used for output.

This is about the simplest form of program organization for buffering; many other techniques are also employed, depending on whether more than one input/output operation can be done simultaneously, the size of the tape blocks, the amount of core storage available, special instructions that may be available, etc. These details are unfortunately too complex to be discussed here; the programmer should obtain information about his particular computer to make the best use of buffering methods.

To round out our photographic survey of com-

puting equipment we have two representative complete systems. Figure 2.20 shows the IBM System 360, Model 40, and Figure 2.21, the Univac 9300 System.

2.6 Operating Systems

A large computer usually operates under the direction of a set of programs embedded in what is called an operating system. An operating system directs and coordinates the actions of a number of special-purpose programs as well as the user's program. The operating-system programs may reside on magnetic tape (for a tape-operating system, abbreviated TOS) or on magnetic disks (for a disk-operating system, or DOS).

When a computer is placed under control of an operating system by appropriate actions on the

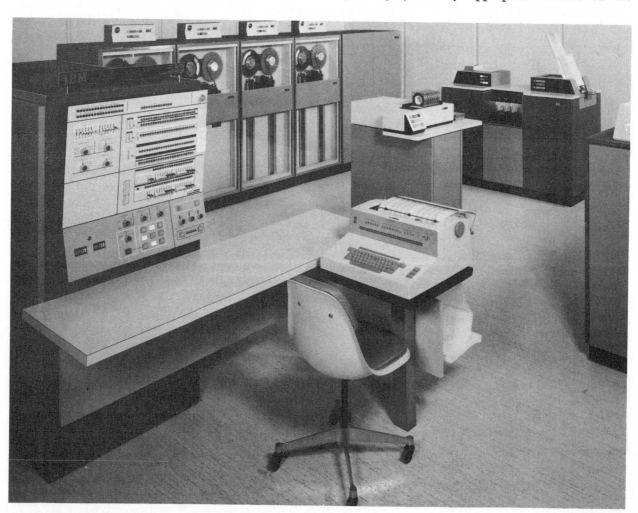

Figure 2.20. A typical configuration of the IBM System 360, Model 40. (Courtesy IBM.)

Figure 2.21. A typical configuration of the Univac© 9300 System. (Courtesy Sperry Rand Corporation.)

part of the (human) computer operator, one of its components, the supervisor, is transferred into core storage. The supervisor has the job of recognizing what tasks need to be done and calling into action other sections of the operating system. How does the supervisor know what needs to be done? That is, what constitutes signals that some action is required? There are a number of types of signal.

The most direct type of demand for action is the one that impels us to bring the subject up: a control card placed in the job deck by the COBOL programmer. Almost all computer installations require that every COBOL deck be preceded and followed by job-control cards that "communicate" to the operating system what the programmer wants done with his deck. We return to this subject in Section 9.2.

Our survey of computer and punched-card equipment is now completed. Presumably no reader will have been tempted to think that we have covered the subject thoroughly or that he knows everything about it he will ever need to know. This much, however, will serve nicely to get us started, and most of the further specifics will come from ma-

terials that treat a particular machine rather than the generalities, as we necessarily have done.

With this foundation, then, we move on to actual COBOL programming.

REVIEW QUESTIONS

1. True or false:
   a. A computer is usually equipped with a card reader, a printer, some tape drives, and possibly some disk drives.
   b. Normally, a COBOL program is punched on cards, and the cards are read by the card reader of a computer.
   c. The input to a computer is invariably a deck of punched cards, and the output is always a printed report.
   d. A reel of magnetic tape may contain one million characters at the most.

2. True or false:
   a. Characters are represented in core storage by unique bit configurations.
   b. The blocking factor is the number of characters in a record.
   c. Disks and tapes are both used as direct access media in random access applications.

ANSWERS

1. a and b are true; c is false; in fact, the trend today is to replace punched cards with encoded magnetic tapes (and printed reports with microfilms and CRT devices) or to enter data directly into the computer; d is false: the proper figure is of the order of 15 million characters.

ANSWERS (Continued)

2. a is true; b is false: the blocking factor is the number of logical records in a physical record or, more simply, the number of records per block; c is also false because tape is not a direct-access medium and records on tape may not be accessed "directly."

3. THE PROCEDURE DIVISION

3.1 The Parts of a COBOL Source Program

In Chapter 1 we said that a COBOL source program is composed of four DIVISIONS:

IDENTIFICATION DIVISION
ENVIRONMENT DIVISION
DATA DIVISION
PROCEDURE DIVISION

and we briefly described their respective functions.

These four divisions must be present in the source program in the order stated. We are going to study them in the reverse order, however, which seems to be the more meaningful approach. The IDENTIFICATION DIVISION and ENVIRONMENT DIVISION are almost trivial to complete in practice and need not detain us at this point. The DATA DIVISION is, in fact, the place at which the real work of writing a source program must begin, but much of it will not make sense until we have a better understanding of what is done in the PROCEDURE DIVISION.

Since the goal now is to get a general picture, the reader is forewarned that in this chapter not every detail of the topics discussed is presented. Subsequent chapters provide important additional elements.

3.2 Basic PROCEDURE DIVISION Elements

Let us review briefly and expand what we saw in the sample program in Chapter 1.

Statements. The COBOL PROCEDURE DIVISION is made up of a series of statements, each of which calls for some kind of action to be taken. The bulk of this chapter considers the various kinds of statement available and what they do; here are some examples of the kinds of things we shall be studying:

(1) ADD OVERTIME-PAY TO STRAIGHT-TIME-PAY.
(2) MULTIPLY RATE BY TIME GIVING DISTANCE.
(3) IF QUANTITY-ON-HAND IS LESS THAN QUANTITY-ORDERED GO TO SHORTAGE-ROUTINE.
(4) READ TRANSACTION-FILE, AT END GO TO EOJ.
(5) WRITE OUTPUT-LINE.
(6) MOVE SPACES TO OUT-RECORD.
(7) MOVE 'AB-885' TO PART-NO.

Statements may be *imperative* or *conditional*. A conditional statement contains a condition, either in the obvious format of IF followed by a comparison or in a less obvious format such as AT END GO TO. Imperative statements, instead, indicate actions that are not subject to any condition, like OPEN INPUT PAY-FILE.

Sentences. A COBOL sentence consists of one or more statements and is *terminated* by a *period* and a *space*. When a sentence contains several statements, they may be set off by any of the following *separators*:

,   ;   THEN

Separators are allowed simply for readability: their presence or absence has no effect on the compiled object program. A separator must be followed by a space. The use of some words like IS and ARE (the latter pertaining to the DATA DIVISION) is also optional: the statements

IF HOURS-WORKED IS LESS THAN 7
IF HOURS-WORKED LESS THAN 7

receive identical treatment by the compiler.

EXAMPLES OF SENTENCES

(1) ADD OVERTIME-PAY TO STRAIGHT-TIME-PAY.
(2) MOVE DIVIDEND TO OUTPUT-AREA-3; MOVE DISCOUNT TO OUTPUT-AREA-4.
(3) IF ON-HAND IS LESS THAN REORDER-POINT, MOVE PART-NUMBER TO REPORT-1; MOVE REORDER-QUANTITY TO REPORT-2; WRITE REORDER-RECOMMENDATION.
(4) IF MAN-NUMBER EQUAL TO PREVIOUS-MAN-NUMBER GO TO SUMMARIZE; ELSE GO TO MAN-TOTAL.

Paragraphs. It is frequently expedient to group several sentences into a paragraph so that the group can be given a name and referred to by statements in the same or other paragraphs.

We may also occasionally wish to break a long series of sentences into several paragraphs just for convenience and clarity—and never refer to these paragraph names in the entire program. In any event, a *paragraph* can always be defined as *one or more sentences preceded by a paragraph name.*

PROCEDURE DIVISION reference format. A COBOL source program must be written on a page in a precise format according to some rather simple rules. A special form is not actually required, but many programmers will find it easier to write their programs on a printed form (usually called a *coding sheet*) to avoid ambiguity when the program is punched on cards. Figure 3.1 shows such a form with the illustrative program of Section 1.5 written on it.

The first six positions of each line of the reference format (and therefore of the coding sheet) are reserved for a *sequence number,* which may be used at the programmer's discretion to identify the program cards and keep them in the proper sequence. On the form shown here these six positions are divided into a three-digit *page number* and a three-digit *line number.* The seventh position is reserved for indicating (by writing a hyphen) that the first character on this line is a continuation of a word from the preceding line.*

Position 8 is called the *A margin* and position 12, the *B margin. Paragraph names always begin at the A margin.* The paragraph name must be fol-

* Many programmers will probably choose to avoid this situation simply by not starting a word at the end of a line unless all of it can be written on that line.

PROGRAM: STUDENT SAMPLE - A SYSTEM: SHEET 1 OF 1
PROGRAMMER: STANDARDS GROUP - NEW YORK - ESSO MATH & SYSTEMS DATE: JAN. 1970 IDENT. (73–80): SAMPLE-A

```
001010 PROCEDURE DIVISION.
001020 HOUSEKEEPING.
001030     OPEN INPUT FILE-IN.
001040     OPEN OUTPUT FILE-OUT.
001050 READ-ROUTINE.
001060     READ FILE-IN, AT END GO TO END-RUN.
001070     MOVE RECORD-IN TO RECORD-OUT.
001080     WRITE RECORD-OUT.
001090     GO TO READ-ROUTINE.
001100 END-RUN.
001110     CLOSE FILE-IN.
001120     CLOSE FILE-OUT.
001130     STOP RUN.
```

Figure 3.1. The sample program of Section 1.5, written on a coding sheet. (Form courtesy Esso Mathematics and Systems, Inc.)

lowed by a period and a space, as shown in Figure 3.1. The first sentence of the paragraph may begin anywhere thereafter on the same line or on the next line, the latter choice being preferable in the interest of clarity. The subsequent lines of a paragraph may not begin to the left of the B margin. A good practice is to start every sentence in position 12 and, if the sentence takes more than one line, to start the continuation in position 16 or 15. Again this will improve readability. A coding sheet position, by the way, is usually called a column, which is abbreviated as *cc.* (for card column) or *col.*

The most common input medium for a source program is cards, making the maximum length of a line 80 characters. However, a COBOL program line, including the period, if any, at the end of it, may not extend beyond col. 72.* The remaining columns (73 to 80) may be used to enter a short program name (program identification) that will be common to all the cards in the program.

The first line of the PROCEDURE DIVISION. Each of the four divisions of the source program must begin with one line that identifies the division to the compiler, which is also illustrated in Figure 3.1. Nothing else may be written on this line.

Character set. Any programming language must specify the characters it accepts and requires.† The complete COBOL character set, and the names used for the special symbols, are as follows:

0, 1, 2, 3, 4, 5, 6, 7, 8, 9.
A, B, C, D, E, F, G, H, I, J, K, L, M, N, O, P, Q, R, S, T, U, V, W, X, Y, Z
Space or blank (written "b" in text examples)
+ Plus sign
− Minus sign or hyphen
* Asterisk
/ Slash
= Equal sign
$ Dollar sign

, Comma
. Period or decimal point
; Semicolon
' or " Quotation mark
(Left parenthesis
) Right parenthesis
> "Greater than" symbol
< "Less than" symbol

Note that only upper case (capital) letters are permitted.

Some computers do not have all of these characters, in which case substitutions of other characters or of letter combinations can be made. For instance, GR may be substituted for the "greater than" sign or a percent sign may be used in place of the semicolon. These substitutions, which are called *transliterations* in the trade, are defined by each manufacturer whenever necessary.

On the same subject notice that the quotation mark may be represented by either ' or ". The character one should use depends on the equipment. The RCA-3301 computer would require ", whereas the IBM 360 wants '. Some differences go right down to the punch-card positions; for example, a left parenthesis is represented by a 5-8 punch combination for RCA-3301 equipment, but for the IBM 360 the combination is 12-5-8; the right parenthesis is 6-8 for RCA-3301, 11-5-8 for the IBM 360.

Data names. As discussed in Section 1.4, it is crucial in COBOL (or any other computer language, for that matter) to be able to refer to data by a name. With this facility we can write procedures in terms of names—assigned in the DATA DIVISION—that stand for whatever values may be associated with the names when the object program is run later.

In making up a data name we must adhere to a few simple rules:

—a name may not be composed of more than 30 characters;
—it may contain only letters, digits, and hyphens (special characters, such as $ or % are *not* allowed);
—hyphens may appear only in the body of the name, not at the beginning and not at the end;
—at least one character must be a letter;
—COBOL reserved words must not be used for data names or for any other purpose than that

* Incidentally, we may finish a sentence in col. 71 and enter a period in col. 72, ignoring the requirement that a space must follow the period; col. 73, regardless of its actual contents, will act *as if* it contained a space.

† To avoid confusion let it be clear that this restricted character set applies to the COBOL source-programming language itself and not to the data that we may read or originate. As we shall see very soon in connection with non-numeric literals, we could print out, for instance, a percent sign next to a number, even though the percent sign is not a character in the COBOL set.

specified.* Note that a space is not allowed within a data name (since a space constitutes a name separator, it would look like two data names with a space).

EXAMPLES OF DATA NAMES

GROSS-PAY
QUANTITY-ON-HAND
ALLOWANCE-FOR-TRIMMING
USAGE-DATA
R6492750257
R58-83-22Z
8WXYZ

The following are *not* legal data names:

6492750257 (must contain at least one letter)
666-82 (must contain at least one letter)
GROSS PAY (space not permitted)
STOCKNUMBER- (must not end with hyphen)
USAGE (this is a COBOL reserved word!)
DATA (so is this)
$-TOTAL (special character not permitted)
-EMPL-NUMBER (must not begin with hyphen)
ALLOWANCE-FOR-TRIMMING-AND-WASTE
    (more than 30 characters)

Paragraph names.   These may be formed in the same way as data names; in contrast to data names they may be composed of digits only.

Literals.   Data is most frequently referred to by a data name so that we can write procedures that will process whatever data the program itself reads from input devices. Sometimes, however, we want to use data that does not change, such as page headings, the number 1 to be added to a counter, or a constant multiplier of 1.5 for use in computing overtime pay. Such constants are called *literals*; the term is meant to suggest that we write the thing *itself* rather than refer to it by name.

When a literal is used in a PROCEDURE DI-VISION statement (e.g., MOVE 'AD431' TO PART-NO or ADD 78 TO GROWTH-RATE), it is called a *procedure literal*. We may use literals

in the DATA DIVISION as well, as we shall see in connection with the VALUE clause in Chapter 5.

Literals are of two types: numeric and non-numeric.

A *numeric literal* is composed of digits, with (perhaps) a plus sign, a minus sign, or a decimal point. If there is no decimal point, the literal is assumed to be an integer (whole number). If there is a sign, it must appear as the leftmost character of the literal without a space between it and the first digit; if there is no sign, the literal is assumed to be positive. A decimal point may appear anywhere except as the rightmost character (to avoid confusion with the period marking the end of a sentence). The length of a numeric literal may not exceed 18 digits.

EXAMPLES OF NUMERIC LITERALS

1
100000
123.456789
−5
40.09
+40.09

EXAMPLES OF INCORRECT NUMERIC LITERALS

1. (must not end with decimal point)
− 8.93 (no space allowed after sign)
78,000 (commas not allowed)

We must be clear on exactly what a decimal point in a numeric literal means: its only function is to show the compiler how to set up the instructions that do arithmetic with the constant. The decimal point is *not* stored as a character in storage; it is therefore called an *implied* or *assumed* decimal point. The basic idea is that the object program instructions compiled to add 1.25 to a data item will ordinarily be quite different from those compiled to add 12.5 to the same data item, and both will depend on where the (implied) decimal point of the data item is.

The handling of the decimal point is just one application of a more general principle: a numeric literal defines a *value* independent of the characters used to represent it. When we write the numeric literal −78.904, we have little idea just how the value represented may be set up by the compiler: it might be in pure binary or the sign might be represented in some way that depends on machine

---

* A list of COBOL reserved words is given in the appendix and can be found in the appendix of every manufacturer's COBOL manual. Avoiding reserved words while forming data names may be a bother. Two systematic methods of staying out of trouble may be suggested for consideration. 1. Observe that only a few reserved words are hyphenated (these can be remembered) and hyphenate every name you invent. 2. Observe that few reserved words contains digits and put a digit in every invented name.

details. For another example consider these numeric literals:

12
+12
12.0000
000012.0

All of these represent the same *value* and are therefore equivalent. The idea that a numeric literal represents a value independent of its representation in the machine is quite important in understanding the difference between a numeric and a non-numeric literal.

A *non-numeric literal* stands for the characters of which it is composed and nothing more. It may contain any characters in the character set of a computer except a quotation mark. The reason for this omission is that the entire *literal must be enclosed in quotation marks* to avoid confusion with data names, numeric literals, and reserved words. The length of a non-numeric literal may not exceed 120 characters.

EXAMPLES OF NON-NUMERIC LITERALS

(1) 'PAGE NUMBER'
    '−5'
(2) 'CONTROL TOTAL ON CLOCK CARDS DOES NOT BALANCE.'
(3) 'USAGE DATA'
(4) 'QUANTITY-ON-HAND'
(5) '50%'
(6) '$ & CENTS'

Note that spaces are allowed just like any other character, that reserved words are *not* excluded, that what is enclosed in quotes may be a data name elsewhere in the program without confusion, and, except for the quotes, a non-numeric literal may have the same appearance as a numeric literal.

But the two are not the same! Consider these two literals:

−14.62

'−14.62'

The first (a numeric literal) would be stored in the object program as the negative *number* 1462 in one of the available arithmetic representations defined by the USAGE clause in the DATA DIVISION. It would then be used with appropriate instructions to line up the (implied) decimal point properly; the minus sign would be stored in whatever man-

ner the particular computer uses. The non-numeric literal '−14.62', on the other hand, would be stored as the six characters −14.62 and it would be impossible to do arithmetic with them, since object program arithmetic instructions cannot deal with such things as the coded representation of the minus sign and the decimal point.

Figurative constants. Certain constants are frequently needed in many programs; some of them have been given fixed names that will be recognized by the compiler and corresponding constants will be set up in the object program. ZERO, ZEROS, and ZEROES all stand for the numeric value zero. SPACE and SPACES stand for one or more spaces, the exact number being determined by the compiler in each situation. For instance, if we write MOVE SPACES TO FIELD-A, where FIELD-A is defined in the DATA DIVISION as six characters, six spaces will be moved. If FIELD-A had been defined as having 13 characters, 13 spaces would have been moved. The compiler makes this type of determination by combining the DATA DIVISION specifications with the PROCEDURE DIVISION statements.

The figurative constant QUOTE is a bit tricky in an interesting sort of way. Suppose we wanted to write the characters 'SPECIAL' on the printer, *including the quote marks*. How would we indicate such a non-numeric literal? It would not do to enclose it in quote marks like this

' 'SPECIAL' '

because the compiler would regard the second quote as meaning that the end of the literal had been reached. The figurative constant QUOTE solves this problem; it calls for the output of a quote mark. To get the characters 'SPECIAL' printed, we would write in the PROCEDURE DIVISION the phrase DISPLAY QUOTE 'SPECIAL' QUOTE. The compiler would interpret the first QUOTE as meaning that a quote mark should be printed; 'SPECIAL' would be treated as an ordinary non-numeric literal, with the quote marks meaning only that this is a non-numeric literal and therefore *not* printed; the second QUOTE would cause another quote mark to be printed.

This kind of precision of intended meaning is rather typical of the way things are in working with a computer. We must always distinguish most carefully between a symbol that stands for itself and a symbol that denotes something about other information, just as we must distinguish between a data item and its name.

A special kind of figurative constant is provided by the ability to write the word ALL followed by any literal, such as

ALL 9
ALL 'Q'

ALL 'ABC'

These forms generate as many characters as are required by the situation, as described in connection with SPACES.*

Other figurative constants are the following:

HIGH-VALUE or HIGH-VALUES represents the largest value in a computer's collating sequence,** that is, the character that is "larger" than all others when alphanumeric characters are compared.

LOW-VALUE or LOW-VALUES represents the "smallest" value in a computer's collating sequence.

Just what character(s) is represented by these figurative constants is a matter of computer hardware and of agreement at each installation. In the IBM 360, for instance, HIGH-VALUE is represented by hexadecimal FF: one F in the upper 4 bits and the other in the lower 4 bits of the same byte. LOW-VALUE is represented by hexadecimal 00.

REVIEW QUESTIONS

1. How many statements may a sentence contain?

2. True or false: a statement must always be followed by a statement separator.

3. True or false: a sentence must always be followed by a period and a space.

4. True or false: it would be legal (and perhaps sometimes convenient) to write a program in which each paragraph contained one sentence and each sentence contained one statement.

5. True or false: a paragraph must have a name.

---

* Odd situations can come up, though. What happens if we say MOVE ALL 'ABC' TO DATA-1, where DATA-1 is defined in the DATA DIVISION to have five characters? The answer, in some compilers, is that the literal is repeated from the beginning until the data item is filled; the characters transmitted in this case would be ABCAB.

** See also Section 3.5.

6. True or false: data names and paragraph names are formed according to exactly the same rules.

7. Is this a legitimate format for a paragraph?
PARAGRAPH-1.
    MOVE QUANTITY TO
    ORDER-QUANTITY.
    MOVE CUSTOMER-NAME TO RE-
    PORT-LINE.

8. Is this a legitimate paragraph format?
12345. MOVE QUANTITY TO ORDER-
    QUANTITY.
    MOVE CUSTOMER-NAME TO RE-
    PORT-LINE.

9. Identify the characters that are *not* in the COBOL character set.
+ , : * % R # $. ; ÷ 0

10. Some of the following are *not* allowed as data names. Identify them and state why they are not allowed.

NET-PAY
RATE-3
RATE/3
65432
SIX5432
NUMBER-OF-DEPENDENTS
ASTERISK***
HYPHEN-
QUANTITY ON HAND
DIVISION
MULTIPLICATION
DATA DIVISION
DATA-DIVISION

11. Identify and explain the errors in writing numeric literals in some of the following.

1862.990
88.44—
— 88.44
1,000,000
1000000
+22.5830
—23459.
+234598.0
453
453. 09

12. Do all of the following represent the same value?

692.00
+692
692.
692.000000

13. Criticize the following statement: the literal 'USAGE DATA' is illegal because USAGE and DATA are both reserved words and a space is not allowed in a data name.

14. Is there any error in this non-NUMERIC literal?
'TOTAL EXCEEDS THE $100.00
LIMIT-CORRECT AND RE-ENTER.'

15. With which of these literals could arithmetic be done?

88.230	'SIXTEEN'
'88.230'	SIXTEEN
+12	—.00063

16. How many characters would the compiler generate from the figurative constant ALL 'Q'?

17. True or false?

    a. A non-NUMERIC literal must always be enclosed in quotation marks.

    b. A NUMERIC literal is never enclosed in quotation marks.

    c. A non-NUMERIC literal must contain at least one non-NUMERIC character.

    d. The PROCEDURE DIVISION precedes the DATA DIVISION in a COBOL source program deck.

    e. We could start a sentence in col. 24 of a COBOL coding sheet and end it in col. 74.

    f. We could enter a paragraph name starting in col. 12 of the COBOL coding sheet.

3.3 The MOVE Verb and the Arithmetic Verbs

Now we are finally ready to consider some of the actual ways of writing PROCEDURE DIVISION statements to accomplish useful processing. The subject can be broken into the study of a number of *verbs,* so called because in analogy with verbs in grammar they lead to some kind of action. As it happens, all statements begin with verbs, followed by other words of a type and sequence dictated by the allowable format of each verb. We have seen in our sample program in Chapter 1 some of these verbs: OPEN, CLOSE, MOVE, READ, WRITE, STOP. Our task for the rest of this chapter, in a nutshell, is to learn in a systematic manner

---

ANSWERS

1. Any number, from one up to however many you want to write.

2. False: the use of separators is optional.

3. True, except that when the period at the end of a sentence appears in column 72 the contents of column 73 are immaterial.

4. True.

5. True.

6. False: anything allowed as a data name would be an acceptable paragraph name, but paragraph names may also consist of digits only—which data names may not.

7. Yes: the paragraph name may be on a line by itself.

8. Yes: the paragraph name (12345) is acceptable and the first sentence may begin on the same line as the name.

9. : % # ÷

10. RATE/3 contains a character that is not allowed.
    65432 does not contain a letter.
    ASTERISK°°° contains a character that is not allowed.
    HYPHEN- ends with a hyphen.
    QUANTITY ON HAND contains spaces and would be treated as three words.
    DIVISION is a reserved word, as in DATA DIVISION
    DATA DIVISION contains a space and both are reserved words.
    ALL the others are acceptable, including DATA-DIVISION, which is *not* a reserved word.

11. 88.44— ends with a minus sign; the minus sign must be the first character of a NUMERIC literal.

ANSWERS (Continued)

    — 88.44 there must not be a space between the sign and the first digit.
    1,000,000 commas not allowed.
    —234593. ends with a decimal point.
    453. 09 contains a space.

12. Trick question. The *legal* ones do, but 692. is not legal in COBOL.

13. Completely false! A non-NUMERIC literal may contain any characters in the character set (except quotes). It is just to avoid such confusion as this question raises that quote marks are written around a non-NUMERIC literal.

14. No.

15. With the numeric ones: 88.230, +12, and —.00063. SIXTEEN, of course, is not a literal at all, but a data name.

16. Depends entirely on what is being done with the literal and in particular on the length of the data item that it is being used with.

17. a. True.
    b. True.
    c. False: '23456', for instance, would be a legal non-NUMERIC literal.
    d. False: the order in which the four divisions must be present in a source program is IDENTIFICATION, ENVIRONMENT, DATA, and PROCEDURE.
    e. False: it would be legal to start a sentence in col. 24 (although col. 12 would be a better choice), but it is illegal to go beyond col. 72.
    f. False: a paragraph name must start in col. 8.

---

what some of the more common verbs do and what formats may be used with them.

MOVE. One of the most common operations in a COBOL source program is to move a data item from one place in core storage* to another. In our sample program in Chapter 1, for instance, we wrote MOVE RECORD-IN TO RECORD-OUT. The format of a MOVE, as we shall study it now, is shown in the box.

$$\text{MOVE} \begin{Bmatrix} \text{data-name-1} \\ \text{literal} \end{Bmatrix} \text{TO data-name-2} \begin{bmatrix} \text{data-name-3} \end{bmatrix} \dots$$

A word or two about the generalized style in which the allowable formats will be displayed may be in order. Any word in capitals is a *reserved word*, which may not be used for any other purpose. If, in addition, it is underlined, this means that it is a *key word*, which *must* be written when the verb is used. There are no reserved words in the MOVE format that are not underlined, but other verbs have them: these are *optional* reserved words.

An optional word may be written or not, as the programmer wishes. (But it is still a reserved word and it must still be spelled correctly.) Naturally, the underlining is for use only in studying the reference formats; it is not necessary to underline key words in writing an actual COBOL source program.

Braces { } are used to enclose two or more things from which a choice must be made; in this case we obviously are required to write either a data name or a literal between the MOVE and the TO. Items enclosed in square brackets[ ] are options, to be used or not as the situation demands; we can MOVE the same data item or literal to *two* different receiving fields and write, for instance

MOVE SPACES TO MAN-NAME, MAN-TITLE.

Finally, the ellipsis (three periods) designates that the preceding group may be repeated as many

* The main storage, or internal storage, as distinguished from mass file storage. This was discussed in Chapter 2.

times as necessary. We can therefore have three or more receiving fields.

EXAMPLES OF MOVE STATEMENTS

(1) MOVE TRANSACTION-QUANTITY TO OUTPUT-QUANTITY.
(2) MOVE 'PAGE NUMBER' TO OUTPUT-RECORD.
(3) MOVE ZERO TO TOTAL-A.
(4) MOVE 1 TO PAGE-COUNTER.
(5) MOVE ZEROS TO COUNTER-A COUNTER-B COUNTER-C.

ADD. This important and much used arithmetic verb can be written in a variety of ways, but most of the time it will be in one of the two forms shown in the box.

$$\text{ADD} \begin{Bmatrix} \text{data-name-1} \\ \text{literal} \end{Bmatrix} \text{TO data-name-2}$$

$$\text{ADD} \begin{Bmatrix} \text{data-name-1} \\ \text{literal-1} \end{Bmatrix} \begin{Bmatrix} \text{, data-name-2} \\ \text{literal-2} \end{Bmatrix} \text{GIVING data-name-3}$$

EXAMPLES

(1) ADD HOURS-WORKED TO TOTAL-HOURS.
(2) ADD 1 TO COUNTER.
(3) ADD ON-HAND, ON-ORDER GIVING TOTAL-AVAILABLE.
(4) ADD A, 2 GIVING B.

The difference between the GIVING and TO options can be stated thus: when two quantities should be added and *one of them* replaced with the sum, use TO; when two quantities should be added and *some other data* item made equal to the sum, use GIVING.

Actually, as we shall see from the more complete format that will be presented after we discuss the available options, we are not restricted to *two* quantities but can, in fact, use any number, as in these examples:

ADD A, B TO C.
ADD A, B, C GIVING D.

The first example will form the sum of the data items named A, B, and C and replace C with the sum. The second will form the sum of A, B, and C and replace D with the sum. In the first example the original value of C is lost; in the second example the value of C is not changed.

The comma here is called a *series separator*, to give it a fancy name. Its use is at the discretion of the programmer. This freedom in writing series separators applies wherever a comma is shown in the reference format for any verb.

We should mention two options that apply to all five arithmetic verbs, even though the discussion will have to anticipate some aspects of DATA DI-

data item for the answer is not disturbed and whatever statement follows the words ON SIZE ERROR is executed. Ordinarily, what follows will be a GO TO statement leading to a routine set up by the programmer to handle the error condition.

These two options will probably not be required too often; care should be exercised to determine when they are really needed; for instance, the ON SIZE ERROR OPTION is clearly unnecessary if we add two 1-digit numbers and place the result in a two-digit field.

Now that the choices available in using the ADD verb are presumably understood, we may show (in the box) the way a COBOL reference manual would present them in one condensed general format.

ADD $\left\{ \begin{array}{l} \text{literal-1} \\ \text{data-name-1} \end{array} \right\}$ $\left[, \left\{ \begin{array}{l} \text{literal-2} \\ \text{data-name-2} \end{array} \right\} \cdots \right]$ $\left\{ \begin{array}{l} \text{TO} \\ \overline{\text{GIVING}} \end{array} \right\}$ data-name-n

[ROUNDED] [; ON SIZE ERROR any imperative statement]

VISION matters. Whenever a result is computed, it obviously must be stored somewhere; the data description for this data item will have considerable influence on just how the result is stored and, for that matter, on the computation itself. First, the decimal-point location of the result data item will determine how the final answer is positioned. Second, if there are more decimal places in the answer than there are in the data item assigned to the answer, the extra places will simply be dropped (which is technically called *truncation*) unless we use the ROUNDED option, in which case the answer will be rounded off. For an example of truncation versus rounding suppose that 784.369 is to be stored in a location that has room for only two decimal places. The *truncated* result would be 784.36, whereas the *rounded* result would be 784.37. Third, if there are more integral places in the answer (digits to the left of the assumed decimal point) than in the data item assigned to the answer, the extra digits at the left will be dropped. Some compilers generate object programs that will *stop* the execution of the program when such a situation occurs.

In other words, if the result is too big, we're in trouble. This possibility can be tested before storing if we write the ON SIZE ERROR option. When this is done, the answer is checked to see if it will fit in the space allocated to it; if it will not fit, the

Notice that it is mandatory to use either TO or GIVING, but it is illegal to use both. For instance, ADD A, B is illegal, and so is ADD A TO B GIVING C.

EXAMPLES OF ADD VERBS

ADD A B GIVING C.

	A	B	C
Before	1	2	50
After	1	2	03

ADD A TO B.

	A	B
Before	4	3
After	4	7

ADD A, B, C GIVING D.

	A	B	C	D
Before	2	3	4	67
After	2	3	4	09

ADD A, B, C TO D.

	A	B	C	D
Before	2	3	4	05
After	2	3	4	14

ADD 1 TO COUNTER-4.

	COUNTER-4.
Before	16
After	17

$$\text{SUBTRACT} \begin{Bmatrix} \text{literal} \\ \text{data-name-1} \end{Bmatrix} \text{FROM data-name-2}$$

$$\text{SUBTRACT} \begin{Bmatrix} \text{literal-1} \\ \text{data-name-1} \end{Bmatrix} \left[, \begin{Bmatrix} \text{literal-2} \\ \text{data-name-2} \end{Bmatrix} \cdots \right] \text{FROM} \begin{Bmatrix} \text{literal-n} \\ \text{data-name-n} \end{Bmatrix}$$
$$\text{[GIVING data-name-m]} \text{ [ROUNDED]} \text{ [; ON SIZE ERROR any imperative statement]}$$

SUBTRACT. This verb will most often be used in the form shown in the first box.

If it is desired to subtract one data item from another and store the difference in some other data item, the GIVING option may be used.

The presence of the option to have additional operands before the FROM means that it is possible to do the following: form the *sum* of several oper-

SUBTRACT A, B FROM C GIVING D.

	A	B	C	D
Before	1	3	5	29
After	1	3	5	01

MULTIPLY. This arithmetic verb is used to multiply two numeric quantities and make one of them, or a third, equal to the product.

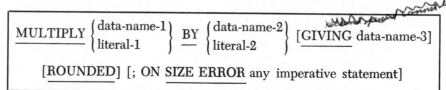

$$\text{MULTIPLY} \begin{Bmatrix} \text{data-name-1} \\ \text{literal-1} \end{Bmatrix} \text{BY} \begin{Bmatrix} \text{data-name-2} \\ \text{literal-2} \end{Bmatrix} \text{[GIVING data-name-3]}$$
$$\text{[ROUNDED]} \text{ [; ON SIZE ERROR any imperative statement]}$$

ands; then subtract this sum from another operand. Thus SUBTRACT A, B FROM C would mean to subtract the *sum* of A and B from C.

Note in the following examples that negative numbers are automatically handled according to the rules of algebra, as they are in all arithmetic verbs.

EXAMPLES OF SUBTRACT VERBS

SUBTRACT A FROM B.

	A	B
Before	3	8
After	3	5

SUBTRACT A FROM B.

	A	B
Before	8	2
After	8	−6

SUBTRACT A FROM B GIVING C.

	A	B	C
Before	2	6	39
After	2	6	04

SUBTRACT A FROM B.

	A	B
Before	6	−07
After	6	−13

If the GIVING option is not used, the second operand must not be a literal and the product replaces the *second* operand. The ON SIZE ERROR option can always be avoided with the MULTIPLY verb by determining the maximum length of the result field. The simple rule is that the number of digits in the product of two numbers never exceeds the sum of the number of digits of the original numbers.

EXAMPLES OF THE MULTIPLY VERB

MULTIPLY X BY Y.

	X	Y
Before	8	09
After	8	72

MULTIPLY UNITS BY PRICE GIVING COST.

	UNITS	PRICE	COST
Before	23	147	4444444
After	23	147	0003381

DIVIDE. This arithmetic verb is used to divide one numeric quantity into another and to make the second operand (or a third) equal to the quotient. If the GIVING option is not used, the second operand must not be a literal and is set equal to the quotient.

$$\boxed{\underline{\text{DIVIDE}} \left\{ \begin{array}{l} \text{data-name-1} \\ \text{literal-1} \end{array} \right\} \underline{\text{INTO}} \left\{ \begin{array}{l} \text{data-name-2} \\ \text{literal-2} \end{array} \right\} [\underline{\text{GIVING}}\ \text{data-name-3}]}$$

$$[\underline{\text{ROUNDED}}] [;\ \text{ON}\ \underline{\text{SIZE ERROR}}\ \text{any imperative statement}]$$

Some compilers accept BY instead of INTO but only in conjunction with the GIVING option.

The ON SIZE ERROR option should always be used with the DIVIDE verb, since a division by zero always results in a size error condition.

EXAMPLES OF THE DIVIDE VERB *Note use of the caret ($\wedge$) to indicate location of (implied) decimal point*

Further Equivalent

The COMPUTE Verb. Many business applications of computers involve only a little arithmetic and that little is usually quite simple. Nevertheless, some jobs do require more complex arithmetic operations, and in these cases the use of the ADD, SUBTRACT, MULTIPLY, and DIVIDE verbs can lead to rather cumbersome programs. The COMPUTE verb offers a much more compact way of specifying arithmetic operations.

$$\boxed{\underline{\text{COMPUTE}}\ \text{data-name-1}\ [\underline{\text{ROUNDED}}]\ =\ \left\{ \begin{array}{l} \text{date-name-2} \\ \text{formula} \end{array} \right\}}$$

$$[;\ \text{ON}\ \underline{\text{SIZE ERROR}}\ \text{any imperative statement}]$$

DIVIDE 5 INTO TOTAL GIVING AVERAGE.

	TOTAL	AVERAGE
Before	589207 $\wedge$	333333 $\wedge$
After	589207 $\wedge$	117841 $\wedge$

DIVIDE 18.75 INTO BOND-DEDUCTION GIVING NUMBER-OF-BONDS.

	BOND-DEDUCTION	NUMBER-OF-BONDS
Before	3580 $\wedge$	08
After	3580 $\wedge$	01

(original contents of NUMBER-OF-BONDS unimportant; operand has two digits and no decimal places)

The second example shows how it can happen that we would *not* want an arithmetic result to be rounded. In this situation we would be interested in knowing the *maximum* number of bonds that the employee can purchase; dividing 18.75 into 35.80 gives a quotient of 1 and a remainder of 17.05. All we care about is the 1; it is of no interest to know that the employee is more than halfway toward being able to buy a second bond. Therefore we set up the NUMBER-OF-BONDS item as an integer and do not round. The next step in a procedure to use this sentence would be a few sentences to compute and move the $17.05 (remainder) to a storage location where it could be written on tape as the employee's balance for buying bonds.

When the data-name-2 option shown in the format is used, the COMPUTE verb is simply an alternative way of doing what a MOVE does; used in conjunction with ROUNDED, however, this option serves the purpose of rounding data-name-2.

The normal use of this verb is with a *formula*, or *arithmetic expression*, which is a combination of data names, arithmetic operators, and possibly literals and parentheses, combined according to a few reasonable rules. There are five arithmetic operators, each of which is represented by a symbol:

+ for addition
− for subtraction
* for multiplication
/ for division
** for exponentiation.

Exponentiation means raising to a power; thus Z^2, which means Z times Z, is written

$$Z ** 2.$$

An arithmetic operator must always be preceded and followed by a space, but this is no more than saying that every data name and literal must also be preceded and followed by a space. Thus an "expression" like A-B would be misinterpreted as a single data name and A*B would be regarded as illegal for having a character not allowed in data names. This is entirely reasonable.

For arithmetic expressions containing combinations of operators but no parentheses we must have rules to determine which operations are performed first; these rules are just the same as in ordinary algebra:

All exponentiations, if any, are performed first.
All multiplications and divisions are performed next.
All additions and subtractions are performed last.

Thus, in an expression like $A + B / C + D * E ** F - G$, E would be raised to the F power, B divided by C, and D multiplied by E to the F; then the additions and subtraction would be performed. In other words, the expression would be treated as though written

$$A + (B / C) + (D * (E ** F)) - G.$$

In an expression containing a combination of additions and subtractions, or a combination of multiplications and divisions, but no parentheses, the operations are carried from left to right. Thus certain expressions that are considered ambiguous in ordinary algebra are permitted in COBOL: $A / B * C$ is treated as though written $(A / B) * C$ and $A / B / C$ means $((A / B) / C)$.

Rather seldom will things of this nature occur in normal business data processing, and anyway it is always possible, with no important penalties, to indicate explicitly what is meant by writing parentheses even when they are not strictly needed.

EXAMPLES

Suppose we have already determined that HOURS-WORKED is greater than 40; we want to get OVERTIME-PAY by multiplying the hours over 40 by the pay rate times 1.5:

COMPUTE OVERTIME-PAY = (HOURS-WORKED − 40) * RATE * 1.5.

Suppose we want to update a year-to-date sales amount with the extended price of a number of units sold:

COMPUTE YEAR-TO-DATE-SALES
    = YEAR-TO-DATE-SALES
    + QUANTITY * UNIT-PRICE.

This is *not* an equation in the algebraic sense, but it is perfectly legitimate in COBOL: it means to perform a multiplication, add the product to the item named YEAR-TO-DATE-SALES, and store the sum as the new value of YEAR-TO-DATE-SALES.

Suppose that we want to compute the average of the usage of a stock item for the first three months of the year:

COMPUTE QUARTER-AVERAGE
    = (JAN + FEB + MAR) / 3.

Note that the parentheses here are not just to make the meaning clear; they are essential: without them MAR would be divided by 3 and the quotient added to JAN and FEB, which is not what we want at all. As a simple example of the convenience provided by the COMPUTE verb, consider what the last illustration would be without it:

(1) ADD JAN, FEB, MAR GIVING
    TEMPORARY.
(2) DIVIDE 3 INTO TEMPORARY GIVING
    QUARTER-AVERAGE.

The COMPUTE version is seen to be not only less trouble but considerably easier to read. Because of its versatility, we could, of course, use the COMPUTE verb instead of any of the other arithmetic verbs. In the case of a subtraction, for instance, we could write

COMPUTE NET-SAL = GROSS-SAL
    − TAX-AMOUNT.

rather than

SUBTRACT TAX-AMOUNT FROM
    GROSS-SAL GIVING NET-SAL.

This would be legal COBOL, but would it be a good practice? The answer is that since different object-program instructions may be compiled for the two verbs, object-program efficiency may be affected by the choice. The determination of these matters usually rests with expert programmers who are capable of analyzing the object-program instructions and are normally members of the standards group of an installation. Suffice it to say here that several installations have adopted the standard practice of using ADD and SUBTRACT only for simple additions and subtractions and COMPUTE for *all* other arithmetic calculations.

Summary of action of arithmetic verbs. Table 3.1 may be helpful as a reference to summarize what each of the five arithmetic verbs does under the various options.

TABLE 3.1

Arithmetic Statement	Value *After* Execution of the Statement			
	A	B	C	D
ADD A TO B	A	A + B		
ADD A, B, C, TO D	A	B	C	A + B + C + D
ADD A, B, C GIVING D	A	B	C	A + B + C
SUBTRACT A FROM B	A	B − A		
SUBTRACT A, B FROM C	A	B	C − (A + B)	
SUBTRACT A, B FROM C GIVING D	A	B	C	C − (A + B)
MULTIPLY A BY B	A	A × B		
MULTIPLY A BY B GIVING C	A	B	A × B	
DIVIDE A INTO B	A	B/A		
DIVIDE A INTO B GIVING C	A	B	B/A	
COMPUTE C = A + B	A	B	A + B	
COMPUTE A = A + B	A + B	B		
COMPUTE C = A − B	A	B	A − B	
COMPUTE C = A * B	A	B	A × B	
COMPUTE C = A / B	A	B	A / B	

REVIEW QUESTIONS

1. Each of the following contains at least one *syntactic* error; that is, aside from what the writer may have *meant* by the statements, they do not follow the rules for proper *format*. Identify the errors.

    a. MOVE TO A FROM B.
    b. ADD COUNTER TO 1.
    c. ADD A, B, C TO D GIVING E.
    d. SUBTRACT QUANTITY-ON-HAND FROM ZERO.
    e. MULTIPLY X TIMES Y GIVING Z.
    f. DIVIDE R BY S.
    g. DIVIDE A INTO 6.
    h. ADD A TO B WITH ROUNDING.
    i. MULTIPLY L BY M GIVING N; IF SIZE ERROR GO TO ERROR-CASE.

2. Fill in the "after" line in each of the following statements.

    a. MOVE A TO B.

	A	B
Before	165	274
After		

    b. ADD A TO B.

	A	B
Before	6	3
After		

    c. ADD A, B, C GIVING D.

	A	B	C	D
Before	1	2	3	4
After				

    d. ADD A B TO C.

	A	B	C
Before	3	2	9
After			

    e. SUBTRACT A FROM B.

	A	B
Before	1	9
After		

    f. SUBTRACT A FROM B GIVING C.

	A	B	C
Before	1	9	5
After			

    g. SUBTRACT A B FROM C GIVING D.

	A	B	C	D
Before	2	5	3	8
After				

    h. MULTIPLY A BY B.

	A	B
Before	2	4
After		

    i. MULTIPLY A BY B GIVING C.

	A	B	C
Before	2	3	4
After			

    j. DIVIDE A INTO B.

	A	B
Before	3	15
After		

    k. DIVIDE A INTO B GIVING C.

	A	B	C
Before	3	15	20
After			

    l. DIVIDE A INTO B ROUNDED.

	A	B	
Before	3	11	(A and B have no decimal places, i.e., they are integers.)
After			

<h1>48 COBOL PROGRAMMING</h1>

m. DIVIDE A INTO B.

<table>
	A	B
Before	3	11
</table>

(A and B are integers.)

After

n. MULTIPLY A BY B GIVING C ROUNDED.

	A	B	C
Before	6	346	562

(C has one decimal place.)

After

3. Are the following legal COBOL arithmetic expressions?

    a. 0.03125 * EARNINGS
    b. 4800.00 — PREV-YTD
    c. 4 / 3 * PI * R ** 3

---

executed. The statement is about the simplest there is: the only rule is that it must refer to the name of a paragraph. There is no provision for transferring to any sentence in a paragraph except the first one, since only the beginning of a paragraph can be named. As examples we may use two statements that we wrote in our sample program in Chapter 1:

    ...AT END GO TO END-RUN.
      GO TO READ-ROUTINE.

The PERFORM verb has quite a number of options, of which we now wish to consider only the simplest. In this version we write a statement having the format given in the box.

PERFORM procedure-name-1   [THRU procedure-name-2]

---

    d. (4 / 3) * PI * (R ** 3)
    e. 0.18*(GROSS — 1300 * DEPENDENTS)
    f. A * B / * C + D
    g. 67.8 * 6 — 12.0 / 14.87
    h. (HOURS — 40.) * 1.5

4. Do the following pairs of statements accomplish the same thing?

    a. 1. ADD CURR-MONTH TO YTD-69.
       2. COMPUTE YTD-69 = YTD-69 + CURR-MONTH.
    b. 1. COMPUTE SUMA = ZERO
       2. MOVE ZERO TO SUMA
    c. 1. COMPUTE X = A * B — C / D
       2. COMPUTE X = (A * B) — (C / D)
    d. 1. COMPUTE Y = A — B * C — D
       2. COMPUTE Y = (A — B) * (C — D)
    e. 1. COMPUTE Z = A / B * C — D * E / F
       2. COMPUTE Z = (A / B) * C — (D * E) / F
    f. 1. COMPUTE Z = A / B * C — D * E / F
       2. COMPUTE Z = A / (B * C) — D * (E / F)
    g. 1. COMPUTE DISCOUNT-PRICE = 0.98 * PRICE
       2. COMPUTE DISCOUNT-PRICE = PRICE — 0.02 * PRICE

5. Can you think of an example in which use of the COMPUTE verb might save object program instructions? (Cheat: no examples were given in the text.)

3.4 The GO TO, PERFORM, and STOP Verbs

The GO TO verb, as we saw in Section 1.5, provides a way of breaking out of the one-after-the-other sequence in which sentences are ordinarily

---

If the second procedure name is not written, the execution of this statement is as follows: the paragraph named procedure-name-1 is executed and control returns to the statement following the PERFORM statement. An example of how this verb may be used is shown in the sample program at the end of this chapter. When the routine consists of two or more consecutive paragraphs, the THRU option must be used to name the last paragraph in the set to be PERFORMed.

We shall see in Chapter 8 that the PERFORM verb is capable of doing a great deal more than this.

The STOP statement is used to terminate—either temporarily or permanently—the execution of the object program. It does *not* stop the compilation of the source program in which there may very well be more than one STOP statement.

STOP { literal / RUN }

If a literal is written with the STOP, that literal will be displayed on the console typewriter, and after the necessary operator action the execution of the object program will continue with the statement following the STOP. This form could be used, for instance, to signal some sort of error condition from which the operator might be able to recover and then continue. The STOP RUN version, as we saw in the sample program in Chapter 1, causes instead the termination of the execution of the object program.

3.5 The IF Statement and Related Matters

Tests and decisions are an important part of any data-processing procedure, both because they are themselves a desired part of the processing and because they are required by the way we approach data processing with a computer. In COBOL the IF statement* and its variations are used to effect these actions.

The IF statement. We have already seen a number of examples of IF statements, such as IF QUANTITY-ON-HAND LESS THAN QUANTITY-ORDERED GO TO SHORTAGE-ROUTINE. The general format of this type of IF statement is

IF   condition   statement(s)

where a "condition" may be any one of a variety of things, as we shall investigate shortly. The "statement" written after the condition may be whatever is needed. We could write, for instance,

IF TRANSACTION-QUANTITY IS LESS THAN ON-HAND MOVE 'OUT OF STOCK' TO PRINTER-AREA.

Let us now investigate what possibilities there are for writing IF statements.

Relation tests. The examples of IF statements that we have seen so far have already introduced the most important type of condition, a relation test. This requires the comparison of two operands, either of which may be a data name, a literal, or a formula. (An example of a formula would be ON-HAND + ON-ORDER; these are the same as the expressions that follow the equal sign in a COMPUTE.) The "relation" here is simply one of equality or relative size; the forms that are allowed are shown in the format for a full relation test. Most compilers would accept also the symbols >, <, and = for GREATER THAN, LESS THAN, and EQUAL TO, respectively.

---

* We said earlier that all statements begin with verbs, of which IF is not an example. It is useful, however, to classify IF as a verb for COBOL purposes, since it shares the universal characteristic of COBOL verbs: the creation of object program instructions to carry out action on data.

Now we should explore a few of the implications of the form of the data being compared: whether NUMERIC or not and whether the two items are of the same length.

For NUMERIC items a comparison establishes that the value of one of the items is LESS THAN, EQUAL TO, or GREATER THAN the other. This comparison is based on the *values* of the two, completely apart from their form of representation. Thus 45, 0045, and +45.000 would be considered equal. The comparison is algebraic, which means that signs are considered according to the following familiar rules: any positive value is greater than any negative value, and a "small" negative value is algebraically greater than a "large" negative value. Thus 45 is greater than 34; 45 is greater than −34 and also greater than −56; −65 is greater than −76. Zero is considered to be a single unique value, regardless of sign, length, or implied decimal point.

For *non*-NUMERIC *items* we must begin by defining what we mean by "greater" and "less." Is the letter A† greater or less than the letter B and is a letter greater or less than a digit? These questions are answered by the *collating sequence* that is built into each machine. According to the collating sequence for IBM equipment, for instance, a space is "smaller" than all letters, all letters are "smaller" than all digits, and the various other characters fit in at odd places among the letters and digits. In the equipment of several other manufacturers the positions of the letters and digits are reversed. The collating sequences for different machines are in very few cases the same. In working with any one machine this is no problem, of course, but it can have a significant effect on compatibility if a user changes computers.

If we assume any fixed collating sequence, the general idea of a non-numeric comparison is that the two items are compared character-by-character, starting from the left, until either the rightmost characters are reached or until a nonmatching pair of characters establishes that one item is greater or less than the other; for instance, if we write

---

† We mean the letter A *itself*, of course, not the letter A considered as a data name.

$$\text{IF} \left\{ \begin{array}{l} \text{data-name-1} \\ \text{literal-1} \\ \text{formula-1} \end{array} \right\} \left\{ \begin{array}{l} \text{IS [NOT] GREATER THAN} \\ \text{IS [NOT] LESS THAN} \\ \text{IS [NOT] EQUAL TO} \end{array} \right\} \left\{ \begin{array}{l} \text{data-name-2} \\ \text{literal-2} \\ \text{formula-2} \end{array} \right\}$$

IF NAME-1 IS GREATER THAN NAME-2

and the two names are SMITH and JONES, the comparison stops as soon as the object program determines that S is "greater" than J. If the names had been SMITHERS and SMITHSON, then the comparison would have had to continue until it is found that E is "less" than S. With regard to data items consisting only of letters, we can simply state that a comparison consists of determining which of the two items would "alphabetize" as smaller. For items of equal length this simplified description applies even if there are spaces at the right end of one or both data items: SMITHbbb is "smaller" than SMITHSON and SMITHbbbbb is "smaller" than SMITHSONbb.

If the two data items are not of equal length, the following reasonable rule applies: if the characters of the shorter item are exactly the same as the same number of characters at the left end of the longer, then the shorter is considered to be smaller unless all remaining characters of the longer are spaces, in which case they are considered to be equal. Thus WILLIAMS is "smaller" than WILLIAMSON but "equal" to WILLIAMSbbbbb.

ANSWERS

1. a. No such format. Must be MOVE A TO B or MOVE B TO A, whichever is meant.
   b. Last operand must not be a literal. Should be ADD 1 TO COUNTER.
   c. The TO and GIVING options cannot both be used.
   d. Last operand cannot be a literal or a figurative constant.
   e. Should be MULTIPLY X BY Y GIVING Z.
   f. There is no such format. The presumed meaning would be given by DIVIDE S INTO R.
   g. Last operand must not be a literal.
   h. The format is ROUNDED, not WITH ROUNDING.
   i. The format is ON SIZE ERROR; OK otherwise.

2. a. | A | B |
      |---|---|
      | 165 | 165 |

   b. | A | B |
      |---|---|
      | 6 | 9 |

   c. | A | B | C | D |
      |---|---|---|---|
      | 1 | 2 | 3 | 6 |

   d. | A | B | C |
      |---|---|---|
      | 3 | 2 | 14 |

   e. | A | B |
      |---|---|
      | 1 | 8 |

   f. | A | B | C |
      |---|---|---|
      | 1 | 9 | 8 |

   g. | A | B | C | D |
      |---|---|---|---|
      | 2 | 5 | 3 | —4 |

   h. | A | B |
      |---|---|
      | 2 | 8 |

   i. | A | B | C |
      |---|---|---|
      | 2 | 3 | 6 |

   j. | A | B |
      |---|---|
      | 3 | 5 |

   k. | A | B | C |
      |---|---|---|
      | 3 | 15 | 5 |

   l. | A | B |
      |---|---|
      | 3 | 4 |

ANSWERS (Continued)

   (3 into 11 gives 3.666 . . . which rounds to 4.)

   m. | A | B |
      |---|---|
      | 3 | 3 (no rounding) |

   n. | A | B | C |
      |---|---|---|
      | 6 | 346 | 208 |

3. a. Yes.
   b. Yes. Note that PREV-YTD is a single data name; the hyphen is *not* a minus sign, since it is not preceded and followed by spaces.
   c. Yes.
   d. Yes, and the meaning is the same as in (c).
   e. No, but the only error is the absence of spaces around the first asterisk.
   f. No: it is meaningless and illegal to have two operation symbols side by side.
   g. Yes, but why do it? The object program would have to carry out this computation every time; you could work out the value of the expression with a desk calculator once before writing the source program.
   h. No, but only because of the decimal point at the end of the first numeric literal, which is illegal.

4. a. Yes.
   b. Yes.
   c. Yes.
   d. Not at all: with the parentheses, the subtractions are carried out first; without them, the multiplication is done first.
   e. Yes.
   f. No: A / B * C means $\frac{A}{B}$ C, not $\frac{A}{BC}$. However, D * E / F and D * (E / F) *are* equivalent.
   g. Yes: this is just algebra. The first version is preferred, however, since it requires less object program arithmetic.

5. In the example in which we computed (JAN + FEB + MAR) / 3 some machines would be able to do the division without ever storing the sum temporarily, as the ADD and DIVIDE formulation would require.

With regard to data items that are not made up entirely of letters, the action is a little less rational appearing but still consistent: each character comparison is based on the machine's collating sequence. If in a particular computer the digits are all greater than the letters, then ABC852 is greater than ABCDEF but smaller than 634ABC.

We quite often need to test a data item to determine whether it is less than, equal to, or greater than zero .This can be done, of course, simply by comparing the data item with the figurative constant ZERO, but COBOL provides an alternative way to do the same thing. Once again we must be

$$
\text{\underline{IF}} \left\{ \begin{array}{c} \text{data-name} \\ \text{formula} \end{array} \right\} \text{IS [\underline{NOT}]} \left\{ \begin{array}{c} \text{\underline{POSITIVE}} \\ \text{\underline{NEGATIVE}} \\ \text{\underline{ZERO}} \end{array} \right\}
$$

specific: zero is neither positive nor negative in this context. To be positive an item must be greater than zero, and to be negative it must be less than zero.

Class tests. It is sometimes convenient to be able to determine whether a data item that should contain either digits or letters does in fact contain only one or the other. We may recall from Chapter 1 that a data item that *may* contain NUMERIC, ALPHABETIC, and/or special characters is called alphanumeric and that the designations NUMERIC, ALPHABETIC, and alphanumeric are called the class of the data. A class test is of the form shown in the box.

$$
\text{\underline{IF}} \quad \text{data-name} \quad \text{IS} \quad \text{[\underline{NOT}]} \left\{ \begin{array}{c} \text{\underline{NUMERIC}} \\ \text{\underline{ALPHABETIC}} \end{array} \right\}
$$

Condition names and conditional variable tests. A condition name is a name assigned to a specific value, set of values, or range of values within the complete set of values that a data name may assume. The data name itself is called a *conditional variable* and the values it may assume are referred to by *condition names;* for instance, suppose that a payroll application includes a data item named PAYROLL-PERIOD, in which a 1 indicates weekly, 2 indicates semimonthly, and 3 indicates monthly. When we process a payroll record, we shall need to determine which of these three it is; this can naturally be done by tests:

IF PAYROLL-PERIOD IS EQUAL TO 1 GO
    TO WEEKLY-ROUTINE.
IF PAYROLL-PERIOD IS EQUAL TO 2 GO
    TO SEMIMONTHLY-ROUTINE.
IF PAYROLL-PERIOD IS EQUAL TO 3 GO
    TO MONTHLY-ROUTINE.

COBOL provides another and more readable way to do the same thing. In the DATA DIVISION we can give condition names to the three possible values of the variable PAYROLL-PERIOD; let us call them WEEKLY, SEMIMONTHLY, and MONTHLY. Now we can write

IF WEEKLY GO TO WEEKLY-ROUTINE.
IF SEMIMONTHLY GO TO SEMIMONTHLY-
    ROUTINE.
IF MONTHLY GO TO MONTHLY-ROUTINE.

The compiler will set up object program instructions to do just what the explicit tests do. The sentence IF WEEKLY GO TO WEEKLY-ROUTINE, for instance, will result in instructions to test whether the conditional variable named PAYROLL-PERIOD currently has the value 1 and transfer to the routine named if true. We shall see in Chapter 5 how to set up condition names that refer to sets and ranges of values of a conditional variable.

Switch status tests. Many computers have switches on their consoles that may be tested by the object program and the result used to control the processing; for instance, if a certain switch is up, it might mean to put the output on tape, but if it is down the output should be printed directly. Through the ENVIRONMENT DIVISION (see Chapter 6), the *status* of such switches can be given condition names, which may then be tested just as conditional variables are tested by condition names; for instance, we might write IF TAPE-OUTPUT or IF PRINTER.

Full conditional sentence. The simplest version of a conditional sentence, as we have seen, contains a condition and a statement that describes what to do if the condition is satisfied. By default, if the condition is not satisfied, the statement is not executed, and the program control passes automatically to the next sequential instruction, which is to say the next sentence.

A more comprehensive version of the IF sentence allows us to state, in addition, what to do if the condition is *not* satisfied.

$$\text{IF } \underline{\text{condition}} \begin{Bmatrix} \text{statement-1} \\ \underline{\text{NEXT SENTENCE}} \end{Bmatrix} \begin{Bmatrix} \text{OTHERWISE} \\ \text{ELSE} \end{Bmatrix} \begin{Bmatrix} \text{statement-2} \\ \underline{\text{NEXT SENTENCE}} \end{Bmatrix}$$

If the condition is found to be true, either statement-1 or the next sentence, whichever is indicated, will be executed and statement-2 skipped over. If the condition is found to be false, statement-2 or the next sentence, whichever is indicated, will be executed next. Notice that to terminate the sentence by the combination ELSE NEXT SENTENCE is pointless, for, as we have just said, if a condition is not satisfied, control passes to the next sentence *automatically*.

EXAMPLES

(1) IF AMOUNT IS NEGATIVE MOVE 'CR' TO OUT-7.

(2) IF MARRIED ADD 1 TO MARRIED-COUNT.

(3) IF AGE IS LESS THAN 21 ADD 1 TO MINOR-COUNT ELSE ADD 1 TO MAJOR-COUNT.

(4) IF COD IS LESS THAN 10 NEXT SENTENCE; OTHERWISE MOVE 'BAD CODE' TO OUT-1; MOVE COD TO OUT-2; MOVE SPACES TO OUT-3.

REVIEW QUESTIONS

1. Identify the syntactic errors, if any, in the following sentences.

   a. IF BILL IS NOT EQUAL TO JACK MOVE A TO B.

   b. IF BILL EQUAL TO GEORGE MOVE C TO D.

   c. IF BILL DOES NOT EQUAL JOE MOVE E TO F.

   d. IF BILL EQUAL TO 21 MOVE G to H.

   e. IF 17 EQUALS 17 GO TO EQUAL.

2. Two numeric literals are given in each of the following. If they were the values of two data items, would the first be considered to be less than, equal to, or greater than the second?

a.	+12	12.000
b.	−78	−93
c.	77	−1239
d.	12.00	12.001
e.	77	−76
f.	11.9999	−12.0001
g.	−78	−76
h.	4	+4
i.	+4	−4

3. Same as Question 2, except that the literals are non-numeric. Assume that digits are "larger" than letters.

a.	'78FR'	'FR78'
b.	'789'	'678'
c.	'JOEbbb'	'JOSEPH'
d.	'JOE'	'JOEbbb'
e.	'NIXbON'	'NIXON'
f.	'KEN'	'KENNEDY'
g.	'GOOSE'	'GEESE'
h.	'7'	'EIGHT'
i.	'JOHNbbbbbb'	'JOHNSON'

4. Which of the following statements are true, if any?

   a. An item that passes the IF ALPHABETIC test may contain spaces.

   b. If an item does not pass the IF NUMERIC test, then it could certainly pass the IF ALPHABETIC test.

   c. If an item does not pass the IF NUMERIC test and then does not pass the IF ALPHABETIC test, we can conclude that it is alphanumeric in content.

   d. An item that contains a special character will fail both the IF NUMERIC and the IF ALPHABETIC test.

5. In a statement like IF WEEKLY GO TO WEEKLY-ROUTINE, how would the compiler know that WEEKLY is a condition name rather than a data name?

6. In a statement like IF TAPE-OUTPUT GO TO TAPE-WRITING how would the compiler know that TAPE-OUTPUT is a switch-status name rather than a condition name or a data name?

7. Consider the following sentence:

IF A IS LESS THAN B MOVE 2 TO S; ELSE MOVE 3 TO S.

If A is currently 41 and B is 37, what would be placed in S?

8. Consider the following sentence.

IF A IS GREATER THAN B MOVE 5 TO X, MOVE 6 TO Y; OTHERWISE MOVE 7 TO X, MOVE 8 TO Y.

If A is currently 41 and B is 37, what would be placed in X and Y?

9. Consider the following sentence.

IF A IS EQUAL TO B MOVE M TO N, MOVE P TO Q; ELSE GO TO R-1.

If A is not equal to B, what would be placed in N and Q?

3.6 Input and Output

Getting data into the computer storage and results out of it is a major portion of the work of any data-processing system; if the programming is done in the machine's language, it is a large part of the programming effort also. With COBOL we have six verbs ...ectively; a ...eds of ob-

...DISPLAY, ...and have ..., OPEN, ...ely powerful ...a great ...s. Since ...under- ...L PRO- ...e every ...hat the

...small ...om an (The ...with The

...e]

...e it ...the ...ON-

...eral-2} ...ta-name-2} ... [UPON mnemonic-name]

...n ...y ...e ...s ...n ...information

from cards, but if we want to enter data from the console typewriter we need to say ACCEPT data-name FROM CONSOLE.

Only one data name may be written, but as we shall see in Chapters 5 and 7 in connection with the WORKING-STORAGE SECTION of the DATA DIVISION it is possible for a single data name to represent a whole *group* of smaller data items. There are some restrictions in the number of characters that a data item may contain. If the latter is on a card, for instance, its length obviously cannot exceed 80 characters: if we need to enter more than 80 characters, we have to write two (or more) ACCEPT statements. Some compilers restrict the maximum number of characters ACCEPTed by the console to 72.

EXAMPLES

(1) ACCEPT TODAYS-DATE.
(2) ACCEPT CONTROL-TOTAL FROM CONSOLE.
(3) ACCEPT EXTRACT-CODES FROM CARD-READER-100.

We assume, for the last example, that the standard input device is something other than a card reader —for instance, a tape drive. Incidentally, it may sometimes be necessary to establish in the ENVIRONMENT DIVISION a "tie-in" between names such as CARD-READER-100 and actual hardware devices.

DISPLAY. This corresponds to ACCEPT in handling low volumes of output. The format is slightly more extensive because here we are permitted to list several data names or literals. As before, the

...eral-2} ...ta-name-2} ... [UPON mnemonic-name]

mnemonic-name option is necessary when we do not display the information on the system's standard output device. (The latter is usually the printer.)

If there are several operands, they are displayed in succession in the output, from left to right. Ordinarily the program will be organized so that a DISPLAY verb will not involve more characters than will fit on one card, one line, or whatever. If there are too many characters, another card or line will be written or the excess characters may in some cases be deleted.

EXAMPLES

(1) DISPLAY COMPUTED-CONTROL-TOTAL.

(2) DISPLAY 'COMPUTED CONTROL TOTAL IS', COMPUTED-CONTROL-TOTAL.

(3) DISPLAY 'DISMOUNT REEL ON TAPE UNIT 6' UPON CONSOLE.

(4) DISPLAY 'ITEM', PART-NUMBER, 'BACK ORDERED'.

(5) DISPLAY 'JOB FINISHED' UPON PRINTER.

(6) DISPLAY PART-NUMBER, QUANTITY-ORDERED, QUANTITY-ON-HAND, DESCRIPTION UPON SYSPUNCH.

OPEN. As we have seen in the sample program in Chapter 1, before data can be read from a file or anything written on it the file must be *opened*. This prepares the file and the object program for reading or writing and also carries out operations associated with *labels*.

A label is a special record at the beginning and/or end of a file which contains such things as the file name, the volume number, the date the file was written, and perhaps the date after which the information will no longer be valid.* Labels are used to avoid the almost inevitable mixups that will happen occasionally in an installation with hundreds or thousands of reels of tape—which is not an exaggerated number—or dozens of disk

---

* This is, of course, in addition to the paper label pasted on the outside of the reel or disk pack itself, which is sometimes called the *external* label to distinguish it from what we are talking about, which is then called the *internal* label or *magnetic* label.

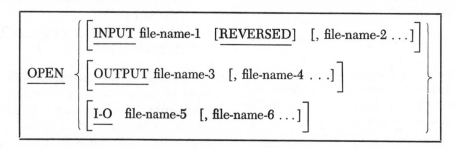

ANSWERS

1. c. The DOES NOT EQUAL is not allowed; should be IS NOT EQUAL TO.

  e. The comparison of two literals is forbidden, as it happens, even though it looks legal enough in the format; of course, it is pointless because the relation will always be satisfied or always not satisfied. Also EQUAL—a reserved word—is used as a procedure name. Finally, EQUALS is not legal: the legal form is EQUAL TO.

2. a. Equal.
  b. Greater.
  c. Greater.
  d. Less.
  e. Greater.
  f. Greater.
  g. Less.
  h. Equal.
  i. Greater.

3. a. Greater.
  b. Greater. And these *are* non-NUMERIC literals, as written.
  c. Less.

ANSWERS (Continued)

  d. Equal.
  e. Less.
  f. Less.
  g. Greater.
  h. Greater.
  i. Less.

4. a, c, and d are true; b is false. Spaces are regarded as ALPHABETIC characters. Special characters are neither ALPHABETIC nor NUMERIC, and an item containing one or more of them would fail both tests. So, incidentally, would any item which contains both digits and letters.

5. This would be specified in the DATA DIVISION.

6. This would be specified in the ENVIRONMENT DIVISION.

7. 3.

8. 5 in X, 6 in Y.

9. Nothing would be placed in N and Q by this statement; their values would remain unchanged from their previous values. Control would be transferred to the paragraph named R-1.

packs. For tapes there are four possible types of label, which go by the standard names of begin-

READ. This verb performs a large number of operations, despite its fairly simple format.

| READ file-name RECORD [INTE data-name] $\begin{Bmatrix} \text{; AT END} \\ \text{INVALID KEY} \end{Bmatrix}$ any imperative statement |

---

ning-file-label, beginning-tape-label, ending-tape-label, and ending-file-label. The first tape of a file can have two labels at the beginning, and the last tape of a file can have two at the end. It will probably not be too common to use all four; in fact, the most common approach requires only beginning tape labels. Some installations do not use tape labels at all.

The absence of labels is natural for card files. Disk packs, on the other hand, always contain a label that indicates the volume serial number and refers to an area that contains the standard labels of all the files on the pack.

For files that do contain labels the amount and nature of the checking performed when a file is read are also subject to wide variation. The contents of the labels for each file are specified in the DATA DIVISION. Often a standard type of label will be used for all files. Certain standard checking procedures may be established for an installation, such as making sure that the tape is taken from the proper file, that it has the correct reel number, and, for an OUTPUT tape, that it is not being improperly used before its expiration date.

For an INPUT file the OPEN verb automatically supplies whatever "standard" label checking has been established. Additional checks may be done by a routine supplied by the programmer in connection with the USE verb described in Chapter 8. For an OUTPUT file OPEN automatically writes a standard label and/or follows the procedure defined by another USE. Any files that have no labels will be so described in the DATA DIVISION, and all the label processing will naturally be bypassed.

The OPEN verb does *not* read the first data record; this is done by a READ. Every file *must* be opened before the first READ or WRITE for it, whether it has labels or not.

The REVERSED option applies to systems in which it is possible to read a tape backward, a very useful feature on occasion; it can be used only for files consisting of a single reel of tape.

The I-O option refers to random access files and is treated in Section 7.7.

Note that RECORD here is an optional word, since it is not underlined. Nevertheless we should begin by emphasizing that READ (and WRITE) operate with *records*. The primary function of the READ is, in fact, to make available the next record of a file. This presents no problems if we READ a file that consists of a deck of cards: each execution of a READ instruction will make available the next card. In the case of an unblocked* file on magnetic tape, it would, likewise, make available the next record.

What happens when we have a tape file on which the records are blocked? The answer is still the same: each execution of a READ would make available for processing the *next logical record*, whether that record is simply the next one from a block that has already been read from the external medium or whether a new block must be read because all records from the preceding block have already been processed. In short, the object program instructions created from a READ automatically handle all the data record manipulations associated with blocked records.

If an error is detected in reading a block, the tape is automatically backspaced and reread on the assumption that the trouble may have been nothing more than a speck of dust and that a second or third reading may show no trouble. If after a few readings the error persists, the object program will branch to the error routine specified by a USE verb, if there is one, and will stop if no error routine has been provided.

If the INTO option is used, the action is that of a READ followed by a MOVE of the entire record to the area specified, which might be a temporary working storage or an output area. When this is done, the record is still available in both places.

If in attempting to read a block the object program recognizes the signal that the end of the

---

* The material on the READ and WRITE verbs will depend heavily on a clear understanding of the difference between a record and a block. See Section 2.5 for a review of this matter.

reel has been reached,* the object program will perform a standard routine for processing the end of the reel label (if there is one) and any special routine that may have been specified by a USE. Then, if the file has been set up to use two alternate tape units, as is frequently the case, to avoid wasting computer time while tape reels are changed, it will start the rewinding of this reel and perform the label checking for the reel on the alternate unit. Finally, it will go ahead and read the first block on the next tape and make its first record available for processing. All of the operations described in this paragraph can be done in a fraction of a second, except for the rewinding, which is finished while processing of the next tape continues.

When the signal indicating the end of the file (as distinguished from the end of one reel of the file) is detected, the object program will perform whatever is dictated by the AT END statement and whatever is indicated by a USE, if any.

EXAMPLES

(1) READ ORDER-FILE, AT END GO TO END-OF-JOB.
(2) READ MASTER-IN INTO MASTER-OUT; AT END MOVE 'Y' TO END-CONTROL, GO TO REPROCESS-2.
(3) READ ORDER-FILE RECORD AT END GO TO END-RUN.
(4) READ TRANSACT-IN AT END GO TO MASTER-WRITING.
(5) READ FILE-IN, AT END CLOSE FILE-IN, CLOSE FILE-OUT, STOP RUN.

vice we want to read? As we shall see, this would be specified in the ENVIRONMENT DIVISION, in which we relate each file to a specific device.

What about the INVALID KEY option? Like the I-O option after OPEN, it applies to disk files when used in the random access mode. Random access handling presents several peculiar intricacies, and the entire subject will be treated separately, because, at this stage, it would interfere with the understanding of the most important—and most practical—features of the COBOL language.

In fact, a few reassuring statements are perhaps in order at this moment. First of all, magnetic tapes are still by far the most common file medium, which means that we can and should concentrate on them without letting our minds wander in too many directions. Also most tape files are on one reel, which means that all the details about multireel files may be set aside for the moment. Finally, most tape files have either standard labels or no labels at all. These two alternatives are taken care of by two very simple options in the FILE SECTION of the DATA DIVISION: LABEL RECORDS ARE STANDARD and LABEL RECORDS ARE OMITTED.

Thus reassured, the reader—if any—may now turn his or her attention to two other verbs that we have seen in the sample program in Chapter 1, WRITE and CLOSE.

WRITE. This verb enables us to write records on any type of output files: printed output, cards, tapes, and disks. WRITE performs its functions in a manner similar to that of READ. We must remember, however, that we READ a file-name, but we WRITE a record-name.

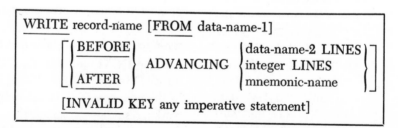

A few more words on READ will also clarify some points on certain other sections of COBOL. We said that the READ verb can be used to read files on cards, tapes, or other media, but how would the computer know from which input de-

The ADVANCING option has to do with files for printing; this is considered subsequently.

The basic actions, returning now to the common case of tape files, are quite similar to those of READ. Once again the primary function of the verb is to write a *record*, with all special actions required by blocked records taken care of auto-

---

* For a review of this matter see page 31.

matically. If writing a record fills the block, the block is written out to tape. If this record does not fill the block, nothing is put on tape, but things are arranged so that the next record will go into the next record position in the block.

Some computers are able to detect errors in writing, using special equipment in the tape units. On such computers error-checking procedures are automatically supplied as part of the WRITE, with the block being rewritten if an error is detected.

If, during writing, the object program detects the physical end of a reel, it will write the tape-ending label, if any, start the tape rewinding, switch to the alternate tape unit if the file is set up that way, write a label on the new tape if so specified, and prepare to write the next block on the new tape.

If the FROM option is used, the verb in effect becomes a MOVE and WRITE just as a READ with the INTO becomes a READ and MOVE.

EXAMPLES

(1) WRITE SALES-REPORT.
(2) WRITE PAYROLL-JOURNAL.
(3) WRITE PAYROLL-JOURNAL FROM AREA-2.
(4) WRITE MASTER-OUT FROM MASTER-IN.
(5) WRITE HEADING AFTER ADVANCING 0 LINES.
(6) WRITE TOTAL-LINE AFTER ADVANCING 2 LINES.
(7) WRITE SECOND-HALF BEFORE ADVANCING 1 LINES.

CLOSE. From a practical standpoint all we need to know about this verb is that in a COBOL program we must sooner or later CLOSE all the files that we have previously OPENed. If a file is on cards or a disk or is printed, there is very little else to say. For tape files there are a few details worth mentioning.

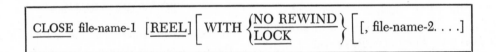

CLOSE file-name-1 [REEL] [WITH { NO REWIND / LOCK }] [, file-name-2. . . .]

If the file is to be printed, which would be specified in the ENVIRONMENT DIVISION, the options listed allow the programmer to control the spacing of lines on the page. These options permit the paper to be advanced a fixed number of lines (the integer option) or a variable number of lines, depending on a variable in the program (the data-name-2 option), or to a predetermined position on the page (the mnemonic-name option). This last refers to printers in which there is a loop of punched paper tape called the *carriage control* tape. A signal from the program will cause the carriage to move to any of several predetermined positions, such as the first or last printing lines. Typical mnemonic names here might be PAGE, for the top of the page, or BOTTOM, for the last printing position. These page-advance operations may be specified to take place either before or after the printing.

Most commonly, the AFTER ADVANCING option is used with 1 LINES, 2 LINES, and 3 LINES. Several compilers will recognize the option AFTER ADVANCING 0 LINES (where 0 is a zero, not an alphabetic O) as an instruction to go to the beginning of the next page.

When the processing of a reel or complete file is completed, certain things need to be done to close out the work with the file: rewinding the reel, label operations, and possible provision of a *rerun point*.

For an input file the first thing done as a result of the CLOSE is to check the ending reel or file label. As we said before in connection with the READ verb, the type and contents of such a label are specified in the DATA DIVISION entry for the file; any nonstandard checking is called for by a USE.

For an output file any partially filled blocks are written first, and then any labels are written, as specified by the appropriate entries.

The CLOSE REEL version is used for two rather different purposes. The first is the provision of a *rerun point*, that is, a point in the processing at which it would be possible to start the work again if subsequently it had to be stopped because of an uncorrectable machine or operator error or because the work was interrupted by a higher priority job. Providing a rerun point involves "dumping" (writing) the entire contents of core storage on tape, plus certain other actions; starting again from a rerun point requires a special *restart procedure*.

In order for CLOSE REEL to initiate the dumping of core storage this action must be mentioned in an appropriate section of the ENVIRONMENT DIVISION. If this has been done, then whenever a reel is closed, either for input or output, the rerun procedure is carried out and the processing of the next reel is initiated (if this is a multiple reel file, of course). Label checking is not done as a part of the verb with this option, but it can still be done with the AT END option of the READ verb.

The other usage of CLOSE REEL, and perhaps the more common one, is to CLOSE a reel before its end has been reached. This could become necessary, for instance, because the job had to be stopped or because the information on a tape was found to be invalid.

The CLOSE REEL is the same, whether a rerun point is desired or the tape is being closed before reaching the end; the choice is governed by the ENVIRONMENT DIVISION for the file in question.

It should be emphasized that it is *not* necessary to write a CLOSE REEL verb for every reel of a multiple-reel file unless rerun points are desired. A normal part of the READ and WRITE verbs is the processing of the ending labels and the other actions required when the end of a reel is reached and more reels remain.

Whether or not the CLOSE REEL option is used, the final action in closing is to rewind the reel, unless, of course, the NO REWIND option has been written. If the LOCK option is used, the reel is rewound in such a way that the file cannot be read or written again without special action by the computer operator.

We have not listed all the conventions for the handling of a number of special situations. The material presented here will cover the large majority of practical applications; the interested reader may consult a reference manual on his system for the few remaining details.

EXAMPLES

(1) CLOSE PAYROLL-JOURNAL.
(2) CLOSE PAYROLL-MASTER WITH LOCK.
(3) CLOSE TIME-CARD REEL WITH LOCK.

QUALIFICATION. As a general rule, paragraph names, file names, record names, and data names need to be unique, which means that no two of them may be spelled exactly in the same manner within the same COBOL program. This seems reasonable enough: if we gave the same name, let us say XYZ, to two different paragraphs and then said GO TO XYZ, how would the compiler know to which paragraph we really want to transfer?

The case for uniqueness seems to be overwhelming, yet there is something in COBOL called *qualification* that permits us to assign nonunique names and then work with them without any problem. The rule is that a nonunique name, when used in the PROCEDURE DIVISION, must be followed by either IN or OF and the higher order name to which it belongs. As an example, let us say that we have PART-NUMBER in both the SALES-RECORD and the PRICE-RECORD. We could then write

IF PART-NUMBER IN SALES-RECORD IS
    EQUAL TO PART-NUMBER
    IN PRICE-RECORD . . .

or

MOVE PART-NUMBER OF PRICE-RECORD
    TO WORK-AREA-2.

We can also qualify record names by specifying the *file* to which they belong. We can even qualify paragraph names if we group paragraphs into sections. (The latter is a COBOL option that is seldom needed. If we use it, we can also refer to the SECTION name in a GO TO or PERFORM statement.)

Of course, we may always make all our names unique if we prefer to do so. Some installations, in fact, have adopted "uniqueness" as one of their COBOL standards and have ruled out qualification altogether.

REVIEW QUESTIONS

1. Which of these are *not* acceptable sequences of verbs, when each is assumed to apply to *one* file?
    a. READ, READ.
    b. OPEN, READ, CLOSE.
    c. OPEN, ACCEPT, CLOSE.
    d. OPEN, READ, CLOSE, OPEN, READ, CLOSE.
    e. OPEN, DISPLAY, CLOSE.

2. True or false: a single ACCEPT could not be used to input both a date and a control total because the format permits only one data name.

3. In a statement such as DISPLAY FINAL-TOTAL UPON PRINTER, what is the word PRINTER called? How is this made to correspond to a physical device?

4. Can a single DISPLAY be used to output both a data item and a literal?

5. Consider the following sentence:

DISPLAY 'JOB FINISHED.'.

How many periods would be printed?

6. Consider the following sentence:

DISPLAY 'THIS IS A', QUOTE, 'HORSE', QUOTE,'.'.

Exactly what would be printed?

7. Must every file have a label?

8. What five verbs mentioned in this section may, in some situations at least, be involved with processing labels?

9. True or false?

a. An OPEN *always* either checks or writes a label.

b. A CLOSE *always* rewinds a tape.

c. A READ or WRITE *always* causes a tape to move.

d. An OPEN must *always* precede the first READ or WRITE for a file.

e. After AT END we may write more than one imperative statement.

f. The statement OPEN INPUT MAST-FILE, OUTPUT PRINT-FILE is legal in COBOL.

g. The statement WRITE RECORD-A, RECORD-B is legal in COBOL.

10. Suppose that a certain tape has blocks consisting of five records each. Would a block be read from tape the first time a READ for that file is executed? How about the second? The fifth? The sixth?

11. Same as No. 10, except the verb is WRITE.

12. When records are blocked, the block is not written onto tape until the block is full. Suppose that when a file is closed the block in core storage is *not* full. How do the last records get written onto tape?

13. Must a data name be unique within a COBOL program?

e. True.

f. True.

g. False: WRITE may *not* be followed by more than one record name.

3.7 Programming Examples

So far we have been learning how some of the COBOL verbs work; now we must try to put them together to do useful processing. Most beginners in programming find that this is a big jump in difficulty; there is a great difference between seeing how someone else has done a job and being able to do it yourself. Therefore in the examples that follow we try to determine "how to go about it" rather than merely displaying a finished program and explaining its operation.

As a first example, suppose that we are given SALES and QUOTA; we are to compute COMMISSION, according to the following rules:

If SALES are less than or equal to QUOTA, the COMMISSION is 2% of SALES.

If SALES are greater than QUOTA, the COMMISSION is 2% of QUOTA plus 3% of the amount over QUOTA.

The calculation is not difficult, but we must decide how to set up the program to make the choice between the two computations. The most straightforward way is to begin with a statement IF SALES IS GREATER THAN QUOTA GO TO FORMULA-2, in which FORMULA-2 is the name of a separate paragraph to handle that condition.* Following this IF statement, we can write the statements to handle the case in which SALES are less than or equal to QUOTA.

Let's review. We begin with a conditional statement to determine the formula to use and jump to a second paragraph if the second one should be used; immediately following the IF, in the same paragraph, will be the computation according to the first formula. Is that all? No! If we write the two paragraphs in sequence, as described, what would happen at the completion of the first? Answer: control would pass on to the second, where we would recompute the commission according to the second formula, which could be all wrong. In other words, the commission would *always* be computed by the second method. It will therefore be necessary to put one final statement at the end of the first paragraph: GO TO CONTINUE, where CONTINUE is the arbitrarily chosen name for the paragraph following the second one.

Looking at the completed program segment in Figure 3.2 we see that the "flow of control" for the two possibilities is as follows. If the SALES are greater than QUOTA, control jumps to the second paragraph and its computation, after which the paragraph named CONTINUE (whatever it does) will be executed. If SALES are not greater than QUOTA (less than or equal), the rest of the first paragraph is executed, including the GO TO that jumps around the second paragraph.

---

* SALES IS? SALES ARE? Unfortunately, "ARE" is not acceptable in this format. Well, we said *similar* to ordinary English. One solution might be to observe that the IS is optional and write IF SALES GREATER THAN QUOTA.

```
PROGRAM
PROGRAMMER                                                      SYSTEM            SHEET      OF
                                                               DATE              IDENT.   73      80
PAGE  LINE  A       B
      0 7 0  SALES-COMMISSION.
      0 8 0      IF SALES GREATER THAN QUOTA GO TO FORMULA-2.
      0 9 0      MULTIPLY SALES BY 0.02 GIVING COMMISSION.
      1 0 0      GO TO CONTINUE.
      1 1 0  FORMULA-2.
      1 2 0      MULTIPLY QUOTA BY 0.02 GIVING REGUL-COMMISS.
      1 3 0      SUBTRACT QUOTA FROM SALES GIVING OVER-QUOTA.
      1 4 0      MULTIPLY OVER-QUOTA BY 0.03 GIVING EXTRA-COMMISS.
      1 5 0      ADD REGUL-COMMISS, EXTRA-COMMISS GIVING COMMISSION.
      1 6 0  CONTINUE. (whatever follows)
```

Figure 3.2. Program segment for the sales commission calculation example.

The point is, and it is an important one, that in the absence of explicit instructions to do otherwise control always "flows" sequentially through the program. Without the GO TO the computer would have no way of knowing that it would be nonsense to compute the commission according to both formulas; it would forge ahead blindly and do just that.

A few words now about our data names. We said that we were given QUOTA and SALES. This means that we will obtain them from some input file that we READ. We may also assume that COMMISSION is a field of an output file and that it is a field of a record that we will eventually WRITE. What about REGUL-COMMISS, EXTRA-COMMISS and OVER-QUOTA? These are *temporary*

ANSWERS

1. a. No: an OPEN must be executed before reading or writing. (However, a READ may follow a READ *after* the file has been opened.)
   b. OK.
   c. No: ACCEPT cannot be used with a file; it is restricted to minor amounts of data not organized into a file.
   d. OK. This amounts to reading a file, rewinding it, and reading it again. Note, however, that once a file has been closed it must be reopened before any further processing can take place.
   e. No: DISPLAY cannot be used for files.
2. False: the ACCEPT permits only a single data name, but this might have been set up in the DATA DIVISION to consist of two smaller data items.
3. It is a mnemonic name, made to correspond to a physical device by an appropriate entry in the ENVIRONMENT DIVISION.
4. Certainly.
5. One: the one inside the quote mark; the one outside the quote mark is simply the period at the end of the sentence.
6. THIS IS A'HORSE'. To get a space between A

ANSWERS (Continued)

and HORSE there should have been a space after the A in the literal.
7. *COBOL* does not require every file to have a label; at a particular installation it may be required, at least for tape files. Disk files, however, always have labels.
8. OPEN, CLOSE, and USE are probably obvious. READ and WRITE also initiate processing of labels when the end of a tape is reached and more tapes remain in the file.
9. a. False: the file might not have labels.
   b. False: the NO REWIND option may prevent this.
   c. False: if records are blocked, there is tape motion only when a *block* is read or written; READ and WRITE deal with *records*.
   d. True.
10. A block would be read the first, sixth, eleventh, etc., times the READ is executed, but not for the second, third, fourth, fifth, seventh, eighth, etc.
11. A block would be written for the fifth, tenth, fifteenth, etc., WRITE operations, but not for others.
12. This is handled by the CLOSE.
13. No, but if not we must remember to "qualify" it when we use it in the PROCEDURE DIVISION.

fields that will hold intermediate results. The assignment of temporary fields is a frequent necessity in programming. As we shall see in Chapter 5, we reserve these "working-areas" in the WORKING-STORAGE SECTION of the DATA DIVISION.

Could we reduce the number of statements in this sample without upsetting its logic? Certainly! Notice that if we use the verb COMPUTE the entire second paragraph can be written as

COMPUTE COMMISSION = QUOTA
    * 0.02 + (SALES − QUOTA) * 0.03.

This approach would have the further advantage of not needing any temporary working storage, thereby streamlining the working storage portion of the DATA DIVISION of the program.

For a second programming example suppose we have a card deck containing payroll data on a group of employees for one week and that we are required to produce a report in which the names and earnings of those who have earned more than $300 in the week, together with a count of the number of such workers, are listed. Assuming that for the workers in question such weekly earnings are abnormal, the purpose of the report might be to check for input errors (miscoding, mispunching, etc.). This kind of report would also be a way to try to prevent fraud.

The input consists of a card deck containing for each employee a card giving his name (EMPL-NAME), hourly rate (HOURLY-RATE), and the number of hours worked (HOURS-WORKED).

The desired form of the report may be seen in Figure 3.3.

The logic of the program in Figure 3.4 is not complex. We begin by opening both files, which must always be done before we can READ or WRITE. Next we need to write the desired page heading at the top of the first page. We do so with a PERFORM in the BEGIN-PROGR paragraph that calls into play the PAGE-HEADING paragraph. Accordingly, we discuss the latter-named portion of the program next, temporarily skipping over the MAIN-LINE segment that does the actual processing of the input data.

We assume that we have reserved in the DATA DIVISION (shown at end of Chapter 6) two WORKING-STORAGE areas. One would contain the literal 'REPORT ON WEEKLY SALARIES OVER $ 300' and the other would contain 'NAME' and 'WEEKLY SALARY' suitably spaced out. Suppose these constants have been named HEADING-LINE-1 and HEADING-LINE-2 and that the record name in the output file is DETAIL-LINE. Then we can print the two heading lines by moving them, one at a time, to the output record and writing, as shown in the paragraph named PAGE-HEADING.

The WRITE verbs here use the ADVANCING option to control line spacing. As noted in Section 3.6, in many compilers the AFTER ADVANCING 0 LINES causes the printer to advance the paper to a position some four to six lines below the physical top of the page. The ADVANCING option in the second WRITE provides the desired blank line between the two heading lines. Next we move SPACES to DETAIL-LINE and WRITE it to get a blank line between the second heading line and first line of the body of the report when it is printed later.

The next action in the PAGE-HEADING paragraph has to do with another matter related to headings. The page heading is not desired just at the top of the first page but at the top of every page. Since the maximum number of lines that a page can accommodate is limited by the page

```
          REPORT ON WEEKLY SALARIES OVER $ 300


          NAME                              WEEKLY SALARY

     HILBERG DONALD E                        49,950.00
     ABDULWANIS TURKI                           454.50
     GONZALES RAFAEL                            400.00
     STREET ROBERT H                            310.00


 NUMBER OF PEOPLE WITH WEEKLY SALARY OVER $ 300      4
```

Figure 3.3. Output produced by the program of Figure 3.4, which lists employees with indicated earnings of more than $300.

```
001630 PROCEDURE DIVISION.
001640 BEGIN-PROGR.
001650     OPEN INPUT CARD-FILE.
001660     OPEN OUTPUT PRINTER-FILE.
001670     PERFORM PAGE-HEADING.
001680 MAIN-LINE.
001690     READ CARD-FILE AT END GO TO EOJ.
001700     COMPUTE WEEKLY-SALARY ROUNDED = HOURLY-RATE * HOURS-WORKED.
001710     IF WEEKLY-SALARY IS GREATER THAN 300 PERFORM WRITE-DET-LINE.
001720     GO TO MAIN-LINE.
001730 PAGE-HEADING.
001740     MOVE HEADING-LINE-1 TO DETAIL-LINE.
001750     WRITE DETAIL-LINE AFTER ADVANCING 0 LINES.
001760     MOVE HEADING-LINE-2 TO DETAIL-LINE.
001770     WRITE DETAIL-LINE AFTER ADVANCING 2 LINES.
001780     MOVE SPACES TO DETAIL-LINE.
001790     WRITE DETAIL-LINE AFTER ADVANCING 1 LINES.
001800     MOVE 4 TO LINE-CTR.
001810     MOVE SPACES TO DETAIL-LINE.
001820 WRITE-DET-LINE.
001830     ADD 1 TO NUMBER-OF-PEOPLE ON SIZE ERROR
001840         DISPLAY 'NO-OF-PEOPLE FIELD NOT LARGE ENOUGH' GO TO EOJ.
001850     IF LINE-CTR GREATER THAN 57 PERFORM PAGE-HEADING.
001860     MOVE EMPL-NAME TO OP-EMPL-NAME.
001870     MOVE WEEKLY-SALARY TO OP-WEEKLY-SALARY.
001880     WRITE DETAIL-LINE AFTER ADVANCING 1 LINES.
001890     ADD 1 TO LINE-CTR.
001900 EOJ.
001910     MOVE NUMBER-OF-PEOPLE TO OP-NO-OF-PEOPLE.
001920     MOVE  TOTAL-LINE TO DETAIL-LINE.
001930     WRITE DETAIL-LINE AFTER ADVANCING 2 LINES.
001940     CLOSE CARD-FILE PRINTER-FILE.
001950     STOP RUN.
```

Figure 3.4. A program to produce a listing of all employees with indicated earnings of more than $300.

length, we must arrange to skip to the top of the next page when the desired maximum number of lines has been printed on one page. Suppose that after considering the size of page to be used (let us say one that has space for 66 lines of printing) we decide for reasons of appearance to limit the actual number of lines to 60. We accordingly set up a WORKING-STORAGE item named LINE-CTR (for line counter) and arrange to add one to it every time a line is printed. When the desired total has been reached, we arrange to carry out the page-heading routine again. Since the heading, including blank lines, uses up four lines, we initialize the line counter to 4.

This is an ideal situation for using the PERFORM verb in that the page-heading routine needs to be called into action from two different places in the program: at the very beginning (uncondition-

ally) and in the body of the program (whenever needed). We accordingly make the heading routine a separate paragraph, making it possible to write PERFORM PAGE-HEADING. When this occurs, control is transferred to the paragraph named, the actions in it are executed, and control returns to the sentence following the PERFORM, whichever one it was.

Returning now to the paragraph named MAIN-LINE, we see that the actual processing is somewhat simpler than the work connected with the appearance of the output (which is not untypical of the work of a programmer).

For each input record we must calculate the weekly earnings, which is done by multiplying the hourly rate by the number of hours. We then compare this result with a constant of 300. If the earnings are greater than $300.00, we print a single-spaced line for that employee and add one to the line counter; if it is not, we simply read another record.

The writing of a line in case of calculated earnings of more than $300.00 is carried out with another PERFORM, this time merely as a matter of convenience in writing the program. The paragraph WRITE-DET-LINE begins by incrementing a counter set up to keep track of the total of those having earnings of more than $300.00. (This is not the same as the line counter.) The ON SIZE ERROR option is used to test the possibility that so many workers were discovered to have earned more than $300.00 (probably because of some systematic error in the input) that the data item called NUMBER-OF-PEOPLE could not hold the total. If this happens, we simply stop and display an error message. Next we check to see if the line counter has reached 57. We said the total number of lines was to be 60; here we use 57 to allow room for the summary lines that will occur on the last page of the report. If the page is full, we PERFORM the PAGE-HEADING routine. Then we move the employee's name and earnings to data items named OP-EMPL-NAME and OP-WEEKLY-SALARY; these would have to be defined in the DATA DIVISION as fields in the record named DETAIL-LINE. After writing the line we increment the line counter. Notice that it would not be good practice to use the EQUAL TO option when comparing a line counter to a constant. This test would fail miserably, for instance, if an AFTER ADVANCING 2 LINES instruction caused the counter to *exceed* the constant *without ever being equal* to it. The comparison with GREATER THAN is much safer. Practice, of course, will teach everybody how to avoid pitfalls of this kind.

The end-of-job (EOJ) routine is required simply to print the number of employees with indicated earnings of more than $300.00 and terminate the run. The former involves no new concepts; the latter is a matter of closing both files and saying STOP RUN. This would return control of the computer to the operating system, which would proceed to the next job in line or signal the human operator appropriately that more work could be accepted.

* * *

This would be a good time to review the complete process of getting a COBOL source program compiled and run, now that we know more about what a source program is and having seen in Chapter 2 a little of what the machine does.

First of all, what we have shown in these examples is only the PROCEDURE DIVISION of a COBOL source program; a complete program also includes the IDENTIFICATION, ENVIRONMENT, and DATA DIVISIONS. The most important is the DATA DIVISION, in which we would describe the files, records, and data items: how the files are organized, how long each data item is, whether any data items require punctuation to be inserted, etc.

The complete source program must be translated into an object program consisting of actual machine instructions; this is the function of the COBOL *compiler* (also called a *translator*). The compiler, which is itself a program of many machine instructions, reads the source program and in a rather complex process that we shall not explore produces actual machine instructions that will do what the PROCEDURE DIVISION says to do with the data described in the DATA DIVISION. The object program must handle every detail of the required processing. It may turn out, for instance, that a simple statement such as MOVE SALES IN IN-REC TO SALES IN OUT-REC will generate quite a number of instructions; the "source" and "receiving" items may be of different length, the receiving area may specify such things as supplying dollar signs, decimal points, and the suppression of unwanted leading zeros.

The sole output of the compiler program is a finished object program, supplemented, particularly during testing, by an optional program listing that may also contain error messages and other information pertaining to the program. *The object program has not yet been executed.* Input data is *not* used during compilation and no output results are produced.

The compiler produces the object program on a magnetic tape or disk and sometimes on a deck of cards. At *execution time* the object program is read into storage, data tapes or disks are mounted, blank tapes or disks are mounted for output, control cards (and possibly data cards) are fed into the card reader, the printer is activated, and the object program is started. Now, finally, the input is read, the processing is carried out, and the output is produced.

This process should be fully understood, which is why we are reviewing it, even though the matter was mentioned in Chapter 1. If there is any doubt about the difference between a source program and an object program or the difference between the purpose of the compiler program as distinguished from the running of the object program, now would be an excellent time to study the matter again. Many important topics will be hard to follow as we proceed if this understanding is not gained now.

EXERCISES.

(Answers to starred exercises are given at the end of the book.)

*1. Write COBOL statements to do the following:

   a. There are data items in storage named TRANSACTION-QUANTITY and QUANTITY-ON-HAND. Write a statement that will make the value of QUANTITY-ON-HAND the same as the value of TRANSACTION-QUANTITY, leaving the latter unchanged.
   b. There is a data item named COUNTER; make its numerical value equal to 1.
   c. There is a data item named HEADING; move the characters PAGE NUMBER to it.
   d. Make the numerical value of the item named HOW-MANY zero.
   e. There are two items in storage, both named QUANTITY; one is in a record called TRANS and the other in a record called MASTER. Move the quantity in TRANS to the quantity in MASTER.
   f. Add the value of the item named CAT to the value of the item named DOG, with the sum replacing DOG, and CAT left unchanged.
   g. Add the value of the item named CAT to the value of the item named DOG, with the sum replacing GOAT, and CAT and DOG left unchanged.
   h. Add the values of the items named HORSE, COW, and MULE (all these left unchanged), with the sum replacing ANIMALS.
   i. Add 50 to the value of the item named POSTAGE.
   j. Subtract 6 from the value of the item named AMOUNT. (If the initial value of AMOUNT were −72, what would it be after executing the object program instructions created from this statement?)
   k. Multiply OVERTIME-HOURS by 1.5, with the product becoming the new value of OVERTIME-DOLLARS.
   l. Divide the value of the item named TOTAL by the value of the item named NUMBER, with the quotient becoming the new value of the item named AVERAGE.

   m. Divide the value of the item named RATE by 2, with the quotient replacing the old value of RATE.
   n. Subtract both X and Y from Z and replace W with the value thus computed.
   n. Form the sum of R and S, with the new value replacing T; if the sum is too large to fit in the space assigned to T, transfer control to a paragraph named ERROR-ROUTINE. (ERROR-ROUTINE is assumed to be elsewhere in the program; you do not write it.)

2. Write COBOL statements to do the following:

   a. Make the value of the data item named B the same as the value of the data item named A, leaving A unchanged.
   b. Make the numerical value of the item named BASE-COUNT equal to 47.
   c. Put the characters OUT OF STOCK in the item named SPECIAL.
   d. Make the *value* of the item named LIMIT 9999999.
   e. Put the characters 9999999 *themselves* in the item named WARNING.
   f. Blank out any previous contents of the item named SPECIAL by moving spaces to it.
   g. There are two items in storage, both named MAN-NUMBER; one is a record called TIME-CARD and the other is in a record called EARNINGS-STATEMENT. Move the man number in the time-card record to a separate storage location named PREVIOUS-MAN-NUMBER.
   h. Add the value of the item named ROBIN to the value of the item named SPARROW, with the sum replacing the previous value of ROBIN, leaving SPARROW unchanged.
   i. Add the value of the item named ROBIN to the value of the item named SPARROW, with the sum becoming the new value of an item named CROW, and ROBIN and SPARROW left unchanged.
   j. Subtract M from N, with the difference replacing N, and M left unchanged.
   k. Decrease the value of an item named COUNTER by 1.
   l. Subtract DISCOUNT from FULL-PRICE, with the difference becoming the new value of BILLING-PRICE.
   m. Multiply Q by 2, with the product replacing Q.
   n. Multiply Q by 2, with the product replacing R.
   o. Divide QUARTER-USAGE by 3, with the quotient going to AVERAGE-USAGE.
   p. Subtract the sum of J and K from L; if the final result is too large to fit in L, transfer control to ERROR-6.
   q. Two amounts, AMOUNT-1 and AMOUNT-2, are both expressed in dol-

lars and cents. AMOUNT-3 is expressed to the nearest dollar. Place the sum of AMOUNT-1 and AMOUNT-2 in AMOUNT-3, rounded to the nearest dollar.

*3. Write statements to do the following:

a. Determine whether HOURS-WORKED is greater than 37.5, and, if so, transfer control to another paragraph (which you do not write) named OVERTIME-ROUTINE.

b. Add 1 to an item named ADULT if AGE is 21 or greater.

c. Transfer control to the paragraph named STOCK-ITEM if PART-1-A contains the letter S.

d. Add 1 to BIG if SIZE-A is greater than 800 and add 1 to LITTLE if SIZE-A is less than or equal to 800.

e. If the item in NAME-1 is greater than the item in NAME-2, move the contents of NAME-1 to TEMPORARY; if the item in NAME-1 is less than the item in NAME-2, move the contents of NAME-2 to TEMPORARY; if the two are equal, move either of them to temporary.

f. If the value of the item named HOURS-WORKED is *anything but* 40, transfer control to NONSTANDARD.

g. Transfer control to BAD-CODE if CODE-X contains anything but digits.

4. a. Determine whether the value of the item named FINAL-BILL is greater than 999.99 and, if so, transfer control to another paragraph (which you do not write) named SPECIAL-APPROVAL.

b. Add 1 to an item named MAJOR-BILLING if TOTAL is 1000.00 or greater.

c. If the item named CODE-A contains the characters AB47Z, move the characters APPROVED to the item named APPROVAL.

d. Move −1 to SIGNAL if MEASURE is negative; move zero to SIGNAL if MEASURE is zero; move +1 to SIGNAL if MEASURE is positive.

e. Transfer control to the paragraph named REGULAR if HOURS-WORKED is exactly 40 and to SPECIAL in any other case.

f. Transfer control to BAD-CODE if CODE-A contains anything but alphabetic characters.

g. If CODEX contains 1, add SALARY to WEEKLY-SALARY; if CODEX contains anything else, add SALARY to MONTHLY-SALARY.

h. If CODE-A contains 1, add SALARY to WEEKLY-SALARY; if CODE-A contains 2, add SALARY to MONTHLY-SALARY; if CODE-A contains neither 1 nor 2, transfer to BAD-CODE.

5. Form the sum of the values of the data items named JAN, FEB, and MAR; then divide by 3 to get the new value of AVERAGE.

*6. A man worked more than 40 hours, for which everything over 40 was paid at the overtime rate of 1.5 times his base rate. Given HOURS-WORKED and RATE, compute GROSS-PAY.

7. A part of a man's GROSS-PAY is NONTAXABLE. Find the taxable portion, then multiply it by 3 1/8% to get his SOCIAL-SECURITY.

*8. A man has N dependents. Compute his TAX from

$$TAX = 0.18 \times (GROSS\text{-}PAY - N \times 12.00)$$

without using the verb COMPUTE.

*9. As in Problem 8, except that before computing the tax check that GROSS-PAY is greater than the number of dependents times $12.00; if the gross pay is not sufficient to cover the dependent allowance, store zero as the tax.

10. Given SET-UP-TIME, TIME-PER-UNIT, and NUMBER-OF-UNITS, compute TOTAL-TIME from

TOTAL-TIME = SET-UP-TIME
    + TIME-PER-UNIT
    × NUMBER-OF-UNITS.

*11. Given NUMBER-SOLD, PRICE, and PREVIOUS-YTD, update PREVIOUS-YTD by adding to it the product of NUMBER-SOLD and PRICE.

12. Given ON-HAND, AVERAGE-USE, and SAFETY-FACTOR, compute

QUANTITY-TO-ORDER = AVERAGE-USE
    × SAFETY-FACTOR - ON-HAND

and replace QUANTITY-TO-ORDER with zero if the value computed from the formula is negative.

13. Write COMPUTE statements corresponding to the following formulas:

a. $Y = (A + B + C) \div D$

b. $R = A \times B + C \div D$

c. $M = A \div 6 - C \times D \div E$

d. $G = 1.5 \times H \times R - 67.74$

e. $Z = (M^2 - N^3) \times P - R \div S$

f. $A = R \times (P - Q + Y \div Z)$

g. $L = A \times B - C$

h. $G = (M - 2.5783) \times A - B \div (C + D)$

i. $O = A \div (E \times I) - U$

j. $L = F^G - H \times (I - J) + K$

14. a. Write a COMPUTE statement to increase YTD-SALES by the product of QUANTITY and UNIT-PRICE.

b. Write a COMPUTE statement to calculate BILL-AMOUNT from MINIMUM plus the product of RATE and KWH.

c. Write a COMPUTE statement to form the sum of PRICE, FINANCING, TAX, and SHIPPING; then divide by 12 to get PAYMENT.

e. Write COMPUTE statements to get the following three items:
OSS-TRUE: the quotient of OSS-ASSESSED and OSS-EQ.

NC-TRUE: the quotient of NC-ASSESSED and NC-EQ.

YT-TRUE: the quotient of YT-ASSESSED and YT-EQ.

f. Write a COMPUTE statement to get TOTAL-TRUE, which is the sum of OSS-TRUE, NC-TRUE, and YT-TRUE.

g. Write a COMPUTE statement to get OSS-RATE, which is obtained as follows: divide OSS-TRUE by TOTAL-TRUE and multiply the quotient by TOTAL-LEVY; divide all of this by OSS-ASSESSED over 1000.

*15. If SHIFT-CODE is 2, add 10% of GROSS-PAY to GROSS-PAY.

16. If SHIFT-CODE is 2, add 10% to GROSS-PAY; if SHIFT-CODE is 3, add 15% to GROSS-PAY.

*17. Given REGULAR-PAY, OVERTIME-PAY, SHIFT-PREMIUM, and BONUS, compute GROSS-PAY, which is simply the sum of all of the foregoing.

18. Given the necessary information, compute NET-PAY from

NET-PAY = GROSS-PAY

— SOCIAL-SECURITY — WITHHOLDING

— BONDS — INSURANCE

— UNION-DUES.

*19. Given PRICE and CODE-B, update one sales total:

If CODE-B = 1, add PRICE to CLASS-1

If CODE-B = 2, add PRICE to CLASS-2

If CODE-B = 3, add PRICE to CLASS-3

If CODE-B = 4, add PRICE to CLASS-4

If CODE-B is none of these, add PRICE to ERROR-TOTAL.

20. Suppose that in a salesman's commission calculation there are five different commission formulas. Which of the five is to be applied is determined by the PRODUCT-CODE:

PRODUCT-CODE	COMMISSION
1	$(0.15) \times (\text{SALE-PRICE})$
2	$(0.40) \times (\text{SALE-PRICE} - \text{BASE-PRICE})$
3	$(0.10) \times (\text{BASE-PRICE}) + (0.50) \times (\text{SALE-PRICE} - \text{BASE-PRICE})$
4	$\$10.00 + (0.05) \times (\text{BASE-PRICE})$
5	$\$15.00$

Given PRODUCT-CODE, SALE-PRICE, and BASE-PRICE, compute COMMISSION.

21. Given ANNUAL-EARNINGS, compute TAX:

ANNUAL-EARNINGS	TAX
Less than $2000.00	Zero
$2000.00 or more but less than $5000.00	2% of the amount over $2000.00
$5000.00 or more	$60.00 plus 5% of the amount over $5000.00.

*22. Suppose a man has a regular weekly gross pay of $162.39. His Social Security tax, computed at 4.8%,

would be $7.79. After 10 weeks his total gross earnings would be $1,623.90 and his accumulated Social Security $77.90. But 4.8% of $1,623.90 is $77.95. Why is it that the sum of the individual contributions is not the same as 4.8% of the total? Is it not true that

$$10 \times (0.048 \times 162.39) = 0.048 \times (10 \times 162.39)?$$

The answer lies in what is called the *accumulation of round-off errors*. The figure of $7.79 is actually "rounded off" from the exact amount of $7.79472, which is almost half a cent higher than the approximate result. In any one week this doesn't matter, but in 10 weeks it accumulates to five cents.

Maybe that doesn't matter either; sometimes it would, sometimes not. If it does, we can reduce the total round-off error to no more than one cent by the following device. Each week compute the tax on the total taxable amount, then subtract the preceding year-to-date tax; the difference is this week's tax with any necessary adjustment for previous round-off errors included.

Given NEW-YTD-GROSS (including this week's pay) and PREVIOUS-SS (not including this week's), compute THIS-WEEKS-SS.

*23. Each record in a file named INPUT-FILE contains a DOLLAR amount, along with other information. Form the sum of the DOLLAR amounts from all records in the file and DISPLAY it on the console.

24. As in Exercise 23, except that each record also contains a CODEM, which is either zero or one. Form the sum of the DOLLAR amount from all records having a code of one and DISPLAY it.

*25. As in Exercise 24, but in addition write a new file, named OUTPUT-FILE, which contains all the records from INPUT-FILE having a code of zero. The records are INPUT-RECORD and OUTPUT-RECORD.

*26. A file named INPUT-FILE is supposed to be in sequence on an item in each record named KEY1. Read the file and *sequence-check* it; that is, determine that no KEY1 is less than the KEY1 of an earlier record (duplicates are acceptable). DISPLAY 'SEQUENCE OK' if there are no sequence errors; if a sequence error is detected, CLOSE the file, DISPLAY 'SEQUENCE ERROR ON KEY' and the KEY of the offending record.

27. Given an input file named DEDUCTIONS, and four output files named TAX, SOCIAL-SECURITY, BONDS, and DUES. Read the input file and write each of its records to one of the output files, depending on the value of a COD in each record:

if COD is	write record to	record name
1	TAX-FILE	TAX
2	SOCIAL-SECURITY-FILE	SS
3	BONDS-FILE	BONDS
4	DUES-FILE	DUES

*28. ACCEPT a CONTROL-TOTAL, then accumulate the DOLLAR amount from each record (named RECORD-1) of a file named FILE-1. If the accumulated dollar amount is the same as the CONTROL-TOTAL, DISPLAY 'OK', otherwise 'NG'.

*29. An input file named SAMPLE has records

named EXAMPLE and items named F1, F2, F3, F4, and F5. For each record in the file check that F1 is NUMERIC, that the value of F2 is positive and less than 18, that F3 is less than F4, and that F5 is not zero. Each record that passes all these *validity checks* should be written to a file named GOOD-FILE having records named GOOD-RECORD; any record that fails any of the validity tests should be written out to a file named BAD-FILE having records named BAD-RECORD.

30. An input file named INPUT-FILE has records named INPUT-RECORD and items named I1, I2, I3, I4, I5, and I6. Check that the file is in sequence on I1, that I2 is either zero or greater than 10, that I3 is not equal to I4, and that I4 plus I5 is greater than I6. Write out the good and bad records as in Exercise 29. Any time a record is found in which I1 is less than I1 in the preceding record, DISPLAY 'SEQ ERR' and the value of I1.

4. CASE STUDY 1: SALES STATISTICS

4.1 The Business Situation

Reports giving information on sales, analyzed in a variety of ways, are one of the most common products of a data-processing operation. Many people in the sales department are concerned with the performance of the various product lines, perhaps compared with a similar period last year or with anticipated or forecasted sales. Production planning needs such information as a guide to future manufacturing requirements. Advertising wants it as a measure of advertising effectiveness and as a guide to products to emphasize in future promotion. The analysis of sales by product may enter, at least indirectly, into management control of the company in an attempt to put the most company effort into the most profitable lines.

Analyzing the sales according to product is only one way to present the results. The same basic data can be reorganized so that it shows the performance of salesman and of branch offices or districts, perhaps as compared with last year or with the budget (forecast). It can be reorganized to show total sales to each customer and can sometimes be used to prepare a prediction of future sales if market trends and seasonal variations in the particular industry are well enough understood to permit a reasonable mathematical formulation of what influences sales.

A full-scale sales-statistics job would clearly be too large for us here, so we shall consider a more limited set of requirements. The job we will do is not so extensive as many that are carried out in industry, but it is still fully representative of what is involved in working with business-data processing and COBOL; furthermore, in some cases it would be an adequate report in itself.

4.2 The Data-Processing Situation

We begin with a list of sales records for all sales made in the last month; each record shows

(1) product number,
(2) the quantity of this product sold,
(3) the salesman number,
(4) the number of the district in which the salesman works.

In an actual data-processing system this information would ordinarily be extracted from sales records prepared for other purposes; the basic data would not be transcribed from source documents to cards or tape more than once. In this case study, however, we shall not be able to explore the ramifications of integrating this application with all of the others being done in the company and therefore we simply assume that the data is available on a deck of cards. Specifically, we assume that there is one card for each product sold by each salesman, each showing his district and how many of this product were sold. We have no knowledge of the order of the cards; they certainly may not be assumed to be in product number order.

The reader may have noticed that most of the information is in coded form: we do not show the *name* of the salesman, but his *number*, etc. This is done to save space in the various files and reports and to reduce the amount of card punching in preparing the transaction file. This practice is widely followed in business-data processing and has led to the development of many systematic methods for assigning the codes to make them easy to remember, or meaningful in themselves (for instance, a 4 in the third position might always mean steel, whereas a 5 would always mean copper), self-checking (by assigning an extra digit so that the sum of all the digits is always a multiple of 9), or to give them other desirable characteristics. In a book on systems design the subject of coding methods would be a chapter in itself: we must pass the matter by, after assuming that all the codes in this example are simply numeric.

Figure 4.1 shows the sample file of *transactions* (sales records) that we shall work with in explaining the processing steps. There are 20 transactions here; a typical report for one month for a medium-sized business would contain many thousands.

We are required to prepare two reports that will present the following information:

Report 1: Total dollar sales of each merchandise item for the month.
Year-to-Date (YTD) dollar sales of each merchandise item sold this month.

Report 2: Total dollar sales of each salesman for the month.
Total dollar sales of each district for the month.
Total dollar sales of the company for the month.

Why must there be two separate reports? The answer is fundamental: because the original transaction records enter into the two reports in different sequences. Several salesmen may have sold a particular item; a report summarizing the sales of each product would not group the sales for each man together. On the other hand, each salesman works out of only one district; once we have arranged all transactions for each salesman together, the sales

PRODUCT	QUANTITY	SALESMAN	DISTRICT
48198	6	50	3
56030	15	36	3
12911	10	52	1
92379	2	18	2
47128	1	41	1
56030	12	39	3
56030	50	18	2
36615	3	32	2
62379	1	18	2
12911	25	69	1
62379	5	69	1
84326	4	36	3
12911	8	32	2
10437	1	52	1
36615	2	39	3
56030	1	69	1
27128	1	41	1
84326	1	50	3
48198	8	32	2
12911	40	41	1

Figure 4.1. Sample data (unsorted) for the sales statistics case study.

for each district will be grouped together, too. (Total sales for the company could be derived from either organization of the data; the decision to place it with the salesman and district breakdown is arbitrary. In fact, we shall see that it is desirable for other reasons to obtain this total in both cases.)

One of the first operations in the preparation of these reports must be to obtain the price of each product sold, since this information does not appear in the transaction records. The price of each product is given in a master file, of which Figure 4.2 is a sample.

PRODUCT UNIT PRICE YTD SALES

PRODUCT	UNIT PRICE	YTD SALES
00961	43.60	1264.40
10229	1.87	523.60
10437	87.50	1487.50
10558	90.00	720.00
12911	2.25	519.75
13061	48.75	2047.50
17850	21.80	1068.20
27128	8.37	878.85
36615	52.00	624.00
36618	40.00	320.00
36619	47.00	705.00
47128	105.00	0.00
48198	1.45	68.15
48614	0.87	381.06
49006	127.50	637.50
53828	75.25	1806.00
56030	1.45	3306.00
60189	1.93	1592.25
62379	15.39	446.31
77083	29.40	323.40
84326	43.10	1163.70
87125	26.60	347.80
92379	59.90	239.60
94864	160.00	160.00
98814	5.39	598.29

Figure 4.2. Sample master file for the sales statistics case study, in product number sequence.

Note that this file contains the accumulated year-to-date (YTD) sales for each product. In addition to preparing the sales report for the current month, we are required to *update* the YTD sales in the master file. This will require writing a new master tape that contains the sum of the previous YTD sales (from the old master) and the sales from this month. For each product sold this month we shall also show the YTD sales, but YTD sales will *not* be reported for products not sold this month; that could also be done if needed.

The master file is in sequence on product number and we assume that it is on magnetic tape.

As we saw in Chapter 1, before the transactions can be processed efficiently they must be put into the same sequence, which is usually called *sorting*. Sorting can be done with the computer and is an important part of the work load of many machines; since our data is on cards, we could sort it instead with a card sorter before putting the transactions on tape. In our simplified situation the choice is mostly economic: which way would cost less? Other considerations are these: card sorting has a greater chance of error; sorting might be required at a point in the work schedule when the computer is heavily loaded with other things; with a small number of transactions the time required to mount the additional tapes needed for computer sorting might cost nearly as much as doing the whole job with a card sorter; if the product number were long, or if it could include letters, card sorting would become much more expensive, whereas computer sorting would not be much affected. In a real application, tied in with other processing, the transaction file might very well have been drawn from another tape in any case, thus making this discussion academic. It is hard to think of a case in which it would be economical to punch out a file, sort it, then put it back on tape—just for the purpose of getting it sorted.

We assume, for concreteness, that the transactions are sorted with a card sorter before they are converted to tape. Figure 4.3 shows the sample data after sorting.

Now comes the first computer action, and it happens to be one that illustrates a number of basic data-processing ideas. In essence, the task is to carry out the following operations:

1. For each transaction get the price of that product from the corresponding master-file record.

2. Multiply the number of units sold by the unit price, giving the total price for that transaction.

PRODUCT	QUANTITY	SALESMAN	DISTRICT
10437	1	52	1
12911	10	52	1
12911	25	69	1
12911	8	32	2
12911	40	41	1
27128	1	41	1
36615	3	32	2
36615	2	39	3
47128	1	41	1
48198	6	50	3
48198	8	32	2
56030	15	36	3
56030	12	39	3
56030	50	18	2
56030	1	69	1
62379	1	18	2
62379	5	69	1
84326	4	36	3
84326	1	50	3
92379	2	18	2

Figure 4.3. Transaction file (sample data) for the sales statistics case study, sorted into product number sequence.

3. Add the total price for that product to the previous year-to-date sales figure in the master-file record.

4. Accumulate the prices from each sale for a product number and print this total with the new year-to-date sales figure when all transactions for a given product have been processed.

5. Accumulate the total sales for the month and print it when all the transactions for the month have been processed. This is the same total that is required as a part of the second report; we are pro-

ducing it here also in order to provide a check on the accuracy of processing. If the total as produced in two rather different procedures is the same, we have some assurance that the processing was not seriously in error. This is an example of a *control total*. In this case it happens to be a meaningful number in itself and furthermore it is required as part of the output. In other cases a control total is often kept *only* for the purpose of ensuring accuracy, even though the total may not be required as output and may not be a meaningful number in itself.*

Figure 4.4 shows the contents of the sales report by product, as printed by the computer.†

The processing required to produce the second report will be considered after we have worked out the COBOL program for the first.

Figure 4.5 is a *run diagram* of the procedures for

PRODUCT	MONTH SALES	YTD SALES
10437	87.50	1575.00
12911	186.75	706.50
27128	8.37	887.22
36615	260.00	884.00
47128	105.00	105.00
48198	20.30	88.45
56030	113.10	3419.10
62379	92.34	538.65
84326	215.50	1379.20
92379	119.80	359.40

1208.66

Figure 4.4. Summary by product number, in sales statistics case study. This is actual computer output, produced when the program of Figure 4.7 was run on an IBM System 360.

* An example of a control total that is not "meaningful": the "sum" of all salesman *numbers*. The "sum" of salesman number 21 and salesman number 32 would be 53, which has no meaning, but in certain situations it would still provide the same kind of checking.

† All the programs presented in this text have been compiled and executed on an IBM 360.

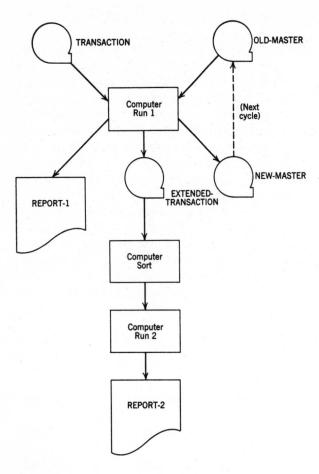

Figure 4.5. Run diagram of both runs of the sales statistics case study.

producing both reports. We see that the TRANS-ACTION file and the OLD-MASTER file are the inputs to the first run. The outputs are REPORT-1, the EXTENDED-TRANSACTION file, and a NEW-MASTER file, the latter becoming the input to the first run the *next* time the job is done. The EXTENDED-TRANSACTION file becomes the input to the second run, from which the only output is REPORT-2. The sorting operation between the two runs is discussed later.

REVIEW QUESTIONS

1. Name the source of each of the following data items:

    a. Quantity sold.
    b. Unit price.
    c. Product number.

2. Why could the information contained in the two reports here not be combined into one report?

3. Why must the transaction file be sorted on product number before processing?

4. What is the "extended price" of a product?

5. What is a control total?

6. Is the file named EXTENDED-TRANSACTION an input or an output file?

4.3   The Summary by Product

We may begin the study of the COBOL program by listing in Figure 4.6 the five files employed in

File	Record	Data Items
OLD-MASTER	OLD-MAST	PRODUCT-NUMBER UNIT-PRICE YTD-SALES
NEW-MASTER	NEW-MAST	PRODUCT-NUMBER UNIT-PRICE YTD-SALES
TRANSACTION	TRANS	PRODUCT-NUMBER QUANTITY SALESMAN DISTRICT
EXTENDED-TRANSACTION	EXT	EXT-PRICE SALESMAN DISTRICT
REPORT-1	REP-1	PRODUCT-NUMBER PRODUCT-TOTAL-FOR-MONTH YTD-SALES

Figure 4.6. Schematic representation of the files in Run 1 of the sales statistics case study, showing record names and items within records.

the first run, together with the file and record names and the names of the data items in each.

This corresponds in a general way to the layout of the DATA DIVISION, which as we saw not only appears before the PROCEDURE DIVISION in the completed source program but is also usually worked out first in approaching the programming task.

We have shown both file and record names here: each file has only one kind of record, but the file name and the record name must nevertheless be different. Then for each record we show the data items it contains by listing the names chosen.

In addition to these data items in the files, we need three locations in working storage for various items that are developed during the processing.

TOTAL-PRICE
PRODUCT-TOTAL
MONTH-TOTAL

A hint now on a few things we shall see in the DATA DIVISION. The input data items, both on the transaction cards and the master tape, do *not* contain decimal points: the latter will be indicated by *implied* decimal points in the data description entries. However, the Report-1 data is printed with a decimal point: how this editing step can be accomplished is shown in Chapter 5.

Figure 4.7 shows the PROCEDURE DIVISION for the preparation of the first report. We have not shown a block diagram of the detailed processing, which should not be too hard to follow from the program.

After opening the five files we write the page headings. Let us assume that this is a one-page report and that we do not have to repeat these steps. Notice that this time we have used a procedure literal (line 001820) rather than a WORKING-STORAGE literal: this is legal and also convenient when the literal is not too long.

We then read a transaction record. This particular reading step is not repeated, since the possibility of several transactions for the same master record forces us to organize the sequence of reading to take account of the fact that we will in some cases read several transactions without reading a new master record. The operations in lines 001790-001860, which are necessary to get things started but are not repeated, are an example of *housekeeping,* as it is commonly called.

At line 001870 we have a new paragraph, which, as always, must have a name; this is made a sep-

arate paragraph so that we can return to it from other parts of the program. The name that is used here will cause no confusion with the following statement, which is similar in appearance: the hyphen between READ and OLD-MASTER makes the whole name a separate entity. Now we make a test: does this master record correspond to the product number in the transaction? Note the qualification of names here: PRODUCT-NUMBER is a name in four files; whenever we use such a name, we must specify which occurrence of it we mean by qualifying the *item* name with the desired *record* name. Note also here the use of *record* names and *file* names: TRANSACTION is a file name, used in the READ statement, but TRANS is a record name, used in the qualification and in the WRITE statement.

If this is the correct (or "matching," as it would usually be called) master record, we go to the paragraph named PROCESS; if not, we go on to the paragraph named TESTING-2. There we ask whether the product number in the old master record is less than that in the transaction, which would indicate that there were master records for which there were no sales during the month. Such master records should simply be written out to the new master file unchanged. (Note the use of the FROM option.) If the master product number is neither equal to nor less than the transaction product number, it must be greater. This represents an error condition, indicating either that a transaction product number has been miscoded or mispunched or that one or both files are out of sequence. In this case we have indicated that a message should be printed and the job stopped. In a real application we would probably close the files and stop the run if the files were out of sequence, and we would display an error message and continue if an individual transaction were wrong. This would require additional instructions and more elaborate programming techniques. Our aim here, however, is to keep our program as simple as possible.

The processing of a transaction record, once the proper master record has been found, is not really complex if we keep in mind the files being used. After multiplying the unit price by quantity to get the total price we need to write a record in the extended transaction file that will be the input to the second part of the job. Therefore we move the total price for this transaction to the extended transaction record (EXT), together with the salesman and district numbers, and write this record. This

```
001760 PROCEDURE DIVISION.
001780 HOUSEKEEPING.
001790     OPEN INPUT TRANSACTION, OLD-MASTER
001800         OUTPUT REPORT-1, EXTENDED-TRANSACTION, NEW-MASTER.
001810     MOVE SPACES TO REP-1, EXT, NEW-MAST.
001820     MOVE '    PRODUCT    MONTH SALES   YTD SALES' TO REP-1.
001830     WRITE REP-1 AFTER ADVANCING 0 LINES.
001850     READ TRANSACTION RECORD, AT END GO TO LAST-TRANSACTION.
001860     MOVE PRODUCT-NUMBER IN TRANSACTION TO SAVE-TRANS-PROD-NO.
001870 READ-OLD-MASTER.
001880     READ OLD-MASTER RECORD, AT END GO TO WRAPUP.
001890 TESTING-1.
001900     IF SAVE-TRANS-PROD-NO IS EQUAL TO PRODUCT-NUMBER
001910         IN OLD-MAST GO TO PROCESS.
001920 TESTING-2.
001930     IF PRODUCT-NUMBER IN OLD-MAST IS LESS THAN
001940             SAVE-TRANS-PROD-NO  WRITE NEW-MAST FROM OLD-MAST
001950         GO TO READ-OLD-MASTER, OTHERWISE STOP
001960        'FILE SEQUENCE ERROR OR INVALID TRANS PRODUCT NUMBER'.
001970 PROCESS.
001980     MULTIPLY UNIT-PRICE IN OLD-MAST BY QUANTITY
001990         GIVING TOTAL-PRICE.
002000     MOVE TOTAL-PRICE TO EXT-PRICE.
002010     MOVE SALESMAN IN TRANS  TO SALESMAN IN EXT.
002020     MOVE DISTRICT IN TRANS TO DISTRICT IN EXT.
002030     WRITE EXT.
002040     ADD TOTAL-PRICE TO PRODUCT-TOTAL.
002050     ADD TOTAL-PRICE TO MONTH-TOTAL.
002060     READ TRANSACTION RECORD, AT END GO TO LAST-TRANSACTION.
002070     MOVE PRODUCT-NUMBER IN TRANSACTION TO SAVE-TRANS-PROD-NO.
002080     IF SAVE-TRANS-PROD-NO       IS EQUAL TO PRODUCT-NUMBER
002090         IN OLD-MAST GO TO PROCESS.
002100 DIFFERENT-PRODUCT.
002105     MOVE SPACES TO REP-1.
002110     MOVE PRODUCT-NUMBER IN OLD-MAST TO PRODUCT-NUMBER IN REP-1.
002120     MOVE PRODUCT-TOTAL TO PRODUCT-TOTAL-FOR-MONTH.
002130     ADD PRODUCT-TOTAL,  YTD-SALES IN OLD-MAST GIVING
002140         YTD-SALES IN REP-1.
002150     WRITE REP-1 AFTER ADVANCING 2 LINES.
002160     ADD PRODUCT-TOTAL TO YTD-SALES IN OLD-MAST.
002170     WRITE NEW-MAST FROM OLD-MAST.
002180     MOVE ZEROES TO PRODUCT-TOTAL.
002190     GO TO READ-OLD-MASTER.
002200 LAST-TRANSACTION.
002210     MOVE HIGH-VALUES TO SAVE-TRANS-PROD-NO.
002220     GO TO DIFFERENT-PRODUCT.
002230 WRAPUP.
002240     MOVE SPACES TO REP-1.
002250     MOVE MONTH-TOTAL TO PRODUCT-TOTAL-FOR-MONTH.
002260     WRITE REP-1 AFTER ADVANCING 3 LINES.
002270     CLOSE TRANSACTION, OLD-MASTER,
002280         REPORT-1, EXTENDED-TRANSACTION, NEW-MASTER.
002290     STOP RUN.
```

Figure 4.7. COBOL PROCEDURE DIVISION for the summary by product, in sales statistics case study.

completes the operations on the only file that is written in this paragraph.

Now we add the total price from this transaction to the total for the product and for the month and read the next transaction record. We immediately determine whether it is for the same product number, which is given by the product number in the old master record still in storage. If the new one is for the same product number as the preceding one, we simply go back to process the new one.

If it is different, however, we go on in sequence to the next paragraph. Where do we stand at this point? All transactions for the preceding product have been processed and records corresponding to them have been written in the extended transaction file. We have built up the total dollar sales for the preceding product but have not yet written the REPORT-1 record for it. The new master record for the preceding product has not yet been written. The transaction now in storage is for the *next* product number—and this will act as a trigger in the unloading of some of the data that we have been accumulating.

Taking one file at a time, we first set up the data items that go into the REPORT-1 record: the product number, the total for the product for the month, and the updated YTD sales figure. The record is written. Now we shall work on the NEW-MASTER record. Since only one item in it (YTD-SALES) is different from the contents of the OLD-MASTER record, the simplest approach is to modify that one

item as it appears there and then use the FROM option on the WRITE.

We are now about ready to get back to work on the new transaction that is waiting patiently in storage, but first we must clear out the old product total, which is no longer of interest. This total is set to zero so that when the total price from the new transaction is added to it the procedure will be properly started, and we go back to READ-OLD-MASTER, where the whole business is repeated for the new transaction.

Now we should investigate what happens when the ends of the two files are reached. Unless there are incorrect transactions or file-sequence errors—possibilities that we ignore this time—the end of the transaction file will be reached first. There may or may not be more master records remaining when this occurs. Since there could be more (as in our sample data), we must arrange to read the rest of the old master records and write them in the new master file. There are many ways to do this; here we will "trick" the testing scheme by putting into the location where we "save" the transaction product number the highest characters in the machine's collating sequence, using the HIGH-VALUES figurative constant. From this point on the comparison at TESTING-2 will always show that the master product number is less than the transaction product number, which will result in writing the master record and going back to read another master. (We assume, of course, that there is no product number

ANSWERS

1. a. Transaction file.
   b. (Old) master file.
   c. Almost a trick question: product numbers are contained in both the transaction and the master files and are used to match a transaction record with the corresponding master record. In a sense the transaction file is the "primary" source of the product number, since we will read a transaction record first and then search the master file for the record with the same product number.

2. Because the source data enters the two reports in quite different sequences: when the data is in product-number sequence, for producing the first report, and the sales for one salesman are not grouped together and cannot be.

3. Actually it *would be* possible to do the job without sorting, but it would be exorbitantly time consuming when the master file is on tape. The idea is that if the

ANSWERS (Continued)

transactions are in product-number sequence we will be able to proceed "straight through" the master file without ever having to "back up" to find the master record corresponding to the next transaction. This means that the whole job can be done in one "pass" of the master file. Disks, on the other hand, allow for both sequential and nonsequential (random) processing.

4. The unit price is the price of *one* of the products; the extended price is the total price of some quantity of the product.

5. The sum of all occurrences of some data item in a file, used, among other purposes, perhaps, to determine that all records have been read correctly and that none has been skipped over in the processing.

6. Both, but not at the same time. It is an output file in the first run, which produces the summary by product; it is an input in the second run, which produces the summary by district and salesman.

that is the same as or greater than HIGH-VALUES; although it is always necessary to verify the validity of this assumption, there is seldom any problem.)

Where are we when the end of the transaction file is detected? We have just processed the last transaction in the file and have asked for another, but have found that no more remain. The report line for the last product number has therefore not yet been written, and neither has the new master record. After putting HIGH-VALUES in SAVE-TRANS-PROD-NO, we accordingly transfer to the paragraph named DIFFERENT-PRODUCT, which writes the two records. At the end of these steps there is a transfer to the READ-OLD-MASTER paragraph, which is just what we want.

When the end of the old master file is detected —perhaps immediately, perhaps after copying the remaining master records onto the new master tape —it remains only to write the final total of the entire month's sales and close all files.

At this point we can also explain why we had to transfer the transaction product number to a "save" area after reading a transaction. With some computers this would not be necessary; we could simply use PRODUCT-NUMBER IN TRANS for the comparisons and move HIGH-VALUES into it at the end. In several of the more modern computers the core storage area reserved to an input file is *no longer available* after the file has reached the end. With the IBM 360 used for testing, if we had moved HIGH-VALUES TO PRODUCT-NUMBER IN TRANS, we would have lost the HIGH-VALUES there right away. Consequently the subsequent comparisons with PRODUCT-NUMBER IN OLD-MAST would have given unpredictable results.

This discussion undoubtedly will seem complex at first reading. *The student is urged to study it until the underlying logic is perfectly clear: what we have done here, except for the details of the application, is absolutely fundamental to all business-data processing based on magnetic tape files.* In later case studies we shall extend the technique somewhat to include additional features, but the basic ideas will be the same *and the later examples will assume that the reader has mastered the ideas in this one.* Trying the procedure on the sample data is an excellent way to gain full understanding.

REVIEW QUESTIONS

1. Can a file and a record within that file have the same name?

2. Can two data items in different records have the same name?

3. In the READ statement we name a file. Do we name a file in the WRITE statement also?

4. This procedure was set up on the apparent assumption that there would be several transaction records for each product number. Is there any difficulty if some product number has only one transaction record? Justify your answer in terms of the sequence of operations in the PROCEDURE DIVISION.

5. Why is it necessary to write an extended transaction record for *every* transaction? Why not group them by product number, as in REPORT-1?

6. When control reaches the paragraph named DIFFERENT-PRODUCT, have the transaction record and the master record then in storage the same product number?

7. Outline briefly what would be required to produce a YTD sales total for the products *not* sold this month. (It's fairly simple.)

8. If there were transactions with product numbers greater than that of the last master, would they be processed like the others?

9. At line 002180 we carefully placed zeros in the working storage location named PRODUCT-TOTAL so that the total price from the next transaction would be added to zero, not the total for the preceding product. What assurance have we that this location will be zero for the first transaction? (Not answered in text. Cheat: look at the answer.)

10. Why were spaces moved to REP-1 in lines 001810, 002105, and 002240? (Cheat again.)

11. Is "PROCESS" a good choice for a paragraph name?

4.4 The Summary by District and Salesman

With the tape for printing the summary by product number out of the way, we may proceed to show how the second report might be prepared. The input for this run will consist of just one tape: the extended transaction tape which was one of the outputs of the preceding run.

Before we can begin to use this tape to prepare the report, however, it must be sorted into sequence on district number and salesman. This phrase "on district number and salesman" means that the tape must be put into order on district and *within each district* it must be in order on salesman. This double sorting is no problem at all, however: it requires only that both district number and salesman number be used as a combined key in sorting, with the district number being treated as the more significant. In card sorting this would require sorting first on *salesman number* and then on district; the second sort on district would not disturb the salesman order, and we would have just what we wanted.

Some COBOL compilers include provision for sorting, as we shall see in connection with the SORT verb in Chapter 8. Let us assume that our compiler does not recognize the verb SORT, which makes it necessary to do tape sorting some other way. Sorting routines that do this job with little effort on the part of the programmer, except for the inconvenience of having to get out of COBOL for the purpose, are available for all business computers. We shall not attempt to describe these routines, since they vary considerably from one computer to another. Suffice it to say that there are generalized programs of machine instructions that, in a sense, can adapt themselves to the particular needs of a file to be sorted. They are generally efficient and save many months of programming time in coding special sort routines, which are quite complex.

We assume that our tape has been sorted by such a sorting program and proceed to a consideration of the processing necessary to produce the second report.

The heart of the work is to accumulate the required totals while making sure that all required salesman and district information is available when needed and that the totals are properly started over after getting the total for each man and district. The COBOL PROCEDURE DIVISION is shown in Figure 4.8.

Another file is involved here, with the following names used.

File	Record	Data items
REPORT-2	REP-2	SALESMAN
		SALESMAN-TOTAL
		DISTRICT
		DISTRICT-TOTAL
		MONTH-TOTAL

Additional working storage will also be required:

DISTRICT-NUMBER
DISTRICT-ACCUM
SALESMAN-NUMBER
SALESMAN-ACCUM
MONTH-ACCUM

In DISTRICT-ACCUM, SALESMAN-ACCUM, and MONTH-ACCUM we will be "accumulating" (adding) the individual items that go to make up the totals.

We begin as always by opening the files. This time we must do two housekeeping operations. In

the main body of program, in the paragraph named TRANSACTION-READING, we will be asking whether each record is for the salesman in the preceding record. Without some special action at the beginning of the program there would be no "preceding" record for the *first* transaction. We therefore read a transaction record here in a position in the program in which the step will never be repeated. Now we wish to get the MONTH-ACCUM started at zero so that we can add district totals to it without worrying about its initial contents.

The next two paragraphs are also used to get things started properly, but in addition they will be repeated from time to time. We move the district number (from the transaction just read) to a working storage location for it, once again to get the comparison system started correctly. Then we move zero to the district accumulator. The paragraph named NEW-MAN does the same thing in getting the salesman number comparison started, but with the salesman accumulator there is a difference. Instead of moving zero to the accumulator, we want to place in it the extended price from the first transaction. This, as it happens, completes the processing of the first transaction.

Now come three paragraphs that do the heart of the work of preparing this report. We read another transaction record and ask if it is for the man in the preceding one; if not, we go to the paragraph that sets up and prints the total for that man. If it is for the same man, we add the extended price to the accumulator for the salesman and go back to read another transaction record. (We do *not* add the total price to the other two accumulators; they will be taken care of later. It would be *possible* to add the total price to all three accumulators at this point but at the expense of some wasted time.)

The paragraph named SALESMAN-RESULT basically sets up and writes the salesman number and total for what is by now the preceding man, but it begins with a step that is not exactly obvious. The record we are writing here contains room for five items; we never write more than two. What happens to the *previous* contents of this record storage when we do not enter anything into item locations that had contained something? Answer: they stay there—and we do not want them. Therefore we begin by moving spaces into the *entire record,* which can easily be done by naming the record instead of all the individual items in it.

```
001480 PROCEDURE DIVISION.
001490 HOUSEKEEPING.
001500     OPEN INPUT EXTENDED-TRANSACTION, OUTPUT REPORT-2.
001510     MOVE SPACES TO REP-2.
001520     MOVE '      SALESMAN      DISTRICT        TOTAL' TO REP-2.
001530     WRITE REP-2 AFTER ADVANCING 0 LINES.
001540     MOVE SPACES TO REP-2.
001550     READ EXTENDED-TRANSACTION, AT END GO TO FINAL-PROCESSING.
001560     MOVE ZEROES TO MONTH-ACCUM.
001570 NEW-DISTRICT.
001580     MOVE DISTRICT IN EXT TO DISTRICT-NUMBER.
001590     MOVE ZEROES TO DISTRICT-ACCUM.
001600 NEW-MAN.
001610     MOVE SALESMAN IN EXT TO SALESMAN-NUMBER.
001620     MOVE EXT-PRICE TO SALESMAN-ACCUM.
001630 TRANSACTION-READING.
001640     READ EXTENDED-TRANSACTION, AT END GO TO FINAL-PROCESSING.
001650     IF SALESMAN IN EXT IS NOT EQUAL TO SALESMAN-NUMBER
001660         GO TO SALESMAN-RESULT.
001670     ADD EXT-PRICE TO SALESMAN-ACCUM.
001680     GO TO TRANSACTION-READING.
001690 SALESMAN-RESULT.
001700     MOVE SPACES TO REP-2.
001710     MOVE SALESMAN-NUMBER TO SALESMAN IN REP-2.
001720     MOVE SALESMAN-ACCUM TO SALESMAN-TOTAL.
001730     WRITE REP-2 AFTER ADVANCING 2 LINES.
001740     ADD SALESMAN-ACCUM TO DISTRICT-ACCUM.
001750     IF DISTRICT IN EXT IS NOT EQUAL TO DISTRICT-NUMBER
001760         GO TO DISTRICT-RESULT.
001770     GO TO NEW-MAN.
001780 DISTRICT-RESULT.
001790     MOVE SPACES TO REP-2.
001800     MOVE DISTRICT-NUMBER TO DISTRICT IN REP-2.
001810     MOVE DISTRICT-ACCUM TO DISTRICT-TOTAL.
001820     WRITE REP-2 AFTER ADVANCING 2 LINES.
001830     ADD DISTRICT-ACCUM TO MONTH-ACCUM.
001840     GO TO NEW-DISTRICT.
001850 FINAL-PROCESSING.
001860     MOVE SPACES TO REP-2.
001870     MOVE SALESMAN-NUMBER TO SALESMAN IN REP-2.
001880     MOVE SALESMAN-ACCUM TO SALESMAN-TOTAL.
001890     WRITE REP-2 AFTER ADVANCING 2 LINES.
001900     MOVE SPACES TO REP-2.
001910     MOVE DISTRICT-NUMBER TO DISTRICT IN REP-2.
001920     ADD SALESMAN-ACCUM TO DISTRICT-ACCUM.
001930     MOVE DISTRICT-ACCUM TO DISTRICT-TOTAL.
001940     WRITE REP-2 AFTER ADVANCING 2 LINES.
001950     MOVE SPACES TO REP-2.
001960     ADD DISTRICT-ACCUM, MONTH-ACCUM GIVING MONTH-TOTAL.
001970     WRITE REP-2 AFTER ADVANCING 2 LINES.
001980     CLOSE EXTENDED-TRANSACTION, REPORT-2.
001990     STOP RUN.
```

Figure 4.8. COBOL PROCEDURE DIVISION for the summary by district and salesman, in sales statistics case study.

After setting up the REPORT-2 line we write it and then add the SALESMAN-ACCUM to the DISTRICT-ACCUM. This process will get us the total for the district: each time we write the total for a salesman we also add it to the district total. Doing this requires many fewer additions than adding each extended price separately to both accumulators (and to the accumulator for the month).

Now where are we? The report line for the preceding man has been written and a new transaction has already been read. Is this new transaction for the same district as the one we have been working on or not? If it is the same district, all we need to do is to move the extended price from the transaction to the salesman accumulator and move the salesman number to its working storage location. These two actions can be accomplished simply by transferring to the paragraph named NEW-MAN: this is just what we had to do at the outset.

If the new transaction is for a new district, then the total for the preceding district should be printed, the district accumulator added to the month accumulator, and we are ready to go back to the paragraph named NEW-DISTRICT, which performs the actions to get started with a new district.

The final processing must write all three totals because at the point at which the end of the transaction file is detected we have not yet written the totals for the last man or the last district. The AT END does not respond to a reading of the *last transaction* but to an attempt to read another transaction after the last one has *already* been read. Furthermore, the district total as it stands at this point does not include the last salesman and the month total does not include the last district. All of these considerations are reflected in the steps in the paragraph named FINAL-PROCESSING. The last action is to close the files and stop the run.

ANSWERS

1. No.

2. Certainly—this is what data name qualification is all about.

3. Sorry, the WRITE statement requires us to name a record. There is a good reason for this difference. Although we do not discuss it in the text, a file may have several types of record, each with different names. When *reading* such a file, it is often impossible to know which will turn up next, so we must give the *file* name, then inspect some item in the record to determine the record type, and proceed accordingly. When *writing* such a file, however, we would know which type of record was being written.

4. No trouble. After processing the one transaction we would read another and discover it was different. This would take us to DIFFERENT-PRODUCT, where a REPORT-1 record would be written, along with a new master record, etc. Some of the "totals" would be for one transaction only, but this is no problem.

5. Because the extended transactions enter into the second report in an entirely different sequence: by salesman within district. This is essentially the same as asking why the two reports cannot be combined into a single report.

6. Not at all: the transaction record is for the *next* transaction, which must be saved until this one is cleared out.

7. Just before or just after the statement WRITE NEW-MAST FROM OLD-MAST in line 001940 we would simply insert statements to pick up the product number and YTD sales from the old master and write a REPORT-1 record.

ANSWERS (Continued)

8. No. The AT END clause in master reading would stop the job without these transactions having been processed. These transactions would represent some kind of error, of course: erroneous transaction product numbers, perhaps, or files out of sequence or missing master records. A realistic program would have to include a good deal of error checking, which we have not done in an effort to keep the program understandable at this stage.

9. As far as you know at this point there is no assurance at all that this has been taken care of. We shall see in Chapter 5, however, that a WORKING-STORAGE location can be given an initial value for just such situations as this.

10. In line 002240: because the locations for PRODUCT-NUMBER and YTD-SALES in the record named REP-1 would have old values left in them from previous WRITE statements. Unless we clear them out by moving SPACES there, the old values would be printed.

In line 001810: because the storage area reserved to REP-1 may contain, at the beginning, any kind of unwanted information which would then be printed to the right of the page headings.

In line 002105: because of the way in which buffering works, it is always advisable to clear an area before moving a new set of data into it. This ensures elimination of characters left over from previous printing from the same buffer. This problem may also be solved by using the WRITE . . . FROM . . . option.

11. Not really: it is a reserved word in many compilers.

(A word to the wise: failure to process the last item of a group is the one of the most common programming errors. Satisfy yourself that everything in the final paragraph is essential and make a mental note to be on the lookout for mistakes in handling the end of a job.)

The report could be as shown in Figure 4.9.

As in the first part of this application, there are fundamental ideas here that should be understood fully before proceeding. The concepts involved are not quite so crucial as the logic of sequential-file processing but they are still important: the scheme for producing summaries within summaries, all the while keeping accumulators and identifications properly in step.

It would be too much to expect the reader to have grasped all of this material so thoroughly that he could attack a similar problem with ease. He should be content if he understands what has been done; the facility for doing it himself will come later after more examples and more practice.

REVIEW QUESTIONS

1. The paragraphs named NEW-DISTRICT and NEW-MAN are repeated on occasion, but the last line of the paragraph named HOUSEKEEPING, which performs a similar function, is done only once. Why?

2. In line 001650 the relational operator is IS NOT EQUAL TO. Is the NOT a mistake?

3. Would this procedure work if a salesman could work out of more than one district?

SALESMAN		DISTRICT	TOTAL
41	203.37		
52	110.00		
69	134.65		
		1	448.02
18	207.69		
32	185.60		
		2	393.29
36	194.15		
39	121.40		
50	51.80		
		3	367.35
			1208.66

Figure 4.9. Summary by salesman and district in sales statistics case study.

ANSWERS

1. The second and third paragraphs deal with district and salesman totals, respectively; as we reach a new district or new salesman, the old total must be erased and the new district or man number moved to working storage. The first paragraph deals with the total for the month, which never has to be started over.

2. No: we want to go on to writing the total for the salesman if the new transaction is for a *different* man, which is what this relation does.

3. Not at all: the whole logical structure depends on the fact that when we reach a new district we know positively that there will also be a new salesman. This is implicit in the transfer to NEW-DISTRICT, after which we automatically proceed to NEW-MAN.

5. THE **DATA DIVISION**

5.1 Introduction

COBOL makes a clear distinction between the description of what processing is to be done, which is the function of the PROCEDURE DIVISION, and the characteristics of the data on which the processing is to be carried out, which is the function of the DATA DIVISION. The two are entirely separate divisions in the source program, which leads to some significant advantages of COBOL. At the same time, however, the two are strongly intertwined in the compiled object program. Before delving into the details of writing the DATA DIVISION it might be well to consider some of the implications of the distinctness in the source program combined with interrelation in the object program.

One of the most important aspects of planning an electronic data-processing system is the provision for flexibility. Almost everything we do in this work is subject to change: the source program must be changed as errors are detected and corrected, programming methods change as new techniques and new compilers are developed, and the processing specifications themselves change as management, labor, and governmental regulations are modified.

COBOL assists in providing this flexibility in a number of ways. The fact that the source program is written in English helps because it is a relatively simple matter to modify a few parts of a COBOL program and recompile it, whereas making equivalent changes in a machine language program can

be a major undertaking. Perhaps the biggest reason why a COBOL program simplifies the change problem, however, is that the PROCEDURE and DATA DIVISIONS are kept rigidly separate.

It may not be obvious to the newcomer to computing that the procedural aspects become strongly intertwined with the data characteristics in the object program. As a matter of fact, virtually everything in the object program depends on how the data is stored and organized. Given exactly the same procedures to be executed, the object program will be greatly different whether or not records on tape are blocked, whether there are two instead of four places to the right of a decimal point, whether a field is numeric or alphabetic, or whether the sorting keys of records are in the first word or the sixth. It is in precisely such matters that many of the changes that we must deal with occur. A program has to be modified to accept a four-digit deduction that was formerly three digits; a part number that was previously numeric will now have two positions that may contain letters; a tax-law revision will now make it possible for an employee to accumulate more than $99.99 state tax in one quarter, requiring a lengthening of a data item.

With COBOL, or any similar high-level language, such changes are relatively simple to make: the DATA DIVISION is modified suitably, the input data formats are reworked if necessary, and the program is recompiled. With machine-language programs there are actual examples of cases in which adding one more digit to a deduction has required weeks of reprogramming.

Similarly, if the processing requirements change, the necessary modification can be made in the PROCEDURE DIVISION and the source program recompiled.

Furthermore, the separation of the procedure and data divisions in COBOL assists the source programmer to do a more rapid and error-free job in the first place. The attempt to keep in mind the influence of the data characteristics on the actual instructions being written often leads to confusion, slow work, and errors. With COBOL these two aspects of the work are kept distinct so that the programmer can concentrate on one thing at a time.

Finally, in considering why it is important for the reader to understand the subject of this chapter, we should mention that the way the data is stored and organized has a major effect on the efficiency of the object program; examples have been constructed in which a simple change in the DATA DIVISION can slow down a program by a factor of 10—to do exactly the same work!

In this chapter we shall learn how to write the DATA DIVISION; at the end of Chapter 6 we include the DATA DIVISION of the sample problems OVER $300 and SALES-1 that we presented in Chapters 3 and 4. Chapter 7 provides another example of a complete DATA DIVISION and Chapter 9 discusses how the DATA and PROCEDURE DIVISION both affect the "efficiency" (speed, approximately) of the object program.

5.2 The File Description

The information that a COBOL compiler needs to have about a file is given in three parts—once again separating things into small pieces that are more easily managed. In the *file description* we specify certain information about its over-all organization: its name, how the data is recorded if there is a choice in the particular machine, the number of records per block, certain things about labels, and the names of the records in the file.

After surveying the format in which this information is presented, we shall turn to an investigation of the second part of the file information, the *record description,* in which we specify how the data is organized into items. The last part of the complete description of a file is given in the

ENVIRONMENT DIVISION, in which we give certain information about the medium on which the file is stored (cards, tape, disks, printer output, etc.). The ENVIRONMENT DIVISION is considered in Chapter 6.

The DATA DIVISION usually consists of a FILE SECTION (which is present with almost no exception) and a WORKING-STORAGE SECTION (which is needed most of the time).*

In theory we could do without the FILE SECTION by using the verbs ACCEPT and DISPLAY to perform our input-output processing: these verbs only require WORKING-STORAGE entries. In practice a COBOL program structured along these lines would be nothing more than an academic exercise. A program is generally written to process a substantial volume of records which are organized in files and are handled by the much more efficient verbs READ and WRITE.

We could also have a program that does not require a WORKING-STORAGE SECTION. This is the case, for instance, of our easy sample program in Section 1.5.

In any event the DATA DIVISION must begin at the A margin (col. 8)† with the words DATA DIVISION, followed by a period. On the next line, starting again at the A margin, we enter the name of the first SECTION. With almost no exceptions we start as follows:

DATA DIVISION.
FILE SECTION.

The first part of the FILE SECTION is composed of the *file descriptions* (abbreviated FD) for each of the files in the program. There are quite a number of options here, which give the complete format a forbidding appearance. It isn't that bad! The most important functions of the file description can be summarized quite briefly: to state the size of the blocks and records in the file, to specify in general what is to be done about labels, and to give the names of the record or records in the file. To give courage to the faint of heart let it be noted

---

* We may also have a CONSTANT SECTION (which is becoming obsolete because, as we shall see, it is perfectly possible to set up constants in the WORKING-STORAGE SECTION), a LINKAGE SECTION (which may be used to receive data from *other* programs), and a REPORT SECTION (which pertains to an extension of COBOL called Report Writer). We shall not delve into any of these.

† See Section 3.2 for a review of the format of the coding sheet.

that a perfectly legitimate file description could consist of just

FD TRANSACTION; LABEL RECORDS ARE STANDARD; DATA RECORD IS TRANS.

Option 1 refers to a *library* of "prefabricated" descriptions which may be available in those compilers that can handle this feature. The idea here is that if many programmers have to use the same files the descriptions of these files can be drawn up once and entered into the library; all programmers can use (COPY) them simply by writing something like

FD PAYROLL-MASTER COPY LIB-23

PAYROLL-MASTER would be the agreed-on name for the file, and LIB-23 would be the name under which it was entered into the library. Physically, the library, when available in a compiler and used by an installation, consists of a tape or disk file, which the compiler reads when a library call is encountered in the source program. (Even though some of the formats do not specifically show it, library calls may be made for nearly every section of a source program.)

RECORDING MODE. Some computers have more than one way of recording information on file media or can handle records of different sizes within one file. If the computer at hand has only one recording mode for a particular file storage medium, this clause need never be written; it may also be omitted if one recording mode has been designated as the standard and this standard is to be used. In any case the words to be used for "mode" are specified for each compiler by the computer manufacturer in a separate publication for each system.

EXAMPLES

(1) RECORDING MODE IS F (for fixed length records).
(2) RECORDING MODE IS V (for variable length records).

BLOCK CONTAINS. The most common need for this clause is simply to state the blocking factor when there is more than one record per block (or logical record per physical record, as some manufacturers' manuals would say). It may be omitted when the blocking factor is equal to 1, which is the

Option 1
FD file-name COPY library-name

Option 2
FD file-name [; RECORDING MODE IS mode]

[; BLOCK CONTAINS [integer-2 TO] integer-3 {RECORDS / CHARACTERS}]

[; RECORD CONTAINS [integer-4 TO] integer-5 CHARACTERS]

; LABEL {RECORDS ARE / RECORD IS} {STANDARD / OMITTED / data-name-1 / library-name-1 IN LIBRARY}

[, {data-name-2 / library-name-2 IN LIBRARY} ...]

[; VALUE OF data-name-2 IS {data-name-4 [HASHED] / literal}]

[, data-name-5 IS ... ...]

; DATA {RECORD IS / RECORDS ARE} data-name-6 [, data-name-7...]

case for card and printed files. The "integer-2 TO" clause refers to a file in which there may be a variable number of records in a block—a rare occurrence.

EXAMPLES

(1) BLOCK CONTAINS 10 RECORDS
(2) BLOCK CONTAINS 5 TO 8 RECORDS

RECORD CONTAINS. This clause is never required because, as we shall see in Section 5.3, the record description entries completely specify the length of each logical record. When it is used, with the meanings being fairly obvious, it can in some cases simplify the work of the compiler and therefore lead to a shorter compiling time.

EXAMPLE

RECORD CONTAINS 80 CHARACTERS

LABEL RECORD. This clause must be written in every file description, even though the file may have no labels, in which case the word OMITTED must be used. As we have already said, for some file media, such as disks, labels are mandatory; for some, such as tape, they are optional; as a rule, card and printed files have no labels. At any rate, label usage, contents, and processing are subject to the standards set up by each installation. In the cases in which there are choices of types of label, the options data-name-1 and library-name-1, etc., may be used. In the first case the format of the label would be described in a separate record description, and in the second the label record description would be available in the compiler library.

VALUE OF. This option is used to check the contents of label item values in an input tape or file label and to insert contents in label item values in the label of output tapes or files. Once very fashionable, this clause is no longer implemented in all compilers.*

EXAMPLES

(1) VALUE OF ID IS 'OCORSMAST'
(2) VALUE OF CONTROL-TOT IS 770033

DATA RECORD clause. This clause states the name or names of the record or records in the file.

---

* For instance, in the IBM implementation of ANSI COBOL (1968), this clause "is treated as comment when present." This means that it would serve only as documentation.

It used to be a required clause, but the trend is to make it optional. Since the name of the record must appear as the first entry after the end of the FD statement, the compiler can always associate a record with its file. This holds true also when a file contains several records with several different data arrangements.

EXAMPLES

(1) DATA RECORD TRANS.
(2) DATA RECORD IS OLD-MAST.
(3) DATA RECORD IS NEW-MAST.
(4) DATA RECORDS ARE TRANS-1, TRANS-2, TRANS-3.

EXAMPLES OF FILE DESCRIPTION ENTRIES

(1) FD   INVENTORY-MASTER
         RECORDING MODE IS F
         BLOCK CONTAINS 25 RECORDS
         LABEL RECORDS ARE STANDARD
         DATA RECORD IS MAST-RECD.
(2) FD   PRINT-FILE
         LABEL RECORDS OMITTED.
(3) FD   FILE-IN
         RECORD CONTAINS 100
         CHARACTERS
         BLOCK CONTAINS 20 RECORDS
         LABEL RECORDS STANDARD
         VALUE OF ID IS 'OCORSMAST'
         DATA RECORD IS RECD-IN.
(4) FD   PAYR-FILE
         RECORDING MODE IS F
         BLOCK CONTAINS 5 RECORDS
         LABEL RECORDS ARE STANDARD
         DATA RECORDS ARE EMPL-DATA,
         PAY-DATA, BENEF-DATA.

Notice that FD must begin at the A margin (col. 8) and the remaining clauses in column 12 or to the right of it. Notice also that a period must be inserted at the end—*and only at the end*—of the file description.

REVIEW QUESTIONS

1. True or false:
   a. The primary functions of a file description entry are to furnish information concerning the physical structure (record blocking, recording mode, etc.), the file identification (if any), and the names of the record(s) appearing in the file.
   b. Every file *must* have a file description.

c. The complete file description entry can be obtained by a simple library call if the compiler can accept library calls and the required description actually is on the library tape.

d. Every file description must have a LABEL RECORD clause, even if it is nothing more than LABEL RECORDS ARE OMITTED.

e. The required clauses of a file-description entry may not be the same for different compilers and different installations.

f. We may start the clause RECORDING MODE IS V in column 10 of the coding sheet.

g. The clause DATA RECORD IS may be omitted for all compilers.

h. The clause BLOCK CONTAINS nn RECORDS may be omitted if the blocking factor is 1.

i. The following FD entry is legal:
FD SALESFILE LABEL RECORDS
STANDARD.
DATA RECORD IS SALES-REC.

2. Why is the RECORD CONTAINS clause always optional?

3. Did the text explain how a file description is entered into the library? (No; cheat.)

5.3 The Record Description

A record is described by a series of entries, most of which may apply to the record itself or to some of its parts:

1. Level number
2. Record-name or data-name or FILLER
3. PICTURE
4. VALUE
5. USAGE
6. REDEFINES
7. OCCURS
8. SYNCHRONIZED
9. JUSTIFIED

Among these entries (1) and (2) are essential; (3) is required in certain cases and must be omitted in others; (4), (5), (6) and (7) may be conveniently used when needed; the last two are used rather infrequently. Let us now discuss them one at a time.

Level structure and level number. So far (in the file description) we have given the compiler only certain information about the over-all characteristics of the file; now we must specify just what is contained in each record of the file and how the items in them are organized.

The entries in a COBOL record description are built around the concept of a *level* of data. The record itself is the highest level and must always have the level number 01 (which may also be written 1). Within a record there may be *groups of items*; these groups, which may consist of other groups of items or *elementary items* (single pieces of data), must have level numbers that are higher than 01. Every record is, in fact, composed of elementary items, which may have level numbers as high as 49.

Consider an example. In a payroll application a record consisting of the information about one man gives the man's name, his employee number, the date, and the number of hours worked. The employee number and hours worked are elementary items, but the name is further subdivided into last name, first initial, and middle initial and the date is divided into month, day, and year. Schematically, the record organization might be as shown in Figure 5.1.

TIME-CARD is the name of the *record*, which must have level 01. NAME is the name of a *group item* at level 02 consisting of three *elementary items* at level 03. MAN-NUMBER is an elementary item at level 02. DATE and HOURS-WORKED follow similar patterns. With this structure, we could do things like the following:

1. Move the entire record to working storage by giving just the name TIME-CARD or blank out the entire record by writing MOVE SPACES TO TIME-CARD.

2. Move the entire name, including initials, by using a sentence such as MOVE NAME TO PREVIOUS-NAME.

3. Move the last name only by a sentence such as MOVE LAST-NAME TO KEY-STORE.

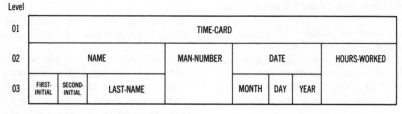

Figure 5.1. Schematic representation of the levels of an illustrative record.

In other words, the level structure of the COBOL DATA DIVISION allows us to work with entire records, groups of elementary items, or elementary items. There may be as many intermediate levels as one likes (up to level 49—far more than would ever be needed); this would amount to having groups of groups.

To summarize what is required: every record must have a name, and must be level 01; every record must eventually be shown as a set of elementary items. The formation of groups of elementary items is at the discretion of the programmer.

What all this means is that COBOL, through the technique of levels, assumes the responsibility for the details of setting up the object program to work either with basic data or with groups of data. The most common thing to write in the PROCEDURE DIVISION is the name of an elementary item, but when it is necessary to work with a group or an entire record the power of the COBOL level structure can be a great convenience.

The level structure is presented in the DATA DIVISION by writing the level number of each record, group, or elementary item before the name. The foregoing example could be written as shown in Figure 5.2, in which we have given only the level number and name, omitting the various clauses that are discussed below.

Level numbers always start with 01 for records, a record being the most inclusive grouping of data. Successively less inclusive groupings are assigned higher—but not necessarily successive—level numbers, ending finally with elementary items, which must have level numbers no larger than 49.*

The indention of higher level entries is at the discretion of the programmer. They need not be in-

---

* Level numbers 77 and 88 are used for special purposes and are considered in Sections 5.6 and 5.11.

```
01 TIME-CARD
   02 NAME
         03 FIRST-INITIAL
         03 SECOND-INITIAL
         03 LAST-NAME
   02 MAN-NUMBER
   02 DATE
         03 MONTH
         03 DAY
         03 YEAR
   02 HOURS-WORKED
```

Figure 5.2. Schematic representation of the way the level structure of Figure 5.1 would be presented in the DATA DIVISION. (Only level numbers and names are shown; complete computer entries would contain other information.)

dented at all; some entries may be indented and others not. In general, the following rules should be observed: 01 should be entered in column 8. The 02 and higher level items should be entered in column 12. *Optionally*, the higher level items *may* be indented, as shown in Figure 5.2. If one entry at a given level is indented, however, all entries at that level should be indented the same amount, for consistent documentation.

NAME.   The level number must be followed by a name. This is a record name for level 01 and a data name or the reserved word FILLER for the other levels. As we shall see very soon in connection with PICTURE, FILLER may be used to indicate any item that will not be referred to in the program.

REVIEW QUESTIONS

1. Is the level structure a function of the PROCEDURE DIVISION or the DATA DIVISION?

2. If QUANTITIES is a name at level 05 and immediately following it in the record description

---

ANSWERS

1. a, b, c, d, and e are all completely true. In fact, these statements summarize the entire section; if you have answered any of these with "false," a review may be in order.

    f. False: we may start in column 12 or to the right of it but not to the left of it.

    g. False: we said the "trend" is to make it optional. It is optional, for instance, in the IBM implementation of ANSI COBOL 1968, but it has been a required clause for many years for many compilers.

ANSWERS (Continued)

    h. True.

    i. False: the period after STANDARD is an error.

2. Because the record description (to be studied next) always specifies the size of the record.

3. No. This is an example of quite a number of things that will not be explained here, since they do not greatly concern the average source programmer and, more importantly, because they depend so much on the details of the machine and the installation.

are QUANTITY-ON-HAND, QUANTITY-ON-ORDER, and QUANTITY-RESERVED, all at level 06, what will happen if we write MOVE QUANTITIES TO TEMPORARY?

3. Must the level number of a record actually be 01 or must it merely be the lowest numbered level?

4. Does it make any difference whether we write a level number as 2 or 02?

5. The text does not give a formal definition of an *elementary item*. Try to formulate such a definition.

6. Could a record description consist of elementary items only, with no group items?

7. In the example in this section could MAN-NUMBER and HOURS-WORKED have been given level 03?

5.4 The PICTURE Clause

A PICTURE, basically, describes the class of characters in an elementary item and the length of the item. How this clause works is perhaps best illustrated by some examples.

Let us say that we have a card record named PRODUCT-REC with the following record layout:

Column 1 through column 5	REPORT-NO
Columns 6–10	MAJOR-PROD
subdivided into	
Column 6–8	PROD-LINE
Column 9–10	PROD-TYPE
Column 65–70	UNIT-PRICE
Column 71–80	UNITS-SOLD

The record description entries could be as follows:

```
01 PRODUCT-REC.
   02 REPORT-NO PICTURE X(5).
   02 MAJOR-PROD.
      03 PROD-LINE PICTURE X(3).
      03 PROD-TYPE PICTURE XX.
   02 FILLER PICTURE X(54).
   02 UNIT-PRICE PICTURE 9999V99.
   02 UNITS-SOLD PICTURE S9(10).
```

PICTURE X(5) after REPORT-NO indicates that this item is five characters long or, as we would usually say, has a size of 5. The X indicates that the field is alphanumeric, which means that it can accommodate any class of characters: alphabetic, numeric, or special characters. If we wrote PICTURE 9(5), the 9 would have indicated that the field is defined as numeric and is meant to accommodate numeric information only: this would be necessary if we wanted to use this item in arith-

metic operations, as is actually the case for both UNIT-PRICE and UNITS-SOLD.

The V in the PICTURE for UNIT-PRICE—a PICTURE that, incidentally, we could have written as 9(4)V9(2) or 9(4)V99—indicates that there is an *implied* decimal point to the left of the last two digits. Finally, the S in PICTURE S9(10) for UNITS-SOLD indicates that this item is *signed*, which means that it may contain either a positive or negative quantity. If we omit the S, the item would always be treated as a positive quantity in any arithmetic operation, which would prevent us from processing correctly a negative adjustment to a sale entered in error.*

Several important things should be noticed. A PICTURE is assigned only to the elementary items (those *not* further subdivided); the sum of all the sizes, as indicated by the notations, adds up to 80, which is the number of columns in a card and the desired length of our record: *neither the S nor the V would occupy any space in storage,* and we do *not* count them in determining the number of characters in an item. A period is required at the end of each entry. Finally, we have used FILLER to bridge the gap between column 10 and column 65: since we are apparently uninterested in whatever exists in card columns 11 through 64, it would have been pointless to assign a real data name to this field.

Additional notations are available for a PICTURE clause. Items that are meant to accommodate only letters or spaces may be defined by one or more symbols A. Thus PICTURE AAA or PICTURE A(3) would both designate a three-character ALPHABETIC field. The symbol P is used to indicate that the implied decimal point is outside the word in storage: if we have the digits 56 in storage and the PICTURE describing this item is VPP99, the arithmetic value of the item would be .0056. The symbol P will seldom be useful in commercial applications. As to the symbol A, we do not really have to use it, because the symbol X does the job equally well. Furthermore, even peoples' names may be nonALPHABETIC; names like O'Neill and Corelli-Barnett, in fact, contain special characters.

The maximum number of characters in a PICTURE is 30. (This is quite distinct from the num-

---

* Even when we do not expect a negative quantity to appear, it is preferable to use the S for a numeric field. In many computers a signed item is treated more efficiently at execution time than an unsigned one.

ber of characters in the item described by the PICTURE. The PICTURE 9(7)V999 has eight characters, whereas the item it describes has 10.)

Before we start discussing another kind of PIC-

TURE (the *editing* PICTURE), let us look at Figure 5.3, which shows a number of PICTURE clauses containing the symbols that we have mentioned so far. The listing shows a number of PIC-

PICTURE	SIZE	CLASS	CHARACTERS IN STORAGE	USED IN PROCEDURES AS
999V99	5	NUMERIC	12345	123₄₅
9(6)	6	NUMERIC	123456	123456ᴧ
9(6)V	6	NUMERIC	123456	123456ᴧ
VPPP999	3	NUMERIC	123	ᴧ000123
9(4)P(4)V	4	NUMERIC	1234	12340000ᴧ
VP9	1	NUMERIC	1	ᴧ01
9PV	1	NUMERIC	1	10ᴧ
99999	5	NUMERIC	23456	23456ᴧ
99V999	5	NUMERIC	23456	23₄56
AAAA	4	ALPHABETIC	WXYZ	WXYZ
XXXXXX	6	ALPHANUMERIC	1M89SS	1M89SS
XXXXX	5	ALPHANUMERIC	12345	12345
X(6)	6	ALPHANUMERIC	12•345	12•345

Figure 5.3. Examples of the use of the PICTURE clause with various nonedited items.

ANSWERS

1. Primarily the DATA DIVISION, certainly as far as the source program is concerned, but the information about data structure conveyed by the levels becomes heavily intertwined with the PROCEDURE DIVISION statements during compilation.

2. The group item consisting of *all three* elementary items would be moved to what is presumably a working storage location.

3. It *must* be 01, which can also be written 1.

4. No.

5. An elementary item is one that is not further subdivided into less inclusive items.

6. Certainly. In fact, a record could, in principle, consist of just *one* elementary item, the record itself. This is uncommon, but RECORD-IN and RECORD-OUT in the program in Section 1.5 show that it can happen.

ANSWERS (Continued)

7. Yes; but this, of course, would make them members of the level 02 group preceding them. About the only thing you cannot do in assigning level numbers is to give an item a number *smaller* than *any* that has previously been used; for instance, this structure would be illegal:

```
01 TRANS
   03 KEY-A
      04 KEY-1
      04 KEY-2
   02 QUANTITY
```

QUANTITY has been given a level number smaller than that of *any* item before it, which is illegal. (Why? Try to draw a schematic diagram of what this might mean and you will convince yourself that there would be no point to it.)

TUREs, assumed characters in storage, the size and class that will be inferred from the PICTURE, and the meaning of the characters thus described when used in procedures, with the implied decimal point assumed to be as shown by the caret ($\wedge$).*

REVIEW QUESTIONS

1. Assume that we have the following entries for a record description:

```
01 SALES-RECORD.
   02 FIELD-A
   03 FIELD-B
   04 FIELD-C
   04 FIELD-D
   03 FIELD-E
   02 FIELD-F
```

Could we say for sure that (answer yes or no)

    a. FIELD-C and FIELD-D should have a PICTURE, whereas FIELD-A should not?

* If there is still any lingering uncertainty about actual versus assumed decimal points, now would be an excellent time to clear it up. Any operand used in an arithmetic verb must be NUMERIC, which means that the *characters* decimal point, comma, dollar sign, etc., *cannot* appear in it. The assumed or implied decimal point in a NUMERIC item governs how the arithmetic is done, for instance, in terms of how operands are aligned before addition or subtraction, but does *not* appear as a character. By analogy it is as though in doing pencil and paper arithmetic we did not *write* the decimal point but merely kept a mental note of where it was at all times. It *is* still possible to keep the character "." in storage, with the digits of an item, but such an item is automatically alphanumeric (since it contains a character other than a digit or a letter) and *cannot* be used in arithmetic.

    b. FIELD-C is an elementary item?
    c. FIELD-A, FIELD-B, and FIELD-C all start in position (column, if you prefer) 1 of SALES-RECORD?
    d. If FIELD-A ends in position 20, FIELD-F starts in position 21?
    e. The size of FIELD-D is less than that of FIELD-B?
    f. The size of FIELD-E is greater than that of FIELD-B?
    g. FIELD-F should have a PICTURE?

2. Yes or no:

    a. MOVE FILLER TO SAVE-A would be a legal instruction in the PROCEDURE DIVISION.
    b. FIELD-R's PICTURE is X(5). Would it be legal to write ADD 3 TO FIELD-R and would it work if FIELD-R contained only digits?
    c. An assumed decimal point takes up no space in storage and is therefore not counted in determining the size of an item.
    d. FIELD-X has a PICTURE of 999. Could we write MOVE 'ABC' TO FIELD-X?
    e. The entries PICTURE XXX and PICTURE X(3) are equivalent.

5.5 Editing Pictures

The PICTURE clauses we have just reviewed provide information about how the compiler should set up storage for data: what kind of representation to use, where the decimal points are, and how many characters there are. The editing PICTUREs to be considered now go a step further: applied

---

ANSWERS

1. a. Yes. The level numbers indicate that both FIELD-C and FIELD-D are elementary items, and, as such, they should have a PICTURE. FIELD-A is a group item and therefore should not.
    b. Yes.
    c. Yes. If you do not believe it, draw a schematic diagram of the level-number structure in this record.
    d. Yes. Do you need a diagram *this* time?
    e. Yes. FIELD-B (level number 03) consists of both FIELD-C and FIELD-D (level number 04). Therefore FIELD-D must be shorter than FIELD-B.
    f. No. No, we cannot tell for sure, that is. The level structure in this case is not sufficient to indicate their relative sizes. We would need two PICTUREs to tell for sure.
    g. Yes.

ANSWERS (Continued)

2. a. No: FILLER is used to refer to an item that is *not* going to be referred to in the program. Furthermore, since we can use FILLER as many times as we like in any record description, how would the compiler know which of the items named FILLER we want to MOVE?
    b. No and no. FIELD-R is defined as alphanumeric and therefore may *not* be used in an arithmetic operation, no matter what it actually contains. Incidentally, if you do things of this sort, the compiler will give you nasty error messages at the end of your program listing; and on finding a predetermined number of errors, it would not permit the execution of the program.
    c. Yes. This would also apply to the symbols S and P.
    d. No. FIELD-X is defined as NUMERIC, and we may not MOVE a non-NUMERIC literal into it. See also incidental note to 2b above.
    e. Yes.

to a receiving area, they specify actions to be taken when the object program is run; furthermore, the precise nature of the action depends on what the data is.

Editing, in this context, refers to the preparation of data for printing in a more easily read form than it appears in storage and to the insertion of dollar signs and asterisks.

The actions here, which may refer to elementary items only, must refer to a *receiving area*; that is, an area (data item) that "receives" data as the result of a MOVE or arithmetic verb. In a statement such as MOVE A TO B, A is a *source* area and B is a *receiving* area. The insertion and/or replacement occurs at the time the object program is run, when data is transmitted to the item by a MOVE or an arithmetic verb.

As a rule, only NUMERIC *information may be edited.* Here are some examples of editing PICTUREs:

PICTURE ZZZ, ZZZ. 99
PICTURE $999
PICTURE $$$9
PICTURE -99
PICTURE 999CR
PICTURE ***99

We shall now explain the function of each available editing symbol and the rules governing its use.

Z. The character Z specifies suppression of leading zeros: we can indicate just how many positions are to be suppressed by the number of Z's written.

EXAMPLES

SOURCE ITEM	PICTURE	EDITED RESULT
12345	ZZ999	12345
01234	ZZ999	1234
00001	ZZ999	001
00000	ZZ999	000
10023	ZZ999	10023
10000	ZZ999	10000
00010	ZZZZZ	10
00000	ZZZZZ	(BLANK)

$. A single dollar sign as the leftmost character of a PICTURE specifies that a dollar sign should be placed in the edited item *in that position.*

EXAMPLES

SOURCE ITEM	PICTURE	EDITED RESULT
1234	$9999	$1234
0023	$9999	$0023
0023	$ZZ99	$ 23
0004	$ZZ99	$ 04
0050	$ZZZZ	$ 50
0000	$ZZZZ	(BLANK)

Zero suppression with a *floating dollar sign* is specified by placing a dollar sign in each leading position to be suppressed; the rightmost character suppressed will be replaced by a dollar sign in the edited result. Zero suppression with the floating dollar sign is specified only if *more than one* dollar sign is written.

EXAMPLES

SOURCE ITEM	PICTURE	EDITED RESULT
00123	$$999	$123
01234	$$$$$	$1234
00002	$$999	$002
00000	$$$$$	(BLANK)
00000	$$$99	$00

, (comma). When a comma is written in a PICTURE, it will be inserted in the position shown without loss of digits from the source data. If all

EXAMPLES

SOURCE ITEM	PICTURE	EDITED RESULT
123456	999,999	123,456
000078	999,999	000,078
000078	ZZZ,ZZZ	78
000000	ZZZ,ZZZ	(BLANK)
000078	ZZ,9999	0078

characters to the left of the comma(s) in the source data are zeros and zero suppression is called for, the comma(s) will be replaced by space(s).

. (decimal point). When a decimal point is written in a PICTURE, it will be inserted in the position shown without loss of digits from the source data. This, of course, is an *actual* decimal point, which occupies a character position in the edited result and which will be printed. An item may never contain more than one actual (or assumed) decimal point.

When the source data is moved to a data item for which the PICTURE contains a decimal point, the assumed decimal point of the source item is considered; that is, the source item is placed in the receiving item with the actual decimal point in the receiving item aligned with the assumed decimal point in the source item. This can cause the insertion of zeros in the edited result, as the examples show.

EXAMPLES

SOURCE ITEM	PICTURE	EDITED RESULT
1234.56	9999.99	1234.56
1.23456	9.99999	1.23456
1.23456	99.999999	01.234560
00.0123	ZZ.ZZZZZZ	.012300
000009	ZZZZ.ZZ	.09
000009.	ZZZZ.ZZ	9.00
000009	ZZZ9.99	0.09
1234.56	Z,ZZZ.99	1,234.56
000009	Z,ZZZ.99	.09
000000	Z,ZZZ.ZZ	(BLANK)
123456.	$ZZZ,ZZZ.ZZ	$123,456.00

— (minus sign). If a single minus sign is written as the first or last character of a PICTURE, a *display* minus sign (one that occupies a character position in storage and will be printed) will be inserted into the edited item where written if the data is negative. If the data is not negative, the minus sign will be replaced by a space.

EXAMPLES

(A sign over the units position indicates an operational sign.)

SOURCE ITEM	PICTURE	EDITED RESULT
123	-999	-123
123	999-	123-
123	-999	123
123	999-	123
000	-999	-000
000	-999	000

In the foregoing examples a sign over the units position of a number is used to indicate an *operational* sign, as opposed to the *edited result* sign.*

Zero suppression with a *floating minus sign* is specified by placing a minus sign in each leading position to be suppressed; the rightmost character suppressed will be replaced by a minus sign in the edited result if the source item is negative. This applies only if *more than one* minus sign is written in the PICTURE.

EXAMPLES

SOURCE ITEM	PICTURE	EDITED RESULT
1234	---99	-1234
0012	----9	-12
0012	----9	12
0008	---99	-08
0000	---99	00
0000	-----	(BLANK)
0012	-----	-12
0002	---99	-02

* Now would be an excellent time to remove any lingering confusion on *this* matter, too. An *edited result sign* (or *display sign*, as we may also call it) is a separate character (+ or −) stored in a separate, distinct character position. The presence of a display sign makes an item Alphanumeric, and therefore it is impossible to do arithmetic with it. An *operational sign* is stored in some manner or other, the precise method varying widely with different computers; an operational sign does not in most cases take up a separate character position. Printing a number that has an operational sign does *not* result in printing a plus or minus sign in front of it—unless the item is *first* edited.

+ **(plus sign).** If a single plus sign is written as the first or last character of a PICTURE, a *display* plus sign will be inserted into the edited item where written if the data is positive; if the data is negative, a minus sign will be inserted. If the source data has no sign, it is considered to be positive.

EXAMPLES

SOURCE ITEM	PICTURE	EDITED RESULT
-12345	+99999	-12345
+12345	+99999	+12345
12345	99999+	12345-
12345	99999+	12345+
00000	+99999	+00000
-00000	99999+	00000-

Zero suppression with a *floating plus or minus sign* is specified by placing a plus sign in each leading position to be suppressed; the rightmost character suppressed will be replaced by a plus sign if the source data is positive or has no sign and by a minus sign if the source data is negative. This applies only if *more than one* plus sign is written.

EXAMPLES

SOURCE ITEM	PICTURE	EDITED RESULT
1234	+++99	+1234
0023	+++99	+23
-0023	+++99	-23
0004	+++99	+04
0000	+++++	(BLANK)

CR and DB. The credit and debit symbols CR and DB may appear only as the rightmost two characters of a PICTURE. If the source data moved to such an item is negative, the edited result will contain whichever symbols are written; if the source data is positive or has no sign, the symbols will be replaced by spaces.

EXAMPLES

SOURCE ITEM	PICTURE	EDITED RESULT
1234	9999CR	1234
-1234	9999CR	1234CR
0002	9999DB	0002DB
-0002	ZZZZCR	2CR

The actions of the various types of display sign for positive and negative data are shown in the table of Figure 5.4.

PICTURE Characters	Edited Results if Data Is Positive	Edited Results if Data Is Negative
—	blank	—
+	+	—
CR	2 blanks	CR
DB	2 blanks	DB

Figure 5.4. Summary of the action of the PICTURE clause in handling signs for printing.

* **(asterisk).** The asterisk is used to indicate check protection; as with Z for zero suppression, the number of positions of replacement is controlled by the number of asterisks, and if *only* asterisks (or other suppression characters) are used and the data is zero the edited result will be blank.

EXAMPLES

SOURCE ITEM	PICTURE	EDITED RESULT
1234	**99	1234
0023	**99	**23
0000	**99	**00
0000	****	(BLANK)
0080	**99	**80

0 (zero). The character zero in a PICTURE will cause a zero to be inserted in the corresponding position of the receiving item without loss of characters from the source data.

EXAMPLES

SOURCE ITEM	PICTURE	EDITED RESULT
1234	990099	120034
1234	999900	123400
0012	ZZZZ00	1200

B. The character B in a PICTURE will cause a space (blank) to be inserted in the corresponding position of the receiving item without loss of characters from the source data.

EXAMPLES

SOURCE ITEM	PICTURE	EDITED RESULT
123456	99BBB9999	12 3456
010203	99B99B99	01 02 03
535221583	999B99B9999	535 22 1583

Before closing with an extended set of examples, let us summarize certain information about PICTURE clauses.

The characters allowed in a picture may be classified as follows:

DATA CHARACTERS

X represents an alphanumeric character
9 represents a NUMERIC character
A represents an ALPHABETIC character
(n) represents the number of times a character is repeated

OPERATIONAL SYMBOLS NOT REPRESENTING CHARACTER POSITIONS

S indicates that item may be negative or positive
V assumed decimal point position
P assumed decimal point scaling position

ZERO SUPPRESSION CHARACTERS REPRESENTING NUMERIC CHARACTERS TO BE SUPPRESSED OR REPLACED WHEN ZERO

Z standard suppression (replacement by blanks or spaces)
* check protection (replacement by asterisk)

INSERTION CHARACTERS

$ dollar sign (floating when more than one is written)

, comma
. actual decimal point
B blank or space
0 zero

DISPLAY SIGNS
$\left.\begin{array}{c} + \\ - \\ CR \\ DB \end{array}\right\}$ handled as shown in Figure 5.4

An item can have only one algebraic sign and only one actual or assumed decimal point.

All characters except operational symbols are counted in determining the size of an item from its PICTURE.

Since a numeric literal or an operand in an arithmetic operation may not exceed 18 digits (a restriction that hardly matters in commercial applications), an editing PICTURE should reflect this limitation.

An edited item, at a later time, may become a source item. This would be a rare program requirement, but, if it occurs, we must remember that an edited item more often than not will be alphanumeric in content and therefore not usable in arithmetic operations.

EXAMPLES

The listing in Figure 5.5 shows a number of examples of both nonediting PICTUREs (on the left) and editing PICTUREs (on the right). The Edited Result column shows what the edited field would contain if we had used the verb MOVE to transfer the item on the left to the receiving area.

We may also edit the result of an arithmetic operation, and this is an example of how it would work:

UNIT-PRICE PICTURE 999V99. (Actual content: 00552.)
SOLD-QTY PICTURE 999. (Actual content: 012.)
TOTAL-PRICE PICTURE ZZZ,ZZZ.99.
MULTIPLY UNIT-PRICE BY SOLD-QTY
    GIVING TOTAL-PRICE.

The execution of this instruction would place in TOTAL-PRICE bbbbb66.24 which would then be printed as 66.24.

Notice the leading zeros in the operands: spaces are not allowed in numeric items. Notice also the interaction between the implied (V) and the edit-

	SOURCE AREA		RECEIVING AREA	
PICTURE	SAMPLE DATA		PICTURE	EDITED RESULT
999999	123456	−	$ZZZ,ZZZ.99	$123,456.00
9999V99	123456		$ZZZ,ZZZ.99	$ 1,234.56
9(4)V99	000123		$ZZZ,ZZZ.99	$ 1.23
9(4)V9(2)	000006		$ZZZ,ZZZ.99	$ .06
9999V99	000123		$$$$,$$$.99	$1.23
9999V99	000000		$$$$,$$$.99	$.00
9999V99	000000		$$$$,$$$.$$	
9(6)	102030		$ZZZ,ZZZ.ZZ	$102,030.00
9(6)	000100		$$$$,$99.99	$100.00
9(6)	000008		$$$$,$99.99	$08.00
9999V99	123456		$***,***.99	$**1,234.56
9999V99	000123		$***,***.99	$******1.23
9999V99	000098		$***,***.99	$*******.98
9999V99	000000		$***,***.99	$*******.00
9999V99	000000		$***,***.**	
99999V9	001234		$$$$,$$$.99	$123.40
9999V99	000123		Z,ZZZ.ZZ	1.23
9999V99	000123		Z,ZZZ,ZZZ.ZZ	1.23
9(6)	123456		−999999	123456
S9(6)	123456 −		−9(6)	−123456
S9(6)	000123 −		−9(6)	−000123
S9(6)	000123 −		−−−−−−9	−123
S9(6)	000123 −		9(6)−	000123−
S9(6)	000123 −		Z(6)−	123−
9(6)	123456		+9(6)	+123456
S9(6)	123456 −		+9(6)	−123456
S9(6)	000012 −		+(6)9	−12
9999V99	001234		$*,***.99CR	$***12.34
S9999V99	001234 −		$*,***.99DB	$***12.34DB
S9999V99	001234 −		$$,$$$.99CR	$12.34CR
S9999V99	000000 −		$$,$$$.99CR	$.00CR
S9999V99	000000 −		$$,$$$.ZZCR	
9(6)	001234		ZZZBBB999	1 234
9(6)	123456		9B(4)9(5)	1 23456

Figure 5.5. Examples of nonediting and editing applications of PICTURE clauses.

ing (.) decimal point. Finally, notice that the result field contains a period and is therefore alphanumeric. Consequently a statement like MULTIPLY TOTAL-PRICE BY COMMIS-RATE would be illegal.

REVIEW QUESTIONS

Fill in the "edited result" column in each of the following.

5.6 The VALUE Clause (in FILE SECTION)

The VALUE clause, when used to assign literals to data names, may be used only in WORKING-STORAGE.* It may *not* be used in the FILE SECTION for both technical and logical reasons. As an example of the latter, it would be pointless to as-

* This is discussed in Section 5.11.

	SOURCE AREA		RECEIVING AREA	
	PICTURE	SAMPLE DATA	PICTURE	EDITED RESULT
1.	9(6)	000123	ZZZ,999	
2.	9(6)	000008	ZZZ,999	
3.	9(6)	123456	ZZZ,ZZZ.00	
4.	9999V99	123456	ZZZ,ZZZ.ZZ	
5.	9999V99	001234	$$,$$9.99	
6.	9999V99	000078	$$,$$9.99	
7.	9999V99	000078	$Z,ZZ9.99	
8.	9999V99	000078	$Z,ZZ9.99CR	
9.	S9999V99	045678 (−)	$Z,ZZ9.99CR	
10.	S9(6)	123456 (−)	-999,999	
11.	S9(6)	123456 (+)	-999,999	
12.	S9(6)	123456 (+)	+999,999	
13.	S9(6)	123456 (−)	+999,999	
14.	S9(6)	123456 (−)	----,--9	
15.	S9(6)	123456 (+)	----,--9	
16.	S9(6)	123456 (+)	++++,++9	
17.	9(6)	123456	99B99B99	
18.	9(6)	123456	Z(6)00	
19.	9(6)	000092	Z(6)00	

sign a literal to a data item which is meant to accommodate input data: the actual data that we READ would obviously replace whatever we might previously have entered in that field.

There is, however, one particular VALUE clause —known as the *condition name* VALUE—that may be used in the FILE SECTION.

Condition names were mentioned briefly in Section 3.5, in which we saw that it is possible to give a name to a value or set of values for a variable. The various condition names obviously must somehow be associated with the values for which they stand; this is done with a special level entry.

To establish the correspondence between values of a data name and its condition names, we write an entry for the data name and follow it with as many *level 88* entries as are needed to define the

condition names. Each level 88 entry lists a condition name for the data name and gives the value, set of values, or range of values to be associated with the condition name. The format for a VALUE clause in a condition name entry is shown in the box.

Figurative constants may be used in place of literals, as desired; for instance, consider the example given on page 51. The DATA DIVISION entries for this might be as follows; the 05 level for PAYROLL-PERIOD is, as usual, chosen arbitrarily.

05 PAYROLL-PERIOD; PICTURE 9.

   88 WEEKLY VALUE IS 1.

   88 SEMIMONTHLY VALUE IS 2.

   88 MONTHLY VALUE IS 3.

$$\left[\; ; \left\{ \begin{array}{l} \underline{\text{VALUE IS}} \\ \underline{\text{VALUES ARE}} \end{array} \right\} \text{literal-1} \quad [\underline{\text{THRU}} \text{ literal-2}] \quad [, \text{literal-3} \ \underline{\text{THRU}} \ \text{literal-4} \ldots] \right] .$$

For another, consider the following example, in which the meanings are fairly obvious.

      03 GRADE PICTURE 99.

         88 FIRST VALUE IS 1.

         88 SECOND VALUE IS 2.

         88 THIRD VALUE IS 3.

         88 FOURTH VALUE IS 4.

               .

               .

         88 GRADE-SCHOOL VALUES ARE 1 THRU 6.

         88 JUNIOR-HIGH VALUES ARE 7 THRU 9.

         88 HIGH-SCHOOL VALUES ARE 10 THRU 12.

         88 GRADE-ERROR VALUES ARE 0, 13 THRU 99.

Note in this example that one value may be associated with more than one condition name: the value 1 goes with the condition name FIRST and

is also one of the values of GRADE-SCHOOL. Observe also the use of a condition name to cover all other values of the data name other than the ex-

---

ANSWERS

1.	123	6.	$0.78
2.	008	7.	$ 0.78
3.	123,456.00	8.	$ 0.78
4.	1,234.56	9.	$ 456.78CR
5.	$12.34	10.	-123,456

ANSWERS (Continued)

11.	123,456	16.	+123,456
12.	+123,456	17.	12 34 56
13.	-123,456	18.	12345600
14.	-123,456	19.	9200
15.	123,456		

pected ones: we do not like to assume that all data provided to the data-processing system will be correct.* The PROCEDURE DIVISION which uses these condition names could begin with a check that the value read in was reasonable by use of a statement like IF GRADE-ERROR GO TO PURGE-DATA.

It is worthwhile to note what the object program would do as a result of such a statement. The compiler would set up the object program with instructions to test the actual (object time) data value against zero and against the range of values from 13 to 99; if it were any of these, the transfer to the error routine would be executed.

5.7 The USAGE Clause

This clause is used in machines in which data may be stored in two or more different forms, one of which is more convenient for printing and punching (DISPLAY) and another of which is suitable for arithmetic operations (COMPUTATIONAL).

$$\left[\; ; \text{ USAGE IS } \left\{ \frac{\text{COMPUTATIONAL}}{\text{DISPLAY}} \right\} \right]$$

If the clause is not written, the item is assumed to be DISPLAY. The USAGE clause may be written at any level; if it is written at the group level, it applies to all elementary items within the group.

The USAGE clause specifies only the *dominant* purpose of the data: it does not restrict how the data may be used or what verbs may be used with it. However, this does not mean that it makes no difference whether the clause is written or not; for instance, if a DISPLAY item is used in arithmetic, the object program must convert from DISPLAY form to COMPUTATIONAL form and in many cases reconvert the result back to DISPLAY. *This can waste huge amounts of time in the object program.* Careful consideration of what USAGE clause to use is strongly recommended.

In some computers—very few nowadays—there may be only one form of representation of data, and the clause need not be written at all. On the

other hand, as we said in Section 2.3,* there are computers in which characters may be stored in several forms. For the IBM 360, for instance, there are five USAGE clauses that correspond to an equal number of data representation forms:

USAGE	Representation
DISPLAY	One character per byte
COMPUTATIONAL-3	Packed decimal (also called internal decimal)
COMPUTATIONAL-2	Long precision floating point
COMPUTATIONAL-1	Short precision floating point
COMPUTATIONAL	Binary

We shall ignore the floating point representations because they would seldom be useful in a commercial application. The other three, however, deserve a detailed analysis.

DISPLAY. This USAGE may apply to any data item and is compatible with any PICTURE definition: NUMERIC, alphanumeric, ALPHABETIC, or NUMERIC edited. The DISPLAY form is based on a one-character-per-byte representation: the upper four bits and the lower four bits of a byte are used jointly to represent just *one* character. As shown in Figure 5.6, the character A is represented as follows:

Upper bits	1	1	0	0
Lower bits	0	0	0	1

Notice that the upper bits contain a hexadecimal C and the lower bits, a hexadecimal 1.

What happens if the PICTURE of a DISPLAY item is NUMERIC? In that case the upper bits contain a hexadecimal F, and the lower bits, the hexadecimal value of the corresponding digit. Thus F-1 indicates a 1, F-5 indicates a 5, and so on. Since the upper four bits are sometimes called the "zone" bits, a NUMERIC item in DISPLAY format is also called zoned decimal. (It is also called external decimal, with the obvious purpose of confusing even the best of us.)

From Figure 5.6 it is also possible to realize why, in the EBCDIC data representation, 0-0 and F-F represent, respectively, LOW-VALUE and HIGH-VALUE in the collating sequence—a statement

---

* The option containing THRU and the one showing more than one VALUE for an item are not recognized by some compilers.

* A review of Section 2.3 is recommended at this point, since the discussion on the USAGE clause will complement what we have said there.

Decimal	Hexadecimal	Graphic symbol	Punched Card Code	System/360 8-bit Code
0	00	None	12-0-9-8-1	0000 0000
12	0C	+	12-9-8-4	0000 1100
13	0D	—	12-9-8-5	0000 1101
64	40	Space	No punches	0100 0000
193	C1	A	12-1	1100 0001
194	C2	B	12-2	1100 0010
195	C3	C	12-3	1100 0011
196	C4	D	12-4	1100 0100
197	C5	E	12-5	1100 0101
198	C6	F	12-6	1100 0110
199	C7	G	12-7	1100 0111
200	C8	H	12-8	1100 1000
201	C9	I	12-9	1100 1001
209	D1	J	11-1	1101 0001
210	D2	K	11-2	1101 0010
211	D3	L	11-3	1101 0011
212	D4	M	11-4	1101 0100
213	D5	N	11-5	1101 0101
214	D6	O	11-6	1101 0110
215	D7	P	11-7	1101 0111
216	D8	Q	11-8	1101 1000
217	D9	R	11-9	1101 1001
226	E2	S	0-2	1110 0010
227	E3	T	0-3	1110 0011
228	E4	U	0-4	1110 0100
229	E5	V	0-5	1110 0101
230	E6	W	0-6	1110 0110
231	E7	X	0-7	1110 0111
232	E8	Y	0-8	1110 1000
233	E9	Z	0-9	1110 1001
240	F0	0	0	1111 0000
241	F1	1	1	1111 0001
242	F2	2	2	1111 0010
243	F3	3	3	1111 0011
244	F4	4	4	1111 0100
245	F5	5	5	1111 0101
246	F6	6	6	1111 0110
247	F7	7	7	1111 0111
248	F8	8	8	1111 1000
249	F9	9	9	1111 1001
255	FF		12-11-0-9-8-7	1111 1111

Figure 5.6. EBCDIC representation of 41 selected characters, out of the total of 256.

that we made in a somewhat casual fashion in Section 3.2. And we may see why digits are "greater" than letters: digits have a hexadecimal F in the upper bits. What if the item is a *signed* NUMERIC? The F in the low-order digit is replaced by a minus (hexadecimal D) if the item happens to be negative and by a plus (hexadecimal C) if it is positive.

COMPUTATIONAL-3. This USAGE may be associated only with an item defined as NUMERIC.

COMPUTATIONAL-3 stores the digit in packed decimal format (also known as internal decimal), which means that each byte usually accommodates two digits: one in the upper bits and one in the lower bits. We say "usually" because the lower bits of the low-order byte contain a sign (F for unsigned, C or D for signed items). Consequently the number +7654 would actually require three bytes rather than two:

Byte 3	Byte 2	Byte 1
0-7	6-5	4-C

The USAGE in question is most efficient in arithmetic operations and is recommended whenever an item is used in a number of them.

COMPUTATIONAL. This USAGE, like COMPUTATIONAL-3, may be associated only with an item defined as NUMERIC. The binary representation that is related to this USAGE is efficient from the standpoint of both storage economy and execution of arithmetic operations; for instance, the number 1234 (PICTURE 9999) would take four bytes in storage if USAGE IS DISPLAY, three if USAGE IS COMPUTATIONAL-3, but only two if USAGE IS COMPUTATIONAL.

How is this possible? For those who want to know, here is the explanation. In binary the bits of two bytes would represent the following values:

Byte 2	Byte 1
32768	128*
16384	64*
8192	32
4096	16*
2048	8
1024*	4
512	2*
256	1

Now, if the bits that are marked with an asterisk are "on" and we add up their values, we shall have the pleasant surprise of finding that their sum is equal to 1,234. Imagine now what we could do with eight bytes! What happens if the item is a signed NUMERIC? A negative item has a 1 in the highest bit of the high-order byte.

5.8 The REDEFINES Clause

This clause is used to indicate a memory area that may be referred to by more than one data name. As an elementary example, let us assume that we have records with two different formats in an input file. The first 20 columns—except for column 1, which contains the record type code—are identical. Columns 21 to 40, however, contain an employee name in one type of record; in the other type columns 21 to 30 contain his department name, and columns 31 to 40, the name of his section. The REDEFINES clause would work as follows:

```
01  PERS-RECD.
    02 RECD-TYPE          PICTURE X.
    02 COMMON-INFO        PICTURE X(19).
    02 EMPL-NAME          PICTURE X(20).
    02 EMPL-DEPT-SECT      REDEFINES
                          EMPL-NAME.
       03 EMPL-DEPT       PICTURE X(10).
       03 EMPL-SECT       PICTURE X(10).
```

We could now write, for instance:

```
IF RECD-TYPE EQUAL TO '1',
    MOVE EMPL-NAME TO OUT-1.
IF RECD-TYPE EQUAL TO '2',
    MOVE EMPL-SECT TO OUT-2.
```

The REDEFINES clause may be usefully applied in many circumstances. Other examples are given at the end of this chapter and also in Chapter 8 in connection with the verb EXAMINE and within the context of table searching.

When used in conjunction with other clauses, REDEFINES must precede them all; in other words, it must be the first entry after level number and data name. Thus

```
02 EMPL-WORK-CITY    PICTURE X(20).
02 EMPL-HOME-CITY    REDEFINES
                     EMPL-WORK-CITY
                     PICTURE X(20).
```

is a legal entry, whereas 02 EMPL-HOME-CITY PICTURE X(20) REDEFINES EMPL-WORK-CITY is not allowed.

The REDEFINES clause is subject to several restrictions. Among the most important

—REDEFINES may not be used at the 01 level in the FILE SECTION. If we are faced with a situation that would make redefinition at the 01 level desirable, we may enter multiple-record names at the end of the FD statement (RECORD NAMES ARE RECD-1, RECD-2, RECD-3 . . .); we may then describe their different formats under separate record descriptions, each starting with an 01 level entry.

—The data name that REDEFINES must have the same level number of the data name it REDEFINES, and the redefinition must be entered at the first opportunity.

—A VALUE may not be assigned to an area that is redefined.

5.9 The OCCURS Clause

This clause is used to indicate a series of repeated data items and is widely used in table searching in a manner that is fully illustrated in Chapter 8. However, there are also some elementary applications of this clause, which are shown by the following example.

Let us assume that at the end of each week a card is punched for each workman in a factory. The first 10 columns contain the workman identification number. The remaining 70 columns are divided into seven fields, each containing a number of hours: the first field, let us say, refers to the hours worked on Monday, the second provides the same information for Tuesday, and so on. We may apply the OCCURS clause as follows:

```
01 TIME-RECORD.
   02 IDENTIF-NO PICTURE X(10).
   02 HOURS-WORKED OCCURS 7 TIMES
      PICTURE 9(10).
```

The OCCURS clause has the effect of making out of HOURS-WORKED a "subscriptable" data name. This means that this data name may be followed by an expression in parentheses, called a subscript, that specifies the item of the series we actually want to refer to. In its most elementary form a subscript is just a number in parentheses. Thus the instruction

```
ADD HOURS-WORKED (1)
   TO MONDAYS-TOTAL.
```

would select the first of the seven fields and would add its contents to MONDAYS-TOTAL. The instruction

```
ADD HOURS-WORKED (3)
   TO WEDN-TOTAL.
```

would work in a similar manner for the *third* field.

A subscript may also be represented by a data name, which enables us to use it in a great variety of applications. As we shall see, subscripting is one of the most powerful features in the COBOL language.

5.10   The SYNCHRONIZED and JUSTIFIED Clauses

SYNCHRONIZED.   In machines of fixed word length, when the SYNCHRONIZED clause is not used, successive data items are assigned to successive character positions, regardless of the fact that this may cause one data item to extend across two computer words even when it could fit into one or that one word will contain parts of two or more data items. This results in efficient use of storage, both core and tape, but it can slow the execution of the object program by a considerable amount. The SYNCHRONIZED clause specifies that the elementary item to which it refers should occupy the minimum possible number of computer words and that nothing else should be placed in those computer words.

$$; \text{SYNCHRONIZED} \begin{bmatrix} \underline{\text{LEFT}} \\ \underline{\text{RIGHT}} \end{bmatrix}$$

When SYNCHRONIZED LEFT is used, the first character of the elementary item is placed in the leftmost character position of the *next* word, even though this may require positions at the right of the preceding word to be unused and may leave unused positions at the right of the storage locations for this item. When SYNCHRONIZED RIGHT is used, the last character or digit of this item is stored in the rightmost position of the next word (or group of words, if necessary), even though this may leave unused positions at the left of the word or group of words.

Consider an example. Suppose that a certain record consists of six elementary items as described in the following record description.

```
01 RECORD-1.
    02 A PICTURE 9(4).
    02 B PICTURE 9(4).
    02 C PICTURE 9(5).
    02 D PICTURE 9(4).
    02 E PICTURE 9(2).
    02 F PICTURE 9(5).
```

Now suppose that we are working with a computer in which a word consists of six characters. Schematically these six items would be assigned to four computer words, in which "AAAA" stands for the four characters of the data item named A, etc., as follows:

AAAABB	BBCCCC	CDDDDE	EFFFFF

What has happened? Every computer word contains parts of at least two data items, and three of the items are split across two computer words. The object program can certainly be set up to handle such a situation, but extracting an item from other characters in a word and the "assembly" of an item that runs across two words are *very* time-consuming operations. They may be justified if storage space is the overriding consideration, but it is likely that what is saved in storage space may be more than offset by the loss of time in processing the items.

We can instruct the compiler to assign storage locations so that each item fits in just one word with the SYNCHRONIZED clause.

If we enter the SYNCHRONIZED LEFT clause after each PICTURE clause in our example, the assignment of items to computer words would be changed as follows:

AAAA	BBBB	CCCCC	DDDD	EE	FFFFF

Six computer words are used instead of four, but the object program would be able to operate much more rapidly. The extra character positions at the right end of each word would simply not be used. The PROCEDURE DIVISION statements that we write would be exactly the same whether this were done or not; it is a matter of what the object program does, not what the source programmer writes in the PROCEDURE DIVISION.

If the clause had been SYNCHRONIZED RIGHT, the unused positions would, of course, have been at the left end of each word.

The SYNCHRONIZED clause is always optional and has no meaning in a computer with variable word length. In a fixed word-length machine, however, its use should be carefully considered, especially for an item that is used a great deal in arithmetic operations.

JUSTIFIED.   It can often happen that an item of data to be moved within core storage as the result of a MOVE, an arithmetic verb, or other action is shorter than the storage space assigned to the item. When this occurs, the *normal* action (in the absence of a JUSTIFIED clause) is as follows:

1. Numeric data is positioned according to the assumed decimal point of the data, with any unused positions on the right or left filled with *zeros*.

2. When no decimal point is specified for numeric data, the data is assumed to represent an integer; it is "right justified" with *zero* fill on the left; that is, the rightmost position of the data is stored in the rightmost position of the storage location.

3. For ALPHABETIC or alphanumeric data, the data is "left justified" in the storage positions and the unused positions at the right are filled with *spaces*.

In brief, ALPHABETIC data is justified left and NUMERIC data is justified right unless an assumed decimal point overrides.

If these normal actions are *not* desired, the JUSTIFIED clause can be used to override them; for

example, suppose that NAME has been defined in the DATA DIVISION to have a size of 15 ALPHABETIC characters. If we write MOVE CARD-NAME TO NAME and CARD-NAME happens to be eight characters and contain SMITHSON, NAME will contain

SMITHSONbbbbbbb

On the other hand, if the entry for NAME had read

PICTURE X(15) JUSTIFIED RIGHT.

the result of the MOVE would be

bbbbbbbSMITHSON

This example illustrates the most common application of the JUSTIFIED clause. The trend is to drop the JUSTIFIED LEFT option altogether.

JUSTIFIED and SYNCHRONIZED have a somewhat similar appearance but are not the same. SYNCHRONIZED indicates where to assign the *character positions* for an item within the words of a fixed word-length computer, regardless of how many characters there may turn out to be in an actual piece of data. JUSTIFIED, on the other hand, indicates where to put an *actual* piece of data within the character positions assigned to the data

item, no matter how they might be split across computer words.

REVIEW QUESTIONS

1. True or false:
   a. All of the clauses discussed in this section, when required, must be written in an *entry*, which will have a level number.
   b. SYNCHRONIZED refers to the way *storage space* is assigned, regardless of what data appears in the item when the object program is run; JUSTIFIED refers to how the characters of actual data are positioned within the storage space, no matter how the allotted characters are distributed across computer words.
   c. In a machine with only one form of character representation USAGE has no relevance and need not be written.
   d. An alphanumeric item may contain any character in the computer's character set. No difficulty would result if an item that had been classified as alphanumeric were in fact to contain only digits or only letters.
   e. A VALUE clause as described so far makes it possible to assign condition names to selected data items.
   f. REDEFINES may not be used at the level 01 in the FILE SECTION.
   g. In general, a number in COMPUTATIONAL-3 format occupies less storage than the same number in DISPLAY format.
   h. FD entries do not specify whether a file is to serve as input or output.
   i. An assumed decimal point takes up no space in storage and is therefore not counted in determining the size of an item.

2. Identify the errors in the following FILE SECTION entries:
   a. 02 FIELD-REP PICTURE XXX USAGE COMPUTATIONAL.
   b. NAME-ID-3 PICTURE 99 USAGE DISPLAY.
   c. 01 RECORD-1 PICTURE X(30).
       02 LEFT-R PICTURE X(15).
       02 RIGHT-R PICTURE X(15).
   d. 02 H-TIME HAPPENS 20 TIMES PICTURE 9(5).
   e. 03 ITEM-4 PICTURE X(9).
       03 ITEM-4R PICTURE 9(5) REDEFINES ITEM-4.

3. Is it permissible to use a DISPLAY item with arithmetic verbs?

5.11 The Working-Storage Section

So far we have been discussing the FILE SECTION of the DATA DIVISION. As we shall see, much of the preceding material applies to the WORKING-STORAGE SECTION as well. The FILE SECTION entries reserve in core storage an input area that accommodates the records that we READ, and an output area that holds the records that we WRITE. The entries in the WORKING-STORAGE SECTION, on the other hand, reserve space in core storage to hold such items as these:

1. Numeric and non-numeric literals that remain constant throughout the execution of the program: page headings, arithmetic constants, etc.

2. Data items, literals, and intermediate results that flow in and out of their assigned fields according to specific program instructions: "save" areas for keys, as we have seen in the programs presented in Chapter 4; condition indicators, also called program switches, as we shall see in Chapter 7; partial results of arithmetic operations.

3. Data items that we enter into core storage by means of the verb ACCEPT (when we use READ, the record is stored in the core storage area reserved by the FILE SECTION entries).

4. Entire records that we MOVE TO or READ INTO a WORKING-STORAGE area.

5. Entire records that we prepare in WORKING-STORAGE and then write, using the options WRITE FROM or MOVE TO followed by WRITE. [Incidentally, these options would also be employed to write the page headings mentioned in (1).]

The WORKING-STORAGE SECTION must begin with the section name in column 8 of a separate line. The name must be written exactly, WORKING-STORAGE SECTION: *omission of the hyphen will cause a multitude of error messages to appear during compilation.* All the rules and options that apply to record-description entries apply in the WORKING-STORAGE SECTION as well. A PICTURE clause, for instance, must be included, along with the level number and the data name (or FILLER), for every elementary item.

In WORKING-STORAGE we have two additional features which are illustrated by the following examples:

77 HEADING-1   PICTURE X(10)
                               VALUE 'REPORT ABC'.
77 DISTRICT-ACCUM PICTURE 9(5)V99
                               VALUE ZEROS.
77 SPECIAL-INDIC   PICTURE 9 VALUE 3.

Level number 77 may be used for independent items; an *independent item* is one that is elementary and at the same time is not part of a group item. Level 77 entries must precede all other entries in WORKING-STORAGE.

The VALUE clause, as we have hinted several times earlier, enables us to assign an *initial* value to a WORKING-STORAGE data item. The precise format of this clause is

VALUE IS literal-1.
Note the following:

—The PICTURE and the literal must be compatible: a NUMERIC PICTURE calls for a NUMERIC literal; for an alphanumeric PICTURE the literal must be enclosed in quotation marks.
—The size as indicated by the PICTURE must agree with the size of the literal.
—Figurative constants are allowed, as shown by VALUE ZEROS for DISTRICT-ACCUM.

It should be emphasized that the initial VALUE we assign remains in that location in storage *as long as no instruction disturbs it.* When we place some other value there, the original value is lost and is *not* automatically replaced.

One restriction that applies to the FILE SECTION is no longer binding in the WORKING-STORAGE SECTION: here the REDEFINES clause may be associated with level 01 entries.

5.12 Compatibility Requirements

This is perhaps the proper moment to mention a few general rules concerning the relation be-

---

ANSWERS

1. All are true; review is indicated if there was any doubt about them.
2. a. USAGE COMPUTATIONAL may not be used with an item defined as alphanumeric.
   b. The level number is missing. Otherwise o.k.: a PICTURE 99 may be used with a DISPLAY clause.

ANSWERS (Continued)

   c. The level 01 entry should not have a PICTURE.
   d. The right word is OCCURS, not HAPPENS.
   e. REDEFINES must *precede* PICTURE.

3. Yes. An item in the DISPLAY format, however, is less efficient than one with the COMPUTATIONAL format and in some programs this may slow down the execution speed.

tween the VALUE and PICTURE clauses on one side and some PROCEDURE DIVISION statements on the other.

We have just seen that there is a compatibility requirement between PICTURE and the literal entered after VALUE. The same sort of requirements apply to the relation between a PICTURE and a PROCEDURE literal in conditional and MOVE statements. It is fairly obvious that if we have an ITEM-A with a PICTURE of 999 it would be illegal to say

MOVE SPACES TO ITEM-A

or

MOVE 'ABC' TO ITEM-A.

A few other things are not quite so obvious; for instance the two statements

IF ITEM-A EQUAL TO '2'. . .
IF ITEM-A EQUAL TO 2. . .

are not equivalent: the former should be used when ITEM-A is defined as alphanumeric (PICTURE X), the latter when ITEM-A is defined as NUMERIC (PICTURE 9).

Likewise, MOVE '2' TO ITEM-A is the correct choice if ITEM-A's PICTURE is X, whereas MOVE 2 TO ITEM-A is required if its PICTURE is 9.

However—and this may be the confusing part—these restrictions do *not* apply to group items; namely, items that are combinations of elementary items and, *as a group*, have no PICTURE. A group item MOVE is always regarded as an alphanumeric MOVE. We could therefore say MOVE SPACES TO RECORD-OUT, RECORD-OUT being a group item, even when *all* the elementary items that make it up are defined as NUMERIC.

Similar restrictions and rules apply to MOVE instructions concerning two data items. It is illegal to MOVE an alphanumeric data item (so defined by its PICTURE X) into a NUMERIC data item (so defined by its PICTURE 9), *and vice versa*. In these cases a "class violation" warning would be flagged by most compilers.

We can circumvent most of these restrictions, however, if necessary, by means of the REDEFINES clause, as shown in the following example:

```
02 QUANTITY PICTURE X(5).
02 QUANT-R REDEFINES QUANTITY
      PICTURE 9(5).

02 FIELD-N   PICTURE 9(5).
02 FIELD-X   PICTURE X(5).
```

We could now MOVE FIELD-X TO QUANTITY and MOVE FIELD-N TO QUANT-R without violating any compatibility rule. Likewise, we could MOVE SPACES TO QUANTITY, but not to QUANT-R.

Would a seemingly odd manipulation of this kind be of any practical value? Yes, indeed! And we might elaborate right now on a situation that will present itself in the case study in Chapter 7.

5.13 Validation Routines

An input card, as we know, may contain coding or punching errors. A very common type of error that causes real trouble at execution time is the presence of leading blanks (spaces) in a field that is to be used in arithmetic operations.*

What happens when we READ a card containing such erroneous data? The answer may come as a shock to some readers, but here is the whole truth: irrespective of how we have defined the data item in our record description, the erroneous information will get there! Even if we have used a NUMERIC PICTURE? Yes: a NUMERIC PICTURE does not ensure that the contents of an item will be NUMERIC. (This is the reason why, incidentally, we have used, when dealing with these matters, two distinct expressions: "defined as NUMERIC" and "NUMERIC in contents." Now the reader may appreciate the difference.)

Fortunately, we have some defense at our disposal. In the first place we can use the verb EXAMINE. The full format and story on this verb are given in Chapter 8. For now, all we need to know is that we can write, for QUANTITY and QUANT-R of our example, two statements like

EXAMINE QUANTITY REPLACING LEADING SPACES BY ZEROS.
ADD QUANT-R TO. . . .

The point is that the data name that follows EXAMINE must in this case be defined as alpha-

---

* A space, as we know, is not a numeric character. What happens when the computer is instructed to perform an arithmetic operation with a non-numeric data item? Most compilers would instruct it to stop program execution right in the middle of the run (as some compilers do when an overflow occurs without the protection of the ON SIZE ERROR clause) and write a message to the effect that it is asked to execute an impossible step. Such a situation, as the reader may appreciate, is most awkward, and effort to eliminate its occurrence is well spent.

numeric: since the instruction deals with both SPACES and ZEROS, this is a fairly natural requirement. Then we use the numeric redefinition QUANT-R in our arithmetic statements.

This manipulation will solve the problem of unwanted leading SPACES, but how do we protect ourselves against some other kind of non-NUMERIC information that may exist in the same card field? The answer is very simple: by using the class test IF NOT NUMERIC.

We can finally present an example of a full validation routine in the context of a series of program statements:

```
READ-ROUTINE.
      READ CARD-FILE, AT END . . .
VALIDATION-ROUTINE.
      EXAMINE QUANTITY REPLACING
            LEADING SPACES BY ZEROS.
      IF QUANT-R NOT NUMERIC DISPLAY
            'INPUT ERROR IN RECORD',
            RECORD-NUMBER, GO TO
            READ-ROUTINE.
PROCESS-ROUTINE.
      ADD QUANT-R TO . . .
```

A final comment: the IF NOT NUMERIC test would work correctly with either the numeric or the alphanumeric definition of an item: IF QUANTITY NOT NUMERIC would have served equally well in our example.

A final recommendation: a similarly constructed validation routine should be used with any item that is destined to become an operand in an arithmetic statement. The writing of such a routine will cost only a few minutes of programming time and will save many an embarrassing moment during the execution of a program.

REVIEW QUESTIONS

1. Find the errors, if any, in the following entries:

    a. WORKING STORAGE SECTION.
    b. FILE-SECTION.
    c. 02 ITEM-A PICTURE 999 VALUE '800'.
    d. 02 ITEM-B PICTURE XXX VALUE 800.
    e. 77 ITEM-C PICTURE X(3). VALUE '4LT'.
    f. 03 ITEM-D PICTURE XX VALUE 'ABC'.

2. Suppose we have the following entry in WORKING-STORAGE:

    77 SWITCH-A PICTURE X VALUE ZERO.
    Is it correct to say that
    a. SWITCH-A is an independent item?

    b. At the end of program execution time SWITCH-A will contain a zero?

3. True or false:

    a. If we write the statement ACCEPT ITEM-C, we must have defined ITEM-C in WORKING-STORAGE.
    b. In the WORKING-STORAGE SECTION we may use the REDEFINES clause with level 01 data names, whereas in the FILE SECTION we may not.

4. At the end of Chapter 6 we have inserted the still unseen DIVISIONs of the sample programs 'OVER300' and 'SALES-1'. Look at the DATA DIVISION entries of these two programs, compare them with the PROCEDURE DIVISION entries (shown in Chapters 3 and 4) and reply to the following questions:

    a. In 'OVER300' does the description of PAYROLL-REC indicate that HOURLY-RATE and HOURS-WORKED are punched, respectively, in columns 41 to 45 and 51 to 53 of the input card?
    b. All 77 level entries in WORKING-STORAGE precede the other level entries. Is this optional?
    c. Do the editing PICTUREs contain zero suppress symbols?
    d. Do we obtain the report headings in the same manner in both programs?
    e. Are the sizes of the fields that accommodate arithmetic results compatible with the sizes of the operands?

EXERCISES

*1. Write file descriptions for files with the following characteristics:

    a. Name PAYROLL-MASTER; unblocked records with 758 characters; standard labels in which the file identification (ID) is PAYROLL; the record name is also PAYROLL.
    b. Name PARTS-REQUIREMENTS; 10 records per block; standard labels in which the value of ID is PRTREQ; the records are named PART-REQ.

2. Write file descriptions for files having the following characteristics:

    a. Name DAILY-CHANGES; unblocked records of 80 characters; no labels; record name is CHANGES.
    b. Name STORY; 15 records per block; standard labels in which the value of ID is NAME, the value of CREATION-DATE is the value of an item in the program named TODAYS-DATE, and the value of CONTROL-TOTAL is the value of an item named HAWAII; the records are named PEOPLE.

*3. Write elementary item descriptions at level 02

for the items named, having the characteristics described.

a. SALES; six digits to be used in arithmetic operations; decimal point two places to the left of the right end of item; unsigned.

b. MONTH; two digits to be used in arithmetic and comparison; no decimal places; unsigned.

c. CHANGE; three-place integer to be used in arithmetic; may be positive or negative.

d. NAME; 20 alphabetic characters.

e. UNITS; eight characters which may be letters, digits, or special symbols.

f. RATE; four digits for arithmetic; always positive; decimal point lies two places to left of item (i.e., when used in arithmetic, there will always be two zeros assumed at the left).

g. STATE-CODE; two digits used in printing.

h. HOURLY-RATE; five digits with decimal point between first and second digits (from left); to be stored by itself at the right end of a computer word; used in arithmetic.

i. CITY; 10 letters; to be stored by itself in the minimum number of computer words, with any unused positions at the right.

j. PREVIOUS-PART; a working storage location containing eight letters; to be given an initial value of all blanks.

k. TAX-RATE; a working storage location with five digits and a decimal point at left end of item; to be given an initial value of .15625.

4. Write elementary item descriptions at level 7 for the items named, having the characteristics described.

g. TOTAL-SALES; seven digits; decimal point lies three places to right of right end of item (i.e., three zeros at right are assumed in computations); positive.

h. COUNTER; five-digit positive integer for computation; to be placed at right end of a computer word by itself; to be given the initial value 1.

i. CODE-X; a working storage item of one digit used in comparisons; unsigned; to be given the initial value 4.

*5. A certain file is on punched cards, with each card being a record named NEW-MASTER-RECORD. Columns 1–8 contain the PART-NUMBER, which despite its name ("NUMBER") is alphabetic; columns 9–13 contain a numeric QUANTITY; columns 14–16 contain a numeric CATEGORY; columns 17–32 contain an alphanumeric DESCRIIPTION; columns 33–37 contain a PRICE with three decimal places; columns 38–80 are blank. Write a complete record-description entry.

6. A certain master file contains records named PRICE-RECORD. Positions 1–5 contain a NUMERIC PART-NUMBER; positions 6–11 contain a NUMERIC PRICE with three decimal places; position 12 contains a numeric CODE-A; positions 13–19 contain a NUMERIC YTD-SALES in dollars and cents; positions 20–40 contain an alphanumeric DESCRIPTION; position 41 contains a WHERE-MADE code, which is alphanumeric; position 42 contains a numeric TYPE code distinguishing between raw material, subassembly, and finished good. All NUMERIC items are used for computation and are on the file in COMPUTATIONAL-3 format. Write a complete record-description entry.

*7. Refer to the schematic representation of a record shown. The essential information about each elementary item is as follows:

Level

Level									
01	INVENTORY								
02	PART		YTD-USAGE		DESCRIPTION	CODES			QOH
03	PREFIX	BIN-NUMBER	QTY	DOLLARS		WHERE MADE	MFG. PURCH	HI-LO USAGE	

a. DISTANCE; five-digit integer; always positive; used only in arithmetic verbs.

b. SPEED; four digits; decimal point two places to the right of the right end of the item; always positive; used in processing.

c. FACTOR; six digits with a decimal point in the middle; may be positive or negative; used in arithmetic.

d. CLASSIFICATION; two-place integer used for printing.

e. ADDRESS; 24 digits and/or letters.

f. AVERAGE-USAGE; seven digits with a decimal point between second and third places from right; always positive; used in computation.

PREFIX	2 letters
BIN-NUMBER	4 digits, COMPUTATIONAL-3
QTY	6 digits, COMPUTATIONAL-3
DOLLARS	7 digits with 2 decimal places, COMPUTATIONAL-3
DESCRIPTION	15 alphanumeric characters
WHERE-MADE	1 letter
MFG-PURCH	1 digit, COMPUTATIONAL-3
HI-LO-USAGE	1 digit, COMPUTATIONAL-3
QOH	5 digits, COMPUTATIONAL-3

Write a complete record-description entry.

8. Refer to the schematic representation of a

Level

				PAYROLL						
01										
02	EMPLOYEE		RATE	SEX	SERVICE DATE			YTD			
03	DEPT	MAN			MONTH	DAY	YEAR	GROSS	SS-TAX	WITHHOLDING	PENSION

record shown. The essential information about each elementary item is as follows:

DEPT	2 letters
MAN	5 digits, DISPLAY
RATE	5 digits, 4 decimal places, COMPUTATIONAL
SEX	1 letter
MONTH	2 digits, DISPLAY
DAY	2 digits, DISPLAY
YEAR	2 digits, DISPLAY
GROSS	6 digits, 2 decimal places, COMPUTATIONAL
SS-TAX	3 digits, 2 decimal places, COMPUTATIONAL
WITHHOLDING	6 digits, 2 decimal places, COMPUTATIONAL
PENSION	5 digits, 2 decimal places, COMPUTATIONAL

Write a complete record description.

*9. A tape file named ACCOUNTS-BY-AGE contains records named ACCOUNTS with the following elementary items:

ACCOUNT-NUMBER	5 digits
CATEGORY	1 digit
TOTAL-A	6 digits, 2 decimal places
MONTH	2 digits
DAY	2 digits
YEAR	2 digits
ACCOUNT-LIMIT	6 digits, 2 decimal places

MONTH, DAY, and YEAR are members of a group item named DATE-LAST-PAYMENT.

All of these items are on tape in DISPLAY form and are packed together (no fillers) to conserve tape space. When the tape is read, the item descriptions must reflect the way the information actually appears on tape, but we would not like to process the items so described because it would waste time to make the conversion of NUMERIC items from DISPLAY to COMPUTATIONAL form repeatedly. Therefore we shall set up a working-storage record that describes the items most conveniently for processing and move the items to working storage before beginning the processing. Write a record description for a working-storage record to be named WORK-STORE. (All NUMERIC items should be COMPUTATIONAL.)

ANSWERS

1. a. The hyphen is missing between WORKING and STORAGE. Very costly error at compile time.
   b. There is an incorrect hyphen between FILE and SECTION. Same comment as for a. above.
   c. The PICTURE is NUMERIC, but the literal after VALUE is bounded by quotation marks, hence non-NUMERIC. The correct entry is PICTURE 999   VALUE 800.
   d. Same kind of error: VALUE '800' would be the correct literal with PICTURE XXX.
   e. The period in the middle of the item description is illegal. A period must be entered only at the end.
   f. The size of ITEM-D as indicated by the PICTURE is 2 characters, but the size of the literal is 3!

2. a. Yes.
   b. Not necessarily. At the end of program execution time SWITCH-A will contain a zero only if we have not moved anything else into

ANSWERS (Continued)

SWITCH-A during the execution of the program.

3. a. True.
   b. True.

4. a. Yes.
   b. No, it is mandatory.
   c. Yes, in both programs they contain some Z symbols.
   d. No. In 'OVER300' we set up the heading in WORKING-STORAGE (HEADING-LINE-1 and HEADING-LINE-2), we MOVE them to the DETAIL-LINE (output) record, and then WRITE them. In 'SALES-1' we generate them as PROCEDURE literals.
   e. Well, they are when we can determine the size of the result. In one case, in 'OVER300', where we cannot be absolutely sure, we have used the ON SIZE ERROR option. In 'SALES-1' we have gambled that the sales volume in the company will not exceed $99,999.99. Pretty poor gamble, we may say—or pretty poor company.

10. A tape file named POLICY-MASTER has records named POLICY and elementary items as follows:

POLICY-NUMBER	6 digits
TYPE-A	1 letter
ISSUE-DATE	6 digits
AMOUNT	6 digits, no decimal places
PREMIUM	6 digits, 2 decimal places
PAYMENT-CODE	1 letter
NAME	20 letters
BENEFICIARY	20 letters

Write a complete record description for a working-storage record to facilitate processing, as in Exercise 9.

*11. In each of the five parts of this exercise you are given four source items, a PICTURE clause that describes all of them, and corresponding edited receiving items. For each part write a PICTURE clause for the receiving area that would edit the source items as shown:

a.	99999	12345	12345
		01234	1234
		00123	123
		00012	012

b.	999999	012345	$12345
		000123	$123
		000001	$1
		000000	blank

c.	9999V99	012345	$123.45
		000123	$ 1.23
		000001	$ 0.01
		000000	$ 0.00

d.	9999	1234	+1234
		—	
		0012	−12
		+	
		0004	+4

e.	99999	0000	blank
		01462	1 462
		00192	0 192
		10004	10 004
		98765	98 765

12. Same as Exercise 11.

a.	999	123	123
		123	−123
		—	
		002	−2
		000	0

b.	9999V99	123456	1,234.56
		001234	12.34
		000123	1.23
		000012	0.12

c.	9999	1234	1234.00
		0012	12.00
		0001	1.00
		0000	0.00

d.	999V99	12345	$123.45
		00012	$***.12
		00001	$***.01
		00000	blank

e.	9999	1234	$1234
		0123	$123
		0012	$12
		0001	$01

*13. A record named PRINTER-LINE contains eight items, as described below. Write a record description for this record that will perform the required editing for each item after a MOVE instruction and place the items in printing positions indicated. (Extra

Source Item PICTURE	Receiving Item Name	Printing Positions	Editing Required
99999	CUSTOMER-NUMBER	7–11	Suppress leading zeros
A(20)	CUSTOMER-NAME	16–37	None
99	STATE	44–45	Suppress leading zeros
999	CITY	49–51	Suppress leading zeros
99999	INVOICE-NUMBER	59–60	Suppress leading zeros
99	MONTH	64–65	Suppress leading zeros
99	DAY	68–69	Suppress leading zeros
9999V99	AMOUNT	74–81	Insert decimal point, print dollar sign immediately to left of leftmost digit

space will have to be allowed in each receiving item to provide the blank positions between items when they are printed.)

14. Same as Exercise 13, except that there are only six items and FILLERs should be used to separate them.

Source Item PICTURE	Receiving Item Name	Printing Positions	Editing Required
99999	PAYROLL-NUMBER	1–5	Suppress leading zeros
A(25)	NAME	9–33	None
999V99	GROSS	37–42	Suppress leading zeros, insert decimal point
999V99	NET	46–51	Suppress leading zeros, insert decimal point
999V99	FEDERAL-TAX	55–60	Suppress leading zeros, insert decimal point
99V99	SOCIAL-SECURITY	64–68	Suppress leading zeros, insert decimal point

6. THE ENVIRONMENT AND IDENTIFICATION DIVISIONS

6.1 The ENVIRONMENT DIVISION

The ENVIRONMENT DIVISION, which consists of the CONFIGURATION SECTION and the INPUT-OUTPUT SECTION, involves no real conceptual difficulties in most cases. Furthermore, much of the ENVIRONMENT DIVISION material is left to the discretion of the implementer, so that we have not been able to give the full details for any particular system.

We do, however, present some sample entries from actual programs, and at the end of this chapter we include the ENVIRONMENT and IDENTIFICATION DIVISIONs of the two sample programs 'OVER-$300' and 'SALES-1'.

As with all divisions, the ENVIRONMENT DIVISION must begin with the division name in column 8 of a separate line. On the next line, also in column 8, we begin the CONFIGURATION SECTION, which gives the characteristics of the source computer (the one on which the compilation will be done), the object computer (the one on which the object program will be run), and any special or mnemonic names for hardware items.

EXAMPLES

(1) ENVIRONMENT DIVISION.
    CONFIGURATION SECTION.
    SOURCE-COMPUTER.
        RCA-3301.
    OBJECT-COMPUTER.
        RCA-3301 MEMORY SIZE
        140000 CHARACTERS HSU.
    SPECIAL-NAMES.
        CARD-READER IS
        READER-0100.

(2) ENVIRONMENT DIVISION.
    CONFIGURATION SECTION.
    SOURCE-COMPUTER.
        IBM-360 E30.
    OBJECT-COMPUTER.
        IBM-360 E30.

The SPECIAL-NAMES paragraph may be used to specify mnemonic names for hardware devices, as shown in the first example, or to give names to console switches, as shown in option 3 of the format. This is possible because some computers have two-way switches on their consoles, which may be interrogated by the object program; they are often called *sense switches*. As an example, the programmer might like to use sense switch 3 to determine whether one of his outputs is to go onto the printer or onto tape and to give these choices the names ON-LINE and OFF-LINE, respectively. This could be done with

SENSE-SWITCH-3 ON STATUS IS
        ON-LINE,
    OFF STATUS IS OFF-LINE.

SENSE-SWITCH-3 would have to be the hardware name assigned by the implementer; ON-LINE and OFF-LINE are names invented by the programmer. The same clause could be used to give a different name to the sense switch, if desired.

uation. The RESERVE clause allows the programmer to modify the standard input-output areas allocated by the implementer.

```
Option 1.
        SPECIAL-NAMES. COPY library-name.
Option 2.
        SPECIAL-NAMES. hardware-name-1 IS mnemonic-name-1
                [, hardware-name-2 IS mnemonic-name-2 ...].
Option 3.
        SPECIAL-NAMES. hardware-name-1
                ⎰[IS mnemonic-name-1] [, ON STATUS IS condition-name-1] ⎱
                ⎱                      [, OFF STATUS IS condition-name-2]⎰
        [, hardware-name-2 ...].
```

The FILE-CONTROL paragraph of the IN-PUT-OUTPUT SECTION performs the essential function of assigning files to particular hardware devices. This clause must appear for every file named in the DATA DIVISION; for every file the information about it begins with SELECT and ends with a period. The word OPTIONAL means that an input file may or may not be present. Whenever a file is used both as input and output (usually when information is written onto a tape and then read back), a RENAMING clause may be used with some compilers to indicate that the two files have the same file description. This saves the writing of duplicate file-description entries in the DATA DIVISION. Every file must be assigned to a particular input or output device, using the hardware names specified by the implementer. The integer-1 form is used when the file is on tape and more than one tape unit is to be assigned to it. The FOR MULTIPLE REEL clause is used when there could be more tape reels than there are tape units assigned to the file, which is a frequent sit-

Before discussing the meaning of the ACCESS and KEY clauses, let us look at some examples that show what a FILE-CONTROL paragraph may normally contain:

(1) INPUT-OUTPUT SECTION.
    FILE-CONTROL.
        SELECT FILE-IN ASSIGN TO
            1 RCA-3485 01.
        SELECT MASTER-OUT ASSIGN
            TO 1 RCA-3485 02.

(2) INPUT-OUTPUT SECTION.
    FILE-CONTROL.
        SELECT CARD-IN ASSIGN
            TO 'SYS014' UNIT-RECORD
            2540 R.
        SELECT PRINT-REP ASSIGN
            TO 'SYS013' UNIT-RECORD 1403.
        SELECT FILE-OUT ASSIGN TO
            'SYS007' UTILITY 2400 UNIT.

```
Option 1.
        FILE-CONTROL.  COPY library-name
Option 2.
        FILE-CONTROL.  SELECT [OPTIONAL] file-name-1
        [RENAMING file-name-2]  ASSIGN TO [integer-1]
        hardware-name-1 [, hardware-name-2 ...]
        [FOR MULTIPLE REEL] ⎡, RESERVE ⎰integer-2⎱
                                       ⎱NO      ⎰
        ALTERNATE ⎰AREAS⎱⎤
                  ⎱AREA ⎰⎦[ACCESS MODE IS ⎰SEQUENTIAL⎱ ]
                                          ⎱RANDOM    ⎰
        [Key-specifier KEY is date-name] ...  [SELECT ...].
```

(3)INPUT-OUTPUT SECTION.
    FILE-CONTROL.
        SELECT OLD-MASTER ASSIGN TO
           2 TAPES FOR MULTIPLE REEL.
        SELECT EXCEPTION-REPORT
           ASSIGN TO PRINTER.
        SELECT TRANSACTION ASSIGN
           TO CARD-READER.

Like everything else in the ENVIRONMENT DIVISION, the entries for the ACCESS and KEY clauses may be different for each computer and COBOL compiler. The basic concepts, however, remain the same, and we shall now elaborate on them.

Sequential access, as we already know, means that a file is processed sequentially: in the programming examples that we have presented so far all the records in a file were processed in the order in which they existed in the file. Usually, this order was based on a sorting key that determined the file sequence.

The sequential type of access may be used with any type of device: tapes, card readers, disks, printers, etc. In general, if the ACCESS clause is not written, ACCESS IS SEQUENTIAL is assumed to be the programmer's choice. This is the reason why the sample programs we have presented so far do not include it at all.

Random access, on the other hand, is a technique that can be used only with disks or other direct-access devices. The reason for this limitation will become rather obvious once we go through an oversimplified random-access application.

Let us assume that we have a master inventory file that consists of 20,000 items, numbered from 1 to 20,000, and that we store it on a disk. To make things really simple let us say that this disk contains exactly 20,000 tracks, also numbered 1 to 20,000. When we build up the master file, we store the data for item number 1 on track 1, the data for item number 2 on track 2, and so on.

It is apparent now that if we wanted to update the master file we could use the item number on the transaction record to provide the disk address of the matching master records, thus acquiring the capability of accessing them *directly.*

What we have done so far illustrates one of the requirements in random-access processing: there must be some relation between some data on the record (item number, in our example) and the location of the master record on the direct-access device. In actual applications this relation between the data and the address is not so simple and direct as in our example. Since disks are usually divided into cylinders and tracks, it becomes necessary to perform some arithmetic manipulations on the selected record field to construct the corresponding disk address in terms of *cylinder and track numbers.* Furthermore, as we shall see, there is more than one way in which a master file may be organized for random access and more than one random-access technique.

In any event, we can see that random access would allow us to process a group of transaction records without first sorting them into a predetermined sequence, whereas with tape we are restricted to sequential-file processing techniques. In other words, with tapes the processing must always start at the beginning of the tape; with disks any random-access technique will allow the processing to start at the most convenient disk location: as each record is read, a disk address is obtained or constructed from some field or fields in the record, and the proper master record is speedily accessed by using this address.

To accomplish the above we must inform the compiler of two basic facts:

1. A master file is laid out in such a fashion that it is possible to access a specific record by providing its location on the file. This is accomplished by the clause ACCESS IS RANDOM.

2. That when a transaction record is processed, a specific data name—of a record field or a field in WORKING-STORAGE—is to be used to determine the address of master file records on the device. This is stated in the KEY clause. In our example we would have written something like ACTUAL KEY IS ITEM-NUMBER.

A key type may be defined by other key-specifiers besides ACTUAL. We may have RECORD KEY, SYMBOLIC KEY, NOMINAL KEY, and possibly others. Each of these is related to different file types and organization methods.

The two most important organization methods are referred to by the names of *direct* (conceptually similar to the one described in our example) and *indexed-sequential,* in which the operating system assigns "indexes" to the master records when the file is created. These indexes are then used at program execution time to facilitate locating the records. (In some compilers there is a clause that explicitly mentions these options: ORGANIZATION IS DIRECT and ORGANIZATION IS INDEXED.) In general, ACTUAL KEY is used when the organization is direct, RECORD KEY when it is indexed-sequential.

The I-O-CONTROL part of the INPUT-OUT-PUT SECTION is used to describe a number of unrelated actions. The APPLY clause may be used when there is more than one input-output technique available; the techniques and their meanings would, of course, have to be assigned by the implementer.

EXAMPLES

(1) APPLY 2 BLOCK AREAS USING RECORD AREA FIXED ON LYST-IN.
(2) APPLY END-OF-PAGE TO
FORM-OVERFLOW ON PRINT-REPORT.

In the second example FORM-OVERFLOW is a particular expression recognized by some compilers as indicating the maximum number of lines that can be written on a page. END-OF-PAGE is a programmer-assigned name. This clause would allow the programmer to write in the PROCE-DURE DIVISION a conditional statement like

IF END-OF-PAGE PERFORM
PAGE-HEADING-ROUTINE.

The RERUN clause is very useful in some applications. As we noted briefly in Section 3.6, a *rerun point* is one at which we wish to be able to restart the entire program if there is an unrecoverable machine or operator error or if the program has to be removed for any other reason, such as the arrival of a higher priority job. The main thing to be done at a rerun point is to dump the entire contents of core storage (and all necessary control information) on a tape, which, with the aid of a special restart program, provides enough information to get going again from the point of the dump. The various options available in the RERUN clause are designed simply to give a choice of

where to put the dump and when to do it. Probably the most common technique is to dump storage on the end of each output tape; another frequently used method is to set up one tape to contain nothing but dumps and to provide a rerun point at the end of each input tape. The RERUN clause also allows dumping at the end of every so many records of any file, at the end of a certain time interval (if the computer has some kind of internal clock that can be interrogated by the object program), and when some specified condition (such as a sense switch being turned on) is presented.

The SAME AREA option is used to specify that two or more files are to use the same storage area for processing in a situation in which there are many files, in which there is a shortage of storage space, and in which it can be guaranteed that there will never be records from more than one file in storage at one time. The MULTIPLE FILE TAPE option is used when a single tape reel contains more than one file, which happens occasionally.

6.2 The IDENTIFICATION DIVISION

This short division, which is the first of the four in the completed source program, is *required* to contain only the division name and a program identification; it *may* also contain the author's name, the name of the installation, the date when the program was written, the date it was compiled, the security level of the program, and remarks. The exact format for writing these paragraphs is specified by each implementer.

The four divisions of a source program must be given to the compiler in this order: IDENTIFICATION, ENVIRONMENT, DATA, and PROCEDURE.

As promised earlier, Figure 6.1 and 6.2 show the

```
Option 1.
        I-O-CONTROL.    COPY library-name.
Option 2.
        I-O-CONTROL.    [APPLY input-output technique ON file-name-1 [; APPLY ...]]
    [                            ( (END OF REEL          )            ) ]
    | RERUN [ON {file-name-2   }] EVERY { integer-1 RECORDS } OF file-name-3 |
    |            {hardware-name}        ( integer-2 CLOCK-UNITS           ) |
    [                            ( condition-name        )            ) ]
    [; SAME [RECORD] AREA FOR file-name-4, file-name-5 [, file-name-6] ...]
    [; MULTIPLE FILE TAPE CONTAINS file-name-7 [POSITION integer-3]
        [, file-name-8 [POSITION integer-4] ...] .
```

```
001010  IDENTIFICATION DIVISION.
001020  PROGRAM-ID. 'OV300'.
001030  AUTHOR.              W C BELL   U GARBASSI.
001040  INSTALLATION.   NYU  THE MANAGEMENT INSTITUTE.
001050  REMARKS.      EXERCISE  NO 7  FOR COBOL CLASSES
001060        THIS PROGRAM READS WEEKLY TIME CARDS   AND GENERATES
001070        A LISTING OF EMPLOYEES WHO EARNED MORE THAN 300 DOLLARS.
001080  ENVIRONMENT DIVISION.
001090  CONFIGURATION SECTION.
001100  SOURCE-COMPUTER. IBM-360.
001110  OBJECT-COMPUTER. IBM-360.
001120  INPUT-OUTPUT SECTION.
001130  FILE-CONTROL.
001140        SELECT CARD-FILE ASSIGN TO 'SYS005' UNIT-RECORD 2540R.
001150        SELECT PRINTER-FILE ASSIGN TO 'SYS006' UNIT-RECORD 1403.
001160  DATA DIVISION.
001170  FILE SECTION.
001180  FD   CARD-FILE
001190        RECORDING MODE IS F
001200            LABEL RECORDS ARE OMITTED
001210            DATA RECORD IS PAYROLL-REC.
001220  01   PAYROLL-REC.
001230        02 EMPL-NAME          PICTURE X(30).
001240        02 FILLER             PICTURE X(10).
001250        02 HOURLY-RATE        PICTURE S999V99.
001260        02 FILLER             PICTURE X(5).
001270        02 HOURS-WORKED       PICTURE S99V9.
001280        02 FILLER             PICTURE X(27).
001290  FD   PRINTER-FILE
001300        RECORDING MODE IS F
001310            LABEL RECORDS OMITTED
001320            DATA RECORD DETAIL-LINE.
001330  01   DETAIL-LINE.
001340        02 FILLER             PICTURE X(39).
001350        02 OP-EMPL-NAME       PICTURE X(30).
001360        02 FILLER             PICTURE X(7).
001370        02 OP-WEEKLY-SALARY    PICTURE ZZ,ZZZ.99.
001380        02 FILLER             PICTURE X(48).
001390  WORKING-STORAGE SECTION.
001400  77  WEEKLY-SALARY     PICTURE S99999V99
001410            USAGE IS COMPUTATIONAL-3.
001420  77  LINE-CTR  PICTURE S99   VALUE ZERO
001430            USAGE IS COMPUTATIONAL-3.
001440  77  NUMBER-OF-PEOPLE PICTURE S99999 VALUE ZERO
001450            USAGE IS COMPUTATIONAL-3.
001460  01  HEADING-LINE-1.
001470        02 FILLER             PICTURE X(47)  VALUE SPACES.
001480        02 FILLER             PICTURE X(36)  VALUE
001490            'REPORT ON WEEKLY SALARIES OVER $ 300'.
001500        02 FILLER             PICTURE X(50)  VALUE SPACES.
001510  01  HEADING-LINE-2.
001520        02 FILLER             PICTURE X(43)  VALUE SPACES.
001530        02 FILLER             PICTURE X(4)   VALUE 'NAME'.
001540        02 FILLER             PICTURE X(27)  VALUE SPACES.
001550        02 FILLER             PICTURE X(13)  VALUE 'WEEKLY SALARY'.
001560        02 FILLER             PICTURE X(45)  VALUE SPACES.
001570  01   TOTAL-LINE.
001580        02 FILLER             PICTURE X(28)  VALUE SPACES.
001590        02 FILLER             PICTURE X(46)  VALUE
001600            'NUMBER OF PEOPLE WITH WEEKLY SALARY OVER $ 300'.
001610        02 OP-NO-OF-PEOPLE          PICTURE ZZ,ZZZ9.
001620        02 FILLER             PICTURE X(43)  VALUE SPACES.
```

Figure 6.1. The IDENTIFICATION, ENVIRONMENT, and DATA DIVISIONS for the program of Figure 3.4, which produces a listing of employees with indicated earnings of more than $300.

```
001010 IDENTIFICATION DIVISION.
001020 PROGRAM-ID. 'SALES1'.
001030 AUTHOR. D D MCCRACKEN    U GARBASSI.
001040 REMARKS. THIS PROGRAM UPDATES THE SALES MASTER FILE
001050                PRINTS A MONTHLY SALES REPORT AND
001060                WRITES A TAPE FOR THE INPUT TO THE DISTRICT RUN.
001070 ENVIRONMENT DIVISION.
001080 CONFIGURATION SECTION.
001090 OBJECT-COMPUTER. IBM-360.
001100 SOURCE-COMPUTER. IBM-360.
001110 INPUT-OUTPUT SECTION.
001120 FILE-CONTROL.
001130     SELECT OLD-MASTER    ASSIGN 'SYS011' UTILITY 2400 UNIT.
001140     SELECT NEW-MASTER    ASSIGN 'SYS010' UTILITY 2400 UNIT.
001150     SELECT TRANSACTION
001160         ASSIGN TO 'SYS005' UNIT-RECORD 2540R.
001170     SELECT EXTENDED-TRANSACTION
001180         ASSIGN TO 'SYS004' UNIT-RECORD 2540P.
001190     SELECT REPORT-1  ASSIGN 'SYS006' UNIT-RECORD 1403.
001200 DATA DIVISION.
001210 FILE SECTION.
001220 FD OLD-MASTER
001230     LABEL RECORDS ARE OMITTED
001240     RECORDING MODE IS F
001250         DATA RECORD IS OLD-MAST.
001260 01  OLD-MAST.
001270     02 PRODUCT-NUMBER        PICTURE X(5).
001280     02 UNIT-PRICE            PICTURE 999V99.
001290     02 YTD-SALES             PICTURE 9(5)V99.
001300     02 FILLER             PICTURE X(63).
001310 FD NEW-MASTER
001320     LABEL RECORDS ARE OMITTED
001330     RECORDING MODE IS F
001340         DATA RECORD IS NEW-MAST.
001350 01  NEW-MAST.
001360     02 PRODUCT-NUMBER        PICTURE X(5).
001370     02 UNIT-PRICE            PICTURE 999V99.
001380     02 YTD-SALES             PICTURE 9(5)V99.
001390     02 FILLER             PICTURE X(63).
001400 FD TRANSACTION
001410     LABEL RECORDS ARE OMITTED
001420     RECORDING MODE IS F
001430         DATA RECORD IS TRANS.
001440 01  TRANS.
001450     02 PRODUCT-NUMBER        PICTURE X(5).
001460     02 QUANTITY              PICTURE 999.
001470     02 SALESMAN              PICTURE XX.
001480     02 DISTRICT              PICTURE X.
001490     02 FILLER             PICTURE X(69).
001500 FD EXTENDED-TRANSACTION
001510     LABEL RECORDS ARE OMITTED
001520     RECORDING MODE IS F
001530         DATA RECORD IS EXT.
001540 01  EXT.
001550     02 EXT-PRICE             PICTURE 9(5)V99.
001560     02 SALESMAN              PICTURE XX.
001570     02 DISTRICT              PICTURE X.
001580     02 FILLER             PICTURE X(70).
001590 FD REPORT-1
001600     LABEL RECORDS ARE OMITTED
001610     RECORDING MODE IS F
001620         DATA RECORD IS REP-1.
001630 01  REP-1.
001640     02 FILLER               PICTURE X(5).
001650     02 PRODUCT-NUMBER        PICTURE X(5).
001660     02 FILLER               PICTURE X(5).
001670     02 PRODUCT-TOTAL-FOR-MONTH  PICTURE ZZZZZ.99.
001680     02 FILLER               PICTURE X(5).
001690     02 YTD-SALES            PICTURE ZZZZZ.99.
001700     02 FILLER               PICTURE X(97).
001710 WORKING-STORAGE SECTION.
001720 77 TOTAL-PRICE        PICTURE 9(5)V99   VALUE ZEROES.
001730 77 PRODUCT-TOTAL      PICTURE 9(5)V99    VALUE ZEROES.
001740 77 MONTH-TOTAL        PICTURE 9(5)V99   VALUE ZEROES.
001750 77 SAVE-TRANS-PROD-NO     PICTURE X(5).
```

Figure 6.2. The IDENTIFICATION, ENVIRONMENT, and DATA DIVISIONS for the sales statistics program of Figure 4.7.

114

IDENTIFICATION, ENVIRONMENT, and DATA DIVISIONs for the programs 'OVER 300' and 'SALES 1'.

REVIEW QUESTIONS

1. True or false?
   a. The following is a general outline of the sections and paragraphs of the ENVIRONMENT DIVISION:

      ENVIRONMENT DIVISION.
      CONFIGURATION SECTION.
      SOURCE-COMPUTER. . . .
      OBJECT-COMPUTER. . .
      SPECIAL-NAMES. . .
      INPUT-OUTPUT SECTION.
      FILE-CONTROL. . .
      I-O-CONTROL. . .

   b. In a large majority of cases the source and object computers will be the same machine, but the descriptions here might still be slightly different, for instance, when different amounts of core storage are allowed to the two.

   c. All the formats show an Option 1 that consists of copying information from a "library." This library, which would ordinarily be on magnetic tape or disk, will be set up with all the information that is needed in most programs, making the completion of the ENVIRONMENT DIVISION largely a matter of specifying the file assignments in the FILE-CONTROL paragraph.

   d. Random access is a technique that allows us to process records in a nonsequential manner.

   e. The clause ACCESS IS RANDOM, if present, will be included in the FILE-CONTROL paragraph of the INPUT-OUTPUT SECTION.

   f. A file for which we enter the clause ACCESS IS RANDOM may not be assigned to magnetic tape.

   g. The KEY clause provides a necessary item of information for the processing of records in a random access application.

   h. The four divisions of a source program *must* be present in the order stated, but they obviously need not be written that way. A common way to develop the source program would be as follows: work out most of the DATA DIVISION, write the PROCEDURE DIVISION, and at the same time fill in the rest of the DATA DIVISION (working storage and constants), then do what little is required for the ENVIRONMENT DIVISION and at any convenient moment dash off the IDENTIFICATION DIVISION.

2. The four divisions of a COBOL source program can be ranked in the degree to which they depend on the machine used for the execution of the object program. Match the entries in the two columns.

   a. IDENTIFICATION DIVISION.
   b. ENVIRONMENT DIVISION.
   c. DATA DIVISION.
   d. PROCEDURE DIVISION.

   1. No machine dependence at all.
   2. Slight machine dependence.
   3. Slight-to-moderate machine dependence.
   4. Almost complete machine dependence.

3. Provision for reruns is virtually mandatory in any program that runs longer than an hour and is often wise even for shorter runs. How does dumping core storage guarantee that when the program is restarted such things as working storage and control totals will be returned to the status they had when the program was stopped?

ANSWERS

1. All are true.
2. A-1, B-4, C-3, D-2.
3. Trick question, perhaps. It doesn't guarantee that things will be returned to where they stood at the time the program was stopped, but to their status at the last rerun point before that. With this qualification everything will be exactly as it was when core storage

ANSWERS (Continued)

was dumped, since working storage, control totals, intermediate results, etc., are all contained in core storage. Getting all tapes remounted and repositioned exactly where they were when storage was dumped is another matter requiring careful use of block counters that in effect specify where the tapes were. This is one of the major functions of a *restart program*.

7. CASE STUDY 2: INVENTORY CONTROL

7.1 The Business Situation

Accurate and up-to-date information on the inventory of a concern is important in several ways. The stock of raw materials, subassemblies, and finished goods represents a major investment in most businesses; the interest charges on the capital invested are themselves important. If there is more stock in the stockroom than is needed, money is being tied up unnecessarily. The waste of expensive storage space is costly, too, as are insurance, taxes, and fire protection.

On the other hand, it can obviously be expensive to have too little stock on hand: sales can be lost, shipments delayed, higher shipping charges incurred, and overtime made necessary. The goal of scientific inventory management is to balance the cost of excessive stock against the risk of sometimes running out. The mathematical techniques by which this balance can be achieved are beyond the scope of this book but they produce rules that specify how low each stock item should be allowed to go (the reorder point) before ordering more. Similar analyses govern the amount to be purchased or manufactured (the reorder quantity).

An electronic data-processing system is most commonly employed to keep the day-to-day records of how much of each item is on hand and to carry out some of the routine decision making, such as when to reorder.

As in many data-processing applications, the basic task is almost trivially simple, but the volume of data, the exceptions that must be handled, and the precautions that must be taken to prevent and detect errors make the job much more difficult (and challenging) than the bare problem statement would indicate.

7.2 The Data-Processing Requirements

For each item that is stocked we are given a master file record that contains the following:

1. The key that identifies the item, which we call the *part number*.

2. A short alphanumeric description.

3. The quantity on hand (QOH) the last time the master file was processed.

4. The quantity on order (QOO), which tells how many have been ordered from a vendor or from manufacturing but which have not arrived.

5. The reorder point (RP); if the quantity on hand plus the quantity on order falls below the reorder point, more should be ordered.

6. The reorder quantity (RQ), the amount that should be ordered.

7. The unit in which the quantity is measured—pounds, feet, an actual count, etc.

8. A code that specifies whether this is raw material (code 1) or finished goods (code 2).

9. The price of one unit.

10. The sales of this item so far this year (YTD sales) if it is finished goods.

The master file is in ascending sequence on part number.

Each working day we are required to update this file; that is, we must produce an entirely new master file tape that reflects all the "transactions" that have occurred since the last processing cycle. These transactions will enter the computer on a transaction tape that contains the following six types of transaction (although all six would never occur for any one item in one cycle).

Code 1. An addition; that is, an entirely new record being added to the file for some item not previously stocked.

Code 2. An adjustment; that is, an increase or decrease resulting from a recount, spoilage, or any other cause except a normal transaction of one of the other types.

Code 3. A receipt from manufacturing or from a vendor.

Code 4. An order, which is a notification from purchasing or manufacturing that a previous recommendation to obtain more stock is being acted on.

Code 5. An issue, either to shipping or manufacturing.

Code 6. A deletion; that is, the part number of a record that should no longer be kept in the master file.

All transactions contain a part number and a transaction code; all except a deletion contain a quantity; an addition must contain everything that is to appear in the new master record. These transactions are punched from source documents; the cards are sorted before entry into the computer.

A number of outputs are required.

1. A complete new master file must be produced each day. This will reflect all changes introduced into the preceding day's master file by today's transactions; it will be the input to tomorrow's processing.

2. A listing of all items for which it is recommended that more be manufactured or purchased.

3. A listing of all records deleted from the file.

4. A listing of all items for which issue requests could not be filled because there was not enough stock on hand. This Shortage report will be printed on line, whereas the Order recommendation and the Deletion listings will be written on tape for subsequent printing.

In addition to these formal reports there will be occasional messages to the operator printed on the console typewriter. Since the Shortage report is the only one printed on line, it will be convenient to include in it the error messages originated during the run.

Figure 7.1 is a run diagram of our task.

The handling of the master file here illustrates an important concept in file processing. Suppose that today we use copy A of the master as input to produce a new master which we call copy B. Copy A should never be needed again: copy B is now the input the next time the job is run. Suppose that when the job is next run copy B is destroyed; perhaps it is written over incorrectly, a tape breaks, or the file is lost. These possibilities are unlikely, of course, but if copy A has not been saved they can be almost catastrophic.

With copy A securely in a fireproof safe, however, things are not so bad. We retrieve the transactions from the last time, which must be saved for the purpose, and rerun the job with copy A as input to produce another copy B, after which the normal processing can be continued. Rerunning a complete cycle is inconvenient, certainly, but an inconvenience is better than a complete breakdown in the system.

This technique is almost always used as one of the methods of protecting essential master-file data. Commonly used terminology refers to the technique as the *grandfather* concept: if today's input is the "father" which produces a "son," then the copy saved yesterday for protection is the "grandfather."

7.3 Checking Methods

As we have mentioned several times earlier, these questions of data protection and the methods used to ensure accuracy of processing are of major importance. Consequently, a number of checking routines are usually included in a program for the specific purpose of validating files, records, and selected record fields. In many cases they represent a significant part of the total effort of system design and programming.

As an illustration of the types of things that can

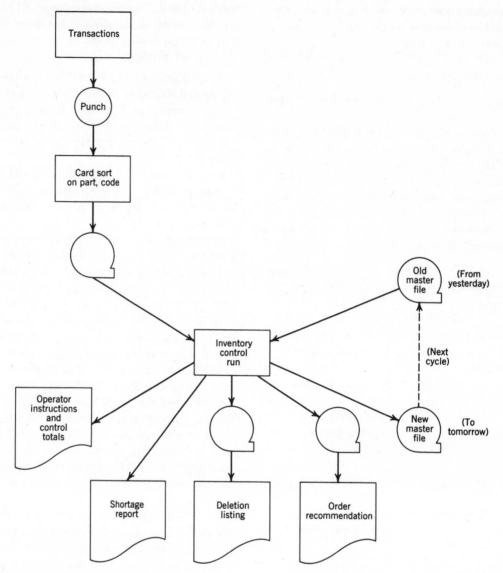

Figure 7.1.   Run diagram of the inventory-control case study.

be built into a program, we use several checking methods in this case study.

One obvious thing to check, as we have already discussed, is that the correct file is being used. One way of dealing with this problem is to let the automatic label checks assess the situation. But what if an installation uses unlabeled tapes? Would we have to give up this important control? Not at all: as we shall see when reviewing the PROCE-DURE DIVISION of the program, we can create a special record at the beginning of the master tape file. This record can then be used to ascertain that we have the right master file mounted at the beginning of the run.

Starting with the right master is obviously pretty

important, but hardly sufficient. We also would like to have some assurance that the processing is done properly and smoothly. To this end we shall include in our program three types of check: a record count verification, a number of transaction plausibility tests, and a series of validating steps on NUMERIC fields.

The record count does not require too much of an effort. As we read the old master, we keep a count of the number of records in it. We also keep a similar count for the new master, as we write it. At the end of the run we verify that the difference between the two totals is justified by the number of additions and deletions that were processed during the run.

This is an example of what we may call a *balancing formula*; writing it as an equation, we have

number of records in new master
= number of records in old master
+ number of addition records
− number of deletion records

This type of check on the accuracy of processing could be made virtually ironclad by doing a similar thing with the control totals of quantity on hand, except that the balancing formula would be a little more complex.*

An example will help to make the scheme clearer and will also suggest some things to keep in mind as we work out the PROCEDURE DIVISION. Figure 7.2 shows some selected fields in three sets

* The formula for this control, which we shall not include in our program, would look like this:

new master control total
= old master control total
+ sum of addition quantities
+ sum of adjustment quantities
+ sum of receipt quantities
− sum of issue quantities
− sum of deletion quantities

The logic of this formula is just the same as that of the record-count formula: the difference between the new and the old control total should be justified by the changes caused by all the transactions. But then we should also make allowance for discrepancies caused by shortages and erroneous negative adjustments.

of sample records belonging to (a) the old master file, (b) the transaction file, and (c) the new master file.

In this example the number of records in the old master is 14. There are four transactions that will modify it: three additions and one deletion. (There *is* another deletion in the transaction file, that for part number 7, but it is an invalid record, since there is no master file record for part number 7. The invalid record is excluded from the checking.) Therefore the number of records in the new master, at the end of the run, should be 16. Any other result would indicate faulty processing.

Figure 7.2 also provides some hints of what will be required in the PROCEDURE DIVISION to handle the transactions properly. One major concern must be with what happens when there are several transactions for one item. The most common example would be a receipt and an issue on the same day. In such a case we clearly want to process the receipt first; otherwise, it might appear that there was not enough stock on hand to fill the issue request; this would happen for part number 8, for instance. Similarly, we want to process an addition before any other kind of transaction to avoid a false indication that the part number of a transaction is wrong, and we want to process a deletion *after* all other transactions for a part number. Adjustments should be processed before everything except an addition. Order acknowledgments are not crucial; they are included in the

A		B				C	
Old Master Records		Transaction Records				New Master Records	
Part Number	Quantity	Part Number	Code	Type	Quantity	Part Number	Quantity
2	10	1	1	(addition)	0	1	25
4	20	1	3	(receipt)	25	2	5
5	30	2	5	(issue)	5	4	35
6	40	4	3	(receipt)	15	5	30
		7	6	(deletion)		6	40
8	50	8	3	(receipt)	60	8	40
10	60	8	5	(issue)	70	10	60
12	70	12	2	(adjust.)	+30	12	100
15	80	15	2	(adjust.)	−40	15	40
16	90	18	1	(addition)	85	16	90
17	100	18	5	(issue)	45	17	100
20	110	20	6	(deletion)	110	18	40
22	120	22	4	(order)	150	22	0
24	130	22	5	(issue)	100	24	130
25	140	22	5	(issue)	60	25	140
		26	1	(addition)	20	26	20

Figure 7.2. Sample files for an inventory-control case study.

decision whether to recommend ordering, but this is not to be done until all transactions for an item have been processed. Therefore the sequence is not important.

Getting the transactions for any part number into proper sequence on the code is a simple matter of making the code a part of the key on which the transaction file is sorted before processing. Since we want this file to be arranged in transaction number order *within* part number, the transaction code must be treated as less significant than the part number in this sorting.*

We are now about ready for the processing of the transaction file against the old master file, but should we process each transaction record without first subjecting it to some plausibility and validity tests? Well, we could—if we wished to waste computer time and produce reports that contain quite a bit of ridiculous information. Both aims, to be sure, are occasionally pursued by some programmers, but this is not a tendency that ought to be encouraged.

In our application sound processing rules would demand that we perform at least the following plausibility checks on a transaction record:

1. If the transaction is an addition, we should *not* have a matching record in the old master file. If we do, we should flag this condition as an error and exclude this record from further processing.

2. In all other cases (deletions, issues, etc.) we *should* find a matching record in the old master. If we do not, we should flag the error condition.

At this point we must recall that a computer would terminate the execution of the program if asked to perform an arithmetic operation with non-numeric data.† Since coding or key-punching mistakes are always possible, we must ensure that several fields in each transaction record contain only valid numeric data. To this end we replace leading spaces with zeros and execute a series of IF NOT NUMERIC tests on these fields, excluding from further processing the faulty records. For good measure we also check whether the contents of some of these fields are compatible with the

transaction type; for instance, in an addition, a negative quantity amount is not logically acceptable, and, if we let it enter our file, we would be opening the door to many erroneous results.

As we shall see, these checks will require a considerable number of instructions in our program. In a more complex system these kinds of check may take up hundreds of instructions. As a general rule, however, the time taken by writing them and the computer time needed to process them are both well spent. They are most likely to save countless hours of subsequent error hunting and computer reruns.

REVIEW QUESTIONS

1. State in words the criterion used to determine if more of a stock item should be ordered.

2. The Reorder Point (RP) and Reorder Quantity (RQ) are given in the master record for each item. How are these numbers obtained? (Cheat.)

3. All we are required to do in this job, basically, is to *update* the master file; that is, modify the previous contents according to the information in the transaction file. Then why write an entirely new file, which forces us to copy the records for items that have no changes?

4. It is stated that the reorder determination will be made after all the transactions for an item have been processed. Why not do it after each transaction?

5. Outline how you would recover if an input master tape were accidentally destroyed.

6. How do the methods described here guarantee that if there are a receipt and an issue for the same item on the same day the receipt will be processed before the issue and why does it matter?

7. We said that we can sort the transaction cards and then transfer them to tape, or sort the transaction records on tape, after having transferred the unsorted cards to tape. Which method would you think is preferable? Could we also sort the cards and read them from the card reader, without using tape at all for the transaction file?

8. True or false?
   a. The number of records in the new master file should always be the same as the number of records in the old master file.
   b. It will be seen later that the master file has a blocking factor of 20; the number of records in the file must therefore always be a multiple of 20; that is, the last block is not allowed to be partly filled.
   c. We have decided that in our program we shall not check whether the quantity field in a transaction record contains numeric information.
   d. If a transaction is a deletion, it hardly matters to check whether we have a matching record in the old master file.

---

* In the case of card sorting this would mean that the first sort pass should be on transaction code. If we use a tape sort (after transferring the unsorted cards to tape), the sorting field priority would be indicated by the order in which we would enter the sort parameters on the control card calling for the tape sort program.

† A review of Section 5.13 may prove useful for a better understanding of what follows.

7.4 The IDENTIFICATION and ENVIRONMENT DIVISIONS

These two divisions are shown in Figure 7.3, to indicate the general contents. The reader is cautioned against taking them too literally, however, since the hardware names will vary with the equipment type and the computer model. In our case 'SYS010', for instance, is a name that is recognized by the operating system of a given computer as identifying a certain tape drive. It may be worthwhile to point out that if we used the same computer but with a different operating system the same type drive could have a different identification, perhaps 'SYS025'. In view of this it should be evident that writing the ENVIRONMENT DIVISION of a COBOL program requires precise guidance from the manufacturer's manuals and the installation's standards group.

7.5 The DATA DIVISION

The DATA DIVISION for this problem, shown in Figure 7.4, is relatively straightforward; it will give a good review of some of the principles in-

volved. The records in the master files should be blocked to save tape time and space. The only question is what the blocking factor should be. We have chosen to put 20 records in a block, but 10, 15 or perhaps 40 might have worked equally well —a point to which we return in Section 9.3. The record descriptions have a simple structure, based on levels 01 and 02 only. We have decided to make the master records equal in length to the transaction records, even though the master records could have been shorter. This will simplify the processing and save us some MOVE instructions in the PROCEDURE DIVISION at the cost of some minor waste in tape and core storage space.

The item length assignments have been made more or less arbitrarily; in some industries four digits might not be enough for the quantity on hand or eight might be too few for the year-to-date sales. Note that the unit price has been set up with four decimals to allow a sufficiently accurate price for inexpensive items that are stocked and sold in large quantities. Note also that the year-to-date sales item has no decimal places: this implies that sales will be kept to the nearest dollar only.

The record and item descriptions for the Shortage

```
001010 IDENTIFICATION DIVISION.
001020 PROGRAM-ID. 'INVUPD'.
001030 AUTHOR.  U GARBASSI.
001040 REMARKS. THIS PROGRAM UPDATES THE SALES MASTER FILE AND
001050            PRINTS A SHORTAGE  REPORT, IN ADDITION TO PREPARING
001060            A REORDER RECOMMENDATION REPORT AND A DELETED ITEM
001070            REPORT ON TAPE FOR SUBSEQUENT PRINTING
001080        THE SHORTAGE REPORT WILL ALSO CONTAIN WARNING MESSAGES
001090            ON TRANSACTIONS WHICH ARE FOUND TO CONTAIN INVALID
001100            OR QUESTIONABLE DATA DURING PROCESSING.
001110 ENVIRONMENT DIVISION.
001120 CONFIGURATION SECTION.
001130 SOURCE-COMPUTER. IBM-360.
001140 OBJECT-COMPUTER. IBM-360.
001150 INPUT-OUTPUT SECTION.
001160 FILE-CONTROL.
001170     SELECT NEW-MASTER   ASSIGN 'SYS010' UTILITY 2400 UNIT.
001180     SELECT OLD-MASTER   ASSIGN 'SYS011' UTILITY 2400 UNIT.
001190     SELECT SHORTAGE-REPORT  ASSIGN TO
001200                        'SYS006' UNIT-RECORD 1403.
001210     SELECT  ORDER-RECOMMENDATION
001220                 ASSIGN 'SYS008' UTILITY 2400 UNIT.
001230     SELECT TRANSACTION-FILE
001240                 ASSIGN TO 'SYS005' UTILITY 2400 UNIT.
001250     SELECT  DELETION-LISTING
001260                 ASSIGN 'SYS009' UTILITY 2400 UNIT.
```

Figure 7.3. IDENTIFICATION and ENVIRONMENT DIVISIONS for the inventory-control case study.

report have two different formats: one to accommodate the basic data on shortages, the other (PO-REC) to accommodate the error messages as well as the record count at the end of the run. The FILLERs are used simply to spread out the printed results, thereby improving the report readability. The record length is 133 characters on the assumption that the printer has 132 printing positions and that an additional character (the leftmost in the record) is required for carriage control purposes; neither assumption is universally true. In any event, there usually would not be any problems—or any advantages—if we set the record length to less than 133 characters.

The instruction WRITE PO-REC AFTER ADVANCING (1, 2, 3, or 0) LINES places a *carriage control* character in the leftmost position of the record to be printed; this character instructs the printer's carriage to advance a specified number of lines, to skip to the next page, etc. It is worth mentioning that it would be an error to MOVE pertinent output information to this first position of the record because it would be *replaced* by the carriage control character and *never printed*.

It will occasionally be useful to know what the meanings of the valid carriage control characters are. In a convention that is nearly universal, a

---

ANSWERS

1. If the quantity on hand plus the quantity on order is less than the reorder point, place an order.

2. These are computed in a separate operation, perhaps using the computer and perhaps done "by hand." The goal in these computations is to balance the cost of storing more than necessary against the cost of running out and to balance the cost of placing many small orders against the cost of storing a large order. This is one of the basic ideas of scientific inventory management and the subject of numerous books. We assume here that these calculations have already been done in setting up the master file and that some other procedure is available to change them in the light of experience.

3. Two reasons, both basic. First, it is not possible to write one block in the middle of a tape without disturbing the block before or the block after (at least not *dependably*). Second, it would be impossible to add new records to the file unless new records were always assigned part numbers that made them fall at the end of the file. A third problem would be data protection: there would be no way to set up a grandfather system. This, however, can be solved by occasionally making a duplicate copy of the file for protection. In fact, all three problems can be solved in a *random access* file medium, such as disk storage, in which we do precisely what the question suggests: alter only the records that have "activity." This technique has been used for many years but is only now beginning to assume major proportions.

4. Because doing so could result in multiple orders: if the first issue caused the QOH plus QOO to fall below the reorder point, then all succeeding issues would also result in orders. If all of them were actually acted on, far too much stock would be ordered, obviously.

5. Retrieve the grandfather tape and the transactions that were used when it was the input and rerun. This amounts to repeating the preceding day's run and produces a new copy of the file that was destroyed.

ANSWERS (Continued)

6. It matters because without this sequence we might get an erroneous indication that there is not enough stock on hand to fill an issue request. It is automatically handled by including the transaction code in the sorting key, which guarantees that for each item receipts will always appear before issues.

7. In general, sorting records on tape is much faster than sorting cards on a sorter, which makes tape sorting preferable. However, in an installation with a limited number of tape drives and plenty of sorters card sorting may be more convenient. Card sorting is also preferable if the error correction method calls for retrieving erroneous cards from the file and for reprocessing them after the invalid data has been corrected. This method, by the way, would be applicable to our inventory control system: we could read the error messages printed during the run, correct the cards, and make a short run to produce a "clean" new master and error-free reports. This way of doing things may be convenient in some applications, expensive and somewhat clumsy in others.

As to the last point raised in the question, we could indeed read the sorted cards from the card reader, but this would slow down the execution of the program to a considerable extent. Therefore this method should be used only during the testing of the program, when a very small number of transactions is read and processed.

8. a. False: additions increase the length of the new master and deletions shorten it.
   b. False: the last block of a file *is* allowed to be partly filled.
   c. False. We shall check not only the quantity field but also all the other fields that are likely to be used in arithmetic operations.
   d. False. It does matter because this error condition suggests that the part number in that deletion has been coded or punched incorrectly. The error message that we shall print will enable the inventory department personnel to investigate the case and take corrective action.

```
001270 DATA DIVISION.
001280 FILE SECTION.
001290 FD  OLD-MASTER
001300.     RECORDING MODE IS F
001305      BLOCK CONTAINS 20 RECORDS
001310      LABEL RECORDS ARE OMITTED
001320      DATA RECORD IS OM.
001330 01  OM.
001340      02 PART               PICTURE X(6).
001350      02 FILLER             PICTURE X(5).
001360      02 DESCRIPTION        PICTURE X(15).
001370      02 QOH                        PICTURE 9(4).
001380      02 QOO                        PICTURE 9(4).
001390      02 RP                         PICTURE 9(4).
001400      02 RQ                         PICTURE 9(4).
001410      02 UNITS                      PICTURE X(4).
001420      02 UNIT-PRICE        PICTURE 9999V9999.
001430      02 YTD-SALES         PICTURE 9(8).
001440      02 CODX              PICTURE 9.
001450      02 FILLER            PICTURE X(11).
001460      02 FIRST-REC-CHECK-DATE    PICTURE 9(6).
001470 FD  NEW-MASTER
001480      LABEL RECORDS ARE OMITTED
001490      RECORDING MODE IS F
001495      BLOCK CONTAINS 20 RECORDS
001500      DATA RECORD IS NM.
001510 01  NM.
001520      02 PART               PICTURE X(6).
001530      02 FILLER             PICTURE X(5).
001540      02 DESCRIPTION        PICTURE X(15).
001550      02 QOH                        PICTURE 9(4).
001560      02 QOO                        PICTURE 9(4).
001570      02 RP                         PICTURE 9(4).
001580      02 RQ                         PICTURE X(4).
001590      02 UNITS                      PICTURE X(4).
001600      02 UNIT-PRICE        PICTURE 9999V9999.
001610      02 YTD-SALES         PICTURE 9(8).
001620      02 CODX              PICTURE 9.
001630      02 FILLER            PICTURE X(11).
001640      02 FIRST-REC-CHECK-DATE    PICTURE 9(6).
001650 FD  TRANSACTION-FILE
001660      RECORDING MODE IS F
001665      BLOCK CONTAINS 20 RECORDS
001670      LABEL RECORDS ARE OMITTED
001680      DATA RECORD IS TRANS.
001690 01  TRANS.
001700      02 PART               PICTURE X(6).
001710      02 TRANS-CODE         PICTURE 9.
001720          88 ADDITION           VALUE 1.
001730          88 ADJUSTMENT         VALUE 2.
001740          88 RECEIPT            VALUE 3.
001750          88 ORDER              VALUE 4.
001760          88 ISSUE              VALUE 5.
001770          88 DELETION           VALUE 6.
001780      02 TN-QUANTITY                 PICTURE S9999.
001790      02 TX-QUANTITY REDEFINES TN-QUANTITY      PICTURE X(4).
001800      02 DESCRIPTION        PICTURE X(15).
001810      02 TN-QOH                       PICTURE 9(4).
001820      02 TX-QOH          REDEFINES TN-QOH        PICTURE X(4).
001830      02 TN-QOO                       PICTURE 9(4).
001840      02 TX-QOO          REDEFINES TN-QOO        PICTURE X(4).
001850      02 TN-RP                        PICTURE 9(4).
001860      02 TX-RP           REDEFINES TN-RP         PICTURE X(4).
```

Figure 7.4. DATA DIVISION for the inventory-control case study.

```
001870          02 TN-RQ                        PICTURE 9(4).
001880          02 TX-RQ          REDEFINES TN-RQ          PICTURE X(4).
001890          02 UNITS                        PICTURE X(4).
001900          02 TN-UNIT-PRICE    PICTURE 9999V9999.
001910          02 TX-UNIT-PRICE          REDEFINES TN-UNIT-PRICE   PICTURE X(8).
001920          02 TN-YTD-SALES     PICTURE 9(8).
001930          02 TX-YTD-SALES     REDEFINES TN-YTD-SALES     PICTURE X(8).
001940          02 CODX             PICTURE 9.
001950          02 FILLER           PICTURE X(17).
001960 FD  SHORTAGE-REPORT
001970     RECORDING MODE IS F
001980     LABEL RECORDS ARE OMITTED
001990     DATA RECORD IS SHORTAGE, PO-REC.
002000 01  SHORTAGE.
002010          02 SO-CARR-CONTR    PICTURE X.
002020          02 PART             PICTURE X(6).
002030          02 FILLER           PICTURE X(5).
002040          02 QUANTITY                 PICTURE ZZZZ.
002050          02 FILLER           PICTURE X(5).
002060          02 QOH                      PICTURE ZZZZ.
002070          02 FILLER           PICTURE X(108).
002080 01  PO-REC.
002090          02 PO-CARR-CONTR    PICTURE X.
002100          02 PO-MESSAGE       PICTURE X(80)   JUSTIFIED RIGHT.
002110          02 FILLER           PICTURE XX.
002120          02 PO-PART          PICTURE X(6).
002130          02 PO-COUNTER       PICTURE ZZ,ZZ9.
002140          02 FILLER           PICTURE X(38).
002150 FD  DELETION-LISTING
002160     RECORDING MODE IS F
002170     LABEL RECORDS ARE OMITTED
002180     DATA RECORD IS DELETION-LINE.
002190 01  DELETION-LINE            PICTURE X(80).
002200 FD  ORDER-RECOMMENDATION
002210     RECORDING MODE IS F
002220     LABEL RECORDS ARE OMITTED
002230     DATA RECORD IS ORDER-REC.
002240 01  ORDER-REC.
002250          02 ORDER-DATA       PICTURE X(80).
002260 WORKING-STORAGE SECTION.
002270 77  MAST-SW                  PICTURE 9     VALUE ZERO.
002280 77  LOTAG                    PICTURE X(6)      VALUE SPACES.
002290 77  W-MAST-TAG               PICTURE X(6)      VALUE SPACES.
002300 77  W-TRANS-TAG              PICTURE X(6)      VALUE SPACES.
002310 77  W-OUT-TAG-SAVE           PICTURE X(6)      VALUE SPACES.
002320 77  W-WARNING                PICTURE X(46)        VALUE
002330          'INVALID OR QUESTIONABLE ENTRY FOR PART NUMBER '.
002340 77  OLD-MAST-COUNTER    PICTURE 9(5)    VALUE ZEROES.
002350 77  NEW-MAST-COUNTER    PICTURE 9(5)    VALUE ZEROES.
002360 77  TRANS-COUNTER       PICTURE 9(5)    VALUE ZEROES.
002370 77  DELET-COUNTER       PICTURE 9(5)    VALUE ZEROES.
002380 77  ADDIT-COUNTER       PICTURE 9(5)    VALUE ZEROES.
002390 77  ERROR-COUNTER       PICTURE 9(5)    VALUE ZEROES.
002400 77  NEGAT-CHECK         PICTURE S9(10)  VALUE ZERO.
002410 77  QOH-QOO             PICTURE 9(5)    VALUE ZERO.
002420 01  DATES.
002430          02 YESTERDAY-DATE            PICTURE 9(6).
002440          02 TODAY-DATE                PICTURE 9(6).
002450 01  REPORT-HEADING.
002460          02 FILLER           PICTURE X(35)            VALUE
002470          ' PART          DESCRIPTION   QOH QOO '.
002480          02 FILLER           PICTURE X(37)            VALUE
002490               'RP  RQ UNIT UN-PRIC YTD-SALX RP-DATE '.
002500          02 H-REP-DATE       PICTURE 99B99B99.
```

Figure 7.4. *(Continued)*

blank specifies normal single spacing, a *zero* specifies double spacing, and a *one* calls for skipping to the top of the next page—or, more precisely, to the position designated for printing the first line, which is ordinarily a few lines down from the top. It is sometimes convenient to control spacing by placing the appropriate carriage control character directly in the output area rather than by using the AFTER ADVANCING option. On the other hand, the unintentional placement of output values in this position can lead to undesirable results, such as printing only one line on each page. This creates quite a scene at the printer as the paper spews out at many feet per second, an entertainment that every programmer should experience—once, as the result of somebody else's mistake.

Note that the use of a FILLER clause does *not* insert spaces in a record when the object program is run but merely allows room between the items. The insertion of spaces must be done explicitly in the PROCEDURE DIVISION. Note also the use of editing PICTUREs for QUANTITY, QOH, and PO-COUNTER to make these numbers a bit easier to interpret.

For simplicity's sake the records in the deletion listing and the order recommendation report are set to contain unmodified master records to be written on tapes. The assumption is that these tapes will subsequently be printed off-line (using either a standard print-program or a tailor-made one) and that report readability may be overlooked at this point.

The transaction file can contain rather different kinds of record: there may be only a part number and a code, as in a deletion; most records also have a quantity; an addition record has all the items in a master record. The file could have been set up with three different kinds of record, but we preferred to set it up with just one kind of item layout, leaving some of the items blank when they are not used. The transactions come in on cards. After the cards are transcribed to tape, we assume that all records are left 80 characters long—although in some cases it would be possible and desirable to condense them somewhat. The volume of transactions would not ordinarily be great enough, however, to make this an important consideration.

As to the WORKING-STORAGE SECTION, about the only new concept illustrated here is the making of the two dates into a record so that they can be read in from one card with an ACCEPT. Most of the level 77 entries have VALUE clauses to start them off with the desired values without having to write MOVE verbs to do the same thing. Note that NEGAT-CHECK is set up with an S ("signed") as the first character of its PICTURE; this can be a negative number. (TN-QUANTITY in the transaction record was signed for the same reason.) The two dates do not contain VALUE clauses because something is placed in them by an ACCEPT instruction before their contents are used.

REVIEW QUESTIONS

1. Is it *required* that the DATA DIVISION and FILE SECTION headers be on separate lines, as shown in Figure 7.4?

2. In describing the two data records in SHORTAGE-REPORT, could we have said 01 PO-REC REDEFINES SHORTAGE?

3. Is it essential that a file name such as OLD-MASTER be distinct from the name of the records in the file such as OM?

4. State exactly what information is conveyed to the compiler by the clause PICTURE IS 9999V9999.

5. What is a level 88 entry called and what does it do?

6. In the record description for SHORTAGE, QUANTITY and QOH have PICTUREs of ZZZZ. What should the PICTURE clause be if we wanted this quantity to be printed with leading zeros suppressed but with one zero printed if the quantity is zero?

7. WORKING-STORAGE contains two items, under DATES, that are organized as a record. Why was this done and would it make any difference if this record entry were written before the level 77 entries?

8. By examining the blocking factors and the record length for each file, determine how many positions in core storage will be reserved to the input/output areas.

7.6 The PROCEDURE DIVISION

This job is sufficiently complex—as indeed most data-processing tasks are—to make it desirable to start the analysis of what the PROCEDURE DIVISION must do by drawing a flow chart.

Figure 7.5 shows the main outlines of the program flow.

A few comments on the date-checking method might be in order before we pass on to discuss the particular file-processing technique used in this program. As we mentioned in Section 7.3, a special

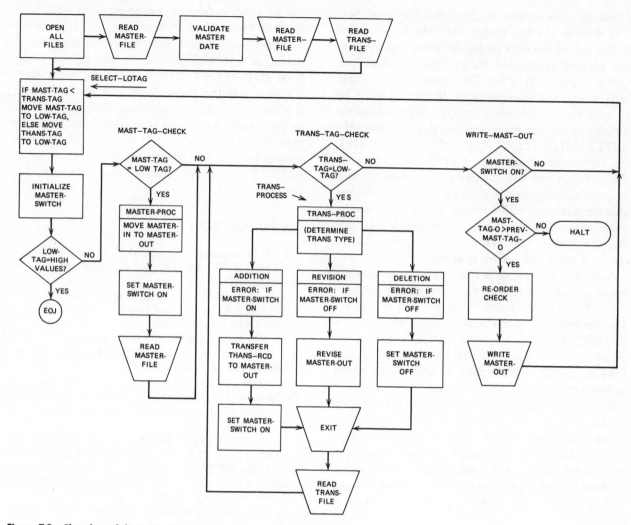

Figure 7.5. Flow chart of the main processing logic of the inventory-control case study.

ANSWERS

1. Yes.

2. No. The REDEFINES clause is not allowed at the 01 level in the FILE SECTION.

3. Absolutely.

4. The length is eight digits; the class is NUMERIC; there is an assumed decimal point in the middle of the item; the item has no sign. (A COMPUTATIONAL USAGE is *not* implied; if this is necessary, it must be stated explicitly.)

5. A condition name entry; in conjunction with PROCEDURE DIVISION statements it generates instructions to test the item for which the condition names are given against the values written in the condition entries.

6. PICTURE ZZZ9.

ANSWERS (Continued)

7. It was done because we want to get *two* dates with *one* ACCEPT, and ACCEPT permits only one data name to be written; all level 77 entries *must* be written *first*.

8. The three input files all have a blocking factor of 20 and a record length of 80. Thus for the input area we have $1600 \times 3 = 4800$. The output files are all unblocked, with record lengths of 133, 80, and 80. The total number of positions for both the input and output areas is therefore 5093. We must remember, however, that in most cases buffering will double this figure. Even so, this is probably not an excessive amount of core storage to tie up for this purpose, although it would strain the capacity of some of the smaller computers.

record at the beginning of the master file, in the absence of label checking, can help us to ascertain that we have the correct tape. This method is quite simple: every time we create a new master we place TODAY-DATE into its first record (in the field FIRST-REC-CHECK-DATE, which was set up for this purpose). The next day, when this file becomes the old master, we check this field against YES-TERDAY-DATE. If they agree, we continue; otherwise, we print a message and stop the run.

Both DATES are accepted as a single entry from the console: a two-line DISPLAY message instructs the operator to enter these dates and makes the computer pause until a "continue" key is depressed. Notice that all this must be done *after* we open the files because the first records of both the input and output master must be available to our checking routine. We then complete our housekeeping by writing the headings for the output reports.

We are now ready for the processing of the files, which, in this program, is done according to a technique called *balance line.**

The balance line is a standardized file processing method that can be usefully applied to master-file updating and other applications—such as merging and matching—that require the coordinated processing of two or more sequenced files.

The processing of sequenced files is not new to us. In our case study in Chapter 4, for instance, SALES-1, we had a year-to-date tape that we updated according to the contents of a transaction file, both files being in ascending sequence on product number. That application, however, was somewhat less complete than the one we have here, which includes the processing of addition and deletion records. Furthermore, we want to do some checking here to make sure that the contents of transactions are consistent with what is found in the master.

The balance-line technique will simplify the work of devising the program to do all these things.

An important concept in the balance-line method is that of the *tag*. In one sense tag is just a synonym for what we have previously called the key: the field or combination of fields on which a file is sequenced. We introduce the new terminology partly because it is customary in circles that use the balance-line technique and because we are expanding the concept slightly.

* This programming technique was devised several years ago by Melvin H. Grosz of Esso Mathematics and Systems, Inc. Since then, it has grown in popularity and has been successfully adopted by other installations.

In particular, the tag idea is used to describe certain relationships between transaction and master records as they come into the computer from tape. At any given moment during the execution of the program there will be several input records in core storage, at least one from each file. In deciding what to do next it is almost always essential to know whether the tag (key) of the transaction record is less than, equal to, or greater than that of the master record. In the balance-line method much of the logic of the sequence of processing records is simplified by having available the tag that is the lowest (in the file sequence sense) of all those currently in core storage. This tag is called the *low tag*. Part of the processing task, of course, is to make sure, as new records are read and old ones disposed of, that the field holding the low tag (called LOTAG in our program) actually does contain the correct tag.

(In out application there is only one transaction file. The balance-line technique will be useful enough even here, but it really comes into its own when there are many transaction files. Without the balance line or some similar technique the logic of record processing then becomes extremely complicated.)

Another essential feature of the balance-line technique is a program switch (MAST-SW in our program) that indicates whether or not we currently have in core storage the master record corresponding to the tag in LOTAG. Every time we place a new tag in LOTAG, MAST-SW is set to zero ("off"); it is set to one ("on") whenever (a) we find the master record with the same tag as LOTAG or (b) we find that the transaction record is an addition.

Let us now follow, in Figure 7.5, the main flow of a generalized balance-line program with two input files (transaction and old master) and one output file (new master). The entries outside some of the boxes are paragraph names used in the program and may be ignored for the moment.

After opening all files, checking the dates, and reading a master record and a transaction record we place a value in LOTAG. This value is the tag of the master record if it is less than the tag of the transaction record; otherwise it is the tag of the transaction record. Note carefully that if the transaction and master records have the *same* tag we still place a value in LOTAG; since they are equal, it is of no importance *which one* goes in LOTAG, but it is very important indeed to realize that "LO-TAG" in that case still has a value. Perhaps the name ought to be LO-OR-EQUAL-TAG, except that that is a mouthful.

Next the master switch is initialized to the off position for the time being, which may seem like a contradiction of the definition given above, since in some cases we shall indeed have in core storage a master record whose tag is equal to LOTAG. This problem is only a temporary one, however, which will be resolved correctly very shortly, with no damage having been done.

The test of LOTAG against HIGH-VALUES determines whether the job is finished. Since on reaching the end of a file we place HIGH-VALUES in its tag, LOTAG will be equal to HIGH-VALUES when both files have reached the end. Then we could go to the end of job routine.

Now, if the master tag is equal to LOTAG, we either have a situation in which there is a master with no matching transaction, which master should be written out unchanged, or a situation in which there is a master with transactions to be processed against it. Either way, unless the transaction turns out to be a deletion (a possibility we handle explicitly later), this master will have eventually to be written out. We accordingly move this master record to the output area, from which—perhaps after further processing—it can be written out, set the master switch on to indicate that we have a master record waiting in the output area, and read another master record. This new master record will not be disturbed for a while, but it will be ready for use when the master in MASTER-OUT has been processed. Now we go on to see whether the transaction tag is equal to LOTAG. Before proceeding, however, we might note that if master tag is *not* equal to LOTAG and there are no file or data errors the only legitimate explanation is that we have a transaction record that is an addition, which will create a new master record. Note that when this happens we go through the portion of the flow chart that deals with transaction processing with MAST-SW *off*.

Next we reach the test whether the transaction tag is equal to LOTAG. If by following the possible paths so far discussed it is not, it means that we have a master record for which there were no transactions and which should now be written out unchanged. If the transaction is equal to LOTAG we now decide what kind of transaction it is.

If it is an addition, the master switch had better be off: the transaction tag ought to be higher than the master tag, so we should not have gone through the path where the master switch was turned on. Assuming no errors, we transfer the addition record to the master out area, set the master switch on to signal the presence of a master to be written out, and exit from this section.

If the transaction is a revision (i.e., an issue, a receipt, an adjustment, or an order acknowledgment), we check to be sure that the master switch is on, do the appropriate revision of the record in the master-out area if so, and exit.

If the transaction is a deletion, we should find the master switch on; we turn it off and exit, which is all that has to be done. Why is it so simple? A deletion is a transaction with the same tag as a master, so that both master and transaction are equal to LOTAG. We had already moved that master to the output area and set the master switch on, but if, in fact, the master is *not* to be written to the new output master file because this record is to be deleted all we have to do is signal that we do *not* have a master to be written. This signal is given simply by turning MAST-SW off.

In all cases, after processing the transaction record, we read another record to be ready for subsequent processing. In some cases this will get us another transaction for the same master we have already been dealing with, so we want to go back through TRANS-PROCESS; this fact will be signaled if the new transaction tag is still equal to LOTAG. Bear in mind that at this instant LOTAG has *not* been altered. If they are not equal, it means the new transaction we just read had a different part number, and we go to the section that deals with the master record now in MASTER-OUT.

Now when we reach the test whether the master switch is on or not, the answer will be "yes" with the one exception of a deletion transaction. All possible work on the master record now being complete, we can check for a sequence error, do the reorder calculation and write out an order recommendation if needed, and finally write the record in MASTER-OUT (NM in our program) onto the new master.

Where do we stand at this point? There are several possibilities to be considered:

—We have just written out a master record for which there was no activity, that is, no matching transactions. The transaction record in the input area has not been dealt with, but we have read a new master.

—We have just written out a master for which

there was activity; we have already read a new master and a new transaction.

—We have just written out a master which came from the transaction file, being an addition record. We have already read a new transaction, and the preceding master record is still waiting to be dealt with.

—We have just skipped past the master-writing routine because the transaction was a deletion. A new master and a new transaction have already been read.

In all cases, therefore, we have a master and a transaction waiting to be processed. We can accordingly go back to determine which tag is LO-TAG and go around again. We don't know, at this point, whether MAST-SW is on or off, but it doesn't matter, since in any case we want it turned off, which will be done as we again initialize it.

To make this logic as clear as possible it may be helpful to go through a simple illustration. Suppose we have an updating job with records that consist only of a product number and a year-to-date dollar sales amount. The transaction records may consist of additions, deletions, and updates. For the purpose of this illustration suppose the master contains the following three records:

Product number	$ Sales
128	280
156	210
175	45

Against this file we want to process three transactions:

Product number	$ Sales
132	25
156	35
181	55

Let us follow the processing of these transactions through the balance-line logic.

After opening the files we read a record from the master and one from the transaction, placing their tags in two WORKING-STORAGE areas that we shall call W-MAST-TAG and W-TRANS-TAG. At this point W-MAST-TAG contains 128 and W-TRANS-TAG contains 132.

The comparison of these two tags will place the master's tag, 128, into LOTAG. Since W-MAST-TAG is then equal to LOTAG, the master leg will be executed: the master in the input area is moved to the output master area (MAST-OUT), the mas-

ter switch is set on, the next master record is read into the input master area, and its tag (156) is moved to W-MAST-TAG.

We now check whether W-TRANS-TAG is equal to LOTAG. Since it is not, the transaction leg is bypassed and we go to WRITE-MAST-OUT. The master switch is on, and we write the waiting master record from MAST-OUT; this is the master for product number 128, with its sales of $280. In short, the old master record, for which there was no transaction activity, has been written out to the new master unchanged.

Now the logic sends us back to SELECT-LO-TAG, where we find that W-MAST-TAG contains 156, whereas W-TRANS-TAG still has 132. The latter therefore goes to LOTAG. The master switch is again turned off. The master leg this time is bypassed, since W-MAST-TAG is not equal to LO-TAG, but W-TRANS-TAG is equal to LOTAG and the transaction leg is executed. We assume that the record contains a code to indicate that this transaction is an addition, with no matching master, which is also implicit in the fact that the master switch is off. The transaction record is moved to MAST-OUT, since it is now to become a new master record. The master switch is turned on, the next transaction is read, and its tag (156) moved to W-TRANS-TAG. Now we go to WRITE-MAST-OUT: the master switch is on and we write the (addition) record that we have just moved to MAST-OUT. Thus we have added a new record to the master file.

Back we go to SELECT-LOTAG. Both W-MAST-TAG and W-TRANS-TAG are presently equal to 156, which means that 156 is moved to LOTAG and that both the master leg and the transaction leg are executed. The master for product 156, with its sales of $210, is moved to MAST-OUT, the master switch is set on, the next master is read, and its tag (175) is moved to W-MAST-TAG. In the transaction leg we find that the master switch is on, meaning that a matching master is awaiting revision. At this point an instruction like ADD TRANS-DOLLARS TO MAST-OUT-DOLLARS will add $35 to $210. The next transaction is read and its tag (181) is moved to W-TRANS-TAG. We now go to WRITE-MAST-OUT, where we write the record in MAST-OUT; this is the one we have just updated. Thus we have written out a revised master record onto the new output file.

Back to SELECT-LOTAG. This time W-MAST-TAG (175) is lower than W-TRANS-TAG (181) and therefore 175 is moved to LOTAG. The master leg is executed: the old master is moved to MAST-OUT, the master switch is turned on, and an attempt is made to read another master. At this point the end of the master file has been reached, which causes HIGH-VALUES to be moved to W-MAST-TAG. The transaction leg is bypassed, since W-TRANS-TAG (181) is not equal to LOTAG (175). The master for 175 is written out unchanged onto the new master.

Back to SELECT-LOTAG. W-MAST-TAG now contains HIGH-VALUES, so W-TRANS-TAG (181) is moved to LOTAG. The master leg is therefore bypassed, but the transaction leg is executed. We find that this is another addition record; the master switch is turned on, and we attempt to read another transaction. The end of the file has been reached, however, and HIGH-VALUES are moved to W-TRANS-TAG. The new master record for product 181 is written onto the new master file.

Now when we go to SELECT-LOTAG both W-TRANS-TAG and W-MAST-TAG contain HIGH-VALUES, and that is what is moved to LOTAG. This signals the end of the job, so we CLOSE all files.

The reader may wish to devise other combinations of master and transaction records to satisfy himself that various other conditions would be properly handled:

—The last master has a tag higher than the last transaction.

—The last transaction calls for deletion of the last master.

—Multiple transactions for one master.

—An addition immediately followed by revisions for the same record.

—Two successive masters with no matching transaction.

These various kinds of special situation should always be checked carefully in any file-processing system.

We now turn to the consideration of the PROCEDURE DIVISION of our program in Figure 7.6. We have omitted flow charts for the detailed operations of processing each of the transaction types, since the processing is not logically complex.

The READ-MAST-RTN and READ-TRANS-RTN segments have similar structures. We move the tags to WORKING-STORAGE, as we did for

the Sales program in Chapter 4 and for the same reason that we explained in Section 4.3. The EXIT allows us to PERFORM this routine up to the end of the file: at the end we place HIGH-VALUES in the tag and go to the EXIT, thus leaving the HIGH-VALUES undisturbed.* The file that is first to reach the end will not be read again (as indeed it must not be), since its tag will never again be the lower of the two. When both tags contain HIGH-VALUES, we go to the end of the job (EOJ-RTN).

SELECT-LOTAG, MAST-TAG-CHECK, and TRANS-TAG-CHECK—three of the key routines in the balance line method—have already been explained. Notice the very powerful statements that are packed in TRANS-TAG-CHECK: almost half the main logic of the program is right there!

Let us now go through the transaction leg, which, from TRANS-PROCESS to TRANS-LEG-EXIT, contains 10 paragraphs. In TRANS-PROCESS we merely edit the numeric fields of the transaction record and bypass, printing an error message, those records that contain non-numeric or implausible data. This is in accordance with what we proposed to do in Section 7.3. We then inspect the transaction code and go to the appropriate paragraph. If the code is not legitimate, an error message is printed and that transaction is bypassed.

The ADDITION-ROUTINE and the DELETION-ROUTINE do not do anything more than what they are expected to do in a balance-line program. Notice that we print an error message if an addition has a matching master or if a deletion has not: the latter applies to all the remaining transaction types.

The ADJUSTMENT-ROUTINE contains a few twists. Let us ignore for the moment the two conditional sentences 003420 and 003430 (there is a review question on them), but what about NEGAT-CHECK in the sentences that follow? Very simple: we do not want to accept a negative TN-QUANTITY, which, because of an error, is greater in absolute value than QOH in the master. This would result in an erroneous QOH in the new master.† Thus sentences 003440 through 003470 are there to

---

* The use of the format PERFORM P-name THRU P-name-EXIT and the verb EXIT is fully explained in Section 8.5.

† Since QOH is defined as $9(4)$ (unsigned), it can never contain a negative value. In this instance it would contain the absolute value of QOH + TN-QUANTITY. Thus, if TN-QUANTITY were -70 and QOH were 20, the result in QOH would be 50.

```
002510 PROCEDURE DIVISION.
002520 START-RTN.
002530     OPEN INPUT OLD-MASTER  TRANSACTION-FILE
002540         OUTPUT  NEW-MASTER SHORTAGE-REPORT  DELETION-LISTING
002550             ORDER-RECOMMENDATION.
002560     PERFORM READ-MAST-RTN THRU READ-MAST-EXIT.
002570     DISPLAY 'ENTER YESTERDAY AND TODAY DATES AS IN' UPON CONSOLE.
002580     DISPLAY 'THE FOLLOWING EXAMPLE 062269062369' UPON CONSOLE.
002590     ACCEPT DATES  FROM CONSOLE.
002600     IF FIRST-REC-CHECK-DATE IN OM NOT EQUAL TO YESTERDAY-DATE
002610         DISPLAY 'WRONG INPUT MASTER' UPON CONSOLE GO TO EOJ-RTN.
002620     MOVE SPACES TO NM.
002630     MOVE TODAY-DATE TO FIRST-REC-CHECK-DATE IN NM, H-REP-DATE.
002640     WRITE NM.
002650     MOVE SPACES TO W-MAST-TAG.
002660     MOVE ZEROES TO OLD-MAST-COUNTER.
002670     MOVE SPACES TO SHORTAGE  DELETION-LINE  ORDER-REC NM.
002680     MOVE '    ORDER RECOMMENDATION REPORT' TO ORDER-REC.
002690     WRITE ORDER-REC.
002700     MOVE '  DELETION REPORT' TO DELETION-LINE.
002710     WRITE DELETION-LINE.
002720     MOVE REPORT-HEADING TO DELETION-LINE, ORDER-REC.
002730     WRITE ORDER-REC.
002740     WRITE DELETION-LINE.
002750     MOVE '  SHORTAGE AND QUESTIONABLE TRANSACTIONS REPORT' TO
002760         SHORTAGE.
002770     WRITE SHORTAGE AFTER ADVANCING 0.
002780     MOVE ' PART        Q-ORD      QOH' TO SHORTAGE.
002790     WRITE SHORTAGE AFTER ADVANCING 1.
002800 READ-MAST-RTN.
002810     READ OLD-MASTER AT END MOVE HIGH-VALUES TO W-MAST-TAG
002820         GO TO READ-MAST-EXIT.
002830     MOVE PART IN OM TO W-MAST-TAG.
002840     ADD 1 TO OLD-MAST-COUNTER.
002850 READ-MAST-EXIT.
002860     EXIT.
002870 READ-TRANS-RTN.
002880     READ TRANSACTION-FILE AT END MOVE HIGH-VALUES TO W-TRANS-TAG
002890         GO TO READ-TRANS-EXIT.
002900     EXAMINE PART IN TRANS     REPLACING LEADING SPACES BY ZEROES.
002910     MOVE PART IN TRANS TO W-TRANS-TAG.
002920     ADD 1 TO TRANS-COUNTER.
002930 READ-TRANS-EXIT.
002940     EXIT.
002950 SELECT-LOTAG.
002960     IF W-MAST-TAG LESS THAN W-TRANS-TAG
002970         MOVE W-MAST-TAG TO LOTAG
002980         ELSE MOVE W-TRANS-TAG TO LOTAG.
002990     MOVE ZERO TO MAST-SW.
003000     IF LOTAG EQUAL TO HIGH-VALUES GO TO EOJ-RTN.
003010 MAST-TAG-CHECK.
003020     IF W-MAST-TAG EQUAL TO LOTAG NEXT SENTENCE
003030         ELSE GO TO TRANS-TAG-CHECK.
003040     MOVE OM TO NM.
003050     MOVE 1 TO MAST-SW.
003060     PERFORM READ-MAST-RTN THRU READ-MAST-EXIT.
003070 TRANS-TAG-CHECK.
003080     IF W-TRANS-TAG EQUAL TO LOTAG PERFORM TRANS-PROCESS
003090         THRU  TRANS-LEG-EXIT
003100         PERFORM READ-TRANS-RTN THRU READ-TRANS-EXIT
003110         GO TO TRANS-TAG-CHECK
003120         ELSE GO TO WRITE-MAST-OUT.
```

Figure 7.6. PROCEDURE DIVISION for the inventory-control case study.

```
003130 TRANS-PROCESS.
003140     EXAMINE TX-QUANTITY       REPLACING LEADING SPACES BY ZEROES.
003150     EXAMINE TX-QOH            REPLACING LEADING SPACES BY ZEROES.
003160     EXAMINE TX-QOO            REPLACING LEADING SPACES BY ZEROES.
003170     EXAMINE TX-RP             REPLACING LEADING SPACES BY ZEROES.
003180     EXAMINE TX-RQ             REPLACING LEADING SPACES BY ZEROES.
003190     EXAMINE TX-UNIT-PRICE     REPLACING LEADING SPACES BY ZEROES.
003200     EXAMINE TX-YTD-SALES      REPLACING LEADING SPACES BY ZEROES.
003210     IF TN-QUANTITY NOT NUMERIC OR TN-QOH NOT NUMERIC OR TN-QOO
003220         NOT NUMERIC OR TN-RP NOT NUMERIC OR TN-RQ NOT NUMERIC OR
003230         TN-UNIT-PRICE NOT NUMERIC OR TN-YTD-SALES NOT NUMERIC
003240         PERFORM ERROR-PRINT-RTN GO TO TRANS-LEG-EXIT.
003250     IF NOT ADJUSTMENT AND TN-QUANTITY LESS THAN ZERO
003260         PERFORM ERROR-PRINT-RTN GO TO TRANS-LEG-EXIT.
003270     IF ADDITION GO TO ADDITION-ROUTINE.
003280     IF ADJUSTMENT GO TO ADJUSTMENT-ROUTINE.
003290     IF RECEIPT GO TO RECEIPT-ROUTINE.
003300     IF ORDER GO TO ORDER-ROUTINE.
003310     IF ISSUE GO TO ISSUE-ROUTINE.
003320     IF DELETION GO TO DELETION-ROUTINE.
003330     PERFORM ERROR-PRINT-RTN GO TO TRANS-LEG-EXIT.
003340 ADDITION-ROUTINE.
003350     IF MAST-SW EQUAL TO 1
003360         PERFORM ERROR-PRINT-RTN GO TO TRANS-LEG-EXIT.
003370     MOVE 1 TO MAST-SW.
003372     MOVE TRANS TO NM.
003374     ADD 1 TO ADDIT-COUNTER.
003380     GO TO TRANS-LEG-EXIT.
003390 ADJUSTMENT-ROUTINE.
003400     IF MAST-SW EQUAL TO ZERO
003410         PERFORM ERROR-PRINT-RTN GO TO TRANS-LEG-EXIT.
003420     IF TN-RP NOT EQUAL TO ZERO MOVE TN-RP TO RP IN NM.
003430     IF TN-RQ NOT EQUAL TO ZERO MOVE TN-RQ TO RQ IN NM.
003440     ADD TN-QUANTITY  QOH IN NM  GIVING NEGAT-CHECK.
003450     IF NEGAT-CHECK LESS THAN ZERO MOVE ZERO TO QOH IN NM
003460         PERFORM ERROR-PRINT-RTN GO TO TRANS-LEG-EXIT.
003470     MOVE NEGAT-CHECK TO QOH IN NM.
003480     GO TO TRANS-LEG-EXIT.
003490 RECEIPT-ROUTINE.
003500     IF MAST-SW EQUAL TO ZERO
003510         PERFORM ERROR-PRINT-RTN GO TO TRANS-LEG-EXIT.
003520     ADD TN-QUANTITY TO QOH IN NM   ON SIZE ERROR  DISPLAY
003530         'QOH FIELD NOT LARGE ENOUGH' UPON CONSOLE GO TO EOJ-RTN.
003540     SUBTRACT TN-QUANTITY FROM QOO IN NM GIVING NEGAT-CHECK.
003550     IF NEGAT-CHECK LESS THAN ZERO MOVE ZERO TO QOO IN NM  ELSE
003560         MOVE NEGAT-CHECK TO QOO IN NM.
003570     GO TO TRANS-LEG-EXIT.
003580 ORDER-ROUTINE.
003590     IF MAST-SW EQUAL TO ZERO
003600         PERFORM ERROR-PRINT-RTN GO TO TRANS-LEG-EXIT.
003610     ADD TN-QUANTITY TO QOO IN NM    ON SIZE ERROR  DISPLAY
003620         'QOO FIELD NOT LARGE ENOUGH' UPON CONSOLE GO TO EOJ-RTN.
003630     GO TO TRANS-LEG-EXIT.
003640 ISSUE-ROUTINE.
003650     IF MAST-SW EQUAL TO ZERO
003660         PERFORM ERROR-PRINT-RTN GO TO TRANS-LEG-EXIT.
003670     IF QOH IN NM NOT LESS THAN TN-QUANTITY GO TO NORMAL-ISSUE.
003680     MOVE SPACES TO SHORTAGE.
003690     MOVE PART IN TRANS TO PART IN SHORTAGE.
003700     MOVE TN-QUANTITY         TO QUANTITY IN SHORTAGE.
003710     MOVE QOH IN NM TO QOH IN SHORTAGE.
003720     WRITE SHORTAGE  AFTER ADVANCING 2 LINES.
003730     IF QOH IN NM EQUAL TO ZERO GO TO TRANS-LEG-EXIT.
003740     MOVE QOH IN NM TO TN-QUANTITY.
```

Figure 7.6. *(Continued)*

132

```
003750 NORMAL-ISSUE.
003760     COMPUTE QOH IN NM = QOH IN NM - TN-QUANTITY.
003770     IF CODX IN NM NOT EQUAL TO 2 GO TO TRANS-LEG-EXIT.
003780     COMPUTE YTD-SALES IN NM ROUNDED = YTD-SALES IN NM +
003790        TN-QUANTITY * UNIT-PRICE IN NM ON SIZE ERROR DISPLAY
003800        'SALES SUCCESS BUSTED THE YTD SALES FIELD' UPON CONSOLE
003810        DISPLAY 'CALL FOR THE PROGRAMMER AND A ROUND OF DRINKS'
003820           UPON CONSOLE,          GO TO EOJ-RTN.
003830     GO TO TRANS-LEG-EXIT.
003840 DELETION-ROUTINE.
003850     IF MAST-SW EQUAL TO ZERO
003860        PERFORM ERROR-PRINT-RTN GO TO TRANS-LEG-EXIT.
003870     MOVE ZERO TO MAST-SW   ADD 1 TO DELET-COUNTER.
003880     MOVE NM TO DELETION-LINE.
003890     WRITE DELETION-LINE.
003900     GO TO TRANS-LEG-EXIT.
003910 ERROR-PRINT-RTN.
003920     MOVE SPACES TO PO-REC.
003930     MOVE W-WARNING TO PO-MESSAGE.
003940     MOVE PART IN TRANS TO PO-PART.
003950     ADD 1 TO ERROR-COUNTER.
003960     WRITE PO-REC AFTER ADVANCING 2 LINES.
003970 TRANS-LEG-EXIT.
003980     EXIT.
003990 WRITE-MAST-OUT.
004000     IF MAST-SW NOT EQUAL TO 1 GO TO SELECT-LOTAG.
004010     IF PART IN NM LESS THAN W-OUT-TAG-SAVE
004020        DISPLAY 'FILES OUT OF SEQUENCE' UPON CONSOLE GO TO EOJ-RTN.
004030     MOVE PART IN NM TO W-OUT-TAG-SAVE.
004040     ADD QOH IN NM, QOO IN NM   GIVING QOH-QOO.
004050     IF QOH-QOO LESS THAN RP IN NM  MOVE SPACES TO ORDER-REC
004060     MOVE NM TO ORDER-DATA   WRITE ORDER-REC.
004070     WRITE NM.
004080     ADD 1 TO NEW-MAST-COUNTER.
004090     GO TO SELECT-LOTAG.
004100 EOJ-RTN.
004110     MOVE SPACES TO PO-REC.
004120     MOVE ' SUMMARY ' TO PO-MESSAGE.
004130     WRITE PO-REC AFTER ADVANCING 3 LINES.
004140     MOVE SPACES TO PO-REC.
004150     MOVE ' TRANSACTION RECORD COUNT ' TO PO-MESSAGE.
004160     MOVE TRANS-COUNTER            TO PO-COUNTER.
004170     WRITE PO-REC AFTER ADVANCING 1 LINES.
004180     MOVE 'INVALID TRANSACTION RECORD COUNT ' TO PO-MESSAGE.
004190     MOVE ERROR-COUNTER            TO PO-COUNTER.
004200     WRITE PO-REC AFTER ADVANCING 1 LINES.
004210     MOVE 'OLD MASTER RECORD COUNT '          TO PO-MESSAGE.
004220     MOVE OLD-MAST-COUNTER         TO PO-COUNTER.
004230     WRITE PO-REC AFTER ADVANCING 2 LINES.
004240     MOVE '   ADDITIONS PROCESSED '    TO PO-MESSAGE.
004250     MOVE ADDIT-COUNTER            TO PO-COUNTER.
004260     WRITE PO-REC AFTER ADVANCING 1 LINES.
004270     MOVE '   DELETIONS PROCESSED '    TO PO-MESSAGE.
004280     MOVE DELET-COUNTER            TO PO-COUNTER.
004290     WRITE PO-REC AFTER ADVANCING 1 LINES.
004300     MOVE 'NEW MASTER RECORD COUNT '          TO PO-MESSAGE.
004310     MOVE NEW-MAST-COUNTER         TO PO-COUNTER.
004320     WRITE PO-REC AFTER ADVANCING 1 LINES.
004330     CLOSE   OLD-MASTER  TRANSACTION-FILE ORDER-RECOMMENDATION
004340               NEW-MASTER SHORTAGE-REPORT  DELETION-LISTING.
004350     STOP RUN.
```

Figure 7.6. *(Continued)*

take care of this possible situation, as well as the normal one. Similar sentences have been included in the RECEIPT-ROUTINE with respect to QOO. In the ISSUE-ROUTINE the processing is a little different, since the same situation would indicate a shortage.

The WRITE-MAST-OUT leg takes care of the writing of the new master record and includes the reorder routine. Finally, the EOJ-RTN takes care of the printing of the record count and closes the files.

This program was run with the sample files that were shown in Figure 7.2. Figure 7.7 is the shortage and questionable transaction report that was produced. We see that the transaction record for part 7, which was identified as a deletion, although there was no corresponding master file record, has been flagged as an invalid transaction. Figure 7.8 then reflects this fact, together with the data for the valid transactions. We see that the record counts are correct, according to the analysis on page 119. Figure 7.7 also shows that for part 22 there were not enough on hand (20) to ship the requested number (60). In Figure 7.9 we have the order recommendations for those parts for which the on-hand plus on-order were found to be less than the

reorder point. It will be noted that we have not concerned ourselves with the spacing of the data in this report, as controlled by the DATA DIVISION entry for the file ORDER-RECOMMENDATION. In a practical application this report would probably be printed on a special form, and we would, of course, arrange the output spacing accordingly. A similar comment applies to the deletion report shown in Figure 7.10.

The reader who has studied this program with great care will realize that, in keeping with the directives contained in the ENVIRONMENT DIVISION, Figure 7.7 and Figure 7.8 were printed together on the on-line printer, making up the file named SHORTAGE-REPORT. This file was described as having two types of records, SHORTAGE and PO-REC; the record count summary was placed in the PO-REC record for printing by the end-of-

```
SHORTAGE AND QUESTIONABLE TRANSACTIONS REPORT
PART        Q-ORD    QOH

                                      INVALID OR QUESTIONABLE ENTRY FOR PART NUMBER    000007

000022        60       20
```

Figure 7.7. The shortage and questionable-transactions report in the inventory-control case study.

```
                          SUMMARY
              TRANSACTION RECORD COUNT              15
      INVALID TRANSACTION RECORD COUNT               1

              OLD MASTER RECORD COUNT               14
                  ADDITIONS PROCESSED                3
                  DELETIONS PROCESSED                1
              NEW MASTER RECORD COUNT               16
```

Figure 7.8. The summary of record counts for the inventory-control case study.

```
     ORDER RECOMMENDATION REPORT

     PART          DESCRIPTION      QOH QOO RP  RQ UNIT UN-PRIC YTD-SALX RP-DATE 06 23 69

     000008        MODEL-3-BOLTS    00400000004500350HUN00321110000123482

     000010        MOD-3-GLASSES    00600000101010101010101010101010122

     000015        FORMULA-X        003900100060001010TONS00602303000202111
```

Figure 7.9. The order-recommendation report in the inventory-control case study.

```
     DELETION REPORT

     PART          DESCRIPTION      QOH QOO RP  RQ UNIT UN-PRIC YTD-SALX RP-DATE 06 23 69

     000020        MOD-15           0110000000202222030505050505050505002
```

Figure 7.10. The deletion report in the inventory-control case study.

job routine EOJ-RTN. Figures 7.9 and 7.10 represent the contents of the files ORDER-RECOMMENDA-TION and DELETION-LISTING, both of which were assigned in the ENVIRONMENT DIVISION to tapes for off-line printing.

REVIEW QUESTIONS

1. Can you guess what the two sentences 003420 and 003430 are supposed to accomplish?

2. With reference to READ-MAST-RTN, on reaching the end of the file why do we go to READ-MAST-EXIT after placing HIGH-VALUES in W-MAST-TAG?

3. In the SELECT-LOTAG paragraph what do we MOVE to LOTAG if W-MAST-TAG and W-TRANS-TAG are equal?

4. Would the end result have been different if in sentence 003330 we had said GO TO ERROR-PRINT-RTN instead of PERFORM ERROR-PRINT-RTN GO TO TRANS-LEG-EXIT?.

5. Why do we regard it as an error condition and print an error message if MAST-SW is equal to zero when the transaction is an adjustment?

6. After instruction 003440 is executed, is it possible for NEGAT-CHECK to contain a positive value?

7. Which instructions would we need to add if we wanted to print out every new master record (as well as shortages and error messages) on the same report?

8. Could it happen that if one of the input files is out of sequence our sequence check for the output master file (sentences 004010-004030) might fail to reveal this erroneous condition?

9. Would it be possible to print different error messages, rather than a standard one, for the various kinds of error condition?

10. Did the clause JUSTIFIED RIGHT (line 002-100, PO-MESSAGE) have any visible effect?

7.7   The Random Access Alternative

In our case studies and programs we have concerned ourselves so far with tapes, cards, and printed files. We did, however, discuss some of the random-access concepts and COBOL options, as well as disks, in Section 6.1. The time has come to look into some of the aspects of a random-access application.

To start with, when does random access become an attractive proposition? We said that disks (not to mention data cells) are much more expensive than tapes. Therefore what is the rationale for using direct access devices?

Perhaps we can better explain this puzzling matter with a step-by-step analysis. Let us define "activity ratio" as the fraction of records of a master file for which there is some activity during an updating run divided by the total number of records in that file. Let us now say that we have a master file with 80,000 records and that at the end of each month this file is updated by 60,000 transactions. The activity ratio (75% in this case) is rather high: sequential processing on tape seems to be a suitable method for the updating of this file because there would be relatively little "passing" of tape without some kind of updating action.

Then company management decides that one month is too long a cycle between updating runs—it creates an information gap—and they ask for a weekly report. What happens to the activity ratio? It decreases to about 18%, since we now have only about 14,000 transactions to be applied weekly against the master file. Tape still looks reasonably convenient, although less so than before, but then the updating run is requested daily: now the activity ratio is less than 3%, and quite a bit of tape would be passed without any kind of updating action. At this point random access starts to look attractive because there is a trade-off between its cost and the computer time that it might save.

This is one of the routes—but by no means the only one—that may lead to adopting random-access files and techniques. Paradoxically, random access is also attractive when the activity ratio is extremely high. In fact, if the transactions are so many that they must be handled immediately, as they come in, the best way is to process them unsorted and randomly against the master. There are other instances in which random access may provide a solution to otherwise unmanageable problems, but we think that we may stop here and look at an actual example of how COBOL may be used in a random-access application.

Figure 7.11 shows a program that will *create* a master file in random form; Figure 7.12 shows a program that will *update* the file once it has been created.

The logic of the master-file-creation program is not complicated when viewed at the level of the COBOL source statements. We read a deck of cards (which must be arranged in ascending sequence on a given key) and write the records on a disk. The underlying process that is actually performed by the computer, however, is rather complex because the operating system is called on to assign indexes to the disk records to permit their

```
IDENTIFICATION DIVISION.
PROGRAM-ID. 'INDXFC'.
AUTHOR.   U GARBASSI.
REMARKS. INDEXED SEQUENTIAL FILE CREATE - THIS PROGRAM READS A
      CARD DECK AND CREATES AN INDEXED SEQUENTIAL FILE ON DISK.
ENVIRONMENT DIVISICN.
CONFIGURATION SECTION.
SOURCE-COMPUTER. IBM-360.
OBJECT-COMPUTER. IBM-360.
INPUT-OUTPUT SECTION.
FILE-CCNTROL.
      SELECT DISK-FILE      ASSIGN 'SYS013' DIRECT-ACCESS 2311
          ACCESS SEQUENTIAL  ORGANIZATION INDEXED
          RESERVE NO ALTERNATE AREA
          RECORD KEY IS D-PART.
      SELECT CARD-FILE ASSIGN 'SYS005' UNIT-RECORD 2540R.
DATA DIVISION.
FILE SECTION.
FD  DISK-FILE
      RECORDING MODE IS F
          LABEL RECORDS STANDARD
          DATA RECORD IS DISK-REC.
01  DISK-REC.
      02  FILLER PICTURE X.
      02 D-PART             PICTURE X(6).
      02 D-DATA             PICTURE X(73).
FD  CARD-FILE
      RECORDING MODE IS F
      LABEL RECORDS ARE OMITTED
      DATA RECORD IS CARD-REC.
01  CARD-REC.
      02 FILLER            PICTURE X.
      02 C-PART            PICTURE X(6).
      02 C-DATA            PICTURE X(73).
WORKING-STORAGE SECTION.
77 RECORD-COUNT        PICTURE   9(5) VALUE ZEROES.
PROCEDURE DIVISION.
      OPEN INPUT CARD-FILE   OUTPUT DISK-FILE.
READ-IN.
      READ CARD-FILE  AT END GO TO EOJ-RTN.
      MOVE CARD-REC TO DISK-REC.
      WRITE DISK-REC    INVALID KEY
          DISPLAY ' INVALID KEY ' C-PART    GO TO READ-IN.
      DISPLAY DISK-REC.
      ADD 1 TO RECORD-COUNT.
      GO TO READ-IN.
EOJ-RTN.
      DISPLAY 'NUMBER OF RECORDS ON DISK ' RECORD-COUNT.
      CLOSE CARD-FILE  DISK-FILE.
      STCP RUN.
```

Figure 7.11. A program for creating a random-access master file for the inventory-control case study.

```
IDENTIFICATION DIVISION.
PROGRAM-ID. 'INDXFU'.
AUTHOR. U GARBASSI.
REMARKS. THIS PROGRAM READS A TRANSACTION FILE IN RANDOM SEQUENCE
         AND UPDATES AN INDEXED SEQUENTIAL FILE ON DISK.
ENVIRONMENT DIVISION.
CONFIGURATION SECTION.
SOURCE-COMPUTER. IBM-360.
OBJECT-COMPUTER. IBM-360.
INPUT-OUTPUT SECTION.
FILE-CONTROL.
     SELECT DISK-MAST      ASSIGN 'SYS013' DIRECT-ACCESS 2311
         ACCESS IS RANDOM
         ORGANIZATION INDEXED
         RESERVE NO ALTERNATE AREA
         SYMBOLIC KEY W-PART
         RECORD KEY IS D-PART.
     SELECT TR-FILE   ASSIGN 'SYS005' UNIT-RECORD 2540R.
DATA DIVISION.
FILE SECTION.
FD  DISK-MAST
         RECORDING MODE IS F
         LABEL RECORDS ARE STANDARD
         DATA RECORD IS DISK-REC.
01  DISK-REC.
    02 D-STATUS             PICTURE X.
    02 D-PART          PICTURE X(6).
    02 FILLER          PICTURE X(5).
    02 D-DESCR         PICTURE X(15).
    02 D-QOH               PICTURE 9(4).
    02 D-QOO               PICTURE 9(4).
    02 D-RP                PICTURE 9(4).
    02 D-RQ                PICTURE 9(4).
    02 D-UNITS             PICTURE X(4).
    02 D-UNIT-PRICE    PICTURE 9999V9999.
    02 D-YTD-SALES     PICTURE 9(8).
    02 D-CODX          PICTURE 9.
    02 FILLER          PICTURE X(16).
FD  TR-FILE
    RECORDING MODE IS F
    LABEL RECORDS ARE OMITTED
    DATA RECORD IS TRANS-REC.
01  TRANS-REC.
    02 FILLER          PICTURE X.
    02 T-PART          PICTURE X(6).
    02 T-CODE          PICTURE 9.
    02 TN-QUANTITY         PICTURE S9999.
    02 TX-QUANTITY REDEFINES TN-QUANTITY    PICTURE X(4).
    02 T-DESCR         PICTURE X(15).
    02 TN-QOH              PICTURE 9(4).
    02 TN-QOO              PICTURE 9(4).
    02 TN-RP               PICTURE 9(4).
    02 TN-RQ               PICTURE 9(4).
    02 T-UNITS             PICTURE X(4).
    02 TN-UNIT-PRICE   PICTURE 9999V9999.
    02 TN-YTD-SALES    PICTURE 9(8).
    02 T-CODEX         PICTURE 9.
    02 FILLER          PICTURE X(16).
WORKING-STORAGE SECTION.
77  W-PART             PICTURE X(6).
```

Figure 7.12. Random-access version of the program to update the inventory-control master file created by the program of Figure 7.11. This program does not duplicate all of the processing performed by the program of Figure 7.6.

```
    PROCEDURE DIVISION.
    START-RTN.
        OPEN INPUT TR-FILE
             I-O DISK-MAST.
    READ-IN.
        READ TR-FILE  AT END GO TO EOJ-RTN.
        EXAMINE TX-QUANTITY          REPLACING LEADING SPACES BY ZEROES.
        IF TN-QUANTITY NOT NUMERIC  DISPLAY
              * TRANSACTION QUANTITY INVALID*
            GO TO READ-IN.
        MOVE T-PART TO W-PART.
        DISPLAY W-PART  TRANS-REC.
        READ DISK-MAST      INVALID KEY GO TO ADD-RTN.
        IF T-CODE EQUAL TO 1 DISPLAY
              *ADDITION - RECORD ALREADY IN FILE *
            GO TO READ-IN.
        IF T-CODE EQUAL TO 4 ADD TN-QUANTITY TO D-QOO.
        IF T-CODE EQUAL TO 6 MOVE HIGH-VALUE TO D-STATUS.
        REWRITE DISK-REC INVALID KEY GO TO NO-WRITE.
        GO TO READ-IN.
    ADD-RTN.
        IF T-CODE NOT EQUAL TO 1  DISPLAY
              * TRANSACTION ERROR - MATCHING RECORD NOT FOUND *
            GO TO READ-IN.
        MOVE TRANS-REC TO DISK-REC.
        WRITE DISK-REC  INVALID KEY  DISPLAY *ADDITION NOT ACCEPTED*
            GO TO EOJ-RTN.
        GO TO READ-IN.
    NO-WRITE.
        DISPLAY * INVALID KEY ON REWRITE * GO TO EOJ-RTN.
    EOJ-RTN.
        CLOSE TR-FILE  DISK-MAST.
        STOP RUN.
```

Figure 7.12. *(Continued)*

subsequent random retrieval. The generation of this elaborate set of object program instructions is triggered by COBOL clauses that we may describe briefly.

ORGANIZATION IS INDEXED. This clause, which is instrumental to the creation of an indexed-sequential file, instructs the compiler to set up the proper object program instructions for generating the indexes and handling the records.

ACCESS IS SEQUENTIAL. This clause (which, incidentally, may be omitted) indicates that the disk file is not accessed randomly in *creating* the file. (It *will* be accessed randomly in the updating program.)

RECORD KEY IS data-name. This entry indicates the field in the incoming data that provides the sequence key to be used to identify the record on disk. Notice that although the keys are actually furnished by the input records the data-name to be used in this clause belongs to the record description of the *disk file*.

INVALID KEY imperative statement. We have mentioned that the input file must be in ascending sequence for *creating* the file, although the updating will be random. Furthermore, the input data must not contain duplicate keys; this is only reasonable. In the file-creation routine the INVALID KEY clause is called into action whenever the incoming file is not in sequence or when duplicate keys are detected. If such a condition develops during the execution of the program it is normally convenient to DISPLAY some identifying fields of the faulty record and then go on to process the next record. This is done in the program of Figure 7.6. (As we shall see shortly, the INVALID KEY clause has somewhat different functions in the updating program.)

A record count is kept for control purposes; it is not an essential feature of file creation. The DISPLAY DISK-REC action is useful for testing purposes but would be eliminated in a running program in which there might be many thousands of records.

(The sharp-eyed reader may notice that the left-most character of each record has been left blank by use of a FILLER. The point of this is discussed below.)

We may now turn to the updating program shown in Figure 7.12. This program reads a transaction file in which the records appear in random sequence and updates the master record corresponding to each, as well as adding new records to the master file when the transaction is identified as an addition. As each transaction record is READ, we MOVE its key to a WORKING-STORAGE area; READ DISK-MAST then obtains the corresponding master record, if there is one. This master record is updated and then written back onto the master file, using REWRITE, a verb that exists for the purpose. An addition, as explained below, is handled by the INVALID KEY clause.

(The reader may have noticed that this routine does not, in the interest of clarity while we investigate new ideas, include all of the checking provisions in the sequential-access version. Simply as a token of what would normally be done in a practical program, we have included one check—the IF NOT NUMERIC test on the quantity field of the

transactions. The types of transaction, again in the interest of simplicity, have been reduced to three: additions, deletions, and one revision, an order. These are coded 1, 6, and 4, respectively, as in the sequential version.)

Could we determine the exact disk location in which this additional record will be inserted? The answer actually has no bearing on our COBOL program but may provide a rudimentary understanding of the mechanics and structure of indexed-sequential files. When such a file is created, we allocate to it a suitable number of cylinders and tracks of a disk. These "limits" of the file are usually called *extents* and are assigned, outside of the COBOL program, by means of job control cards that vary for different operating systems. The allocated cylinders and tracks are grouped into several distinct areas set up to accommodate indexes, "prime" records, and "overflow" records. The addition of new records during an updating run may therefore displace some of the old records from their original "prime" locations and transfer them to "overflow" locations. All this is rather complex (and several volumes have been written on the data management of random files) but what is im-

---

ANSWERS

1. Well, even though the specifications did not explicitly ask for it, we must provide some means of changing the reorder point and the reorder quantity in the master record! The two sentences in question (IF TN-RP NOT EQUAL TO ZERO MOVE TN-RP TO RP IN NM. and IF TN-RQ NOT EQUAL TO ZERO MOVE TN-RQ TO RQ IN NM.) make it possible for an adjustment to modify these quantities by replacing them with new values. You may now add the sentence that would permit the replacing of the unit price.

2. Because otherwise the sentence MOVE PART IN OM TO W-MAST-TAG would not be bypassed and would upset the HIGH-VALUES we have just placed in W-MAST-TAG. The same applies to READ-TRANS-RTN.

3. We move W-TRANS-TAG TO LOTAG, but does it really matter which tag we move when they happen to be equal?

4. No, the end result would have been the same because TRANS-LEG-EXIT immediately follows ERROR-PRINT-RTN.

5. If MAST-SW is equal to zero, it means that there is no old master record for that part number. This is obviously an error if the transaction is an adjustment, an issue, a deletion, a receipt, or an order.

6. Certainly; this would actually be the normal case.

ANSWERS (Continued)

A negative value in NEGAT-CHECK would indicate that the adjustment had been entered for an excessive negative amount.

7. In the paragraph WRITE-MAST-OUT, just before the sentence WRITE NM (004070), we would enter

MOVE SPACES TO PO-REC.
MOVE NM TO PO-MESSAGE.
WRITE PO-REC AFTER ADVANCING 1 LINES.

Notice that if we wrote MOVE NM TO PO-REC we would not print the first digit of PART because it would be "clobbered" by the carriage control character generated by the WRITE statement.

8. Yes, but the final record count would almost certainly show a discrepancy. To play it absolutely safe it is possible to sequence check both input files after the READ routines at the end of their respective legs.

9. Yes, and it would in fact be very desirable because it might save some clerical time and effort to investigate and correct the error. This could be done by MOVing the desired error message (e.g., "DELETION—MASTER NOT FOUND") to PO-MESSAGE before PERFORMing an ERROR-PRINT-RTN which would *not* contain its first two sentences (003920 and 003930).

10. Yes. The effect can be seen in Fig. 7.7, where the W-WARNING message appears right-justified.

portant to us boils down to one basic fact: with an indexed-sequential file the operating system sets up an intricate net of references and cross references that enables it to keep track of all the records in the file and to retrieve them *either randomly or sequentially*. With this drop of knowledge firmly in our grasp, let us now review the various COBOL clauses that are required in a program that updates an indexed-sequential file.

ACCESS IS RANDOM. This clause, which must appear in the SELECT statement for the disk file, enables us to submit the transactions randomly, which means, to put it simply, that we do not have to sort them beforehand.

ORGANIZATION IS INDEXED. This is the same clause that we used in creating the master file. It describes the file organization, so that proper object program routines may be generated for the retrieval of the records.

SYMBOLIC KEY IS data-name. The data-name must be a WORKING-STORAGE area to which we MOVE the transaction key after reading a transaction record.

OPEN I-O file-name. This clause is required for opening a random-access file that is to be updated. (Notice that we used the option OPEN OUTPUT when we *created* this file.)

INVALID KEY imperative statement. The functions performed by this clause in an updating program differ greatly from the ones we saw in the file creation program.

—In conjunction with the READ DISK-MAST statement this condition is activated if no master key is found equal to the current contents of SYMBOLIC KEY. This would normally indicate that we are processing an addition. Therefore, when such a condition occurs in our program, we go to ADD-RTN, where we test whether the transaction has the right code (it should be 1) and, if so, add it to the master.

—In conjunction with the REWRITE DISK-REC statement INVALID KEY would be activated if, because of faulty processing, we tampered with the key after the READ DISK-MAST instruction. This should not happen normally.

—Likewise this clause is not normally activated after the WRITE DISK-REC statement. If an INVALID KEY is detected at this point, it may indi-

cate that the record we are attempting to add to the file cannot be contained within the extents that have been assigned to the master file on the disk. This would call for a reorganization of the file—one of the many challenging problems that belong in the realm of random-access data management.

REWRITE. This is a special COBOL verb to be used only to update a record "in place," that is, to modify it according to the contents of a transaction that bears the same key. In our program we use it after applying an order or a deletion. Why do we REWRITE a master record for which we have just processed a deletion? Because we cannot delete a record from a random-access file as we delete it from a master tape, which is done by simply not writing the record on the updated master. With a random-access file we can "mark" a deleted record only by moving some special character to a specified field in the record; for example, by writing MOVE HIGH-VALUE TO D-STATUS. With certain operating systems a HIGH-VALUE in the leftmost position indicates that the record has been marked for deletion, which would lead to its eventual removal when the file is updated or reorganized. If this feature is not present, we can always delete or ignore the marked record by means of appropriate COBOL instructions.

Could we read and write an indexed-sequential file *sequentially*? Yes by using the clauses ACCESS IS SEQUENTIAL, OPEN INPUT (rather than OPEN I-O) and AT END (rather than INVALID KEY). In this case the file would be read and printed out in sequence by key, regardless of how the records might be physically arranged on the disk. This capability is, in part, what is implied by the phrase "indexed-sequential."

Before we close this review of COBOL, as applied to random-access applications, we should point out that our two sample programs were written for and executed on an IBM 360 with the disk operating system (DOS). The reader should be aware that with other computers, and even with other IBM 360 operating systems, some changes would be needed to make the programs work. The basic concepts remain the same, however.

Another form of random-access file organization is called DIRECT ORGANIZATION. In programs that use this technique the clause ORGANIZATION IS INDEXED would be replaced, naturally enough, by ORGANIZATION IS DIRECT and the clause "ACTUAL KEY IS data-name" would be used instead of "RECORD KEY IS data-name." There would also be still more possible meanings for the INVALID KEY clause: since, in DIRECT processing the ACTUAL KEY indicates a disk location expressed in terms of cylinder and track number and is derived from the record key by means of programmer-controlled formulas, there is always a chance that the calculated value may be outside the file extents or even, in the case of a grievous error, outside the disk itself.

This pretty well sums up all the essential aspects of the relationship between COBOL and random-access processing. The reader may suspect at this stage that a great deal of practice and experimentation is needed before all the related variables can be mastered. This suspicion is well founded, but the programmers who will have occasion to carry out extensive tests on random access will not encounter too many problems beyond those discussed here.

REVIEW QUESTIONS

True or false:

1. In a random access *updating application* the transaction file may be submitted in random sequence.

2. An indexed-sequential file may not be accessed sequentially.

3. In the processing of an indexed-sequential file the INVALID KEY clause is activated by one and only one specific condition.

4. The option OPEN I-O should be used in a program that updates an existing indexed-sequential file.

5. The data-name following SYMBOLIC KEY must be defined in WORKING-STORAGE.

6. The data-name following RECORD KEY is a field in the disk file.

7. When we *create* an indexed-sequential file, the input must be arranged sequentially.

8. All the validation routines that were in the tape update version could be included in the random-access disk update program.

ANSWERS

1. True. This is the primary purpose of random access processing.

2. False.

3. False. In a file creation program it is activated by an out-of-sequence condition or by a duplicate key. In a file updating program it is activated, with different implications, after READ, REWRITE, and WRITE.

ANSWERS (Continued)

4. True.

5. True.

6. True.

7. True.

8. True, although they would appear at different points because of the different logic of the two programs.

8. ADDITIONAL PROCEDURE DIVISION FEATURES

The material presented in Chapter 3 and in the two case studies is a good indication of the general structure of the PROCEDURE DIVISION and includes enough verbs to do much useful work. There are, however, additional features that may be employed to simplify the writing. Few of the things to be discussed here represent operations that cannot be accomplished in some other way, but the new techniques are in many ways much more powerful.

8.1 The MOVE CORRESPONDING Option

In the case study in Chapter 7 we studied some examples in which most of the contents of a record had to be moved to data items of the same name in another record. It may be quite annoying to have to write out all the MOVE verbs required to transfer items from one place to another in such a situation.

The MOVE CORRESPONDING option of the MOVE verb, in conjunction with qualification, makes this unnecessary.

> MOVE CORRESPONDING data-name-1
> TO data-name-2

Both data names must refer to group items (the option makes no sense otherwise); most commonly both are record names. All items within data-name-1 that have the same names as items within data-name-2 are moved, just as though we had written a series of simple MOVEs.

Consider an example. Suppose A and B are the names of two records with the schematic layout of Figure 8.1. The arrows

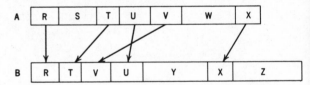

Figure 8.1. Example of the action of a MOVE CORRESPONDING.

indicate the result of writing MOVE CORRESPONDING A TO B. The items named S and W in a record A would not be moved; the items named Y and Z in record B would receive nothing.

At least one of the items in each pair must be elementary, but moving group items in this manner is permitted otherwise. If the descriptions of elementary items in the receiving area specify editing, it is done. Two correspondingly named items in the two records could have different lengths; this is properly handled.

With the exception that at least one elementary item of each pair must be involved, the total effect of MOVE CORRESPONDING A TO B is exactly the same as if we had written:

142

MOVE R IN A TO R IN B;
MOVE T IN A TO T IN B;
MOVE U IN A TO U IN B;
MOVE V IN A TO V IN B;
MOVE X IN A TO X IN B.

This may be a considerable convenience in writing a source program; it may in some cases result in a slower object program. Note that if two records (or two groups) are exactly the same in size and arrangement, MOVE CORRESPONDING *may* be used but *should not* be; it would be faster in the object program simply to MOVE the entire record or group.

8.2 The ADD CORRESPONDING and SUBTRACT CORRESPONDING Options

The ADD CORRESPONDING and SUBTRACT CORRESPONDING options are very similar to the MOVE CORRESPONDING option that we have just discussed.

1. Must E IN J and E IN K be the same length?
2. What would be moved to F IN K?
3. Would it be permissible for B1 IN K to require editing and B2 IN K not?
4. Does the reversal of the elementary items D1 and D2 cause any trouble?
5. Is it not required that at least one item moved be in the same relative position in the two groups?
6. Suppose B2 IN K had had some other name, say D2. Would anything have been moved to it?
7. Is it true that in MOVE CORRESPONDING we may MOVE group items but ADD CORRESPONDING and SUBTRACT CORRESPONDING handle only elementary items?
8. Are the ROUNDED and ON SIZE ERROR options allowed in ADD CORRESPONDING and SUBTRACT CORRESPONDING?

8.3 More Complex Conditionals

In preceding chapters we have seen conditional statements like the following:

IF SALESMAN IN EXT NOT EQUAL TO

ADD CORRESPONDING data-name-1 <u>TO</u> data-name-2
... [ROUNDED] [ON <u>SIZE ERROR</u> imperative-statement]

SUBTRACT CORRESPONDING data-name-1 <u>FROM</u> data-name-2
... [ROUNDED] [ON <u>SIZE ERROR</u> imperative-statement]

With ADD CORRESPONDING the elementary data item in data-name-1 are added to the corresponding elementary data items in data-name-2. With SUBTRACT CORRESPONDING they are subtracted. In both cases the results are stored in data-name-2.

SALESMAN-NUMBER GO TO
SALESMAN-RESULT.
IF W-MAST-TAG LESS THAN W-TRANS-TAG
MOVE W-MAST-TAG TO LOTAG ELSE
MOVE W-TRANS-TAG TO LOTAG.
IF TN-QUANTITY NOT NUMERIC PERFORM
ERROR-PRINT-RTN GO TO
TRANS-LEG-EXIT.
IF ADDITION GO TO ADDITION-ROUTINE.

Conditional statements of this limited type are useful and in principle allow us to do everything we would want to do, but there are more powerful ways to approach more complex tasks.

Formulas in conditionals. All the examples presented so far have used either data names or literals in relation tests; it is also permissible to write formulas, as discussed in Section 3.3 in connection with the COMPUTE verb. All of the fol-

REVIEW QUESTIONS

Questions 1 through 6 refer to the example in Figure 8.2, with the statement MOVE CORRESPONDING J TO K.

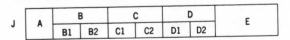

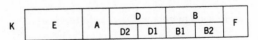

Figure 8.2. Sample records for Review Questions.

lowing are legitimate, for instance; the reader will probably appreciate immediately that making the same tests without formulas would be considerably more work.

(1) If QOH IN MASTER IS LESS THAN REORDER-POINT * SEASONAL-FACTOR GO TO REORDER-ROUTINE.
(2) IF GROSS IS GREATER THAN 13.00 * DEPENDENTS COMPUTE TAX = 0.18 * (GROSS − 13.00 * DEPENDENTS); OTHERWISE MOVE ZERO TO TAX.
(3) IF JAN + FEB + MAR + APR IS GREATER THAN CUTOFF NEXT SENTENCE; OTHERWISE DISPLAY ACCOUNT-NO, 'LOW'.

Compound conditionals. It is often a great convenience to be able to combine two or more tests into one statement or to specify what is to be done if some relation is *not* true. The logical connectives AND, OR, and NOT permit this flexibility. Among the following examples of compound conditionals the first two appeared and were briefly discussed in the case study in Chapter 7:

(1) IF TN-QUANTITY NOT NUMERIC OR TN-QOH NOT NUMERIC OR TN-RP NOT NUMERIC. . .
(2) IF NOT ADJUSTMENT AND TN-QUANTITY LESS THAN ZERO. . .
(3) IF AGE IS GREATER THAN 21 AND AGE IS LESS THAN RETIREMENT-AGE. . .

(4) IF AGE GREATER THAN 21 OR MARRIED. . .
(5) IF STOCK-NO-3 IS EQUAL TO 'A' OR STOCK-NO-5 IS EQUAL TO 99. . .

The following rules define explicitly what AND and OR mean:

1. A compound condition consisting of simple conditions connected by ANDs is satisfied if and only if every simple condition is satisfied.

2. A compound condition consisting of simple conditions connected by ORs is satisfied if any one or more of the simple conditions are satisfied.

What happens in a compound condition containing both AND and OR? The answer is determined by a *precedence rule* (similar to the one that says that in the absence of parentheses multiplications and divisions are performed before additions and subtractions). The rule is simply that AND is a higher ranking operator than OR; that is, ANDs are considered first.

Consider this example:

A = 1 OR B = 2 AND C = 3.

This condition is satisfied (is true) if A is 1, or if B is 2 and C is 3. The punctuation in that sentence is crucial; the condition as written is not necessarily satisfied if A is 1 or B is 2, and C is 3. If we really wanted to write the latter expression, we would insert parentheses, just as in an arithmetic expression: (A = 1 OR B = 2) AND C = 3. Is

A	B	C	A = 1 OR B = 2 AND C = 3	(A = 1 OR B = 2) AND C = 3
1	2	3	Satisfied	Satisfied
1	2	10	Satisfied	Not satisfied
1	10	3	Satisfied	Satisfied
1	10	10	Satisfied	Not satisfied
10	2	3	Satisfied	Satisfied
10	2	10	Not satisfied	Not satisfied
10	10	3	Not satisfied	Not satisfied
10	10	10	Not satisfied	Not satisfied

ANSWERS

1. Not at all. If E IN K were *shorter* than E IN J, some characters would have to be dropped, but if we intended it that way there would be no problem.
2. Nothing. This would presumably be handled by some other statement in the program.
3. Yes.

ANSWERS (Continued)

4. No.
5. No.
6. No; there is no matching D2 of B in the J area.
7. Yes.
8. Yes.

there really a difference? This can be answered best by investigating all of the possibilities for the three variables in the table, in which by 10 we actually intend "anything but the value that satisfies the simple condition."

There are only two lines in which the two are different, but that is enough to make them two different conditions, just as the two arithmetic expressions A + B * C and (A + B) * C are different.

A few more examples may make the possibilities of compound conditions a little clearer.

(1) IF ANNUAL AND POLICY-DATE IS LESS THAN 59 OR POLICY-AMOUNT IS GREATER THAN 10000 AND PREFERRED-RISK. . .
(2) IF A IS EQUAL TO B AND C IS NOT EQUAL TO D OR E IS EQUAL TO F AND G IS POSITIVE OR H IS LESS THAN I * J / 2. . .
(3) IF CLASSIFICATION IS NOT ALPHABETIC AND CLASSIFICATON IS NOT EQUAL TO '2' AND CLASSIFICATION IS NOT EQUAL TO '8' OR CLASSIFICATION IS EQUAL TO 'H'. . .
(4) IF HOURS IS NUMERIC AND HOURS IS NOT GREATER THAN 16 AND HOURS IS NOT NEGATIVE. . .
(5) IF CARD-TYPE EQUAL TO 6 OR CARD-TYPE EQUAL TO 7 GO TO WRITE-A ELSE GO TO WRITE-B.

Compound conditionals which contain a NOT may be a little tricky; for instance, if we wished to use NOT EQUAL TO in sample sentence (5), it would be a mistake to write

(5A) IF CARD-TYPE NOT EQUAL TO 6 OR CARD-TYPE NOT EQUAL TO 7 GO TO WRITE-B ELSE GO TO WRITE-A.

Someone may think that sentence (5) and sentence (5A) are equivalent, but this would be a logical illusion. Actually sentence (5A) is a sort of trap because it will never allow WRITE-A to be executed: if CARD-TYPE is equal to 6, it is *not* equal to 7, and therefore program control will be transferred to WRITE-B; likewise, if CARD-TYPE is equal to 7, it is *not* equal to 6, which means that also in this case we go to WRITE-B; obviously we also go to WRITE-B for any other value of CARD-TYPE.

Is there any way in which we could use NOT

EQUAL TO and still write a logically sound sentence for our example? Yes, by using AND instead of OR as the connective:

(5B) IF CARD-TYPE NOT EQUAL TO 6 AND CARD-TYPE NOT EQUAL TO 7 GO TO WRITE-B ELSE GO TO WRITE-A.

In a program we could use either sentence (5) or sentence (5B) and we would obtain the same result, whereas sentence (5A) would lead us astray. In general, a programmer should beware of such logical pitfalls and keep in mind that in our example an OR used with EQUAL TO had to be changed to an AND with NOT EQUAL TO. Likewise, an AND with EQUAL TO should be changed to OR with NOT EQUAL TO. The reader who is intrigued by such logical twists may enjoy taking up a course in formal logic or playing a game called WFF 'n' PROOF.*

Implied subject. In defining a simple condition we showed each relation test with a subject, a relation, and an object, although we did not use that terminology. In order to simplify writing long expressions, most COBOL compilers (with some exceptions, e.g., IBM's COBOL E) allow the omission of some of these terms in certain forms of compound conditions. To simplify the following discussion let us agree to let the word *operand* stand for a data name, a literal, or a formula.

When a compound condition has the same operand immediately preceding each relation, then only the first of these terms need be written. The omitted subjects are said to be *implied*. Thus the earlier example

IF AGE IS GREATER THAN 21 AND AGE IS LESS THAN RETIREMENT-AGE. . .

could be written

IF AGE IS GREATER THAN 21 AND IS LESS THAN RETIREMENT-AGE. . .

The use of an implied subject is not affected by the presence or absence of parentheses.

Implied subject and relation. When the simple conditions in a compound condition have the same subject and the same relation, then only the first

* Conversely, the reader who is *not* interested in these matters would *not* enjoy attending a course in logic *and* would *not* enjoy playing WFF 'n' PROOF. Most likely he would not enjoy being a programmer, either.

occurrence of the subject and relation need be written. Thus the condition

IF A = 1 OR A = 4 OR A = 5 OR A = 9. . .

could be written, with some compilers,

IF A = 1 OR 4 OR 5 OR 9. . .

This abbreviation applies whether or not there are parentheses and whether or not all logical connectives are the same. Thus

IF A = B OR A = C AND A = D. . .

could equivalently be written

IF A = B OR (A = C AND A = D). . .
IF A = B OR C AND D. . .

Implied connectives. When the subject, relation, and logical connectives in a compound condition are all the same, only the first occurrence of the subject and relation need be written, all objects may be written as a series (preceded by commas if desired), and the logical connective is written immediately preceding the last object. Thus

IF A = 1 OR A = 4 OR A = 5 OR A = 9. . .

which we abbreviated, as before, as

IF A = 1 OR 4 OR 5 OR 9. . .

could finally be condensed to

IF A = 1, 4, 5, OR 9. . .

Again, since these condensed formats are not accepted by all compilers, the programmer will do well to consult the manufacturer's COBOL manual before using them.

Nested conditional statements. We saw earlier that a conditional statement is made in the form shown in the box. In all previous examples statement-1 and statement-2 have been imperative, but they may in fact be conditional also; the result is called a *nested* conditional. There is, in principle, no limit to the "depth" to which a conditional statement may contain other conditional statements, but particular compilers may place restrictions, such as that statement-1 must be imperative or that

if statement-1 or statement-2 is conditional it may not contain another conditional.

Let us explore the possible value of a nested conditional by considering an example. Suppose that at some point in a program we want to do the following, which is written as a series of compound conditionals:

IF MALE AND SINGLE, ADD 1 TO SUM-1;
IF MALE AND MARRIED, ADD 1 TO SUM-2;
IF FEMALE AND SINGLE, ADD 1 TO SUM-3;
IF FEMALE AND MARRIED, ADD 1 TO SUM-4.

In order to write this as a nested conditional, it will be necessary to assume that MALE and FEMALE are the only condition names for the associated variable (which is obviously true unless the data is incorrect) and that SINGLE and MARRIED are the only condition names for that variable (which assumes correct data and that there are no condition names for DIVORCED or WIDOWED). In other words, we want to be able to ask whether the person is SINGLE, for instance, and to be safe in assuming that if the answer is "no" he is married. (This assumption is not so trivial as it sounds, particularly if the incoming data has not been checked for validity.)

The desired operations can now be written a little more compactly:

IF MALE THEN IF SINGLE ADD 1 TO
    SUM-1 OTHERWISE ADD 1 TO SUM-2
    OTHERWISE IF SINGLE ADD 1 TO
    SUM-3 OTHERWISE ADD 1 TO SUM-4.

It should not be too hard to read this statement and to keep track of the OTHERWISE that goes with each IF, since it does exactly what the four compound conditionals did. We would not recommend that this type of construction be used too often, however, because its compact format is achieved at the expense of clarity. In some instal-

IF condition {statement-1 / NEXT SENTENCE} {OTHERWISE / ELSE} {statement-2 / NEXT SENTENCE}

lations, in fact, the use of conditional sentences containing two IFs is strongly discouraged.

REVIEW QUESTIONS

1. Consider the following sentence:
IF AGE IS LESS THAN 40 AND WEEKLY PERFORM ROUTINE-6. True or false?

a. If AGE is exactly 40, ROUTINE-6 will *not* be performed.

b. In order for ROUTINE-6 to be performed, AGE must be less than 40 *and* the employee must be paid weekly.

c. WEEKLY must be a condition name for the sentence to make sense.

2. Would the following two sentences result in the same action?

a. IF A IS EQUAL TO B OR A IS GREATER THAN B GO TO P-16.

b. IF A IS EQUAL TO OR GREATER THAN B GO TO P-16.

3. What will the following sentence do?

IF AGE IS LESS THAN 21 AND GREATER THAN 65 GO TO PARAGRAPH-23.

4. What will the following sentence do?

IF MARRIED OR NOT MARRIED GO TO P-40.

5. Are the following three conditions equivalent?

a. F=1 AND G=2 OR F=1 AND G=6

b. F=1 AND (G=2 OR G=6)

c. F=1 AND G=2 OR G=6

6. Does the following sentence make sense?

IF R=12, 13, AND 17 GO TO P12.

7. Consider the following sentence:

IF (L = 1 OR 2) AND (M = 1 OR 2) AND (N=1 OR 2) GO TO P-67.

Would the condition be satisfied (i.e., would we GO TO P-67) for the following sets of values of L, M, and N?

a. L=0, M=2, N=4.

b. L=1, M=1, N=1.

c. L=2, M=2, N=2.

d. L=1, M=2, N=3.

e. L=1, M=2, N=1.

8. Are the following three sentences equivalent?

a. IF U=1 OR V=6 OR W=12 GO TO P-91.

b. IF (U=1 OR V=6) OR W=12 GO TO P-91.

c. IF U=1 OR V=6 OR W=12 THEN GO TO P-91.

9. Is this a legitimate COBOL sentence?

IF POLICY-AMOUNT IS LESS THAN 50000 OR POLICY-AMOUNT IS LESS THAN 100000 AND (PREFERRED-RISK OR MEDICAL-OK) GO TO STANDARD-RTN ELSE GO TO SPECIAL-RTN.

10. Is this a legitimate COBOL sentence?

IF (A−B) < 0.01 * (A+B) OR (B−A) < 0.01 * (A+B) GO TO EQUAL OTHERWISE GO TO WRITE.

11. Do the following do the same thing?

a. IF REC-CODE IS EQUAL TO 9 AND PROD-CODE IS EQUAL TO 3 GO TO ROUT-A ELSE GO TO ROUT-B.

b. IF REC-CODE IS NOT EQUAL TO 9 OR PROD-CODE IS NOT EQUAL TO 3 GO TO ROUT-B ELSE GO TO ROUT-A.

12. If in the following portion of a program we omitted the period after WRITE RECORD-OUT, would the program logic change considerably?

IF DATA-A EQUAL TO CODE-D MOVE RECORD-IN TO RECORD-OUT WRITE RECORD-OUT.

GO TO READ-RTN.

END-RUN.

CLOSE FILE-IN, FILE-OUT.

STOP RUN.

8.4   Subscripts

In Section 5.9 we introduced the option OCCURS and the concept of subscripting by means of an example:

02 HOURS-WORKED PICTURE 9(10) OCCURS 7 TIMES.

ADD HOURS-WORKED (3) TO WEDN-TOTAL.

We then said that a subscript may be an integer number—like (3) in the above sentence—or a data name. Let us now look at some applications that lend themselves to the use of this powerful feature of COBOL.

We read a file. Each of its records contains some activity data and a state code (STATE-CODE-IN). Let us assume that state code 01 stands for Alabama, 02 for Alaska, 03 for Arizona, and so on. On a report in a field called STATE-NAME-OUT we want to print the state name. Conceivably, we could write in the PROCEDURE DIVISION a series of 50 instructions like

IF STATE-CODE-IN EQUAL TO 01 MOVE 'ALABAMA' TO STATE-NAME-OUT.

IF STATE-CODE-IN EQUAL TO 02 MOVE 'ALASKA' TO STATE-NAME-OUT.

IF STATE-CODE-IN EQUAL TO 03
    . . . etc., etc.

All this would be very tedious. With subscripting we would instead set up the following table in the WORKING-STORAGE SECTION of our program:

```
01 STATE-TABLE.
   02 FILLER PICTURE X(15) VALUE 'ALABAMA        '.
   02 FILLER PICTURE X(15) VALUE 'ALASKA         '.
   02 FILLER PICTURE X(15) VALUE 'ARIZONA        '.
   . . . .
01 TABLE-STATE REDEFINES STATE-TABLE.
   02 STATE-NAME PICTURE X(15) OCCURS 50 TIMES.
```

In the PROCEDURE DIVISION we can then simply write

(READ FILE-IN and other preceding sentences).
MOVE STATE-NAME (STATE-CODE-IN) TO
    STATE-NAME-OUT.
(Whatever follows.)

A few comments. The length of each entry in the table must remain constant for all 50 states: PICTURE X(15), once chosen, must be used for each state, this being a basic requirement of the OCCURS clause. (We could have selected a length of 12 and abbreviated those state names which exceed 12 letters, but in this case PICTURE X(12) would have to be entered for each state.) STATE-CODE-IN in the input record must be defined as a numeric item (PICTURE 99). Also, it would be sound practice to determine whether STATE-CODE-IN actually contains a number in the range 1 through 50 before using it as a subscript.

It is very important to understand fully the direct relationship between the value of the subscript and the position of the corresponding item within the table. In this example, when state code is 01, ALABAMA will be accessed because—and only because—it is the first item in the table. If by some mishap the order of the cards containing ALABAMA and ALASKA is reversed, ALASKA would then become the first item in the table and as such would be called when state code happened to be 01. In essence, the basic things to keep in mind are that *a subscript actually indicates the relative position of an item within a table* and that the number of items in the table is specified by the OCCURS clause.

This example has illustrated one of the ways in which subscripting may be used,* but where this technique is really invaluable is in applications that require table-searching routines.

Let us assume that we have a chart of accounts, the smallest account number being 10000 and the greatest 69999. Not all of the numbers are used: for instance, let us say, we have only seven active account numbers in the 10000 series, 18 in the 20000 series, and so on, for a total of 122 active accounts. We read a transaction file, and, for each record, we wish

* Incidentally, notice the conceptual similarity between the way in which a subscript would access *directly* an item in a table and the direct-access technique in random-access applications discussed in Chapter 6.

ANSWERS

1. a. True.
   b. True, assuming, as is reasonable, that WEEKLY is a condition name referring to the frequency of payment.
   c. True.

2. Yes, with most compilers.

3. Nothing: these two conditions can never be simultaneously true.

4. Always go to P-40; a person must be one or the other.

5. (a) and (b) are equivalent; but (b) and (c) are not; (c) is satisfied when G = 6, regardless of the value of F, whereas (a) and (b) require F to be 1.

6. This is almost a trick question. From the standpoint of syntax (the arrangement of nouns, connectives, etc., according to the rules of COBOL), it is a legal COBOL sentence; but from the standpoint of semantics (what it means), it is nonsense; R could never be equal simultaneously to three different things.

7. a. No.

ANSWERS (Continued)

   b. Yes.
   c. Yes.
   d. No: all three conditions connected by AND must be satisfied for the compound condition to be satisfied.
   e. Yes: it doesn't matter which of the parts of the ORs are satisfied.

8. Yes: the parentheses have no effect here and the THEN is always optional in a conditional statement.

9. Yes, assuming that PREFERRED-RISK and MEDICAL-OK are condition names.

10. No, but the only error is the use of the key words EQUAL and WRITE for paragraph names.

11. Yes.

12. Yes, indeed! Without the period after WRITE RECORD-OUT we would go to END-RUN the first time an unequal condition is encountered. With the period we read all the records and write some of them. Periods in COBOL are always important, but after conditional statements they are even more so!

(a) to ascertain that it contains an active (and therefore valid) account number (ACC-IN);

(b) to process it if test (a) is successful;

(c) to go to an error routine if test (a) fails.

Our primary requirement—to find out whether an account number is a valid one—may be satisfied by a subscripted search routine. We write in WORKING-STORAGE the following entries:

A few comments are in order. For the level 77 entry SUB-A the USAGE is COMPUTATIONAL; namely, this item is stored in binary format. This is preferable because with many compilers a subscript must be in binary format when it is referenced at program execution time. Consequently USAGE IS COMPUTATIONAL avoids time-consuming conversions from other formats to binary.

```
77 SUB-A PICTURE 999 USAGE IS COMPUTATIONAL.
01 TABLE-OF-ACCNTS.
   02 FILLER PICTURE X(19) VALUE '10002EXECUTIVE-EXPS'.
   02 FILLER PICTURE X(19) VALUE '10007DEVELOPMT-EXPS'.
         .
         .
01 ACCNT-TAB REDEFINES TABLE-OF-ACCNTS.
   02 ACCOUNT-DATA OCCURS 122 TIMES.
   03 ACC-NUMBER PICTURE 9(5).
   03 ACC-NAME PICTURE X(14).
```

Notice that this time we have included in the VALUE the account number, whereas there was no state code number in the preceding table. Notice also that the OCCURS clause refers this time to a group item (ACCOUNT-DATA) and that it is not repeated for the elementary items at level 03 (ACC-NUMBER and ACC-NAME). The latter, however, are also subscriptable—as is ACCOUNT-DATA.

Now we can write a searching routine along the following lines:

What happens in our search routine if we have gone through the entire table and have not found an equal condition between ACC-IN and ACC-NUMBER? Very simple: at that point SUB-A will be equal to 123 and consequently program control will "fall through" to ERROR-RTN, which is precisely where we want to be. After we do whatever we have written in ERROR-RTN (write an error message, etc.), we read another record and reset SUB-A to 1, so that another search may begin. (We

```
READ-RTN.
    READ FILE-IN AT END GO TO EOJ-RTN.
         .
         .
    MOVE 1 TO SUB-A.
SEARCH-RTN.
    IF ACC-IN EQUAL TO ACC-NUMBER (SUB-A) GO TO
        PROCESS-RTN.
    ADD 1 TO SUB-A.
    IF SUB-A LESS THAN 123 GO TO SEARCH-RTN.
ERROR-RTN.
         .
         .
    GO TO READ-RTN.
PROCESS-RTN.
    MOVE ACC-NAME (SUB-A) TO X-Y-Z. (or whatever else)
         .
         .
    GO TO READ-RTN.
```

likewise "reinitialize" SUB-A when we read a record after a successful search.)

Is this the only type of subscripted search that we may consider? Fortunately not, because the search executed by this routine is a rather lengthy one. A way in which we can speed up a search is by first sorting the input file on the particular item used in the search. (Incidentally, such an item is usually called an *argument*.) We can then omit resetting the subscript to 1 at the beginning of each search, since the next record can have an argument that is only equal to or greater than the previous one.

What if our processing requirements prevent us from sorting the input file in the most desirable sequence for a search? Among the techniques available for such cases the most important is the "binary search," which, by the way, has nothing to do with binary format. A routine for this type of search splits the table in successive halves at every iteration and directs the search downward or upward in the table according to the result of comparisons between the input and the table arguments. It is not our intention to delve into the intricacies of this technique. Suffice it to say that, as we shall learn when discussing indexes, certain compilers recognize the verb SEARCH ALL and, when encountering it, originate instructions for a binary search.

A few notes on the problems of setting up tables. In our examples so far the table data has been always included in the program. In other words, each table entry was a program card for the WORKING-STORAGE SECTION, which would be cumbersome for very large tables. An alternative method —of which we give an example in this section— is provided by entering in WORKING-STORAGE only the over-all description of the table:

```
01 TABLE-A.
   02 TABLE-ITEM PICTURE X(8)
      OCCURS 1750 TIMES.
```

We could then read each table item from a tape or a deck of cards and use a subscript to direct the item to the proper table location.

We shall now present another example which illustrates how a table may have two "levels" of entries and how, correspondingly, a data name may have two subscripts. Suppose that we need a table of the enrollment of a school system for each grade for each of the years 1958, 1959, 1960, 1961, and 1962. In the WORKING-STORAGE SECTION we can specify that for each enrollment entry (of which there are 12, one for each grade) there are five figures (one for each of these years) by writing

```
01 ENROLLMENT-TABLE.
   02 ENROLLMENT OCCURS 12 TIMES.
   03 YEAR-ENROLLMENT PICTURE 999
      OCCURS 5 TIMES.
```

In this example we have two OCCURS clauses, one for ENROLLMENT and one for YEAR-ENROLLMENT. The table, therefore, will contain 60 three-digit entries. If we assume that the beginning of the table contains 2352462582662712227 . . . , this would mean that grade 1 had 235 students for 1958, 246 for 1959, 258 for 1960, 266 for 1961, 271 for 1962, grade 2 had 227 students for 1958, etc.

We can now call for a particular enrollment figure by using *two* subscripts, one to indicate the grade and one to specify the year within the grade; for instance, YEAR-ENROLLMENT (8, 3) would refer to the enrollment of the 8th grade for 1960, since the 1960 entry is the third one in each set of five assigned to a grade. What would YEAR-ENROLLMENT (2, 1) refer to in our example? To the enrollment for the second grade in 1958, namely, 227 students. Note that the data name we have used is the one at the 03 level. If this were not unique, it could be qualified as usual without affecting the subscripting concept: YEAR-ENROLLMENT IN ENROLLMENT (8, 3). It is similarly permissible to qualify a data name used as a subscript if it is not unique. We might write, for example, YEAR-ENROLLMENT (GRADE, YEAR OF BOND-ISSUE), where BOND-ISSUE could be the name of, let us say, the record of which YEAR is a field. Two things are *not* permitted: a subscript may not itself be subscripted and a data name used as a qualifier may not be subscripted. The latter would be meaningless; the former would be a great deal of work for the compiler and the object program.

COBOL permits a maximum of three levels of subscripting. In our example a third level might be required to distinguish between boys and girls, which could be handled by this data description:

```
01 ENROLLMENT-TABLE.
   02 ENROLLMENT OCCURS 12 TIMES.
   03 YEAR-ENROLLMENT OCCURS 5 TIMES.
   04 ENROLLMENT-BY-SEX PICTURE
      999 OCCURS 2 TIMES.
```

If we agree that 1 stands for boys and 2 for girls,

the number of girls in the fourth grade in 1962 would be called for by writing ENROLLMENT-BY-SEX (4, 5, 2). If a variable named GRADE had previously been given the value 4, a variable named YEAR, the value 5 (not 1962!), and a variable named SEX, the value 2, we would get the same data item by writing

> ENROLLMENT-BY-SEX
> (GRADE, YEAR, SEX).

It is possible to refer to a block of data from a table by writing a higher level name with fewer subscripts; for instance, to get the enrollments for both boys and girls in the ninth grade in 1958 we could write YEAR-ENROLLMENT (9, 1). This does *not* form the sum of the two items! It refers to *both,* and the only meaningful operation on such a group would be to move it to or from a storage space with six digits, in this example. To refer to the group of 10 items (all years, both sexes) in the tenth grade we would write ENROLLMENT (10). To refer to the entire table we could write ENROLLMENT-TABLE (i.e., we could write MOVE SPACES TO ENROLLMENT-TABLE if we wanted to erase it).

How would we go about setting up this table? One method is already familiar to us: we could enter all the figures in a table (FIGURE-TABLE) as we did for the names of the 50 states in an earlier example. We would then use the REDEFINES clause and write

01 ENROLLMENT-TABLE REDEFINES
FIGURE-TABLE.
  02 ENROLLMENT OCCURS 12 TIMES.
  03 YEAR-ENROLLMENT PICTURE 999
  OCCURS 5 TIMES.

Alternatively, we can load this table as follows.

Let us assume that the entire enrollment history of the school, from 1912 to 1970, has been punched on cards. The card design is elementary to the extreme; each card contains three fields: year (YEAR-IN), grade (GRADE-IN), and number of students (STUDENT-IN). We could now load the information from the cards to the table by means of the following routine:

READ-RTN.
> READ CARD-FILE AT END GO
> TO END-JOB.
> IF YEAR-IN LESS THAN 1958 OR
> GREATER THAN 1962 GO
> TO READ-RTN.

IF YEAR-IN EQUAL TO 1958 MOVE
STUDENT-IN TO
YEAR-ENROLLMENT
(GRADE-IN, 1).
IF YEAR-IN EQUAL TO 1959 MOVE
STUDENT-IN TO
YEAR-ENROLLMENT
(GRADE-IN, 2).
IF YEAR-IN EQUAL TO 1960 MOVE
STUDENT-IN TO
YEAR-ENROLLMENT
(GRADE-IN, 3).
IF YEAR-IN EQUAL TO 1961 MOVE
STUDENT-IN TO
YEAR-ENROLLMENT
(GRADE-IN, 4).
IF YEAR-IN EQUAL TO 1962 MOVE
STUDENT-IN TO
YEAR-ENROLLMENT
(GRADE-IN, 5).
GO TO READ-RTN.

Subscripting, as we have just seen, can do many things for us. When employing this technique, however, we should keep in mind some of the most important rules governing the use of subscripts.

1. A subscript may be a literal or a data name; the value of the subscript must be an integer and greater than zero.

2. Subscripts are enclosed in parentheses and written to the right of the subscripted data name, preceded by the space that is always required at the end of a data name.

3. A subscripted data name may be qualified; if this is done, the parentheses enclosing the subscript(s) are written to the right of all qualifiers. A subscript may also be qualified.

4. Neither a qualifier nor a subscript may be subscripted.

5. If a data name appears in the DATA DIVISION with an OCCURS clause, it may not be written in the PROCEDURE DIVISION without subscripts. On the other hand, subscripts may not be used unless the OCCURS clause has been given in the DATA DIVISION.

6. A maximum of three levels of subscripting is permitted. When there is more than one subscript, they must be separated by commas and there must be a space after each comma.

7. An OCCURS clause may not be written at the 01 level.

In some implementations the OCCURS clause may be made dependent on a condition name or a variable to make tables of variable length.

Indexes.   Some compilers can handle indexes* as well as subscripts. An index appears to be similar to a subscript and, on the surface, it works in the same fashion. However, indexes are preferable to subscripts from the standpoint of object program efficiency and should therefore be used whenever they are available.

```
77 INDEX-A USAGE IS INDEX.
01 TABLE-OF-ACCNTS.
   02 FILLER PICTURE X(19) VALUE '10002EXECUTIVE-EXPS'.
         .
         .
         .
01 ACCNT-TABLE REDEFINES TABLE-OF-ACCNTS.
   02 ACCOUNT-DATA OCCURS 122 TIMES INDEXED BY INDEX-A.
   03 ACC-NUMBER PICTURE 9(5).
   03 ACC-NAME PICTURE X(14).
```

Indexes are manipulated by COBOL verbs which differ from those that are used with subscripts. We

```
READ-RTN.
    READ FILE-IN AT END GO TO EOJ-RTN.
         .
         .
         .
    SET INDEX-A TO 1.
    SEARCH ACCOUNT-DATA, WHEN ACC-NUMBER (INDEX-A)
         EQUAL TO ACC-IN GO TO PROCESS-RTN.
ERROR-RTN.
         .
         .
         .
    GO TO READ-RTN.
PROCESS-RTN.
         .
         .
         .
    GO TO READ-RTN.
```

say, for instance, MOVE 2 TO SUB-A, ADD 1 TO SUB-A, SUBTRACT 2 FROM SUB-A (SUB-A being a subscript), but for an index we must say

```
SET INDEX-XYZ TO 2.
SET Q-INDEX UP BY 1.
SET IND-B DOWN BY 2.
```

* English experts would prefer "indices," but COBOL experts generally prefer "indexes." As the reader may surmise, our choice was a hard one to make.

Also, a new clause—INDEXED BY—must be used in conjunction with OCCURS to indicate that the table items will be accessed by means of one or more indexes. Each index requires an entry in the WORKING-STORAGE SECTION: the index name is followed by the clause USAGE IS INDEX, without a PICTURE. Finally, with indexes we can use the verbs SEARCH and SEARCH ALL.

To illustrate all these features let us go back to our search routine for the chart of accounts. Indexing would require the following entries:

With SEARCH, our search routine would be written as follows:

A few points to consider: the object of SEARCH is the data name entered before OCCURS (ACCOUNT-DATA); the conditional IF is replaced by WHEN; notice also that the index is increased automatically: the statement SET INDEX-A UP BY 1 is not required when SEARCH is used. Finally, if we wanted a "binary" search (which, by the way, would work well with this particular example), we could use SEARCH ALL instead of SEARCH.

Indexes, when available, may be used with subscripts within the same program, and an index may be compared to a literal or to another index, as in the following example:

IF RECORD-ITEM (SUB-A) EQUAL TO
    Q-ITEM (INDEX-2) AND INDEX-2
    EQUAL TO 21 OR INDEX-2 EQUAL TO
    INDEX-R . . .

We may close these brief notes on indexing by stating that just about all the restrictions that govern the use of subscripts apply to indexes as well, with one exception: the value of an index may be modified by a literal, as in the following example:

ACCOUNT-NO (INDEX-A + 2).

REVIEW QUESTIONS

1. Which of the following is *not* an advantage of subscripting (or indexing)?
 a. Saves time and effort in writing the DATA DIVISION.
 b. Makes possible shortcuts in writing the PROCEDURE DIVISION.
 c. Simplifies the compilation of the source program.

2. Which of the following best summarizes the subscripting concept:
 a. Subscripting is a way to improve object program efficiency by reducing the number of different data names in a program.
 b. Subscripting is a way to let one data name refer to a whole table of data items, with a particular one (or a group) being specified by the value(s) of the subscript(s) written after the data name.
 c. Subscripting is a way to simplify the writing of the DATA DIVISION, which at the same time makes the PROCEDURE DIVISION easier to write.
 d. Subscripting is a way to write more compact PROCEDURE DIVISION statements.

3. Indexes versus subscripts: is it true that indexes generate more efficient object program instructions and that the verbs SEARCH and SEARCH ALL may be used only with indexes?

4. Identify five errors in the following subscripting example:
 AMOUNT IN TRANS (2) OF TAPEX(0,1,
    RATE + 1)

5. What will the following do?
In DATA DIVISION:

01 SUM-TABLE USAGE IS COMPUTATIONAL.
02 X-SUM PICTURE 9(5) OCCURS 100 TIMES.
In PROCEDURE DIVISION:
    ADD DOLLARS TO X-SUM (CONTR).

6. Assuming the DATA DIVISION of Question 5, what will the following do?
    MOVE ZERO TO TOTAL-A.
        MOVE 1 TO SUBS.
AGAIN. ADD X-SUM (SUBS) TO TOTAL-A.
    IF SUBS EQUAL TO 100 GO TO
        PRINT-RTN.
    ADD 1 TO SUBS. GO TO AGAIN.
PRINT-RTN. DISPLAY TOTAL-A.

7. What will the following put into object program storage when the object program is loaded?

01 NAME-RECORD.
02 FILLER PICTURE X(10)   VALUE 'JONES   '.
02 FILLER PICTURE X(10)   VALUE 'SMITH   '.
02 FILLER PICTURE X(10)   VALUE 'TURNER   '.
etc. for 50 entries.
01 NAME-TABLE REDEFINES NAME-RECORD.
02 NAME-A PICTURE X(10)
    OCCURS 50 TIMES.

8. Refer to the sample routine on page 151 (READ-RTN) that we wrote to load school enrollment figures from a deck of cards. Can you think of a way to reduce the number of IF (conditional) statements from six to one and still accomplish the same results?

8.5 The PERFORM Verb

We have already seen, in Chapter 3 and in the case study in Chapter 7, the simplest version of the PERFORM verb, which simply transfers control to a paragraph or a group of paragraphs and then returns it to the statement following the PERFORM. Valuable as this version often is, it is only the beginning of what can be done with a PERFORM.

For review, and to lay the groundwork for study of the more powerful forms, we may begin with a restatement of the simplest option.

When a PERFORM is encountered, control is transferred to the first statement of procedure-name-1. Exactly when control returns to the statement following the PERFORM depends on whether the optional procedure-name-2 is written and whether these procedure names are paragraphs (usually) or sections.* The precise statement is that control returns as follows:

---

* As we mentioned briefly at the end of Section 3.6, paragraphs may be grouped under programmer-supplied section names.

> *Option 1.*
> <u>PERFORM</u> procedure-name-1 [<u>THRU</u> procedure-name-2]

1. If procedure-name-1 is a paragraph name and procedure-name-2 is not specified, control returns after the execution of the last statement of the procedure-name-1 paragraph.

2. If procedure-name-1 is a section name and procedure-name-2 is not specified, control returns after the last statement of the last paragraph of the procedure-name-1 section.

3. If procedure-name-2 is specified and is a paragraph name (whether procedure-name-1 is a paragraph name or a section name doesn't matter), control returns after the last statement of the procedure-name-2 paragraph.

4. If procedure-name-2 is a section name (in which case procedure-name-1 would often be a section name also but is not *required* to be), control returns after the last statement of the last paragraph of the procedure-name-2 section.

In all cases the last sentence within the PERFORMed procedures must not contain a GO TO statement, nor can there be any GO TO statements that transfer control from within the PERFORMed procedures to some other procedure outside them.

There is no necessary relation between procedure-name-1 and procedure-name-2, except that there obviously must be a "path" leading from the first to the second; that is, if the second does not "follow" the first in the sequence in which the paragraphs appear in the source program, there must be GO TO verbs to form an unbroken sequence. GO TO verbs specifically *are* permitted (as long as control remains within the PERFORMed routines), as are other PERFORMs.

If there are two or more paths leading to the last sentence to be executed (e.g., when alternative procedures are to be followed), procedure-name-2 must be a separate paragraph that consists of a paragraph name and the verb EXIT. This verb can also be used to avoid a violation of the rule that the last executed sentence must not contain a GO TO.

Let us now go through some examples that will clarify these points.

Restating the simplest case, let us assume that we have written the following routine:

NEW-PAGE-RTN.
    ADD 1 TO PAGE-CTR.

ANSWERS

1. (c) might conceivably be true in isolated instances but certainly not in general.

2. (a) is not true at all in general; (b) is completely true; (c) is true to a certain extent, but the meaning of "easier" is subject to argument; (d) is true in most cases, but not always, and it is not the main point in any case.

3. Yes.

4. a. A qualifier must not be subscripted.
   b. There must be a space between data name and the left parenthesis.
   c. A subscript must be greater than zero.
   d. There must be a space following the commas separating the subscripts.
   e. Subscripts cannot be arithmetic expressions; only literals and data names are permitted as subscripts. (Indexes, however, may be followed by a + or a − and an integer.)

5. Add the dollar amount (defined elsewhere) to the element of the SUM-TABLE identified by the current value of CONTR (defined elsewhere).

6. Print the sum of the 100 dollar amounts in the SUM-TABLE. (Assumes, of course, that TOTAL-A and SUBS have been defined elsewhere.)

ANSWERS (Continued)

7. Establish a table of 50 names available to the object program without reading any data cards.

8. Well, here is the "shrunk" routine. (Readers who have found the correct solutions are entitled (a) to feel proud of themselves and (b) to special congratulations.)

READ-RTN.
    READ CARD-FILE AT END GO TO END-JOB.
    IF YEAR-IN LESS THAN 1858 OR GREATER THAN 1962 GO TO READ-RTN.
    SUBTRACT 1957 FROM YEAR-IN.
    MOVE STUDENT-IN TO ENROLLMENT (GRADE-IN, YEAR-IN).
    GO TO READ-RTN.

Incidentally, the sentence IF YEAR-IN LESS THAN 1958 OR GREATER THAN 1962 GO TO READ-RTN. has an implied subject. With some compilers it would be necessary to say: IF YEAR-IN LESS THAN 1958 OR YEAR-IN GREATER THAN 1962 GO TO READ-RTN.

MOVE PAGE-CTR TO PAGE-NO.
MOVE HEAD-1 TO PRINT-REC.
WRITE PRINT-REC AFTER
ADVANCING 0 LINES.
(NEXT-PARAGRAPH).

We are now writing another part of the program:

MOVE GRAND-TOT-LINE TO PRINT-REC.
WRITE PRINT-REC AFTER
ADVANCING 2 LINES.

At this point, if we want to execute the entire NEW-PAGE-RTN, we can just write

PERFORM NEW-PAGE-RTN.
MOVE COMP-CODE TO CHECK-FIELD. (Or any such statement.)

It should be perfectly clear by now that in this example, after writing PRINT-REC, the program would execute all four statements under NEW-PAGE-RTN and would then execute MOVE COMP-CODE TO CHECK-FIELD. The difference between PERFORM and GO TO is evident. If we had written GO TO NEW-PAGE-RTN, the result would have been quite different: the program would have executed NEW-PAGE-RTN, but then it would have continued with the routine following NEW-PAGE-RTN. It would not have come back to MOVE COMP-CODE TO CHECK-FIELD.

Let us go one step farther. Suppose that our original routine said

NEW-PAGE-RTN.
ADD 1 TO PAGE-CTR.
MOVE PAGE-CTR TO PAGE-NO.
MOVE HEAD-1 TO PRINT-REC.
WRITE PRINT-REC AFTER
ADVANCING 0 LINES.
GO TO WRITE-DET-RTN.

If we now wrote

WRITE PRINT-REC AFTER ADVANCING
0 LINES.
PERFORM NEW-PAGE-RTN.
MOVE COMP-CODE TO CHECK-FIELD.

we would actually give contradictory instructions and upset the very logic of the verb PERFORM: at the end of NEW-PAGE-RTN the control would be transferred to WRITE-DET-RTN, and the chances of its ever getting back to MOVE COMP-CODE TO CHECK-FIELD would be pretty dim with any compiler!

The solution in this case is simple: we could remove the GO TO WRITE-DET-RTN instruction from NEW-PAGE-RTN by writing two separate paragraphs:

NEW-PAGE-RTN.
ADD 1 TO PAGE-CTR.
MOVE PAGE-CTR TO PAGE-NO.
MOVE HEAD-1 TO PRINT-REC.
WRITE PRINT-REC AFTER
ADVANCING 0 LINES.

SPEC-PARAG.
GO TO WRITE-DET-RTN.
(NEXT-PARAGRAPH).

But what can we do if we wish to branch out in the middle of a PERFORMed routine by means of an IF statement? The verb EXIT permits us to cope with this case without too much effort, as in the following example:

CHANGE-TRANSFER.
MOVE CODE-IN TO CODE-OUT.
MOVE COMP-IN TO COMP-OUT.
IF CODE-CHECK EQUAL TO 'A' GO
TO CHANGE-EXIT.
MOVE FACTOR-3 TO SIGNAL-OUT.
CHANGE-EXIT.
EXIT.
(NEW-PARAGRAPH).

We can now write PERFORM CHANGE-TRANSFER THRU CHANGE-EXIT without violating any rule and without any conflict of logic. The latter solution would apply equally well with any number of routines, as we had a chance to see in the case study in Chapter 7. In that program the statement PERFORM TRANS-PROCESS THRU TRANS-LEG-EXIT encompassed 10 routines, from which we were branching out with conditional and unconditional statements but *always remaining within the path of the PERFORMed routines.*

Two more points before going to the other options of PERFORM. A procedure that is PERFORMed may itself contain other PERFORM statements. We can write

PERFORM HEAD-PAGE-RTN.

and HEAD-PAGE-RTN may consist of

ADD 1 TO PAGE-CTR.
PERFORM WRITE-M-RTN.

In turn, WRITE-M-RTN may include another

PERFORM, and so on, but a procedure may *not* be PERFORMed within itself: while writing a procedure named TRANSF-RTN we may not include in it the statement PERFORM TRANSF-RTN.*

but it might be useful in some cases with a data name in a situation in which the routine is not needed. In fact, one effective way to employ the TIMES option is simply to let the data name as-

---

Option 2.

PERFORM procedure-name-1 [THRU procedure-name-2] $\begin{Bmatrix} \text{data-name-1} \\ \text{integer-1} \end{Bmatrix}$ TIMES

The TIMES option. The specified number of times, either a literal or a data name, must have a

sume the values zero or one, depending on whether or not the routine is to be performed.

Option 3.

PERFORM procedure-name-1 [THRU procedure-name-2] UNTIL condition-1

---

positive integer value or be zero. The action is straightforward: control is transferred to procedure-name-1 and the following statements executed as many times as the value of the literal or data name. After the specified number of executions control returns as usual to the statement following the PERFORM.

A good example of the usefulness of this option is provided by a compound-interest calculation, in which, for instance, the interest is compounded quarterly but credited only annually. When the interest for the year is to be computed, the calculation must be done four times in succession, or something equivalent (which is the essence of compound interest), rather than by multiplying the interest for one quarter by four. Assuming that INTEREST-CALC is the name for a routine that computes the interest on a given principal and adds the interest to give a new principal, we could easily specify the compounding by writing

PERFORM INTEREST-CALC 4 TIMES.

Suppose that a department store issues as many credit cards to a new customer as he requests for other family members. We can readily see how a statement like this would be a convenience:

PERFORM CREDIT-CARD-ISSUE
    NO-OF-COPIES TIMES.

It would obviously make no sense to call for a routine to be performed zero times with a literal,

The UNTIL option. In this option there is no automatic counting, but instead the routine is performed until condition-1 is satisfied. This "condition" may be any of the types we have discussed: it may, for instance, involve formulas or be compound. The precise mechanism is this: before each transfer to procedure-name-1 the condition is checked; if the condition is *not* satisfied, control is transferred to procedure-name-1, but if it *is* satisfied control continues to the next statement after the PERFORM. Thus, if the condition is satisfied when the PERFORM is first encountered, control will not transfer to procedure-1.

It should be fairly obvious that the condition will almost always involve some variable that changes during the execution of the routine called on by the PERFORM; for example, suppose a reorder calculation has been set up to order a fixed amount, which in some cases might be less than needed. Assuming that REORDER is a routine that increases ON-ORDER if more is needed, we might write

PERFORM REORDER UNTIL ON-ORDER
    + ON-HAND
    = AVERAGE-USE * 2.0 OR
    ON-HAND > AVERAGE-USE * 2.0.

It is worth noting that this version of the PERFORM implies an automatic test of whether to go to the named routine *at all*; if ON-HAND + ON-ORDER is already greater than or equal to twice the average usage, REORDER will not be performed *at all*. Note, incidentally, that it would not be a good idea to specify "equal" rather than "equal to or greater than" because the routine might not

---

* Note that with GO TO, however, we often GO TO the procedure to which the GO TO belongs.

come up with a figure that gives exact equality, in which case REORDER would be performed endlessly! This is called an endless loop and is to be avoided.

The VARYING data-name option. This option is used when it is desired to increase or decrease the value of an item between executions of a pro-

For an example, suppose that we want to print a list showing for a number of values of AMOUNT the corresponding values of RATE. We have a procedure named RATE-FORMULA which computes a rate, given the amount, and prints both; we want to do this for amounts of 50, 55, 60, . . . , up to and including 200. The PERFORM statement could be

---

Option 4.

PERFORM procedure-name-1 [THRU procedure-name-2] VARYING data-name-2

FROM $\begin{Bmatrix} \text{data-name-3} \\ \text{literal-1} \end{Bmatrix}$ BY $\begin{Bmatrix} \text{data-name-4} \\ \text{literal-2} \end{Bmatrix}$ UNTIL condition-1

---

cedure. The format requires specification of a starting value (FROM) for the controlled item, an amount by which it should be increased or decreased between executions of the procedure (BY), and a condition (UNTIL) to determine when executions should stop. The exact mechanism should be stated explicitly because it often matters a great deal exactly what is done when. The block diagram of Figure 8.3 gives the sequence of operations. Note

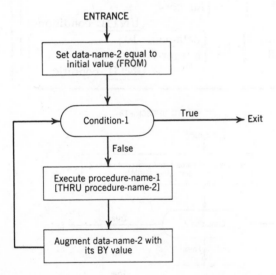

Figure 8.3. The sequence of operations in Option 4 of the PERFORM verb.

that the condition is tested *before* executing the procedure and that at the completion of the procedure the controlled variable has already been augmented so that its value after returning control to the statement following the PERFORM is not the same as the last value used in the procedure.

In contrast with the TIMES option data-name-2 is not required to be an integer, although it may be.

PERFORM RATE-FORMULA VARYING
    AMOUNT FROM 50
    BY 5 UNTIL AMOUNT IS
    GREATER THAN 200.

The RATE-FORMULA routine does *not* have to perform the addition of 5 to AMOUNT each time the routine is executed—indeed, it must not do so. Observe the IS GREATER THAN instead of IS EQUAL TO; since the testing of the condition is done *before* entering the procedure, use of EQUAL TO here would not compute the RATE for an AMOUNT of 200. As it is, the last value used will be 200, as intended; when control passes on to the statement following the PERFORM, the value of AMOUNT will be 205.

If it is desired to perform a procedure with automatic variation of one subscript between repetitions, this option provides a simple method. (If more than one subscript is to be varied in the same procedure, the next option must be used.) For instance, Question 6 in the last group of review questions forms the sum of the 100 data items in a table named SUM-A and prints the total. This could be done more compactly, and perhaps more rapidly in the object program, by using a PERFORM verb:

MOVE ZERO TO TOTAL-A. PERFORM
    ADD-ROUTINE VARYING SUBS
    FROM 1 BY 1 UNTIL SUBS > 100.
    DISPLAY TOTAL-A.

The paragraph named ADD-ROUTINE should be

    ADD-ROUTINE. ADD SUM-A (SUBS) TO TOTAL-A.

Note that the mechanism of the VARYING option is not precisely the same as in the earlier example: there we tested for completion *after* adding a data item and then added 1 to SUBS if we were going to go around again. The VARYING option tests first and, after adding in one more item, augments the subscript in any case. This difference accounts for the test of SUBS for *equality* with 100, whereas here we ask if it is *greater* than 100.

The VARYING subscript-name option. This option is used to augment the value of one or more subscripts in a "nested" fashion between executions of a procedure. By "nested" we mean that in the case of two subscripts the first-named subscript is set to its FROM value and the second-named subscript runs through all its values, after which the first-named subscript is advanced, the second subscript again runs through all its values, and so on until the procedure has been performed for all combinations of the values of the two subscripts. A similar scheme is followed when there are three

MOVE ZERO TO TOTAL-C. MOVE 1 TO YEAR.
　MOVE 1 TO SEX.
　PERFORM SUMMATION VARYING
　GRADE FROM 1 BY 1 UNTIL
　GRADE > 12.

Suppose now that we want the total enrollment of both boys and girls in 1958. This could be done by adding up the boys and girls separately and adding the two sums, but the VARYING option lets us do it with one PERFORM:

MOVE ZERO TO TOTAL-C. MOVE 1 TO YEAR.
　PERFORM SUMMATION VARYING
　GRADE FROM 1 BY 1 UNTIL
　GRADE > 12 AFTER SEX
　FROM 1 BY 1 UNTIL SEX > 2.

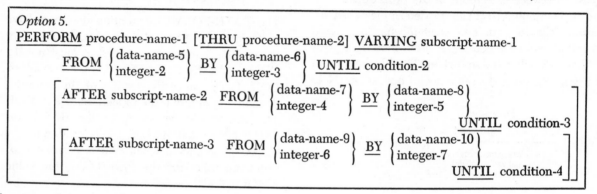

subscripts; the only thing to be careful of is the order in which the two or three subscripts are augmented. This is clearly established by Figures 8.4 and 8.5.

Let us explore some of the applications of this powerful verb by using the school enrollment example in Section 8.3. Suppose that we have a procedure named SUMMATION somewhere in our source program:

SUMMATION. ADD ENROLLMENT-BY-SEX
　(GRADE, YEAR, SEX) TO TOTAL-C.

Recall that ENROLLMENT-BY-SEX is the name we gave to the three-level table, which lists the enrollment in each grade for each of the years 1958–1962, with separate entries for each grade and year for boys and girls. Suppose first that we wanted to get the total number of boys in the school system in 1958. This means that we must hold YEAR constant at 1 (the subscript value corresponding to 1958), SEX constant at 1 (which stands for boys), and let GRADE run through all the values between 1 and 12:

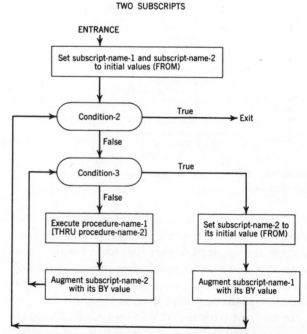

Figure 8.4. Operation of Option 5 of the PERFORM verb with two subscripts.

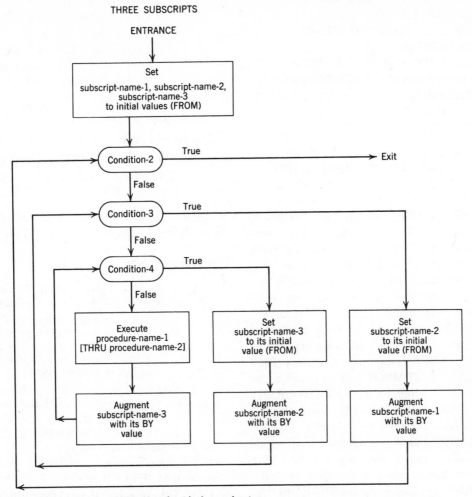

THREE SUBSCRIPTS

ENTRANCE

Set
subscript-name-1, subscript-name-2,
subscript-name-3
to initial values (FROM)

Condition-2 — True — Exit

False

Condition-3 — True

False

Condition-4 — True

False

Execute
procedure-name-1
[THRU procedure-name-2]

Set
subscript-name-3
to its initial
value (FROM)

Set
subscript-name-2
to its initial
value (FROM)

Augment
subscript-name-3
with its BY
value

Augment
subscript-name-2
with its BY
value

Augment
subscript-name-1
with its BY
value

Figure 8.5. Operation of Option 5 of the PERFORM verb with three subscripts.

The way this has been written, the second subscript would be the one varying most rapidly; that is, we would add in both boys and girls for each grade before going on to the next grade. It happens to make no difference at all here, but if we wanted to add up the boys in all grades and then add in the girls in all grades the PERFORM should be

PERFORM SUMMATION VARYING SEX FROM 1 BY 1 UNTIL SEX > 2 AFTER GRADE FROM 1 BY 1 UNTIL GRADE > 12.

Suppose now that we wanted to get the average size of seventh-grade classes, both boys and girls, for all five years:

MOVE ZERO TO TOTAL-C. MOVE 7 TO GRADE. PERFORM SUMMATION VARYING YEAR FROM 1 BY 1 UNTIL YEAR > 5 AFTER SEX FROM 1 BY 1

UNTIL SEX > 2. COMPUTE AVERAGE = TOTAL-C / 5.

To see how three subscripts might need to be varied, suppose we wanted the average school system enrollment for the five years, which requires getting the total of all entries in the table:

MOVE ZERO TO TOTAL-C. PERFORM SUMMATION VARYING GRADE FROM 1 BY 1 UNTIL GRADE > 12 AFTER YEAR FROM 1 BY 1 UNTIL YEAR > 5 AFTER SEX FROM 1 BY 1 UNTIL SEX > 2. COMPUTE AVERAGE = TOTAL-C / 5.

Suppose we wanted the ratio of boys to girls in grades 7 through 12, inclusive, for 1960:

MOVE ZERO TO TOTAL-C. MOVE 3 TO YEAR. MOVE 1 TO SEX. PERFORM

SUMMATION VARYING GRADE
FROM 7 BY 1 UNTIL
GRADE > 12. MOVE TOTAL-C
TO TEMPORARY.
MOVE ZERO TO TOTAL-C. MOVE 2 TO
SEX. PERFORM SUMMATION VARYING
GRADE FROM 7 BY 1 UNTIL GRADE
> 12. COMPUTE RATIO =
TEMPORARY / TOTAL-C.

For one final example of what can be done with the PERFORM verb and subscripts, suppose we wanted to search the table of enrollments for the grade with the largest enrollment, both boys and girls, from 1959 to 1961, inclusive. In addition to the enrollment, we will, of course, want to know what grade and year it was, so that we are actually looking for three things, which we may name BIG-ENROLLMENT, BIG-GRADE, and BIG-YEAR.

One way to do this is to assign to BIG-ENROLLMENT an initial VALUE of zero. We then calculate the enrollment for each grade and year, one by one, storing the result in a field called TEMPORARY, which is compared against BIG-ENROLLMENT: if TEMPORARY is found to be greater than BIG-ENROLLMENT, TEMPORARY is moved to BIG-ENROLLMENT. The first comparison will occur between zero (initial VALUE of TEMPORARY) and the enrollment from grade 1 in 1959: if the latter is not zero, we shall have the enrollment from grade 1 in 1959 in BIG-ENROLLMENT. We then compare BIG-ENROLLMENT with the second grade in 1959; if the second grade has a larger enrollment, we move that to BIG-ENROLLMENT, but if the first grade was larger we leave BIG-ENROLLMENT alone. Then we compare what is in BIG-ENROLLMENT, whether it is from the first or second grade, with the third, etc., always comparing whatever is the largest enrollment so far discovered with the next grade, and similarly for the three years. Each time a grade is found that is larger than that currently in BIG-ENROLLMENT, we move the grade number and the year number to BIG-GRADE and BIG-YEAR, respectively.

The procedure that will be called on by the PERFORM verb may be written as follows:

SEARCH-ROUTINE.
    ADD ENROLLMENT-BY-SEX
        (GRADE, YEAR, 1)
        ENROLLMENT-BY-SEX (GRADE,
        YEAR, 2) GIVING TEMPORARY.

IF TEMPORARY IS GREATER THAN
BIG-ENROLLMENT MOVE
TEMPORARY TO
BIG-ENROLLMENT MOVE
GRADE TO BIG-GRADE MOVE
YEAR TO BIG-YEAR.

The desired search can now be executed by the following PERFORM statement:

PERFORM SEARCH-ROUTINE VARYING YEAR
    FROM 2 BY 1 UNTIL YEAR GREATER
    THAN 4 AFTER GRADE FROM 1 BY 1
    UNTIL GRADE GREATER THAN 12.

The full source program and the concise output are shown in Figures 8.6 and 8.7.

REVIEW QUESTIONS

1. After the completion of the actions called for by a PERFORM, where does control return?
   a. To the statement following the PERFORM.
   b. To the sentence following the one that contains the PERFORM.
   c. To the paragraph following the one that contains the PERFORM.

2. What will be the difference in object program action for these two PERFORM statements?
   a. PERFORM SOME-ROUTINE.
   b. PERFORM SOME-ROUTINE 1 TIME.

3. What will be the effect of this PERFORM statement if the current value of HOW-MANY is zero?
PERFORM THAT-ROUTINE HOW-MANY TIMES.

4. True or false? If procedure-name-1 is a section name and procedure-name-2 is written, the latter must also be a section name.

5. Which of the following statements is *not* true?
   a. If the procedure called on by a PERFORM contains an EXIT verb, the PERFORM *must* be written in the form procedure-name-1 THRU procedure-name-2.
   b. If there is more than one way to reach the end of the procedure called on by the PERFORM, the last paragraph *must* consist of an EXIT verb by itself.
   c. If there is only one way to reach the end of a procedure called on by a PERFORM, an EXIT verb is illegal.
   d. It is not uncommon for a procedure to end in a GO TO that returns control to the beginning of the procedure, but doing such a thing in a procedure called on by a PERFORM is illegal.

6. What would happen in the VARYING data-name option if the procedure called by the PERFORM changed the value of the data-name? Would the original or the changed value determine the number of repetitions?

```
IDENTIFICATION DIVISION.
PROGRAM-ID. 'UG0007'.
AUTHOR. MCCRACKEN AND GARBASSI.
ENVIRONMENT DIVISION.
CONFIGURATION SECTION.
OBJECT-COMPUTER. IBM-360.
SOURCE-COMPUTER. IBM-360.
DATA DIVISION.
WORKING-STORAGE SECTION.
77 TEMPORARY       PICTURE 9999    VALUE ZEROES.
77 BIG-ENROLLMENT       PICTURE 9999    VALUE ZEROES.
77 GRADE               PICTURE 99.
77 YEAR                PICTURE 9.
77 BIG-YEAR            PICTURE 9.
77 BIG-GRADE           PICTURE 99.
01 ENR-TAB.
    02 FILLER          PICTURE X(30)    VALUE
        '050057056053059082046058039067'.
    02 FILLER          PICTURE X(30)    VALUE
        '011012013014015016013019053037'.
    02 FILLER          PICTURE X(30)    VALUE
        '031032053029051023051051042043'.
    02 FILLER          PICTURE X(30)    VALUE
        '00000C0C000000000000000000000000'.
    02 FILLER          PICTURE X(30)    VALUE
        '046043052053051061060071072069'.
    02 FILLER          PICTURE X(30)    VALUE
        '071071075073074029053049021083'.
    02 FILLER          PICTURE X(30)    VALUE
        '052052052052061061072059069059'.
    02 FILLER          PICTURE X(30)    VALUE
        '081043086039059068059051072081'.
    02 FILLER          PICTURE X(30)    VALUE
        '032036054029053081076038063057'.
    02 FILLER          PICTURE X(30)    VALUE
        '050057056053059082046058039067'.
    02 FILLER          PICTURE X(30)    VALUE
        '091084110103005009007006009015'.
    02 FILLER          PICTURE X(30)    VALUE
        '050054056053059082046058039067'.
01 ENROLLMENT-TABLE  REDEFINES ENR-TAB.
    02 ENROLLMENT   OCCURS 12 TIMES.
    03 YEAR-ENROLLMENT   OCCURS 5 TIMES.
    04 ENROLLMENT-BY-SEX   OCCURS 2 TIMES PICTURE 999.
PROCEDURE DIVISION.
    PERFORM SEARCH-RTN VARYING YEAR FROM 2 BY 1 UNTIL YEAR
        GREATER THAN 4 AFTER GRADE FROM 1 BY 1 UNTIL
        GRADE GREATER THAN 12.
    DISPLAY 'BIG GRADE ' BIG-GRADE ' BIG-YEAR ' BIG-YEAR
        ' BIG-ENROLLMENT ' BIG-ENROLLMENT.
    GO TO EOJ-RTN.
SEARCH-RTN.
    ADD ENROLLMENT-BY-SEX (GRADE, YEAR, 1)
        ENROLLMENT-BY-SEX (GRADE, YEAR, 2) GIVING TEMPORARY.
    IF TEMPORARY IS GREATER THAN BIG-ENROLLMENT
        MOVE TEMPORARY TO BIG-ENROLLMENT
        MOVE GRADE TO BIG-GRADE
        MOVE YEAR TO BIG-YEAR.
EOJ-RTN.
    STOP RUN.
```

Figure 8.6. A program using the PERFORM verb to find the largest value in a table.

BIG GRADE 11 BIG-YEAR 2 BIG-ENROLLMENT 0213

Figure 8.7. The output of the program of Figure 8.6.

7. What would happen in the TIMES option if the literal or data-name had a nonintegral value like 2.5?

8. What may be written after the UNTIL in options that use it?

9. When the condition in an UNTIL form is satisfied, is the PERFORM routine called once more or does control pass on to the next statement immediately? In particular, what happens if the condition is satisfied when the PERFORM is first encountered?

10. Referring to the example of computing a RATE from an AMOUNT in PERFORM VARYING, what would the following PERFORM do?

PERFORM RATE-FORMULA VARYING AMOUNT
    FROM 200 BY −5 UNTIL AMOUNT <50.

11. What would be the difference between the results of these two examples?

    a. MOVE ZERO TO TOTAL-A.
       MOVE 1 TO SUBS.
       PERFORM ROUTINE UNTIL SUBS >10.

        .
        .
        .

       ROUTINE. ADD DATA-B (SUBS)
       TO TOTAL-A.
       ADD 1 TO SUBS.

    b. MOVE ZERO TO TOTAL-A.
       PERFORM ROUTINE VARYING SUBS
       FROM 1 BY 1 UNTIL SUBS > 10.

        .
        .
        .

       ROUTINE. ADD DATA-B (SUBS)
       TO TOTAL-A.

12. A PERFORM that executes the procedure more

    a. PERFORM ROUTINE VARYING X FROM
       1 BY 1 UNTIL X = 10.
    b. PERFORM ROUTINE VARYING X FROM
       1 BY 1 UNTIL X > 10.
    c. PERFORM ROUTINE VARYING X FROM
       1 BY 1 UNTIL X < 10.
    d. PERFORM ROUTINE VARYING X FROM
       5 BY 1 UNTIL X > 10.
    e. PERFORM ROUTINE VARYING X FROM
       1 BY 1 UNTIL X = NUMBER-A.

14. Consider the following example:

PERFORM ROUTINE VARYING A FROM 1 BY 1
    UNTIL A > 2 AFTER B FROM 1 BY 1
    UNTIL B > 3.

Write out the six pairs of values that would be taken on by A and B in the order in which they would appear.

15. With reference to the last sample program, which finds the largest enrollment in a table, what would have happened if grade 9 in 1960 (year 3) also had a combined total enrollment of 213?

16. Is it true that the sentence PERFORM ERROR-RTN THROUGH ERROR-RTN-EXIT is a legal COBOL instruction?

8.6   The EXAMINE Verb

As we saw in Section 5.13 and in the sample program in Chapter 7, the EXAMINE verb may be used in validation routines to replace all or leading spaces with zeros.

In more general terms, this verb is used to *tally* (count) the number of appearances of a character in a data item and/or to *replace* it with some other character, with a variety of options. Only DISPLAY items may be used with an EXAMINE.

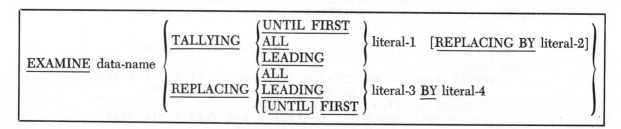

than once is an example of what is usually called a *loop* in programming terminology. A loop has four parts: an *initialization* part, which gives a starting value to some variable; a *compute* part, which does the useful work; a *testing* part, which determines whether there should be more repetitions; and a *modification* part, which changes the value of the variable. Show how the VARYING option has all four of these parts.

13. How many times will the procedure named ROUTINE be executed by these PERFORM statements?

Examination always starts with the leftmost character and proceeds to the right. "FIRST" in the format always refers to the "leftmost."

The TALLYING option produces a "count" or "tally" of the number of occurrences of whatever is requested. This count is placed in a special five-digit register with the name TALLY, which is a reserved word, and is available to the programmer after completion of the EXAMINE action. TALLY does not have to be mentioned in the DATA DIVISION; it may be used for any other purpose if not needed for the EXAMINE verb. The specific contents of the TALLY register after execution of the various EXAMINE options are as follows:

1. When the ALL option is used, TALLY contains the number of occurrences of literal-1, regardless of where they appear in the data item.

2. When the LEADING option is used, TALLY contains the number of occurrences of literal-1 before encountering some character *other than* literal-1.

3. When the UNTIL FIRST option is used, TALLY contains the number of occurrences of characters *other than* literal-1 before the first occurrence of literal-1.

When either of the REPLACING options is used (i.e., with or without TALLYING), the precise actions are as follows:

1. When the ALL option is used, then literal-2 (or literal-4) is substituted for each occurrence of literal-1 (or literal-3), regardless of its position in the word.

2. When the LEADING option is used, the substitution of literal-2 (or literal-4) terminates as soon as a character *other than* literal-1 (or literal-3) is encountered (or when the right end of the item is encountered, of course).

3. When the UNTIL FIRST option is used, the substitution of literal-2 (or literal-4) terminates with the first occurrence of literal-1 (or literal-3) (or when the right end of the item is reached).

4. When the FIRST option is used, only the first occurrence of literal-3 is replaced by literal-4.

EXAMPLES

Figure 8.8 shows a number of examples of how the EXAMINE verb operates.

8.7 The GO TO . . . DEPENDING ON and ALTER Options

Let us assume that we are processing a file that contains three types of record, 1, 2, and 3. For each of them we want to go to a different routine. We could write

IF REC-TYPE EQUAL TO 1 GO TO RTN-A.
IF REC-TYPE EQUAL TO 2 GO TO RTN-B.
IF REC-TYPE EQUAL TO 3 GO TO RTN-C.

The GO TO . . . DEPENDING ON option offers a more compact format to accomplish the same result:

GO TO RTN-A, RTN-B, RTN-C, DEPENDING ON REC-TYPE.

If the value of REC-TYPE is outside the range 1 through 3, program control passes to the statement following the GO TO . . . DEPENDING.

The option ALTER may be used in similar circumstances if we want to modify the logic of the program when a certain condition occurs. Let us assume that we are processing a file that contains many REC-TYPE 1 records, followed by many REC-TYPE 2 records. We can, on reaching the first of the type 2 records, modify the program logic that applied to type 1 records by changing one or

	SAMPLE		Resulting
EXAMINE STATEMENT	Before	After	Value of TALLY
EXAMINE SAMPLE TALLYING ALL '0'	102030	102030	3
EXAMINE SAMPLE TALLYING ALL '0' REPLACING BY SPACES	0016047	16 47	3
EXAMINE SAMPLE TALLYING LEADING '0'	0016047	0016047	2
EXAMINE SAMPLE REPLACING LEADING '0' BY SPACE	0016047	16047	Unchanged
EXAMINE SAMPLE TALLYING LEADING '0' REPLACING BY '*'.	0016047	**16047	2
EXAMINE SAMPLE TALLYING UNTIL FIRST 'Q'.	PT890NQ9	PT890NQ9	6
EXAMINE SAMPLE REPLACING FIRST '*' BY '$'.	***145.82	$**145.82	Unchanged

Figure 8.8. Examples of the action of the EXAMINE verb.

more one-sentence paragraphs containing only a GO TO statement.

> ALTER procedure-name-1 TO PROCEED TO procedure-name-2,
> [procedure-name-3 TO PROCEED TO procedure-name-4,] ...

For instance, if we had a paragraph like PARAGR-1.

GO TO CALC-INTEREST.

we could ALTER it by writing:

IF REC-TYPE EQUAL TO 2 ALTER
    PARAGR-1 TO PROCEED
    TO CALC-CAPIT-GAINS.

In some applications the careful use of the ALTER option may reduce processing time considerably. Since ALTER may be used only to modify paragraphs that contain a single and unconditional GO TO statement, care should be exercised in

establishing these paragraphs at the appropriate points in the program.

8.8 The USE, DEFINE, INCLUDE, and SORT Verbs

As we said briefly in Section 3.6, the USE verb specifies procedures for input/output error and label handling that are, in addition to standard techniques, supplied in the input/output package called into action by OPEN, READ, WRITE, and CLOSE. As we have seen, the standard packages do a great deal and will handle most situations. It will occasionally happen, however, that the programmer will want to specify some action on an error condition or some special label handling that is not provided. All that is required is to write the

---

ANSWERS

1. To the *statement* following the PERFORM. (Of course, if the PERFORM is a sentence by itself or is the last statement in a sentence, then control does return to the sentence following the one containing the PERFORM and a similar statement could be made for paragraphs.)

2. No difference.

3. No effect—the PERFORM is not executed.

4. False: procedure-name-2 could still be a paragraph name.

5. (c). The use of EXIT in this case may be pointless but not illegal.

6. The standard answer to a question like this is, "The action of the compiler and/or object program is unpredicted." Not unpredict*able*, but unpredict*ed*: If anyone considered it important enough, the answer could be determined for any particular implementation. This not having been done, and the action being both pointless and illegal, we just don't know in most cases.

7. This is an invalid source program specification; it would be flagged by most compilers.

8. Any condition, simple or compound, using formulas if desired, etc. The condition could even involve subscripted variables!

9. Immediately; the PERFORM procedure is not executed at all.

10. Just what the earlier example did, but the values of AMOUNT and the corresponding values of RATE

ANSWERS (Continued)

would be printed starting with 200 and working *down* to 50.

11. Absolutely no difference in result but possible difference in object program time.

12. The FROM *initializes* the controlled variable; the BY *modifies* it; the UNTIL condition does the *testing*; the procedure called by the PERFORM does the actual computing work. Note, however, that the last three parts are not done in the order in which they were stated in the question.

13. a. 9.
   b. 10.
   c. None.
   d. 6.
   e. One time less than the value of NUMBER-A.

14. A = 1, B = 1; 1, 2; 1, 3; 2, 1; 2, 2; 2, 3.

15. Grade 9 and year 3 would have been shown as "big grade" and "big year." Grade 11 and year 2 would never have replaced them because their enrollment, when tested, would have been equal to (but *not* greater than) BIG-ENROLLMENT. If this situation does not satisfy you, you may think of some other ways to solve this problem; for instance, by allowing for more than one year and grade to show on the output in case of a tie or by sorting the combined enrollments figures by size, after having written them onto an output tape.

16. No. To the possible dismay of the purists, THRU (and not THROUGH) is the proper spelling in most COBOL compilers.

desired processing in normal PROCEDURE DI-
VISION statements, preceded by a USE that specifies when they are to be applied. There may be
as many USE verbs as necessary, one for each
special procedure.

The procedure to be USEd must be a SECTION,
which is simply a group of one or more paragraphs
headed by a section name and the word SECTION.
On the same line as the section header we write
a USE followed by a few words that indicate when
it is to be applied.

should guide the programmer in making the best
use of this verb for those applications that require
it.

There are three other verbs somewhat akin to
USE in that instead of generating object program
instructions to process data they direct the compiler to do something. (USE *itself* informs the compiler when to apply the section that contains it;
the statements in that section, of course, *do* result
in object program instructions to process data.)

The DEFINE verb (which, like the other two

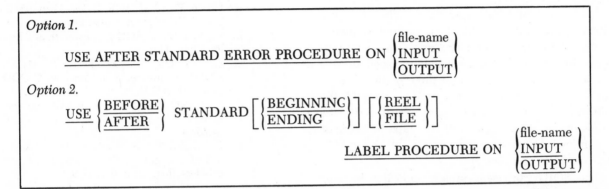

Option 1 applies when it is necessary to do something more than apply the standard error procedures for input and output. We recall that if an
error is detected in tape reading, for instance, the
tape is automatically backspaced and reread a
given number of times; if the error persists, a message is printed, and the supervisory routine may
do something unsuitable to our application. Perhaps all we would like to do in this case is to close
the files and terminate the execution of the program.
This can be accomplished by the following entries:

TAPE-ERROR SECTION.
    USE AFTER STANDARD ERROR
    PROCEDURE ON INPUT.
ERR-RNT.
    CLOSE FILE-1 FILE 2.
    DISPLAY 'UNCORRECTABLE TAPE ERR-
    OR' UPON CONSOLE.
    STOP RUN.

This section would consist of the one paragraph,
which as always must be given a name. The procedure as shown would be called into operation
if such an error developed; in the absence of error, the paragraph would have no effect.

Several compilers contain a number of USE options in addition to the ones shown in the format.
Manufacturers' manuals and installation standards

verbs discussed at the end of this section, is included in only a few implementations) allows us
to set up an entirely new verb with a name and a
function of our own choosing. We might, for instance, have an application that requires frequent
use of a complex formula for computing a discount.
With DEFINE we could set up a new verb called
DISCOUNT and define the format to suit our own
preferences; we might like it to read

DISCOUNT data-name-1 GIVING data-name-2.

DEFINE allows us to establish DISCOUNT as the
name of the new verb and to write this format for
its use: following DEFINE would be a paragraph
detailing the computation of data-name-2 given
data-name-1. The new verb can then be used wherever desired in the source program.

We shall not explore the rules for using the
DEFINE. Those systems that do permit it describe
its use in an appropriate reference manual.

We shall similarly pass lightly over the IN-
CLUDE verb, which, in short, allows us to incor-
porate precoded routines from a library into our
source program. This can be an extremely valuable
feature; the technique is heavily used in scientific
computing, in which, for instance, there are standard functions that nearly everybody needs at one
time or another. It can be almost as useful in com-

mercial data processing for particular types of applications. In some compilers the function of INCLUDE is taken over by an additional option of the COPY verb.

USE, DEFINE, and INCLUDE are called DECLARATIVE operations, which means that they operate under control of the "main body" of the PROCEDURE DIVISION. If present, they *must* be grouped together at the beginning of the PROCEDURE DIVISION, preceded by the key word DECLARATIVES and followed by the key words END DECLARATIVES.

The verb SORT, when available, offers the possibility of arranging a file in a desired sequence *during* the execution of a program. The usual pattern—Run-1, Sort, Run-2—is thus replaced by one single run which performs all three of these steps; for instance, we could read a file, compute the ratio between two fields of each record, write the ratios on an output tape, sort this tape in decreasing order by ratio size, and print it—all this within one COBOL program.

The SORT statement usually indicates at least a fictitious file-name, the sequence key, and the name of the input and output files. Here is an example of its simplest format:

SORT FILE-B ON ASCENDING KEY
    RATIO-P-Y USING TRANS-FILE
    GIVING PRINT-FILE.

TRANS-FILE is the input file; PRINT-FILE is the sorted output file; RATIO-P-Y is the data name of the field that contains the ratio; the KEY may be ASCENDING or DESCENDING; and, finally, FILE-B would not be a file at all, but a special entry that provides a "guide" to the sort feature and is described in some other part of the program.

The SORT feature is subject to several limitations (core storage availability, number of keys, etc.), and before using it it is necessary to refer to the manufacturer's manual and to the installation's standards.

EXERCISES

*1. Write an IF statement to carry out the following: if REORDER-POINT is less than 80% of LEAD-TIME times WEEKLY-AVERAGE, increase REORDER-POINT by 30%.

2. Write an IF statement to carry out the following: if REORDER-POINT is more than 1.3 times LEAD-TIME times WEEKLY-AVERAGE, decrease REORDER-POINT by 20%.

*3. Write IF statements to do the following:
   a. Go to P-69 if AGE is less than 30 and WEIGHT is greater than 170.
   b. Go to 10-YARDS if SPEED-1 is greater than SPEED-2 or if WEIGHT-1 is more than 30 greater than WEIGHT-2.
   c. Go to 2-POINTS if FB-K is greater than FB-C or if FWD-K is greater than FWD-C.
   d. Go to SKATE if ICE is greater than 3 and TEMPERATURE is less than 25.
   e. Go to P-9 if A is greater than 9 and either B equals 8 or C is not equal to 95.

4. Write IF statements to do the following:
   a. Go to P-123 if AGE is less than 65 and SERVICE is greater than 20.
   b. Go to P987 if AGE is greater than 20 and less than 41.
   c. Go to OK if CODX is NUMERIC, CODX is greater than zero, and CODX is less than 10.
   d. Go to NG if ZONE is ALPHABETIC or if ZONE is greater than zero and TYPEX equals 4.
   e. Go to Z-A-3 if X is greater than 1 and A is 2, if Y is greater than 7 and B is 6, or if Z is less than 12 and C is 9.

*5. Two tables of 50 entries each have already been established in the DATA DIVISION; they are named SET-UP and UNIT-TIME. Compute JOB-TIME for the thirteenth entry in each table, in which JOB-TIME is the sum of SET-UP and UNIT-TIME times UNITX.

*6. As in Exercise 5, except compute JOB-TIME for the Nth entry in each table, where N is a data-name in the program to which a value has already been given.

*7. A table named SALES has 50 entries, corresponding to 50 salesmen whose numbers run from 1 to 50. Read a record from a file named SALES-DATA; in this record are a MAN-NUMBER and an AMOUNT. Add the AMOUNT to the table entry for that MAN-NUMBER.

8. An electric-utility billing operation requires that KWH be multiplied by an entry from a table named RATE, where the correct entry in the table is given by the value of SERVICE-TYPE. Perform the multiplication and make the result the new value of an item named BILL.

*9. There is a table named A-TIME with five entries corresponding to the five working days of the week. Use a PERFORM to form the sum of the A-TIMEs and then divide by 5 to get AVERAGE-TIME.

*10. As in Exercise 9, except that TIME has seven entries. Form the sum of the seven entries and also place in COUNT the number of these entries that are nonzero. Divide the total by COUNT to get AVERAGE-TIME.

11. Search the table described in Exercise 7 for

the salesman with the largest sales; DISPLAY his sales and his number.

*12. Write a PERFORM statement to perform a routine named REORDER (which you do not write) repeatedly until ON-ORDER plus ON-HAND is greater than twice MONTHLY-AVERAGE.

13. Write a PERFORM statement to carry out a routine named CALC until $Q^2 - R^2$ is less than $X + 9$.

*14. Write EXAMINE statements to carry out the following operations on a data item named SAMPLE-B:

    a. Change all blanks into hyphens.
    b. Count the number of leading zeros.

    c. Count the number of leading blanks and replace them with periods.
    d. Change all characters up to the first X into X's.

15. Write an EXAMINE statement to carry out the following operation on a data item named EXAMPLE.

    a. Count the number of leading zeros and replace them with blanks.
    b. Change all hyphens into blanks.
    c. Change all characters before the decimal point into 9's.
    d. Change the first R into an S.

9. PROGRAM EFFICIENCY

9.1 Introduction

The cost of getting useful results with a computer is the sum of quite a number of separate factors. We list the most important.

1. The cost of deciding what to do and generally how to do it: the feasibility study and the over-all systems design.

2. The cost of programming: the detailed system design and writing the source program.

3. The cost in computer time to compile the source program into an object program.

4. The cost of locating and correcting any errors in the source program and of proving that the object program really produces correct results for correct data and rejects bad data.

5. The cost of converting the files of the job to magnetic tape or other mass storage medium.

6. The cost of preparing the source data that is processed by the object program.

7. The cost of computer time in running the object program.

8. The cost in personnel and computer time of recovering from errors in the running object program or in the data—errors not detected earlier.

9. The cost of modifying the system as the reporting requirements change.

The cost under item 3—compile time—has been drastically reduced in recent years by improvements that have taken place in both compiler efficiency and operating-system effectiveness. For instance, the compile time for a program like the Inventory Update in Chapter 7 is in the order of one to two minutes; for the other sample programs in this book it is in the order of one minute or less.

As to the other costs, it is not possible to say which of them is "the" most important because that depends on the application. Some computer jobs are "one-shot" affairs, in which the sole goal is one quick set of answers; in this case object program time would not be important at all, but speed of source programming would be crucial. In many business-data-processing applications, however, the cost of running the object program is the over-riding factor because once it is running it is used many times.

In such cases—particularly if the volume of data is substantial—we become concerned with *object program efficiency*, which means simply the speed of the object program, and begin to inquire what can be done in a COBOL source program to improve it.

Even if we accept object program efficiency as the foremost goal, at least for the purposes of this chapter, we must realize that there are still a number of conflicting subgoals to be balanced; for instance, it does not make sense to put so much emphasis on object program speed that source data must be entered in such an awkward form that the computer time savings are more than lost in data preparation. Aside from such technical points, there are a few things that are worth mentioning in connection with the over-all programming effort. We return more specifically to object program efficiency in Sections 9.3 through 9.7.

9.2 Source Program Writing

In recent years we have witnessed a relative decrease in the cost of computer time and a relative increase in the cost of programming time. As a consequence, the efficiency of a programmer—even though difficult to measure—has come under closer scrutiny.

There is no easy formula for efficient programming: this depends on a programmer's aptitude, acumen, and experience. We suggest, here and in Chapter 10, some techniques and practices that may cut down program-writing time and eliminate some potential sources of trouble.

For instance, penciling a COBOL program on a coding sheet may be a tedious job—particularly for those entries that must be rewritten for every program. Furthermore, the improper spelling of some of these entries—for example, WORKING STORAGE SECTION instead of WORKING-STORAGE SECTION—will cause innumerable error messages to appear during the first compilation: every entry in this section will be flagged as an error and will not be recognized in the PROCEDURE DIVISION.

Of course, if there is a COBOL library, the COPY option may alleviate this situation to some extent. But what if there is no library? One solution is to write some special utility programs and use them in a shrewd manner. One such program, called CBLREP by its author,* is shown in Figure 9.1. CBLREP, as the program REMARKS state, reproduces a COBOL deck, inserting sequence numbers into the first six columns of each card and a program name into the last eight. This very simple utility program may be used mainly

(a) to create a good final edition of a program deck when the "provisional" edition was written without card sequence numbers in the interest of speed;

(b) to copy an existing (and working) COBOL deck for the purpose of providing a substantial number of good and tested COBOL entries to a new program that we are about to write.

It is easy to see that such a program is particularly useful in the case of programs using the same input/output files or having a similar processing logic.

* Charles B. Kelley of Esso Standard Libya Inc. Reproduced with author's and company's permission.

We now discuss briefly a few choices that are usually available to a programmer during the compilation and execution of a COBOL program. First of all, let us clarify one important point: once we have in our hands a complete COBOL program, we still need to do a few other things before we can actually run it. In general terms, we must add some instructions to tell the computer what it is expected to do with our program. Instructions of this type must be prepared in a "control" language (not COBOL) which is understood by the operating system of a computer—and would therefore vary with different machines. The main options that may be called on by the "control" cards are usually the following:

1. *Compile.* In this case the computer reads the COBOL instructions, prints the error messages, and, if there are no fatal errors, compiles an object program. This is the proper option to take when compiling the program for the first time.

2. *Compile and go.* If there are no fatal COBOL errors (the error listing may be suppressed if the program has been previously compiled successfully), the computer creates object program instructions, "link-edits" them (this means, roughly, to merge them with input/output instructions provided by the operating system) and executes the "link-edited" object program. Obviously, some input data must be provided when this option is taken.

3. *Catalog.* This option instructs the computer to store the object program in the program library. From then on the execution of the program may be called by one single command if the object program has also been link-edited or two commands (link-edit and execute) if the object program has not been link-edited. (Whether a program has been link-edited or not depends on the type of library in which it is cataloged.) In either case the time-consuming compilation is no longer needed.

Here are some other examples of the kinds of things that an operating system may be informed about and/or called on to do, using appropriate job control commands:

—The source language of this deck is COBOL (or FORTRAN, PL/I, SLIP, BASIC, or whatever language it might be written in, assuming that the operating system includes a compiler for the language in question).

```
001010 IDENTIFICATION DIVISION.
001020 PROGRAM-ID. 'CBLREP'.
001030 AUTHOR.   C B KELLEY.
001040 INSTALLATION. ESSO STANDARD LIBYA INC     TRIPOLI, LIBYA.
001050     REMARKS.     THIS PROGRAM REPRODUCES A COBOL DECK
001060         INSERTING PROGRAM IDENTIFICATION AND SEQUENCE NUMBERS
001070
001080     INPUT
001090     A COBOL DECK, PRECEDED BY A CONTROL CARD CONTAINING
001100         CC 1-6    999999
001110         CC 73-80  PROGRAM IDENTIFICATION
001120
001130     OUTPUT
001140     A DECK WHICH HAS THE PROGRAM IDENTIFICATION
001150         INSERTED IN CC  73-80 AND A SEQUENCE NUMBER
001160         COMPUTED BY INCREMENTS OF 10 INSERTED IN CC 1-6
001170     A LISTING OF THE ABOVE DECK.
001180
001190 ENVIRONMENT DIVISION.
001200 CONFIGURATION SECTION.
001220 OBJECT-COMPUTER. IBM-360.
001210 SOURCE-COMPUTER. IBM-360.
001230 INPUT-OUTPUT SECTION.
001240 FILE-CONTROL.
001250     SELECT CARD-IN ASSIGN 'SYS005' UNIT-RECORD 2540R UNIT.
001260     SELECT CARD-OUT ASSIGN 'SYS007' UNIT-RECORD 2540P UNIT.
001270     SELECT PRINT-LINE ASSIGN 'SYS006' UNIT-RECORD 1403 UNIT.
001280 DATA DIVISION.
001290 FILE SECTION.
001300 FD   CARD-IN
001310     LABEL RECORDS ARE OMITTED, RECORDING MODE IS F,
001320     DATA RECORD IS IN-CARD.
001330 01   IN-CARD.
001340     02 IN-CTL        PICTURE X(6).
001350     02 DATA-FIELD    PICTURE X(66).
001360     02 IN-NAME       PICTURE X(8).
001370 FD   CARD-OUT
001380     LABEL RECORDS ARE OMITTED, RECORDING MODE IS F,
001390     DATA RECORD IS OUT-CARD.
001400 01   OUT-CARD         PICTURE X(80).
001410 FD   PRINT-LINE
001420     LABEL RECORDS ARE OMITTED, RECORDING MODE IS F,
001430     DATA RECORD IS PL.
001440 01   PL               PICTURE X(133).
001450 WORKING-STORAGE SECTION.
001460 01   W-CARD.
001470     02 W-SEQUENCE     PICTURE 9(6)  VALUE 001000.
001480     02 W-COBOL-STAT   PICTURE X(66).
001490     02 W-ID           PICTURE X(8).
001500 PROCEDURE DIVISION.
001510     OPEN INPUT CARD-IN, OUTPUT CARD-OUT, PRINT-LINE.
001520     READ CARD-IN   AT END GO TO END-JOB.
001530     IF IN-CTL NOT EQUAL TO '999999'
001540         DISPLAY 'CONTROL CARD MISSING ' UPON CONSOLE
001550             GO TO END-JOB.
001560     MOVE IN-NAME TO W-ID.
001570 READ-RTN.
001580     READ CARD-IN   AT END GO TO END-JOB.
001590     ADD 10 TO W-SEQUENCE.
001600     MOVE DATA-FIELD TO W-COBOL-STAT.
001610     WRITE OUT-CARD FROM W-CARD.
001620     WRITE PL FROM W-CARD.
001630     GO TO READ-RTN.
001640 END-JOB.
001650     CLOSE CARD-OUT, PRINT-LINE, CARD-IN.
001660     STOP RUN.
```

Figure 9.1. A program to reproduce a COBOL source-program deck, inserting sequence numbers.

—Output should go onto tape B4 instead of the standard tape.

—Data on punched cards follows the source deck.

—The cost accounting number for this job is 3892X9.

—There is no source deck; the object program is on disk 3, cylinders 34 to 38; input is on tape A3; all other options are standard.

The handling of control cards is one of the chores that every programmer must learn and fairly early in the game. Unfortunately, very little about the various operating systems and their control cards is standardized, and we are unable to give the reader specific information on the subject.

From the source programmer's standpoint, recognizing and acting on control cards is the most important function of an operating system, since it is the area in which the programmer has direct contact with the system. But there are other ways the operating system can get into the act, of which the following are representative:

—Reading input and writing output, which require the use of rather involved programs written for the purpose by specialists in such work, are actually quite complex operations. Most operating systems include the routines to do the input and output for all normal programs, even those written in COBOL or some other high-level language.

—Input and output programs include extensive checking for machine malfunction. If an apparent error is detected, other routines are brought into play to try to verify that there definitely is an error and in some cases to attempt to correct it.

—Many modern computers are able to operate in what is known as a multiprogramming mode, which means that two or more programs are in the system at the same time and in some sense "share" the computer. Perhaps one works in core while the other is delayed waiting for input or perhaps there are parallel arithmetic units which allow several things to happen simultaneously. The control of such systems to gain effective use of the equipment is extremely complicated and another task that may be a part of an operating system.

A complete discussion of operating systems would fill volumes, since it is an extensive and complex subject that would require the efforts of many programmers who specialize specifically in that one area. For our purposes here, however, this sketch will have to do. The COBOL programmer has little occasion to study the subject in great depth in any case, and the specifics he needs in order to use COBOL effectively must come from publications related to his particular operating system.

9.3   Input and Output Speed

Let us now go back to object program efficiency.

The primary conditions in optimizing input and output operations in the object program are blocking and buffering. Blocking, as we saw in Chapter 2, refers to the placement of several "logical" or "problem" records in one physical tape block. This speeds up the object program by reducing the amount of time that must be spent in passing over the gaps of blank tape inserted between blocks in almost all magnetic tape systems. Blocking also reduces the amount of tape used, of course.

In order to take advantage of blocking it is necessary to be able to read a complete block into high-speed storage in the case of input or to assemble a complete block in storage before writing it in the case of output. The limitation on the amount of time that can be saved by blocking is therefore the availability of enough core storage to hold the large blocks. Also, the gains diminish after some reasonable blocking factor (the number of problem records in a physical tape block) is reached; for instance, if records are the same length as the interblock gap, a blocking factor of 10 saves about 45% of the total tape time, whereas a blocking factor of 20 saves 47½%, which is not a significant increase over 45%.

Furthermore, if the records are quite long, blocking may not save anything. Suppose we have records of 1000 characters on a tape with 200 characters to the inch and gaps of 0.75 inch. A blocking factor of 10, say, will save about 12% on tape time, which is likely to be completely lost in the internal time necessary to access the records sequentially from the complete block (aside from the fact that not all machines have storage capacity for blocks of 10,000 characters).

The reason for this must be made clear. When we discussed the READ verb, we said that if all records from the block currently in storage have not been processed the next logical record is "made available." This involves moving the next logical record to an intermediate area, modifying all the instructions that refer to the read area so that the next record is accessed, or carrying out an operation with the "index registers" available in some machines. If index registers are not available, in particular, and with bad luck in any case, this apparently simple operation of making the next record available can take considerable time—easily enough to wash out a 12% tape time saving. Like so many other things to be discussed in this chapter, the exact details depend strongly on the particular computer and compiler. It may be hoped that each manufacturer will supply users with a concise summary of the COBOL features that are fast and those that are slow with each system, along with a list of general suggestions for improving object program efficiency. In any event, it is a fairly safe generalization that the object program must be somewhat more complex to handle blocked records; try to determine whether the tape savings are large enough to justify this additional complexity (which they often are, of course; we do not mean to suggest that blocking should always be avoided).

Record blocking is one technique that affects the balance between input/output time and internal processing time; the other is buffering.

Buffering refers to the mode of computer organization and operation in which it is possible to carry out input and/or output operations at the same time that internal operations are being performed on data previously read. As we noted in Chapter 2, this involves transferring data from tape into a special storage device at tape speed and later interrupting internal processing long enough to move the data into core storage at the much faster core transfer rates (or, alternatively and more commonly, transferring one word at a time into the regular core storage, which interrupts internal operation only intermittently). Making effective use of buffering, whatever electronic technique is used to do it, requires additional core storage areas: it is not feasible to try to read into an area while processing the data in it. Instead, two areas are set up, one to hold the previous data that is being processed and another to accept the new data coming in. A similar technique is used for output, one area to hold the results being written and another, the results being developed. More sophisticated techniques make it possible to get most of the advantages of buffering without two separate areas for *each* tape, but the general idea is the same.

Buffering costs something, too: a *complete* overlap between reading or writing and internal processing is not possible. For one thing, internal operations must be suspended long enough to dump the buffer or to fill it; this amounts to perhaps 15% of the tape time, although the figure varies for different computers. For another thing, the alternation of the two buffer areas takes a certain amount of internal processing time, even if the COBOL source programmer hardly need be aware that it is happening.

Despite these costs, however, it would be rare to find an application in which buffering is not worthwhile. About all we can say on this point is that in some cases there may be alternative buffering techniques available to take advantage of special job or machine characteristics; the individual manufacturer must supply information on how to make best use of these methods.

9.4 Item Layout in Fixed-Length Word Machines

A factor that bears heavily on virtually everything having to do with object program speed is the way the data items are laid out on tape and in core storage. This matter is crucial, whether COBOL is used or not; with COBOL it is possible, although extremely ill advised, to ignore it. We touched on this matter in Section 5.10, but it is so important that review and elaboration are in order, beginning with an example.

Suppose we are working with a machine in which a word has eight characters and that we have four-word records laid out as follows:

AAAAAAAA AABBBBCC CCDDDDEE
    EEFFFFFF

To begin with, this is a poor way to assign the six items to four words because three items are split across two words, a problem that cannot be completely avoided without wasting some space but can be reduced to one split word by the following rearrangement:

AAAAAAAA AAFFFFFF BBBBCCCC
    DDDDEEEE

It might be mentioned at this point that the layout of items on tape is not always under the control of the programmer writing the PROCEDURE DIVISION. Since tape must often be processed by several programs, or produced by one and processed by another, data descriptions may be prepared by one person or group and used by all programmers.

It is to be assumed that these people or groups will take into account the factors under discussion, but at any rate these things are not always at the discretion of the PROCEDURE DIVISION writer.

The responsibility for making the best use of the computer does not end with the writing of the DATA DIVISION, however. Suppose that the items on tape simply cannot be organized to lead to the shortest possible object program. Does this mean that the person writing the PROCEDURE DIVISION can do nothing to hold down the computer time? Of course not. Look again at the foregoing example. Even with the rearrangement, each item must still be separated from one other item before it can be processed; if an item must be used more than once in different statements, why make this separation more than once? Suppose, for instance, that CCCC is a quantity-on-hand that appears in half a dozen statements: it is clearly wasteful to carry out the separation of CCCC from BBBB six times. Much better: move it *once* to a working-storage location described as constituting one full word, which will mean filling it out with zeros or spaces (depending on whether the item is NUMERIC or ALPHABETIC). With this one operation out of the way, all subsequent references to the item will involve just one instruction.

This example brings up a rule that ought to be obvious but is nevertheless often violated through carelessness: don't ever do *anything* twice if you can get by doing it once. For a hypothetical but realistic example suppose we had to evaluate the formula

$$X = 2(A + B) - (A + B)^2 + \frac{6}{A + B}$$

We know how to write a COMPUTE statement to evaluate it just as it stands, but why form the sum of A and B three times? Much better:

COMPUTE T = A + B.
COMPUTE X = 2 * T - T ** 2 + 6 / T.

Depending on how A and B are stored, this improvement might mean a small savings or a large one, but the principle is valid in any case. We saw another illustration of this idea in the sample program in Figure 8.6.

9.5   COMPUTATIONAL Versus DISPLAY

In some machines there is no difference in the way in which data items are stored: this section does not apply to them. In the most important group of the machines in use, however, items are represented and stored in different formats—a point we discuss in Chapters 2 and 5. It will not be uncommon, therefore, to have some data items in the DISPLAY format (which is assumed if the USAGE clause is omitted), some in the COMPUTATIONAL format, and still some others in the COMPUTATIONAL-3. This may be necessary and recommendable, but we must be aware that the presence of these different formats creates the need for conversions.

When are these conversions required? Obviously they must be done whenever a data item in one form is moved to a location with which the other form is associated. More than this, however, *any* data item on which arithmetic is to be done *must* be converted to the equivalent of one of the COMPUTATIONAL forms, if it is not already, before the arithmetic can be carried out. This is easy to overlook, since it is permissible to do arithmetic on DISPLAY items, and if a USAGE clause is not written the item is assumed to be DISPLAY. Such conversions can have a bad effect on the running time of an object program.

If it is unavoidable that arithmetic be done on DISPLAY items, common sense dictates that no conversions be repeated on the same item. Furthermore, the conversion is slowed down even more if the item is split across words, which we have seen to be avoidable in some cases.

9.6   Balancing Input/Output and Processing Time

So far we have considered ways to reduce input/output time and, separately, other ways to reduce internal processing time. Any computer run obviously involves both, and we become concerned with the balance between the two; the general principle is to try to make these times equal.

If internal operations must wait for more data or for results to be written, the system is said to be input-output bound (usually abbreviated as I/O-bound). If, on the other hand, the internal processing is so complex that there are long periods in which input-output devices are not moving, the system is said to be process-bound.

The ideal situation in this regard, of course, is to have a system neither I/O-bound nor process-bound; that is, input and output time is just matched by internal time. It is seldom possible to match these times exactly, but careful planning can avoid serious mismatches. This must sometimes be considered early in the system's design; for instance, if a process-bound run is preceded and followed by I/O-bound runs, it may be possible to transfer some of the processing of the "middle" run to the others. This is not strictly a programming concern, being rather in the province of system design, but the alert programmer will be watchful for such situations—especially since they cannot always be foreseen when the system design is begun.

Returning to something that the COBOL source programmer *can* do something about, it can happen that a run will be unavoidably I/O-bound, in which case the programmer should put no great effort into reducing object-program internal-processing time. Anything that gets the job done without excessive waste will be adequate. In the situation in which a run is process-bound, the programmer will concentrate his efforts on removing anything that uses time avoidably; he might, for instance, search for a programming method that could result in an object program that takes more space for instructions but can be executed faster. Such trade-offs are common. Likewise, there may be some way to make use of more storage for data and results to reduce internal processing time.

9.7   An Efficiency Checklist

As noted before, there are few general principles that are entirely independent of the characteristics of the application, the compiler, or the computer. The following checklist must therefore be used in conjunction with certain detailed information about the particular situation, especially the object machine. It will also be helpful, naturally, to have whatever information can be obtained from the manufacturer about how some of these items affect the implementation at hand.

With these provisos in mind, we may suggest a dozen things to consider when trying to conserve object program machine time.

1. *Do* use blocking to conserve tape time (and space).

2. *Do* write everything possible on tape or disk rather than printing, punching on-line, or displaying, if you have the choice.

3. *Don't* split items across words in a fixed-word-length machine any more than necessary. Tape space and time will sometimes force such splits, but always decide whether the tape time saved is worth the additional processing time.

4. *Don't* do anything twice if you can avoid it economically. If an arithmetic expression occurs several times in a formula, or even in the same program segment, compute it once in advance. If an item must be converted from DISPLAY to COMPUTATIONAL or vice versa several times or if it must be extracted from other items in the same word(s), do the time-consuming operations *once* and move the result to a separate working-storage location from which it can be obtained for all subsequent operations.

5. *Do* arrange branches so that the first test is for the most likely condition. If you know that one of the three paths at an IF statement will be taken 95% of the time, the obvious approach is to test for this condition first.

6. *Do* try to balance input and output time and internal processing time, making the two as nearly equal as possible.

7. *Do* arrange your runs so that as much as possible of the set-up (tape mounting, paper changing, etc.) can be done while other parts of the system are productively occupied.

8. *Don't* stop the computer to let the operator make manual corrections to bad data unless there is absolutely no way to proceed otherwise. Even then it is usually better to remove the run entirely than to try to make the corrections under the pressure of having an expensive computer stand idle.

9. *Do* check input extensively for erroneous data: the programming and computer time this takes will generally be more than saved by avoiding rerunning data or in trying to recover from the messes that such data can create with marvelous ease.

10. *Don't* insert unnecessary niceties. If you are going to double a number that you know fits in four characters and put the result in a five-character location, don't use the ON SIZE ERROR option; the overflow could *never* occur in this situation and testing for it wastes both time and space in the object program. Do use it in a division (the divisor may be zero) and in open-ended accumulating fields.

11. *Don't* make rash use of source-program features that may be extremely expensive in your machine. An editing operation that takes just one

instruction in one computer could easily require a complex loop and the execution of dozens of instructions in other machines, whereas a simple data transfer that takes one instruction in some machines might require many in others. *You must either know the basics of machine-language programming for your computer or have a summary of what is simple and what is difficult in your machine.* Three operations that are complex in quite a few cases are editing, subscripting, and the EXAMINE verb.

12. This is directed more to the supervisor of programming than to the programmer, but it is probably the most important of all. *Do* assign your best programmers to the task of laying out the DATA DIVISIONS for the main files well in advance of the actual programming. If careful attention is given to this job, taking due account of system-design problems *and* computer characteristics, the people writing the PROCEDURE DIVISIONS that process these files will be relieved of many of the worries we have considered in this chapter.

10. CASE STUDY 3: PAYROLL– SYSTEM DESIGN TO STARTUP

In this chapter we consider another standard data-processing application to get a better idea of what is commonly done with computers and how the task is approached. The emphasis this time is on the system design*: the over-all organization of computer and methods to obtain the desired results. We attempt to indicate how COBOL assists in the work, but we do not show the COBOL program.

The main thing to be gained from this chapter, therefore, is a general picture of the major steps in going from a bare statement of the requirements to a running system. In the course of this "outline" of the complete job we are able to suggest some areas of study that have been omitted so far, such as program testing, file conversions, and system documentation.

10.1 The Business Situation

The basic idea of a payroll application sounds deceptively simple: given time cards showing the hours worked by each employee and a master file of his hourly pay rate and accumulated payroll totals, compute and print his check for a week's work and up-

---

* Systems design, of course, is a major subject in itself; we shall skim only the highlights. For further study we recommend Laden and Gildersleeve, *System Design for Computer Applications*, Wiley, New York, 1963.

date the totals. Unfortunately the job is far from being as simple as it may sound at first hearing. Consider some of the additional factors that must be taken into account.

—Most industrial concerns need to know how the cost of the work is allocated among the various jobs on which the employee worked during the week. If his time card shows the number of hours spent on each job or if the same information is given by separate job tickets, this *labor distribution* function is a natural by-product of the payroll operations.

—There are, at a minimum, several, and more often dozens, of different deductions that can be taken from the gross salary to arrive at a net check. Each of these deductions must be allotted space in the master file, each must be calculated separately, and provision must be made for the possibility that the employee may not earn enough in some week to cover all the deductions.

—Reports of a wide variety must be produced to document the actions taken.

—There are literally dozens of changes that may have to be made in an employee's master record: pay rate; number of dependents; new, deleted, or modified deductions; adjustments in accumulated totals to correct previous errors; marital status.

—Provision must be made for adding new master records as new employees are hired and for deleting records when employees terminate (but the master record cannot as a rule *actually* be deleted for some time, since it contains tax and deduction information that must be reported later).

As an illustration of the kind of payroll operation that might not occur to the casual observer, an entire run must be set up to *reconcile* checks; that is, to account for every payroll check issued as it is returned from the bank and to prepare a periodic list of checks issued that have not been returned.

To emphasize once more the complexity of this simple-sounding job we may indicate a few of the more or less standard aspects of a payroll application that we shall *not* consider here.

—The salaried payroll for employees who are paid by the week or month rather than by the hour.

—Piecework pay, in which the employee is paid by the amount of work done rather than by the hour (also called incentive payroll), can be *extremely* complex.

—Quarterly and yearly tax reporting, in which the necessary information is extracted from the master file totals and reported to the proper governmental agencies.

—Retirement plans.

—Accrual of vacation pay.

—Explicit provision of an "audit trail" to allow auditing of the correctness of the work.

10.2 The System Design

The person entering into this application would now face the task of system design, by which we mean the set of decisions regarding exactly *what* is to be done and at least approximately *how*. This phase of getting a computer system going involves a number of tasks.

1. Developing a precise statement of what must be done. An indication of the nature of this aspect is suggested by the following questions.

—Just how is each deduction computed?

—If there is not enough gross pay to cover all deductions, which are taken first?

—Is overtime allotted to the job on which it was spent or averaged over all jobs for the week?

—How old must an unreconciled check be before it is listed in the outstanding checks report?

—Will hours be summarized for the week before entering the computer, summarized for the day only, or simply shown for each job each day?

—How much checking is to be done on the validity and reasonableness of the input?

—Will salary garnishees be set up as a "standard" deduction or will they be handled by adjustment cards that subtract the amount of the garnishee from gross, without setting up a special deduction for it?

2. Determining when data will arrive and when results must be supplied. If weekly paychecks are distributed on Friday of the following week, which is not uncommon, time cards and job tickets may arrive at the data-processing center late Monday afternoon; does this provide enough time to prepare checks for distribution to the departments on Thursday afternoon? If not, can some way be worked out to get the data in earlier or to do some preliminary processing (e.g., master-file changes) before the main work begins? In some companies data is presented and preprocessed daily, so that on Monday it is necessary only to process Friday's data and merge it with a summary of the preprocessed data for the first four days of the week. Beyond these questions of over-all timing, what about late or missing data? Payroll data is usually accepted up to some cutoff time and introduced after part of the normal processing has already been done; after that, checks are prepared manually and the master-file totals are adjusted the following week.

In this case study we blithely assume that all data arrives on time on Monday and that enough computer time is available to get the checks out when needed; in practical applications this would be a most unrealistic assumption.

3. Designing card and report formats. This is rather specialized work that requires consideration of a number of factors beyond the obvious necessity of space for everything that must be recorded.

—Any form should be easy to fill out with the spaces arranged so that entries can be made in some logical order; enough room must be provided for handwriting of normal size; any form that is to be typed must account for typewriter characters and line spacing and involve a minimum of resetting margins and tab stops; nothing should have to be filled in that can be preprinted; the spaces for data should be unambiguously labeled; spaces for data on related forms should be laid out in the same sequence to minimize confusion with un-familar forms; if some of the information on the form must be coded later by an editor, there must be space for the code; some consideration must be given to the convenience of the data arrangement when the card is read and processed in the computer.

—Time cards and job tickets are almost always filled out on the punched card that will later be punched and entered into the computer. Such a card format must obviously make it possible for the card-punch operator to see the information as it is being punched (on e.g., IBM card punches a small part of the card is always out of sight behind the punch housing).

—Reports must have headings, either printed by the computer or preprinted, to be readable; the form design must take the printer characteristics into detailed consideration; the information in the report must be arranged in some logical order that makes the report easy to use; thought must be given to separation of the sheets, if as usual they come in a continuous form; the method of binding and/or storing a bulky report must be taken into account.

Good forms design is a specialty in itself. We shall not try to explore all of the ramifications of the subject but simply exhibit some acceptable examples of the forms required in this case study (Figures 10.2, 10.3, 10.5, and 10.6). Anyone interested in further information can consult a book on forms design or see Chapter 9 of the book by Laden and Gildersleeve referred to earlier.

4. Decisions must be reached on the *controls* to build into the system, to give some assurance that processing is proceeding correctly. We have mentioned a number of types of control in preceding chapters: record counts, control totals on some data item within the records in a file, and batch totals on transactions. Batch totals are used in this case study, as discussed more fully later.

5. Since it only rarely happens that a major application can be completed in one run on the computer, the job must be divided into separate runs. The decisions on this point are governed by such considerations as these:

—Each run must use no more than the maximum number of tape and disk units available, taking into account any that are reserved for such things as the object program and the operating system.

—When there is a choice whether to assign a particular function to one run or the one following, the decision may be dictated by an attempt to keep the input and output time in each run balanced with its internal processing.

—The runs should be designed to require a minimum of tape changing and other *setup* operations between runs; setup time generally ties up the computer just as completely as productive work.

—To the extent possible, runs should be designed to require a minimum of run-to-run communication, since, if avoidable, this represents wasted input/output time.

—To a certain extent run design is influenced by the necessity to insert late data into the process after the processing has been started.

—In some applications it is preferable to minimize the number of runs, since doing so will alleviate many other problems, such as input/output time, the need for consistent formats, and control totals to check run-to-run communication accuracy. In some other cases—particularly when many future changes are anticipated—it may prove more convenient to use the "modular runs" approach: several short programs, each performing a distinct system step. It will be much easier, later on, to modify several short and easy programs than tampering with the logic of few, though complex, ones.

6. If both tapes and disks are available, decisions must be made on which file media should be used for the master files and the other files in the systems. For disk files a choice must be made on the technique to use for the updating and processing runs: random access may be the answer in some cases, sequential processing in others.

It should not be thought that system design is a clear-cut series of precise steps, beginning with a definite starting point and proceeding by a nicely logical path to a definite goal. It is, in fact, a somewhat vague process of acquiring information in increasing depth, combined with a host of compromises, many of which are none too satisfactory. Often it is quite impossible to complete one step until some idea is obtained of how a decision at this point would affect later decisions. It is well and good to say that the system designer should minimize the number of runs, but, until he has made a rough guess at how to do it, how can he know what the storage requirements are for each run? Unfortunately it is sometimes necessary to reject perfection in the interest of getting the job done in a practical amount of time. If it should happen that two medium-sized runs could be squeezed into one, 10 minutes of computer time might be saved, but to determine that the combination is possible may require a complete coding of the job, wasting one or two man-months of programming time if it should turn out that they cannot be combined. Dozens of similar examples could be cited to demonstrate that (a) system design is more an art than a science and (b) a good system designer must not only know the computer and the application but be a master of the pragmatic compromise. Perhaps it is such characteristics that make the job so fascinating. Most likely the reader will never appreciate, until he has been through it once,

how many false starts, how many what-would-happen-ifs, how many searches for missing information, how many later-to-be-refined roundhouse estimates, and how many concessions to harsh reality are involved in system design. For this case study we shall not try to fabricate the agonizing, yet intensely satisfying history of the complete project but shall present only the outline of the completed job, realizing that it must look sterile and lifeless when coldly displayed in finished form.

As usual, the best way to get a quick picture of the processing to be done in an application is to study the run diagrams, which are shown for this case study in Figures 10.1, 10.4, 10.7, 10.8, and 10.9.

Time to gross run (Figure 10.1).   Run 1 accepts

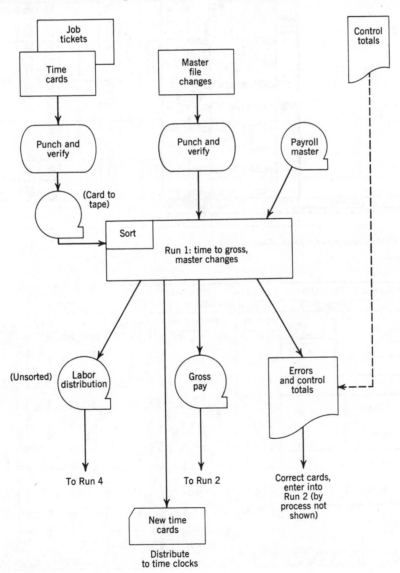

Figure 10.1.   Run diagram of the Time-to-Gross run of the payroll case study.

time cards and job tickets, the payroll master file, and changes to the master; it produces a tape of labor costs, a new deck of time cards for use next week, a tape giving the gross pay for each man, and a listing of errors discovered in validating the input.

The card formats for time cards and job tickets are shown in Figures 10.2 and 10.3.

We see that there is space on each time card for the total hours worked in the week; this number is computed by desk calculator or a tabulator in the payroll section before the time cards are sent to data processing. One reason for doing it this way is that we want to develop a control total. Let us assume that there are 5000 hourly workers in the payroll and that employee numbers have five digits. Then for each "thousand group" of payroll numbers the total hours worked are recorded on paper tape and transmitted to data processing. This means that there will be a control total for the group of time cards for employees whose numbers begin with 00, another for employee numbers be-

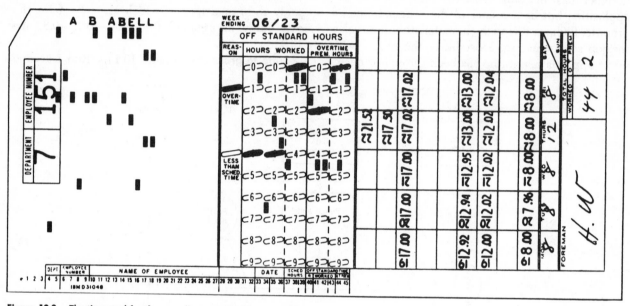

Figure 10.2. The time card for the payroll case study. (Courtesy IBM.)

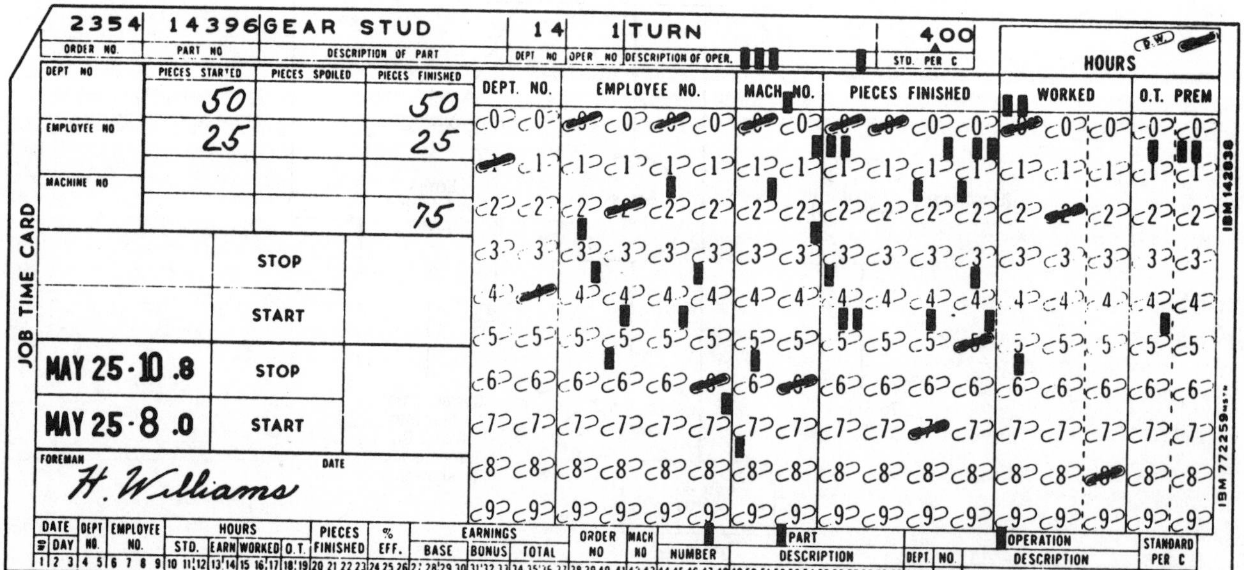

Figure 10.3. The job ticket for the payroll case study. (Courtesy IBM.)

ginning 01, another for employee numbers beginning 02, and so on. There could conceivably be a thousand employees in a group, but ordinarily the employee numbers do not form an unbroken sequence. The average size control group might thus be more like 50 cards, which is a reasonable compromise between the excessive cost of preparing too many control totals if the control groups are too small and the difficulty of finding the error if control groups are too large. The exact details vary, but some such control totals transmitted with the input are common practice and for good reason: they guard especially against lost data, as well as the possibility of dishonest alteration of the data between the payroll office and the computer.

The control totals are received from payroll as an adding-machine tape or a tabulator listing. They are checked against totals produced by the computer on the same listing that details errors in input. If the totals do not check, the differences are tracked down by manual detective work and the errors are corrected.

The time cards that enter the system at this point are prepunched with employee number and department as part of the output of the time-to-gross run in the preceding week; all that needs to be punched now are the hours worked and any special notations such as sick leave, vacation, or overtime. Job tickets are partly prepunched in the case of standard jobs on which a great many people work. The time cards are verified because of the serious morale problems caused by an incorrect paycheck, but the job tickets are not, since an error here would affect only the labor distribution report, which although important is not nearly so sensitive to small errors. Besides, it is easy to check the consistency of the input for each man: the total hours shown on his time card ought to be equal to the total of the hours shown on all his job tickets. If these two are the same, or close, we will not be concerned about the slight chance of two compensating errors in the job tickets for one man: even if it happened, it would not be important enough to justify the considerable extra cost of verifying many thousands of job tickets each week.

The time cards and job tickets are now converted to magnetic tape by using either the mainframe computer or a smaller one off-line and sorted by means of a standard sort program; after sorting, the time card for each man will be ahead of his job tickets.

Almost everything in the master file is subject to change; marital status, name (in case of marriage, usually), number of dependents, bond-purchase-plan participation, accumulated totals (to correct errors or to introduce the data for a manually prepared check), etc., etc. In some computer payroll systems these changes, which could run to several hundred a week in our case, are handled as a separate small run, mostly to get the job out of the way before the peak activity of actually processing the time cards and preparing checks. Here, to keep things simple, we accept them during the time-to-gross run. These change cards can be sorted by a card sorter easily enough.

To avoid having to write two new master tapes these changes are transmitted unchanged to the gross pay tape and written in the master in Run 2. This forces an awkwardness, however: any changes to pay rate must be read from the change before the gross pay is computed. Another, and perhaps more reasonable, solution would be to introduce all master file changes in a separate *file maintenance* run at some other time during the week.

The processing in this run is fairly extensive— in fact, this run as outlined here would probably overextend storage availability and have to be broken down into smaller runs. The input must be sorted into employee-number sequence before processing against the master file. Of course, the time cards are already in sequence (otherwise the control totals could not have been prepared), but there will be many fewer time cards than job tickets and it would probably be faster to carry the time cards through the sorting than to hold them aside while the job tickets were sorted and then merge the two. This sorting would in some systems be set up as a separate run; it will be virtually that here, since the sorting program would take all of core storage, after which the program for the rest of the run's work would be brought in.

After sorting, the processing includes the following.

1. Validation of the input: checking for such things as nonexistent employee numbers (although this particular error will be minimized by having prepared the bulk of the time cards on the computer), impossible hours worked, inconsistent hours on time card versus total hours on job tickets, etc. As we have said before, this kind of checking is strongly recommended. It doesn't take very long —in fact the *net* time to do it may be zero, if, for instance, it can be done during overlapped-card

reading time. Generally, whatever computer time it may cost will be more than saved later by not having to deal with the consequences of these errors. Any bad data discovered during this checking is thrown out for the time being, with an error listing of what happened. The corrected time cards could be entered as a minor input to Run 2 or processed manually; corrected job tickets could be held over to the following week with little inconvenience.

2. Computation of gross pay from hours worked and the hourly rate which can be found in the master file. The gross pay for each man, along with any of his time-card data which must be printed on his earnings statement and any master changes, are written out on a gross-pay tape that will be the main input to Run 2.

3. Once each man's gross pay has been computed his job tickets must be read and the gross pay, "distributed," to the different jobs on which he worked during the week. This is not quite so simple as it sounds: there must at least be a decision regarding the allocation of overtime. It is

usually necessary to charge overtime against the job on which it was spent, which complicates the procedure somewhat. We shall leave this matter unresolved. At any rate, the labor distribution tape contains a record for each job on which each man worked in the order in which the job tickets appeared in the input. Each record gives a job number and a labor cost, and some systems also carry along the labor hours. This tape becomes the input to the labor distribution run.

4. It is a simple matter to punch new time cards at some point in the system; we have shown them as an output of this run. It obviously takes less effort to have the computer punch these cards with employee and department numbers than to punch them manually and there is less chance of error. After punching it might be necessary to sort them by department number to simplify the distribution to time-card racks.

Gross to net run (Figure 10.4). Run 2 accepts the gross-pay tape and the payroll master (again) and carries out the following steps:

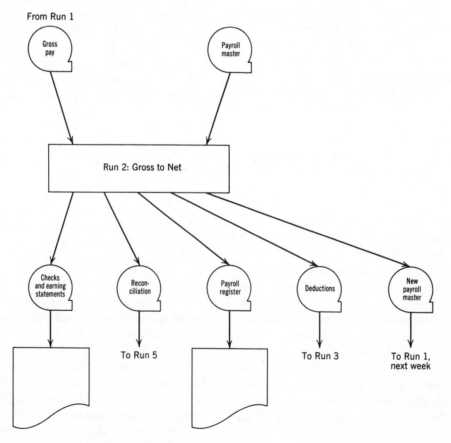

Figure 10.4.   Run diagram for the Gross-to-Net run of the payroll case study.

1. The main function, obviously, is to compute the net pay after subtracting all deductions from gross pay. This is not trivial! For one thing there are typically many possible deductions, 15 or 20 being not at all excessive. Seldom would one man have all of them, but naturally routines must be provided for all. For another thing some of them are complex individually. Finally, it can happen easily enough that a man does not earn enough in a week to cover all the deductions, in which case there must be provision to delay the less crucial ones, along with a precise definition of those that come first.

2. All of the information generated here must be summarized on the earnings statement for each employee; editing this information can be a sizable task in itself. A sample of a continuous earning statement and check form is shown in Figure 10.5.

3. This information generally must be presented also in the form of a payroll register, like that shown in Figure 10.6. The payroll register is kept on file in the payroll section for answering questions from employees, to assist in tracking down errors, and for auditing purposes. The payroll register is not always kept on paper forms; some systems maintain it on magnetic tape for processing

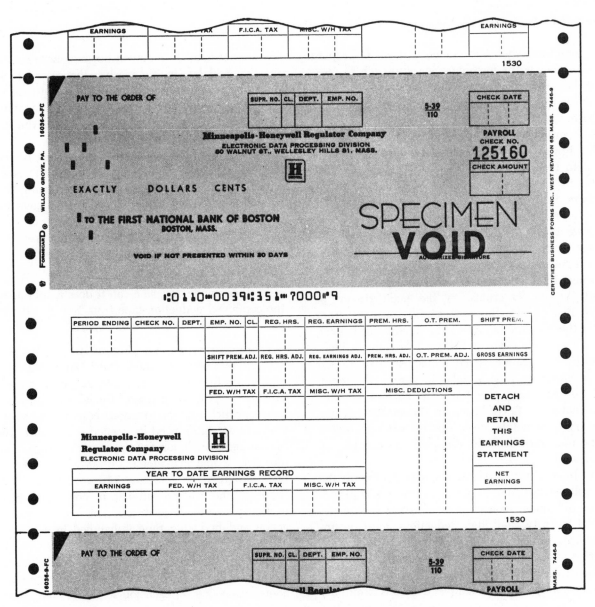

Figure 10.5. Example of a continuous form with earnings statement and check together. (Courtesy Forms, Inc.)

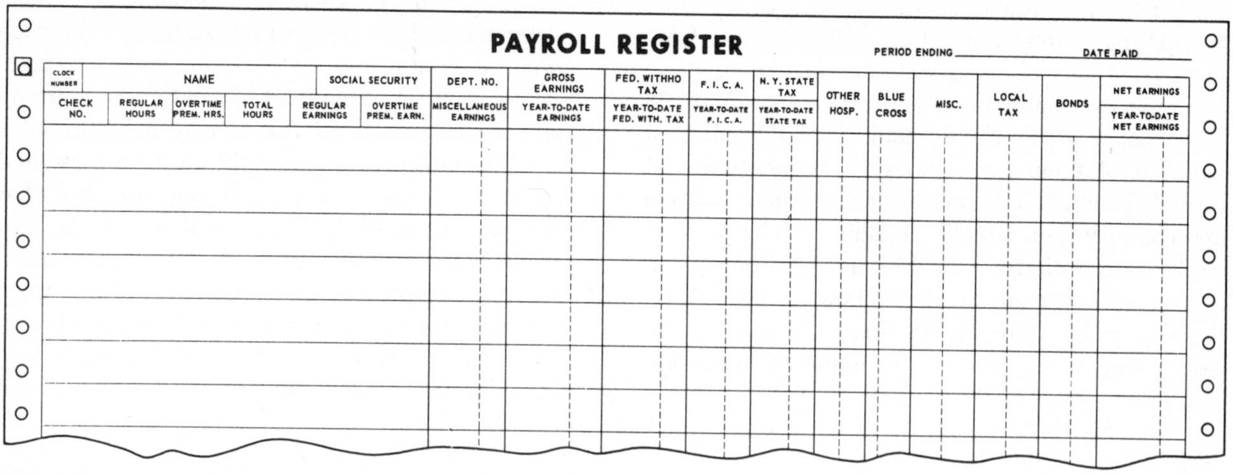
PAYROLL REGISTER
PERIOD ENDING
DATE PAID
CLOCK NUMBER | NAME | SOCIAL SECURITY | DEPT. NO. | GROSS EARNINGS | FED. WITHHO TAX | F. I. C. A. | N. Y. STATE TAX | OTHER HOSP. | BLUE CROSS | MISC. | LOCAL TAX | BONDS | NET EARNINGS
CHECK NO. | REGULAR HOURS | OVERTIME PREM. HRS. | TOTAL HOURS | REGULAR EARNINGS | OVERTIME PREM. EARN. | MISCELLANEOUS EARNINGS | YEAR-TO-DATE EARNINGS | YEAR-TO-DATE FED. WITH. TAX | YEAR-TO-DATE F. I. C. A. | YEAR-TO-DATE STATE TAX | YEAR-TO-DATE NET EARNINGS

Figure 10.6. An example of a payroll register. (Courtesy Moore Business Forms, Inc.)

by computer when information is needed. Keeping it on paper is the more common approach at present, however.

4. Most payroll systems also require deduction registers, which show for each type of deduction the complete list of transactions for each week. This brings up an interesting point: there would seldom be enough tape units to assign a separate tape to each deduction type. What to do? The answer is to write *all* deductions on one tape in whatever order they appear, giving each deduction a code that will identify its type. A separate run (Run 3, in this example) can then sort this tape by deduction type and prepare each report in sequence. Furthermore, since the timing of these reports is not so critical as the main stream of preparing checks, this run can be done at leisure after the pressure of getting the payroll out is over, perhaps on Thursday or Friday. (Payroll is a high-priority application, since employees like to get their checks on time; a delay in getting the input, for instance, or a few hours of machine trouble, can make life fairly hectic in the machine room. We try to schedule lower priority work so that it does not coincide with the peak of the payroll processing.)

5. In our system it is this run that updates the payroll master; Run 1 does not write a new master tape. All totals, such as gross and net pay, taxes, Social Security, and other deductions, must be updated. Any changes to the master file (which were carried along on the gross-pay tape) must now be incorporated in the new master. In contrast with the inventory-control example deletions from the file are not actually removed but merely tagged as inactive and left in the master; the record to be deleted still contains information that must be included, for instance, in quarterly and annual tax reports. At the end of the year a special run can "purge" the file of these inactive records.

6. All checks issued by a company must be *reconciled*, which corresponds approximately to going over the check stubs at the end of the month. One of the outputs of this run is a tape that gives the issue date, check number, and amount of each check written. Run 5, the reconciliation run, accepts this tape as one of its inputs.

Deduction reporting run (Figure 10.7). Run 3 is a rather simple one, since all it does is split apart the combined deduction tape from Run 2 and prepare the individual deduction reports.

Labor distribution run (Figure 10.8). Run 4 is not terribly complex either. The labor distribution tape from Run 1 is sorted into sequence on job number for processing against the labor distribution master, which contains previous costs for each job. Changes are introduced as needed with figures for percentage completion for the important jobs. The idea here is that management often wants to know how progress on certain jobs compares with "budget," the original estimate of how much time it should take to do each job. This comparison of actual and budgeted time is handled in a variety of ways in actual applications.

The output of this run is a labor-distribution report which shows the labor cost (and perhaps hours) expended on each job so far and any "vari-

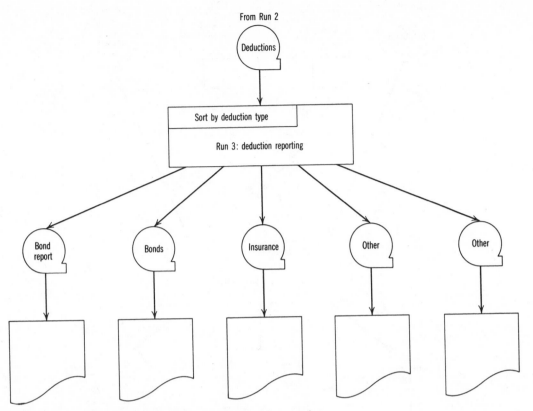

Figure 10.7. Run diagram of the Deduction Reporting run of the payroll case study.

ances" for which there is sufficient data to compute. A validation section might discard some data; this can be corrected and entered as corrections on the next week, since exact accuracy is not usually essential in this report. The run also updates the labor distribution master, which becomes the input master next week.

Check reconciliation run (Figure 10.9). Run 5 "reconciles" the canceled checks returned since the last reconciliation run. This can be done whenever convenient, for it has no necessary time relation to the rest of the job. The reconciliation tape from Run 2, together with all canceled checks, is one of the inputs. An unpaid checks master tape contains a record for all checks previously issued but not yet returned from the banks. The main output of this run, really, is a new unpaid checks master tape. *All* records from the reconciliation tape will be placed in it, since none of the checks just written could have been returned. All returned checks will result in deleting records from the unpaid checks file. The other output of this run is a listing of un-

paid checks older than some maximum, such as six months.

It is customary, as everyone who is paid by punched card check knows, to punch the date of issue and check number into the check, perhaps along with an employee number and the dollar amount. It takes little effort to punch the date of issue and check number but somewhat more to get the amount both punched and printed. For this reason we have shown the punching of the amount as a manual operation after the checks are returned.

The development of a set of run diagrams constitutes what is usually called the *over-all* system design. Carrying the specification of the job on to card and report formats, tape assignments, controls, and error procedures is called *detailed* system design. Some people include the preparation of flow charts in this category also; we prefer to define programming to include flow charting.

Having now learned something of the general nature of a typical payroll application, we shall for the rest of the chapter drop the specific reference to payroll. What follows is a survey of the steps

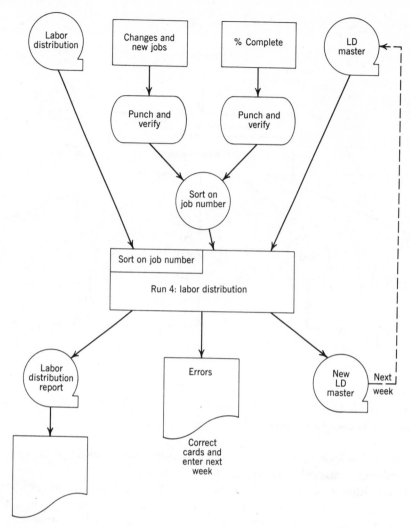

Figure 10.8. Run diagram of the Labor Distribution run of the payroll case study.

from system design through to a running system and applies to any application.

10.3 Programming

Since most of this book has been about programming, the reader presumably has a fair understanding of what this step is all about. It may be appropriate, however, to say a little about how COBOL fits into the scheme of programming techniques.

The first step in programming, as we define the term, is to draw a flow chart of each run or, more precisely, a *set* of flow charts. Most people find it wise to begin with a flow chart that shows the overall strategy, major decisions, and primary inputs and outputs without putting in every last detail.

Then each part of the run is charted in detail. This was the approach taken in the case study in Chapter 7, in which we started with a run diagram and proceeded to an intermediate level to show the file processing logic and the outlines of part of the controls and error conditions. If the processing of each transaction type had been more complex, we could have ended with several detailed flow charts of the major segments of the run. Considering that most data-processing runs are considerably more complex than that case study, it should be clear that working from general to progressively more detailed charts is a good idea.

Furthermore, the beginner ought to be let in on a small secret: flow charts do not drop whole from the pen of the programmer, even the most experienced. Any flow chart, whether general or detailed, is usually produced as a sequence of two,

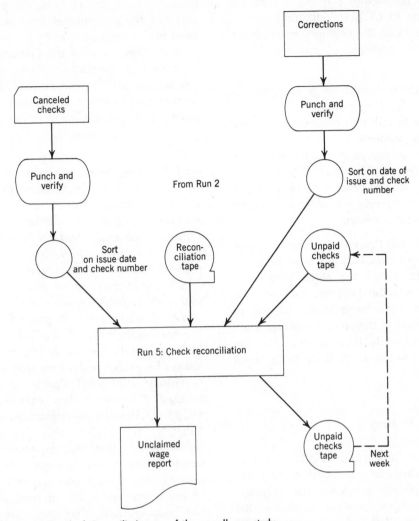

Figure 10.9. Run diagram of the Check Reconciliation run of the payroll case study.

three, or four successively better attempts at a complete product. There seems to be just too much detail to be able to get it right the first time. It is a rare programmer who does not find the eraser on his pencil a useful flow-charting tool.

(Speaking of flow-charting tools, incidentally, templates that greatly simplify the drawing of a neat flow chart are available from all manufacturers.)

COBOL does not in itself offer any advantages in flow charting, but it can still be useful even at this early stage of programming. A number of computer installations have found that if they stay with COBOL terminology in their flow charting it is often possible to punch the source program directly from the flow charts. Naturally it takes a little more effort to do so, and the card punch operators must be trained in certain elementary

COBOL matters, such as the meaning of the A and B margins on the coding sheet. Those who have used the technique, however, say that it is completely feasible and saves the considerable time and effort of writing the actual program on coding sheets. If this is to be done, the flow charts must obviously be written according to COBOL rules, and there must be absolutely no ambiguity about things like paragraph names and the sequence of control.

The fact that it is possible to punch the program directly from a suitably drawn flow chart indicates how near the programming job is to completion when the flow charts are done. We have seen this demonstrated, too: once the flow charts were understood, it was no great effort to follow the programs, which are virtually a transcription of the flow charts even if no attempt is made to have the flow charts conform to COBOL notation.*

Where does this leave the beginner in programming? The essential sequence of learning is the following:

1. What a computer can do: its powers, restrictions, and basic mode of operation.

2. What it takes to talk to a computer: the programming language problem.

3. How to approach the programming task: flow charting, organization of the work.

4. How to approach the general problem of getting a computer into operation to meet a given set of requirements: system design.

Our conviction is that this basic sequence cannot effectively be changed and that anything that simplifies the learning of all the steps is a gain. COBOL, we feel, lets the beginner get into the heart of computer work faster than machine or assembly language and is therefore beneficial. Having had an introduction to these matters, the student will at some point want to learn more about the machine itself.

10.4 Program Testing

Any sizeable data-processing application provides literally hundreds of opportunities to make mistakes that completely invalidate the program. These mistakes may range from simple slips of the pencil that result in illegal data names or misspelled reserved words (these are usually flagged by the compiler) to flow-charting errors that destroy the logic of the method, to misunderstandings of what should have been done. A program is not finished until it has been thoroughly tested to remove all programming mistakes and to establish that the program properly carries out the intentions of the person who defined it. This process of detecting and correcting errors and proving the correctness of a program can easily take weeks.

There is no single way of solving all the problems of testing. We must rely on a combination of

procedures on the part of the programmer, and above all the programmer must exercise good judgment in determining how to go about the checkout process. This is one of the primary areas in which experience is essential to a satisfactory result. We can only point out what some of the standard procedures and tools are and encourage the reader to practice, if possible, under the guidance of an experienced programmer.

Desk checking. There seems to be an almost overwhelming temptation when a program is finished to put it on the machine to see if it works. Yet a programmer should spend some time desk-checking a program to eliminate the most glaring errors. It can easily happen that half a dozen errors of an easily found variety can waste days and cause several unnecessary recompilations.

A listing of the program as punched is a valuable tool in desk checking, since it allows the programmer to check for errors in punching or in interpreting his handwriting at the same time that he is looking for other errors. A few checks that should always be made: make sure that every data name is written as intended, that no reserved words are misused, that every data name in the PROCEDURE DIVISION is defined in the DATA DIVISION, that "ohs" and zeros are properly distinguished, that working-storage contents are never reused before the contents are no longer needed, that there is enough space for all results of arithmetic verbs, that necessary qualifiers have not been omitted, that there are spaces around arithmetic operators and subscript parentheses, that all verb formats have been used correctly, etc., etc.

As we pointed out, the compiler itself will detect quite a variety of errors in *syntax*, that is, errors in the use of verb formats, missing data-name definitions, incorrect use of levels in the DATA DIVISION, or the use of a file name where a record name should have been. The amount of this kind of checking naturally varies from compiler to compiler, but all of them provide some of it. One should, however, avoid the habit of skimping on desk checking on the assumption that the compiler will catch the errors because there are many that cannot be detected in a syntax check: errors in logic, errors in assumptions on data sizes, or such outright blunders as writing a data name that does exist in the program (and therefore looks legal to the compiler) but which is nevertheless incorrect.

Test cases. After a thorough desk check and

---

* It is also possible to work the other way around: a few software firms offer various editions of a program that reads a COBOL source deck and prints a flow chart of the program's logic. These programming aids are very popular with those programmers who put together their COBOL programs directly on cards, bypassing both the flow-charting step and the penciling of the program on a coding sheet.

the correction of any errors detected by the compiler, the source program is compiled. Now comes the basic part of checkout: running the program with sample data to see if it produces correct results. At the outset this test data may be simple: the idea is to see whether the program produces any answers at all: it is not uncommon, in fact, that during the first test something goes so far astray that nothing comes out. Perhaps an arithmetic result is too large to fit in the receiving area, the program tries to read a tape that has not been opened, or the program tries to do arithmetic on an item that was supposed to be NUMERIC but turns out to have letters in it. This kind of error is perhaps somewhat less common with COBOL than with machine or assembly language programming because of the checking the compiler does but it certainly happens.

If the program "hangs up" (the machine stops the execution of the program because of an arithmetic result that is too large or something similar), there may be an indication of what the trouble is on the console or the printer. At this point it may be necessary to fall back on an output that is optionally available from most compilers, a listing of the object program instructions compiled from each source program statement. Then, given the core storage location of the instruction that caused the hang-up, we can locate the offending source statement and perhaps see what the trouble is.

Printing intermediate results. Going to the object program is not really recommended, however, because a technique that is generally needed anyway makes it possible to work almost entirely with the source program. The technique is the provision for printing intermediate results. It often happens that the normal printed output of a program is a rather small part of the total job; the bulk of the work may have to do with producing a new copy of a master file that is not normally printed at all, or a long sequence of operations may lead eventually to a few numbers that are printed. If the final output is missing or incorrect, we obviously need information on what the program did along the way and what it did to things that are not printed, such as new master files. It is generally not too difficult to provide for this kind of intermediate output *if it is planned from the outset.* DISPLAY statements can easily be inserted at appropriate points in the program, along with IF statements that will skip over the printing if a

sense switch is left up or if control signals on an input card provided for the purpose so indicate. If the output is too voluminous to handle effectively with DISPLAY statements, a special output tape may be assigned to hold the intermediate results. This may require that working storage be set up as records, even though it might not need to be otherwise, and it will, of course, require suitable file descriptions.

Particular implementations have features that simplify matters considerably and allow, for instance, specification of the names of data items that should be printed each time a new value is computed for them. Others recognize special instructions to print the paragraph names of all the routines executed during the test, in the order in which they were executed.

With this kind of detailed information on what the program does as it proceeds, step by step, it is usually not too difficult to track down the errors. As a matter of fact, the detective work is often almost fun.

Design of test cases. One of the most important aspects of program checkout is the design of test cases that really do check the program. To do the job there must be test cases to test each branch of every IF; to test the ending conditions on all files; to test editing operations for all the types of data that could appear; to test that labels are correctly generated. There must be *bad* data* to prove that checking procedures built into the program do detect mistakes: file errors, label checking, invalid input, arithmetic overflow, etc.

The design of really thorough test cases is an art in itself, which demands good knowledge of the program, an understanding of the job being done, and a certain amount of imagination. *It does take time.* At the risk of sounding repetitious, however, we must insist that a program will not have been completed until it has been proved to produce correct answers for valid data and to reject invalid data; this assurance can be obtained only by putting in good and bad data and observing what the program does.

The final check that should be made on any data-processing program is called *pilot operation* or a *volume data test.* This consists of using a large quantity of actual transactions from another period.

* This is an important requirement. In fact, it is a good practice to run one test with input data that has been punched *entirely at random.*

Running actual application data provides a better test of possibilities that may not have been thought of in devising the test cases, and the computer results can easily be checked against the results produced by the previous method (if the job has been done before, of course). This final check has another advantage: it gives the system a shakedown on real data but without the time pressures of going directly into full-scale operation and having people waiting impatiently for the results.

A second important advantage of pilot operation is that it provides the personnel in the department for which the work is being done with an opportunity to see whether the program actually does what they intended. It is all too easy for the problem originator to say one thing and mean another, for the programmer to misunderstand what is meant by terms in an area with which he is not familiar, or for either of them to overlook special conditions.

10.5   Master File Creation

At some point it is necessary to create the master file that will be used by the program. If the job has previously been done with manual methods, it will be necessary to punch cards from the present records. If it has been done with punched card techniques, it may be possible to convert the present file to magnetic tape with a separate computer program written for the purpose. Often the data in the cards is rearranged and new information is added.

In many applications this problem of file conversion can be a major undertaking in itself, requiring not only many personnel and a good deal of computer time but careful planning in the scheduling of the conversion to computer operation. (It certainly had better not be left until after the program is checked out!) This planning is made necessary by the fact that the business has to go on running while the computer is put into operation. Often the master file is much too large to permit a complete shutdown of this area of the company's clerical operation while the file is converted.

The usual technique is to prepare the master file as of a specific date and to continue with the manual or punched-card methods until the computer system is ready to go into operation. During the period between conversion of the file and the termination of the previous methods, all transactions are saved (after manual processing). When the system is finally in operation, the first step is to pro-

cess all the accumulated transactions against the new master file. The time pressure in doing this is not extreme, since the results have already been found by previous methods, and the computer's output can be carefully checked against the results, thus giving one more check on the correctness of the program.

If the file is extremely large, and many are, it may be necessary to convert the file in segments by processing part of it manually and part by computer. This can be done by an arbitrary breakdown on the control key; for instance, all accounts beginning with 1 or 2 might be converted first, then all accounts beginning with 3 or 4 next, and so on. If the job has been set up so that the file is processed in segments anyway, it can be converted on the same basis; for instance, an electric utility may have a billing cycle that gives the day or week of the month in which all customers in a certain district are billed or a cycle that depends on the first letter of the customer's name. A large payroll file could be converted a few departments at a time or one complete plant at a time.

Master-file creation or conversion, in addition to its obvious necessity, often produces worthwhile side benefits: errors are often discovered in the previous files—errors that may have been there for years. This is just another example of the principle that the careful *study* devoted to a successful computer operation is valuable in itself, quite apart from the later actual advantages of the computer.

10.6   Startup

After a new program has been properly tested and the file converted, a number of problems still remain before going into full-scale operation.

The first thing that must normally be done is to catch up with transactions that have occurred since the new master file was created. This may uncover a few more errors in the master, either existing errors in the old file or conversion errors. Actually, this process of file clean-up ordinarily continues into the first few weeks (at least) of operation of the system.

A common practice, and one that is recommended, is to continue the use of the previous manual or punched-card system for a few weeks in *parallel operation* with the new electronic system. This provides a backup in case the computer system develops difficulties that require it to be taken out of operation for correction. The parallel operation also provides an excellent test of the accuracy and adequacy of electronic processing, since it is a simple matter to compare the results produced by the two systems.

As we noted before, many master files are so large that they must be converted in segments, since an attempt to convert the entire master file at one time would result in such an accumulation of transactions that it would be difficult to catch up. If the file conversion has been broken into segments by one of the methods suggested earlier, the conversion to computer processing can be effected in the same way.

Any such partial conversion scheme must be carefully planned in advance, so that there will be a minimum of confusion between the data-processing center and those responsible for the previous methods. The difficulty, of course, is that the people who have been running the old system will in most cases be engaged in the new. If the transition is not properly planned, these personnel may be overloaded by having to deal with two systems at once.

It is perhaps obvious that the introduction of various applications to be done with the computer should be spaced out over a period of weeks or months. Any attempt to put several major applications into operation at one time would create peak loads, both at the computer and in the rest of the organization, that could very well cause failure of the whole system.

Once the computer system is running, it is usually possible to transfer to other departments a part of the clerical staff that handled the old system. It should be clearly understood, however, that a few selected employees of this group must remain in their positions to keep the new system under control. Quantity must be replaced by quality: a running computer system, in fact, needs a kind of "superclerk" who combines a perfect knowledge of the system's requirements with a fair understanding of how they are satisfied by the computer. Without this superclerk—who can quickly spot abnormal situations and take corrective action—a computer system may deteriorate rapidly.

10.7 Documentation

A computer system loses much of its value if it is not adequately documented. Many occasions arise when it is necessary to know exactly what the program will do, in order to change it, to predict what it will do in an unusual situation, or to locate previously undetected errors. To provide all the information required for the many people in various parts of the company organization that must use the system several types of documentation are needed.

One of the most important and valuable, when the program has been written in COBOL, is the program itself. Although we do not claim that the English-language feature of COBOL makes a program read like a novel, it nevertheless does greatly simplify the understanding of what the program does. (The reader probably will not really appreciate this fact until he has attempted to make sense out of a program written in assembly language.) Some effort is required to follow the details of a program, no matter what language it is written in; COBOL reduces the difficulty.

This matter of readability long after the program has been completed is so important that it justifies the extra effort needed to make the program readable when it is written in the first place. A lazy programmer who insists on using shorthand data names instead of meaningful ones (A1, ABV, R-4, etc., instead of OLD-MASTER, QUANTITY, TRANSACTION-HEADING, etc.) can destroy readability. Naturally there are some abbreviations that are either standard or fairly obvious, such as QOH for QUANTITY-ON-HAND and OM for OLD-MASTER. We strongly advise against their overuse, however, just because it is so important that it be easy for someone else to figure out what the program does perhaps two years after it was written. Some extra writing is no doubt required, but it is worth the trouble in the long run.

It is also advisable to use the REMARKS clause in the IDENTIFICATION DIVISION to provide a brief description of the program's input, output, and main purpose. Finally, if qualification is not used, it is helpful to use constant prefixes (like I-, PO-, and O-) in making up the data names for input and output files. For the WORKING-STORAGE entries we may choose between prefixes like W- or suffixes like -COUNTER, -SAVE, or -HOLD. By doing this the meaning of many sentences becomes absolutely clear as in the following examples:

MOVE I-EMPL-NUMBER TO EMPL-NO-SAVE.
MOVE I-RECORD TO W-RECORD.

ADD I-SALES TO SALES-COUNTER.
WRITE PO-REC AFTER ADVANCING 2 LINES.

There is also a COBOL verb—NOTE—which may be used in the PROCEDURE DIVISION to enter comments that will not be processed by the compiler; for example, NOTE ABOVE CALCU-LATION APPLIES UNTIL END OF 1970 ONLY.

In addition to the program itself, a number of documents are needed for other purposes, one of which is a complete writeup of the program for use when it is not necessary to follow every detail of the operation. This document, which is often called a *run manual*, normally contains some or all of the following information:

1. A run number and title.
2. The name of the programmer.
3. The date of completion of the program and of the last modification.
4. A sheet summarizing the computer operating instructions for ready reference, including labels and descriptions of tapes and their disposition, error or other special procedures, rerun instructions, average run time, and switch settings.
5. A two- or three-paragraph description of the basic logic of the program.
6. A complete set of flow charts.
7. Completed forms, when applicable, for storage allocation, record designs, and operating instructions for any off-line work.
8. A sample of each input form and of each report produced by the program.
9. Suggestions for future changes and warnings about making changes.

A document of this sort is obviously necessary if intelligent use is to be made of the program and if modifications and revisions are to be made with a minimum of effort.

The programmer should prepare instructions for the computer operator to cover machine setup, console switch settings, tape units required, carriage control tapes, error correction procedures, etc. These instructions, of course, duplicate some of the material in the run book, but there is no room at the console to keep the run books for all the programs in use. Operating instructions for all programs are generally kept in a notebook at the console and the run books are stored elsewhere.

A final type of document might be called a procedures manual, which is used by the people who make use of the computer; that is, the personnel in other departments of the company who originate data and apply the results. Typical contents of such a manual would include the following:

1. Exhibits of input documents, with instructions for their preparation and transmittal.
2. Exhibits of output forms and reports and an explanation of their contents, discussion of the frequency of preparation, etc.
3. Timing schedules for data submission and receipt of reports.
4. Handling of special circumstances.

10.8 Program Maintenance

Newcomers to computing have an apparently universal misconception that once a program is written and checked out it can be forgotten. Unfortunately things are not that simple and some very expensive lessons have had to be learned by people who thought so.

For one thing, errors have a way of hiding, only to be discovered after six months or three years of operation. These errors obviously must be corrected. The main thing that the beginner may not realize, however, is that the jobs themselves change. A new tax law is enacted; a new report is requested by management; a card format turns out to be hard to use and must be changed; additional validation of input becomes necessary because of a high error rate; a new type of deduction must be added; a report item that was thought necessary is found to be of no value. Changes of this general type are so common that major applications often require a *full-time* maintenance programmer.

Beyond making the reader aware of the problem, we can present two factors that should be considered. First, the inevitability of changes must be accepted; the frequently heard phrase "but our problems are different" is simply an indication of lack of experience. Since changes *will* have to be made, it is worthwhile to think about making them simple when the program is first written. This gets rather deeply into machine matters, but we may suggest the following as indications of what can be done.

1. Within reason, allow a little extra space here and there in files for future expansion of sizes and such things as new deductions. This can be over-done, obviously.

2. Make constants in WORKING-STORAGE out of anything that could change, such as an interest rate, factors in a rate formula, and overtime and extra-shift premiums. This is a lot simpler than hunting for all the places in which the same information might have been entered as a procedure literal.

3. Go easy on methods that assume that if all previous tests have failed the item being tested must be the last possibility; for instance, if a code could be 1, 2, 3, or 4, don't test for 1, 2, and 3 and then assume that if it is none of these it must be 4. This is not only bad practice, because it depends on correct data, but it makes the program inflexible. An exception would be a situation in which all but one of the possibilities have been tested. A good example would be the comparison of two control keys: if one is neither less than nor greater than the other, they must be equal.

4. Don't ever take advantage of quirks in the machine or compiler. You might discover, to take an extreme case, that a zero subscript, which is not allowed in the specifications, will in your compiler pick up the last entry in a previous table, which might be useful to you. Don't do it! Not only will such trickery royally confuse anyone who has to modify the program, but if not noticed it could lead to complete chaos if the program were recompiled with the previous table in some other location.

Beyond such considerations, which are common sense, it should be realized that one of the major advantages of COBOL itself is ease of modification. As we have stated before, this is largely because of the rigid separation of the PROCEDURE and DATA DIVISIONS, which keeps data changes and procedure changes independent. This alone is enough to justify the effort of writing the DATA DIVISION, since the matter of lengthening an item, for instance, which is simple in COBOL, can become a major project in assembly language if the item is referred to by many parts of the program.

10.9 Conclusion

Putting a data-processing application on a computer involves a number of steps, carried out at various levels of the organization by many different people. It begins with a study of what the data-processing needs are and of alternative ways of solving them. After it has been established that a particular computer is to be ordered, much work must be done in deciding just how to go about splitting up the company's data-processing requirements into manageable pieces that can be set up on the computer. After this had been done, the general characteristics of each computer run must be planned, including file and record formats. Only at this point is it possible to write a program. When the program has been written, the accuracy of the program must be verified. The file conversion and the startup of the application both require considerable planning. To this list should be added such activities as planning for the physical installation of the computer, the training of the people to program and operate it, indoctrination of personnel in other departments of the company who will make use of the services of the computer, and an education program to introduce the computer to the entire company in a way that will minimize the ever-present fears regarding job security.

Admittedly, in this complete list the subject of programming as we have discussed it in this book is only one part which represents less than a majority of the time required to get into operation. The person who expects to be working closely with computers needs to start his education with the subject of computer programming, for without this knowledge a proper grasp of the more advanced subjects cannot be gained. It should be realized, however, that the area we have introduced here *is* only the beginning and that the person who expects to be a truly professional computer expert has a number of years of apprenticeship and study before him.

Still, the novice to the field should not feel discouraged. The computer field is changing so rapidly that much of yesterday's knowledge may represent more of a burden than an asset. As one experienced data-processing executive recently remarked, "At the present rate of technological change the punk out of college knows as much about computers as I do!" Or, as another computer expert once quipped, "I cannot proofread my articles more than once. If I do, they become obsolete."

Both experts, to be sure, were being a little facetious, but their outlook is, we believe, quite correct. The computer world is indeed constantly changing and is therefore full of opportunities for the old hands as well as the newcomers. In this environment it would seem that the best course of action is to keep an open and questing mind in the spirit of the quotation on the first page of this book.

APPENDIX. **COBOL** RESERVED WORDS

This is a list of some of the reserved COBOL words. It is not a complete "list," nor is it intended to be, because computer manufacturers constantly add new reserved words in their new implementations.

In general a programmer can minimize the possibility of inadvertently using a reserved word as a data name or paragraph name by adhering to one or more of the following rules:

1. Use hyphenated prefixes and suffixes with every programmer-defined name; for example I- for the names of an input file, O- for an output file, and PO- for a print out file. For WORKING-STORAGE entries, in addition to a prefix such as W-, use suffixes like -SAVE, -HOLD, -COUNTER, and -ACCUM.

2. Use one or more digits: very few reserved words contain them.

3. Consult manufacturers' COBOL manuals for all the computers in your installation.

4. Avoid such obvious traps as DATA, SUM, DIVISION and SECTION. It is tempting to use them as data names, especially in a payroll application, but they are all reserved words!

5. For paragraph names use hyphenated suffixes such as -RTN and -ROUTINE. READ and ACCEPT, for instance, are reserved words, but READ-RTN and ACCEPT-RTN are not.

By following these simple rules a programmer will not need to consult this appendix at all and will avoid wasting computer and programming time.

ACCEPT	BEFORE	COMPUTATIONAL
ACCESS	BEGINNING	COMPUTATIONAL-1
ACTUAL	BLANK	COMPUTATIONAL-2
ADD	BLOCK	COMPUTATIONAL-3
ADVANCING	BY	COMPUTE
AFTER		CONFIGURATION
ALL		CONSOLE
ALPHABETIC	CALL	CONTAINS
ALTER	CF	CONTROL
ALTERNATE	CH	CONTROLS
AND	CHANGED	COPY
APPLY	CHARACTERS	CORRESPONDING
ARE	CHECKING	CREATING
AREA	CLOCK-UNITS	CYCLES
AREAS	CLOSE	
ASCENDING	COBOL	
ASSIGN	CODE	DATA
AT	COLUMN	DATE-COMPILED
AUTHOR	COMMA	DATE-WRITTEN

DEFINE	ID	OBJECT-COMPUTER
DECIMAL-POINT	IDENTIFICATION	OCCURS
DECLARATIVES	IF	OF
DEPENDING	IN	OMITTED
DESCENDING	INCLUDE	ON
DETAIL	INDEXED	OPEN
DIRECT	INDICATE	OR
DIRECT-ACCESS	INITIATE	ORGANIZATION
DISPLAY	INPUT	OTHERWISE
DISPLAY-ST	INPUT-OUTPUT	OUTPUT
DIVIDE	INSTALLATION	OVERFLOW
DIVISION	INTO	
	INVALID	
	I-O	PAGE
ELSE	I-O-CONTROL	PAGE-COUNTER
END	IS	PERFORM
ENDING		PF
ENTER		PH
ENTRY	JUSTIFIED	PICTURE
ENVIRONMENT		PLUS
EQUAL		POSITIVE
ERROR	KEY	PRINT-SWITCH
EVERY		PROCEDURE
EXAMINE		PROCEED
EXHIBIT	LABEL	PROCESS
EXIT	LABELS	PROCESSING
	LAST	PROGRAM-ID
	LEADING	PROTECTION
	LESS	
FD	LIMIT	
FILE	LIMITS	
FILE-CONTROL	LINE	QUOTE
FILE-LIMIT	LINE-COUNTER	QUOTES
FILLER	LINES	
FINAL	LINKAGE	
FIRST	LOCK	RANDOM
FOOTING	LOW-VALUE	RD
FOR	LOW-VALUES	READ
FORM-OVERFLOW		READY
FROM		RECORD
	MODE	RECORDING
	MORE-LABELS	RECORDS
GENERATE	MOVE	REDEFINES
GIVING	MULTIPLY	REEL
GO		RELATIVE
GREATER		RELEASE
GROUP	NAMED	REMARKS
	NEGATIVE	REPLACING
	NEXT	REPORT
HEADING	NO	REPORTING
HIGH-VALUE	NOT	REPORTS
HIGH-VALUES	NOTE	RERUN
HOLD	NUMERIC	RESERVE

RESET

RESTRICTED

RETURN

REVERSED

REWIND

REWRITE

RF

RH

RIGHT

ROUNDED

RUN

SA

SAME

SD

SEARCH

SECTION

SECURITY

SELECT

SENTENCE

SEQUENTIAL

SIZE

SORT

SOURCE

SOURCE-COMPUTER

SPACE

SPACES

SPECIAL-NAMES

STANDARD

STOP

SUBTRACT

SUM

SYMBOLIC

SYSIN

SYSOUT

SYSPUNCH

TALLY

TALLYING

TERMINATE

THAN

THEN

THRU

TIMES

TO

TRACE

TRACK-AREA

TRACKS

TRANSFORM

TRY

TYPE

UNIT

UNIT-RECORD

UNITS

UNTIL

UPON

USAGE

USE

USING

UTILITY

VALUE

VARYING

WHEN

WITH

WORKING-STORAGE

WRITE

WRITE-ONLY

ZERO

ZEROES

ZEROS

ANSWERS TO SELECTED EXERCISES

These answers should be taken as showing *one* acceptable way to solve each problem, not as the only way or necessarily the best way. In almost all cases there will be other acceptable answers that are just as good. It makes no difference, for instance, whether we write ADD A TO B or COMPUTE B = B + A or whether we write IF A IS EQUAL TO B or IF B IS EQUAL TO A. Punctuation is in many cases completely at the discretion of the programmer.

The answers given here illustrate many of the options available in verb formats, punctuation, and the order of clauses, but no attempt is made to be complete in this regard.

Chapter 3

1. a. MOVE TRANSACTION-QUANTITY TO QUANTITY-ON-HAND.
   b. MOVE 1 TO COUNTER.
   c. MOVE 'PAGE NUMBER' TO HEADING.
   d. MOVE ZERO TO HOW-MANY.
   e. MOVE QUANTITY IN TRANS TO QUANTITY IN MASTER.
   f. ADD CAT TO DOG.
   g. ADD CAT DOG GIVING GOAT.
   h. ADD HORSE, COW, MULE GIVING ANIMALS.
   i. ADD 50 TO POSTAGE.
   j. SUBTRACT 6 FROM AMOUNT.   (−78).
   k. MULTIPLY OVERTIME-HOURS BY 1.5 GIVING OVERTIME-DOLLARS.
   l. DIVIDE NUMBR INTO TOTAL GIVING AVERAGE.
   m. DIVIDE 2 INTO RATE.
   n. SUBTRACT X Y FROM Z GIVING W.
   o. ADD R S GIVING T; ON SIZE ERROR GO TO ERROR-ROUTINE.

3. a. IF HOURS-WORKED IS GREATER THAN 37.5 GO TO OVERTIME-ROUTINE.
   b. IF AGE IS GREATER THAN 20 ADD 1 TO ADULT. Or: IF AGE IS NOT LESS THAN 21 ADD 1 TO ADULT.
   c. IF PART-1-A IS EQUAL TO 'S' GO TO STOCK-ITEM.
   d. IF SIZE-A IS GREATER THAN 800 ADD 1 TO BIG; OTHERWISE ADD 1 TO LITTLE.
   e. IF NAME-1 IS GREATER THAN NAME-2 MOVE NAME-1 TO TEMPORARY; OTHERWISE MOVE NAME-2 TO TEMPORARY.
   f. IF HOURS-WORKED IS NOT EQUAL TO 40 GO TO NONSTANDARD.
   g. IF CODE-X IS NOT NUMERIC GO TO BAD-CODE.

6. SUBTRACT 40 FROM HOURS-WORKED GIVING
OVERTIME-HOURS.
MULTIPLY 40 BY RATE GIVING GROSS-PAY. MULTIPLY
OVERTIME-HOURS BY RATE GIVING TEMPORARY. MULTIPLY
1.5 BY TEMPORARY. ADD TEMPORARY TO GROSS-PAY.

8. MULTIPLY N BY 12.00 GIVING EXEMPTION. SUBTRACT
EXEMPTION FROM GROSS-PAY GIVING TEMPORARY.
MULTIPLY TEMPORARY BY 0.18 GIVING TAX.

9. MULTIPLY N BY 12.00 GIVING EXEMPTION. IF GROSS-PAY IS
NOT GREATER THAN EXEMPTION MOVE ZERO TO TAX, GO
TO CONTINUE. SUBTRACT EXEMPTION FROM GROSS-PAY
GIVING TEMPORARY.
MULTIPLY TEMPORARY BY 0.18 GIVING TAX.
CONTINUE. ((Whatever follows.))

11. MULTIPLY NUMBER-SOLD BY PRICE GIVING TEMPORARY.
ADD TEMPORARY TO PREVIOUS-YTD.

13. a. COMPUTE Y = (A + B + C) / D.
b. COMPUTE R = A * B + C / D.
c. COMPUTE M = A / 6 − C * D / E.
d. COMPUTE G = 1.5 * H * R − 67.74.
e. COMPUTE Z = (M ** 2 − N ** 3) * P − R / S.

15. IF SHIFT-CODE IS EQUAL TO 2 MULTIPLY 1.10 BY GROSS-PAY.

17. ADD REGULAR-PAY, OVERTIME-PAY, SHIFT-PREMIUM,
BONUS GIVING GROSS-PAY.

19. IF CODE-A EQUAL TO 1 ADD PRICE TO CLASS-1, GO TO HERE.
IF CODE-A EQUAL TO 2 ADD PRICE TO CLASS-2, GO TO HERE.
IF CODE-A EQUAL TO 3 ADD PRICE TO CLASS-3, GO TO HERE.
IF CODE-A EQUAL TO 4 ADD PRICE TO CLASS-4, GO TO HERE.
ADD PRICE TO ERROR-TOTAL.
HERE. ((Whatever follows.))

22. MULTIPLY NEW-YTD-GROSS BY 0.03125 GIVING TEMPORARY.
SUBTRACT PREVIOUS-SS FROM TEMPORARY GIVING
THIS-WEEK-SS.

23.

PARAGRAPH-1. OPEN INPUT INPUT-FILE. MOVE ZERO TO TOTAL.
PARAGRAPH-2. READ INPUT-FILE RECORD; AT END GO TO
PARAGRAPH-3. ADD DOLLARS TO TOTAL. GO TO PARAGRAPH-2.
PARAGRAPH-3. DISPLAY TOTAL UPON CONSOLE. CLOSE INPUT-FILE.
STOP RUN.

25.

P-1. OPEN INPUT INPUT-FILE, OUTPUT OUTPUT-FILE. MOVE ZERO
TO TOTAL.
P-2. READ INPUT-FILE RECORD AT END GO TO P-3. IF CODE-B IS
EQUAL TO 1 ADD DOLLARS TO TOTAL; OTHERWISE WRITE
OUTPUT-RECORD FROM INPUT-RECORD. GO TO P-2.
P-3. DISPLAY TOTAL. CLOSE INPUT-FILE, OUTPUT-FILE. STOP RUN.

26.

P-1. OPEN INPUT INPUT-FILE. MOVE SPACES TO PREVIOUS-KEY.
P-2. READ INPUT-FILE RECORD; AT END GO TO P-4. IF KEY-1 IS LESS

THAN PREVIOUS-KEY GO TO P-3; OTHERWISE MOVE KEY-1 TO
PREVIOUS-KEY GO TO P-2.

P-3. DISPLAY 'SEQUENCE ERROR ON KEY', KEY-1 GO TO P-5.

P-4. DISPLAY 'SEQUENCE OK'.

P-5. CLOSE INPUT-FILE. STOP RUN.

28.

P-1. OPEN INPUT FILE-1. MOVE ZERO TO TOTAL. ACCEPT
CONTROL-TOTAL.

P-2. READ FILE-1 RECORD; AT END GO TO P-3. ADD DOLLARS TO
TOTAL. GO TO P-2.

P-3. IF CONTROL-TOTAL IS EQUAL TO TOTAL DISPLAY 'OK'
OTHERWISE DISPLAY 'NG'. CLOSE FILE-1. STOP RUN.

29.

P-1. OPEN INPUT SAMPLE, OUTPUT GOOD-FILE, BAD-FILE.

P-2. READ SAMPLE RECORD; AT END GO TO P-4. IF F1 IS NOT
NUMERIC GO TO P-3. IF F2 IS NOT POSITIVE GO TO P-3.
IF F2 IS NOT LESS THAN 18 GO TO P-3. IF F3 IS NOT LESS
THAN F4 GO TO P-3. IF F5 IS ZERO GO TO P-3. WRITE
GOOD-RECORD FROM EXAMPLE. GO TO P-2.

P-3. WRITE BAD-RECORD FROM EXAMPLE. GO TO P-2.

P-4. CLOSE SAMPLE, GOOD-FILE, BAD-FILE. STOP RUN.

Chapter 5

1. a.

FD PAYROLL-MASTER; BLOCK CONTAINS 758 CHARACTERS; LABEL
RECORDS ARE STANDARD; VALUE OF ID IS 'PAYROLL'; DATA
RECORD IS PAYROLL.

1. b.

FD PARTS-REQUIREMENTS; BLOCK CONTAINS 10 RECORDS; LABEL
RECORDS ARE STANDARD; VALUE OF ID IS 'PRTREQ',
DATA RECORD IS PART-REQ.

3. a. 02 SALES; PICTURE 9999V99.

b. 02 MONTH PICTURE 99.

c. 02 CHANGE PICTURE S999.

d. 02 NAME; PICTURE A(20).

e. 02 UNITS; PICTURE X(8).

f. 02 RATE; PICTURE VPP9999.

g. 02 STATE-CODE; PICTURE 99.

h. 02 HOURLY-RATE; PICTURE 9V9999; SYNCHRONIZED RIGHT.

i. 02 CITY; PICTURE A(10); SYNCHRONIZED LEFT.

j. 02 PREVIOUS-PART; PICTURE A(8); VALUE SPACES.

k. 02 TAX-RATE; PICTURE V99999; VALUE .15625.

5.   01 NEW-MASTER-RECORD.

02 PART-NUMBER; PICTURE A(8).

02 QUANTITY; PICTURE 9(5).

02 CATEGORY; PICTURE 999.

02 DESCRIPTION; PICTURE X(16).

02 PRICE; PICTURE 99V999.

02 FILLER; PICTURE X(43).

7.   01 INVENTORY.
         02 PART.
            03 PREFIX; PICTURE AA.
            03 BIN-NUMBER; PICTURE 9999; COMPUTATIONAL-3.
         02 YTD-USAGE.
            03 QTY; PICTURE 9(6); COMPUTATIONAL-3.
            03 DOLLARS; PICTURE 99999V99; USAGE IS
            COMPUTATIONAL-3.
         02 DESCRIPTION; PICTURE X(15).
         02 CODES.
            03 WHERE-MADE; PICTURE A.
            03 MFG-PURCH; PICTURE 9; COMPUTATIONAL-3.
            03 HI-LO-USAGE; PICTURE 9; COMPUTATIONAL-3.
         02 QOH; COMPUTATIONAL-3; PICTURE 99999.

9.   01 WORK-STORE.
         02 ACCOUNT-NUMBER; PICTURE 99999; COMPUTATIONAL;
         SYNCHRONIZED RIGHT.
         02 CATEGORY; PICTURE 9; COMPUTATIONAL;
         SYNCHRONIZED RIGHT.
         02 TOTAL-A; PICTURE 9999V99; SYNCHRONIZED RIGHT;
         COMPUTATIONAL.
         02 DATE-LAST-PAYMENT.
            03 MONTH; PICTURE 99; COMPUTATIONAL;
            SYNCHRONIZED RIGHT.
            03 DAY; PICTURE 99; COMPUTATIONAL; SYNCHRONIZED
            RIGHT.
            03 YEAR; PICTURE 99; COMPUTATIONAL;
            SYNCHRONIZED RIGHT.
         02 ACCOUNT-LIMIT; PICTURE 9999V99; SYNCHRONIZED
         RIGHT.

11. a. PICTURE ZZ999.
    b. PICTURE $$$$$$.
    c. PICTURE $ZZ9.99.
    d. PICTURE ++++.
    e. PICTURE Z9B999.

13.   01 PRINTER-LINE.
         02 CUSTOMER-NUMBER; PICTURE B(6)Z(5).
         02 CUSTOMER-NAME; PICTURE B(4)A(20).
         02 STATE; PICTURE B(6)ZZ.
         02 CITY; PICTURE BBBZZZ.
         02 INVOICE-NUMBER; PICTURE B(4)Z(5).
         02 MONTH; PICTURE BBBZZ.
         02 DAY; PICTURE BBZZ.
         02 AMOUNT; PICTURE BBBB$$$$.99.

Chapter 8

1.   IF REORDER-POINT IS LESS THAN 0.80 * LEAD-TIME *
      WEEKLY-AVERAGE, MULTIPLY 1.30 BY REORDER-POINT.

3. a. IF AGE IS LESS THAN 30 AND WEIGHT IS GREATER THAN 170
      GO TO P-69.

   b. IF SPEED-1 > SPEED-2 AND WEIGHT-1 > WEIGHT-2 + 30,
     GO TO 10-YARDS.
   c. IF FB-K > FB-C OR FWD-K > FWD-C GO TO 2-POINTS.
   d. IF ICE > 3 AND TEMPERATURE < 25 GO TO SKATE.
   e. IF A > 9 AND (B = 8 OR C IS NOT EQUAL TO 95) GO TO P-9.

5. COMPUTE JOB-TIME = SET-UP   (13) + UNIT-TIME   (13) *
UNITX.

6. COMPUTE JOB-TIME = SET-UP   (N) + UNIT-TIME   (N) *
UNITX.

7. READ SALES-DATA RECORD. ADD AMOUNT TO SALES
(MAN-NUMBER).

9. MOVE ZERO TO SUM-A. PERFORM AVER VARYING N FROM 1 BY
1 UNTIL N GREATER THAN 5. COMPUTE AVERAGE-TIME
= SUM-A / 5.

.
.
.

AVER. ADD A-TIME (N) TO SUM-A.

10. MOVE ZERO TO SUM-B. MOVE ZERO TO COUNT. PERFORM
AVER VARYING N FROM 1 BY 1 UNTIL N GREATER THAN
7. COMPUTE AVERAGE-TIME = SUM-B / COUNT.

.
.
.

AVER. ADD A-TIME (N) TO SUM-B. IF TIME (N) IS NOT EQUAL TO
ZERO ADD 1 TO COUNT.

12. PERFORM REORDER UNTIL ON-ORDER + ON-HAND >
2 * MONTHLY-AVERAGE.

14. a. EXAMINE SAMPLE REPLACING ALL SPACES BY '—'.
   b. EXAMINE SAMPLE TALLYING LEADING ZEROS.
   c. EXAMINE SAMPLE TALLYING LEADING SPACES REPLACING
BY '.'.
   d. EXAMINE SAMPLE REPLACING UNTIL FIRST 'X' BY 'X'.

INDEX

This index was prepared using *APL PLUS*, a time sharing
service of Scientific Time Sharing Corporation.

COBOL STATEMENT SAMPLES

Page numbers refer to generalized verb formats.

PROCEDURE DIVISION VERBS	PAGE
ACCEPT DATES FROM CONSOLE.	53
ADD 1 TO LINE-COUNTER.	42
CLOSE OLD-MASTER NEW-MASTER TRANSACTION ERROR-LISTING.	57
COMPUTE WEEKLY-SALARY ROUNDED = HOURLY-RATE * HOURS-WORKED.	45
DISPLAY 'WRONG MASTER TAPE--CORRECT AND RESTART' UPON CONSOLE.	53
DIVIDE TIME INTO DISTANCE GIVING RATE; ON SIZE ERROR GO TO ERROR-RTN.	45
EXAMINE TX-QUANTITY REPLACING LEADING SPACES BY ZEROES.	162
EXIT.	154
GO TO TRANSACTION-PROCESSING.	48
IF M-TAG LESS THAN T-TAG MOVE M-TAG TO LOTAG ELSE MOVE T-TAG TO LOTAG.	49
MOVE ' SALESMAN DISTRICT TOTAL' TO REPORT-2.	42
MOVE SALESMAN-NUMBER TO SALESMAN IN REPORT-2.	42
MOVE CORRESPONDING TRANSACTION-IN TO W-TEMPORARY.	142
MULTIPLY UNIT-PRICE IN OLD-MAST BY QUANTITY GIVING TOTAL-PRICE.	44
OPEN OUTPUT NEW-MASTER SHORTAGE-REPORT DELETION-LISTING.	54
PERFORM READ-MASTER-ROUTINE THRU READ-MASTER-EXIT.	48
PERFORM ADD-RTN VARYING SUBS FROM 1 BY 1 UNTIL SUBS GREATER THAN 100.	157
READ CARD-FILE AT END GO TO END-OF-JOB-ROUTINE.	55
STOP RUN.	48
SUBTRACT TN-QUANTITY FROM QOO IN NEW-MASTER GIVING NEGATIVE-CHECK.	44
WRITE PO-RECOMMENDATION-RECORD AFTER ADVANCING 2 LINES.	56

SAMPLE FILE AND RECORD DESCRIPTION

```
FD  SHORTAGE-REPORT
    RECORDING MODE IS F
    LABEL RECORDS ARE OMITTED
    DATA RECORD IS SHORTAGE, PO-REC.
01  SHORTAGE.
    02 SO-CARR-CONT        PICTURE X.
    02 PART                PICTURE X(6).
    02 FILLER              PICTURE X(5).
    02 QUANTITY            PICTURE ZZZZ.
    02 FILLER              PICTURE X(5).
    02 QOH                 PICTURE ZZZZ.
    02 FILLER              PICTURE X(108).
01  PO-REC.
    02 PO-CARR-CONT        PICTURE X.
    02 PO-MESSAGE          PICTURE X(80)  JUSTIFIED RIGHT.
    02 FILLER              PICTURE XX.
    02 PO-PART             PICTURE X(6).
    02 PO-COUNTER          PICTURE ZZ,ZZ9.
    02 FILLER              PICTURE XX.
    02 DATE                PICTURE 99B99B99.
    02 FILLER              PICTURE X(28).
```